The Flavours of History

by

Peter & Colleen Grove

The Flavours of History

First published by Peter J. Grove in 2010

Republished 2011

Copyright Peter & Colleen Grove ©

email : groveint@aol.com

All rights reserved. No part of this book may be reproduced, stored in a retrieval system, or transmitted in any form or by any means for onward transmission, distribution or re-sale without the prior permission in writing of the authors.

Peter & Colleen Grove are also authors of:

Curry Culture (2005 ISBN 0-9548303-0-X)

Curry, Spice & All Things Nice (2000 online)

"Well researched and very interesting. I am sure all enthuisasts of food history would really love to have and benefit from having this book. I wish you and your wife lots of luck with it."

Anjum Anand - TV Presenter/Food Writer

CONTENTS

Introduction	The Father of Organised Food Production	Page 1
Chapter 1	Legend of Osiris	Page 2 - 3
Chapter 2	Dawn of History - the first 2 million years	Page 4 - 14
Chapter 3	A Thousand Years of Conflict - the first thousand years	Page 15 - 18
Chapter 4	Medieval to Modern - the last thousand years	Page 19 - 32
Chapter 5	Medieval Focus - "Pease Pudding and a suck of bacon"	Page 33 - 36
Chapter 6	History of Coffee Houses in Britain	Page 37 - 40
Chapter 7	History of the Ethnic Restaurant in Britain	Page 41 - 58
Chapter 8	Dean Mahomed - First Man of Curry	Page 59 - 62
Chapter 9	Origins of Curry - Is it really English?	Page 63 - 67
Chapter 10	Is it or isn't it? -The Chicken Tikka Masala Story	Page 68 - 74
Chapter 11	On the Trail of the Tandoor	Page 75 - 78
Chapter 12	The 'Currification' of the World	Page 79 - 87
Chapter 13	Compendium of Food terms	Page 88 – 121
Chapter 14	Exotic Foods, Herbs and Spices A – Z	Page 122 – 234
Appendix	Vegetable, Fruits, and Spices used in Western Europe	Page 235
Appendix	Time Lines	Page 236 - 244
	Food Origins	Page 245
	Authors	Page 246 - 247
	Bibliography	Page 248 – 249

"All history is written by someone with a personal agenda - the victor - the enthusiast - the detached intellectual - the critic and, hopefully sometimes, by the seeker after truth and balance in all their shades."

INTRODUCTION

THE FATHER OF ORGANISED FOOD PRODUCTION

Whilst the compilation of this book has been a labour of love as much as a voyage of discovery, it has had, by virtue of the very nature of dealing with times long past, pitfalls and anomalies that lurk around every corner.

Take, for example, the calendar as we know it. Pope Gregory XIII (1502-1585) decided to reform the Julian calendar which was 11 mins 14 sec longer than the solar year causing a loss of 10 days by 1582. The obvious answer was to just drop them and the same was agreed upon when Great Britain adopted the Gregorian calendar in 1752 - although this time we lost 11 days with the next day after September 2nd being September 14th!

USSR did not come on board until 1918 and Greece not until 1923. If this is not enough the Jewish calendar is completely different dating from 3761 BC when the world was created according to the Old Testament and Islam operates on yet another system as does China.

A quoted year can therefore depend on the perspective of the person quoting it. Even the standard 'BC' and 'A.D.' system has its problems with many scholars claiming that Jesus was, in fact, probably born between 7 and 4 BC! With an intervening cushion of two thousand years, these odd few years may not seem too important but as you dip further into pre-history, the problems with precise dating become more acute. Carbon dating and other modern methods have helped considerably but once one looks back beyond 3 - 4000 BC, the variations in dates between experts seem to range from a few hundred years up to an entire millennium.

The dates quoted in this volume are the best consensus of opinion from a multitude of learned works in an effort to give a feeling for the flow of events and a flavour of how food production began and developed throughout history to the present day. As we have neared modern times we have narrowed our area of interest down to the food phenomenon of the latter half of the last century, the ethnic sector which now, for the first time in history, allows the cuisines of the world to impact on all in Britain who wish to enjoy them.

Chapter 1

THE LEGEND OF OSIRIS

One popular school of thought is that civilisation and organised food production developed in three main areas of the World, the Far East, Middle East and the West, completely spontaneously and without outside influence, with 4000 - 3000 BC being the most likely period for the event and quoting civilisations ranging from Sumer to Brittany.

Not only is this rather unromantic but seems to be contradicted by many archaeological facts as we know them. As an interesting and quite plausible alternative we therefore offer the legend of Osiris who could well have been the father of food production worldwide. Osiris, although later to become an Egyptian god and a figure irrevocably interwoven with myth and religious belief, did, according to available evidence, have an historical existence.

Although his legend is based around happenings in the Nile Delta of Egypt, it is known he came from elsewhere, possibly Jordan or Mesopotamia, the cradle of modern civilisation (although even this has been disputed recently in favour of the Nile Delta once again).

The legend of Osiris the deity has been passed on to us by Plutarch and is therefore well documented. Osiris is the Greek rendering of the Egyptian *Ousir*. Originally he was a nature god and embodied the spirit of vegetation and the ebb and flow of the Nile, as one might expect, but later became worshipped as the god of the dead.

Legend has it that he was born in Thebes of Geb and Nut who ascended to rule the heavens on their death. This is supported in Plutarch's *De Iside et Osiride* quoting Osiris as son of Rhea, the Egyptian Nut, the wife of Helios, the Egyptian Ra, by Kronos, the Egyptian Geb. He was handsome, dark-skinned and taller than other men. When he became King of Egypt he married his sister Isis and immediately taught his people to produce grain and grapes for bread and wine. It was he who created the god cult and built temples and gave law to his people.

He then spread civilisation the world over based on non violence leaving Isis to rule in his place but on his return became victim of his evil, jealous brother Set. In the 28th year of his reign Osiris was tricked into a box to meet his death and then cast into the Nile. His loving wife immediately set to searching for the box and when it was found hid it whilst their posthumous son Horus was being born. Unfortunately Set found the hiding place and dismembered the body casting it around the kingdom.

Such was her love that Isis resumed the search once more and found every part of Osiris except for the phallus and with the aid of sorcery brought him back to life. Horus then battled Set and eventually won and when the gods judged the case they found Osiris to be entirely innocent of all blame and deserving of life once more. However, he preferred to leave Horus as king and depart this earthly life to live in the Elysian Fields where he welcomed the souls of the just. His tomb is said to be in Abydos in the Nile Delta. He was worshipped widely as a trinity with Isis and Horus and was identified as Dionysus and Hades, and Isis also took on many other names in other religions such as Demeter, Hera, Selene and even Aphrodite. Osiris, under different names, is represented in the myths of many countries, often in his dragon or serpent incarnation reflecting the winding shape of the River Nile.

Around 10,500 - 10,000 BC life was still nomadic and the population very fluid and based on the hunter-gatherer mode of existence. People had known how to manipulate grains and animals for some time but they still only used what nature provided and moved on to the next natural pantry. This, of course, scarcely lent itself to empire building or the growth of wealth in its natural form so pressures grew for a new system to allow for the final retreat of the Ice Age and gradual population growth.

According to legend, which may have a base in fact, Osiris was possibly the first man to recognise there was another way; a way for the future. It is said to be him, or someone under his direction, who discovered how to cultivate corn and cleverly built up a religion and belief system amongst his people with him as Priest-King, so that the world's first organised abundant supply of food was caused to be grown. Historically speaking, life in the area changed overnight. Instead of small groups ranging far and wide to gather and hunt for food merely to survive, many people were able to live in one area and produce food in excess of their own requirements for the first time ever.

The River Nile had a great influence on this development due to its flood nature, giving abundant water in one season and drought and starvation in another. The importance of the life-giving water was not lost on the people and gradually it merged into a religion centred around Osiris and the river's serpentine shape, with ebb and flow representing good and evil.

The excess of food encouraged Osiris' people to trade and develop further with the Nile as a natural highway. The area became a natural crucible for innovation and invention ranging from the discovery of the potter's wheel by Ptah and a specialised style of boat building. Boat design and navigation knowledge was handed on to the adventurous Phoenicians who traded from Carthage to the British Isles and Spain to the Indian Ocean, even circumnavigating Africa from the Red Sea to Gibraltar in the time of Pharaoh Necho (609 -93 BC).

Influence pushed further afield to the Far East with the same potter's wheel being re-invented in China by Shen-ming and in Japan by a Korean monk named Gyogi. Even Chinese junks seen today, closely resemble the original Egyptian design of Phoenician times.

The serpent myth of Osiris the deified is mirrored throughout the world. In Greece, Dionysis or Bacchus is said to be one and the same as Osiris whilst the serpent of the deep that he was believed to have become after his death is repeated in the famous dragon of China and in India by the drought dragon Indra. As such, Egyptian Pharoahs became avatars of Osiris or Horus and the influence on China is reflected by Emperors becoming an avatar of the dragon or water serpent.

Legend even has Osiris linked with an 'Island of the Blest' where the plant of immortality or something similar grows. This is also repeated in many parts of the world including Britain's Arthurian legends. A belief in Osiris as father of organised food production certainly has an element of fact within it even if considered scientifically fanciful by some more sceptical scholars. However, all known evidence indicates that the area of Rivers Tigris, Euphrates and Nile was the cradle of modern civilisation and of the great diversity of foods and cuisines we enjoy 11,000 years later. So who knows, the legend may be true!

Chapter 2

DAWN OF HISTORY

The first 2 million years - 2,000,000 to 2,000 BC

Fast food is not new - the only difference in pre-historic times was that it ran on two or four legs. The history of Man is reflected in the changes in eating tastes and habits throughout the world, but much of what we think of as innovative and modern, has, in fact, been around for centuries, if not millennia.

Since recorded history began, the food habits of a country have been the result of geography, climate and soil, whether rich or poor, crowded or uncrowded, plus a few imponderables such as religious or tribal taboos. Even now, half the world depends upon wheat, oats, barley, corn and rye and the other on rice.

Homo erectus - the cave dweller of many a fantasy, was using fire as long ago as 500,000 BC, but only from natural happenings such as lightning strikes and had actually been aware of the phenomenon since at least 2,000,000 BC It is from this that the fire ceremonial stems. Man was a gatherer of his food and gradually developed into a hunter-gatherer, who lived off the land around him and plundered Nature's ready supply of resources.

Finds at Chou-K'ou-tien in China, dated back to 500,000 BC, have included evidence of hackberry fruits and the bones of deer.

From 400,000 BC Neanderthal Man evolved in Asia and spread out to colonise Europe. It was not until 250,000 BC that modern Man - Homo sapiens - evolved in sub-Saharan Africa according to many theories and started to move outward to Mesopotamia, the Nile Valley, India, Malaysia, on to Australia, and through Russia to China, whilst others pressed on into Europe.

It has recently been discovered that Charles Darwin's ancient ancestors were among the first group of Homo sapiens Cro Magnon men, leaving Africa 45,000 years ago and reaching Europe around 10,000 years later.

By 125,000 BC, the Ice Age was forcing the Neanderthals into the Near East and Homo sapiens began their migration in the same direction.

By 40,000 BC Homo sapiens were sweeping into Europe in large numbers and by 33,000 BC had spread as far as the Americas overland from Asia. Homo sapiens were the dominant species and suddenly, in historical terms, Neanderthal Man began to disappear and by 30,000 BC, was extinct.

As prehistoric man could shop from Nature's ample larder without applying himself to the soil, the move towards agriculture was very slow as no stimuli existed for many thousands of years to change the status quo to any significant degree. By 50,000 BC areas in China and surrounding locations in what were the USSR and Iran were treating plants and animals as more than mere food, as is evidenced by burial sites and medicines of the time.

By 14,000 BC there is evidence that the beginnings of agriculture took place in the Near East and South East Europe where dogs were starting to be tamed, but the real history of food was marked by the retreat of the Ice Age from around 12,500 BC.

End of the Ice Age

By 12,000 BC early Man was beginning to learn how to manipulate plants and animals as the retreat of the Ice Age presented new opportunities. Then, between 10,500 and 10,000 BC, the end of the Ice Age and the Palaeolithic era moved into the Mesolithic Age. By 9000 BC the first evidence of pottery supposedly appeared from the famous Jonion in Japan, and there was early evidence of wheat, barley and sheep farming in Eurasia.

Modern agriculture dates back to this time, when Neolithic Man learnt how to make fire by friction and intensified his exploration of resources, triggering the start of technological innovation. Man was still a hunter-gatherer, but evidence indicates the beginnings of organised agriculture in Mesoamerica, the Middle East and Far East.

This period of pre-history is one of wide disagreement between historians and archeologists. Man had already spread to most areas of the globe from his birthplace in East Africa long before the ice retreated, so, the claim of some that agricultural development was simultaneous in Southeast and Southwest Asia, the Nile Delta, around the Danube, in Macedonia, Thrace and Thessaly, the Yellow River in China, the Indus in India, the Isthmus of Tehuantepec and Tehuacan in Mexico, could certainly have been possible.

Each of these areas would have been responding to the warmer climate and gradual disappearance of larger animals set against a backdrop of arable land ideally irrigated by major rivers.

Organised agriculture

It is around this time that the Osiris legend would have begun, leading to his becoming the major god in the Egyptian pantheon millennia later. Several modern archeological theories based around astrological alignments linked to around 10,500 BC, from Egypt to South America, Cambodia to Japan lend intellectual support to the Osiris mystery. Indeed the very latest discoveries at Gobekl Tepe in modern northern Turkey also focuses on this pivotal period around 10,000 BC (though with no mention of Osiris). Standing stones and other material being unearthed on an ongoing basis, suggest a level of civilisation previously unimagined by archaeologists who, until recently, considered that time as still part of Man's hunter-gatherer period.

This brings us back to the other explanation that modern agriculture spread around the world from one particular area and there seems little doubt that food production and town life spread from Western Asia in the area between the Himalayas and the Mediterranean not later than 8500 BC

Even this is a 'best guess' based on known information as a new discovery, recently discovered deep beneath the seas in the Gulf of Cambay off the coast of Gujarat in India, suggests an advanced civilisation 9000 BC or even earlier. This and possibly other cities would have been destroyed by flood waters as the Ice Age ended, fitting in with the mystical suggestions of cataclysm around 10,500 BC and even Plato's fabled lost island of Atlantis. There was plenty of impetus for the growth of communities, as excess produce first became the key to trade and then as a sign of wealth and largesse.

This theory is supported by clear evidence that cereal production around the world is descended from three crops which originated in South East Turkey and the Upper Jordan Valley. The best emmer came from the latter and both barley and einkorn from the former to become the ancestors of modern crops.

Usage of Herbs, spices and Vegetables

Mediterranean: (First used BC)	mushroom, beet, radish, turnip, carrot, parsnip, asparagus, leek, onion, cabbage, lettuce, artichoke, cucumber, broad bean, pea, olive, apple, pear, cherry, grape, fig, date, strawberry, basil, marjoram, oregano, mint, rosemary, sage, savory, thyme, anise, caraway, coriander, cumin, dill, parsley, fennel, bay, caper, fenugreek, garlic, mustard, poppy, sesame, saffron.
(Used later)	spinach, celery, rhubarb, cauliflower, broccoli, Brussels sprouts.
Asia: (First used BC)	citron, apricot, peach, cardamom, ginger, cinnamon, turmeric, black pepper.
(Used later)	yam, water chestnut, bamboo, eggplant, lemon, lime, orange, melon, clove, nutmeg, mace, tarragon.
New World: (First used BC)	potato, pumpkin, squash, tomato, kidney bean, lima bean, sweet pepper, avocado, pineapple, allspice, red pepper, chilli pepper, vanilla

Decent sized towns already existed by 8000 BC and Jericho, which has been carbon-dated to 7,800 BC and certainly existed long before, was a town of ten acres by this time. Evidence of elementary farming at Shanidar in Kurdistan dated to 8900 BC further supports this theory. Open settlements in Iraq and Jordan are evident soon after 9000 BC and domestication of animals had already begun in Western Anatolia, Jordan and Khurzistan. Plant domestication came a little after with similar development in Palestine, Lebanon, the Hindu Kush and most highland zones of the Near and Middle East. There is certainly evidence of the beginnings of agriculture in Palestine around 9000 BC and wild wheat, wild barley, wild sheep and wild goats were present in the foothills fringing Assyria.

Communities grow

Between, 8000 – 7000 BC numerous Natufian nomadic groupings gathered together to form communities from the Nile Valley to Anatolia and there is evidence of the domestication of plants, pulse crops (peas, lentils and horse beans), pistacchios, goats and gazelles around Beidha in Jordan.

Elsewhere in the world, development seems to have been behind those in the Middle East and Turkey by as much as a millennium, supporting the theory that they were very much influenced by happenings in those areas. Chilli, for example, was being gathered in South America by 7000 BC but it was not until 5000 BC that evidence indicates organised cultivation. Man had entered the Americas via the Bering Straits overland from 30,000 BC but by 7000 BC immigration began by sea introducing ideas and influences from Asia and the Middle East.

Peasant farming began the story of agriculture in Greece around 6000 BC stretching to the South Balkans by 5000 BC By 6000 BC Catal Huyuk in Turkey was a flourishing town of some 32 acres and pottery appeared at the same time from Zagros in Iran to the East Mediterranean basin.

Alongside the development of agriculture came the development of civilization to a level rarely appreciated today and from 5000 BC civilization advanced rapidly either side of the Syrian Desert in Mesopotamia and Jordan/Egypt.

By 6000 – 5000 BC, millet was cultivated in North China, olive oil was used, chillies and squash were cultivated in Mexico and lima beans in Peru. Cereal farming had grown gradually since the end of the Ice Age to supplement mass fish harvesting techniques and shellfish supplies. The population increased and, as occasional food scarcities occurred, poisons were boiled out of plants for use. Extra food began to be produced as a status symbol and people started to produce food, have more children, and gather in bigger communities.

Lending credence to the Osiris legend, evidence indicates organised agriculture at Fayum in the Nile Valley in 5000 BC with every indication it had been present for some time. The first inhabitants of the Nile Delta were the Tasians followed by the Badanas who had wheat, barley, the hoe, plough and bread, with evidence of storage pits for cereals at Fayum.

The Cradle of Civilization

On the other side of the Syrian Desert in the 'cradle of civilization', the Hassuna culture, from a location some 22 miles south of Mosul on the Assyrian Plain in North Iraq, was very much an agricultural community. In the same area Erhil is still one of the best corn growing areas in Iraq today. Zawi Chemi was one of the first major sites in this region some 2,000 years before the well documented Jarma settlement close to the Tigris River. Another very early farming settlement of the time was Umm Bubaghiyeh on the plains between the Rivers Tigris and Euphrates. It is here that the world's first major civilization, the Sumerians, they of the legendary King-Hero Gilgamesh, appeared, introducing advances that were to shape the world.

Metal worked tools had been known in several areas since 5000 BC and Sumer built up the infrastructure of civilzation including cuniform writing by 3500 BC in 'fabulous' Eridu. The Sumerians of Mesopotamia cultivated dates and, later, cereals as the land improved. Sheep and cattle were kept and donkeys ridden. They were the earliest people to use the wheel widely and, gradually, city states grew up and trade spread as far as India.

The Indus Valley

India was first populated 250,000 years ago but the first major civilization was probably the Harappans who occupied the Indus Valley where Baluchistan was a farming community from 3500 BC Once again, however, this may well have been pre-dated by the 9000 BC Gulf of Cambay civilisation once more is known about it.

By 3000 BC turmeric, cardamom, pepper and mustard were harvested in India. The Harappans, who occupied Harappa and Mohenjodero in the Indus Valley, were of mixed stock, somewhat larger in stature than either the Sumerians or Egyptians denying theories that they were an extension of those communities. They had club wheat, barley, sheep and goats from the Iranian Plateau and cotton from Southern Arabia or North East Africa but were held back by their reliance on flood waters due to general lack of knowledge of irrigation.

Sumer had trade links with the Indus Valley via Hindu Kush by 3000 BC and by sea from 2500 BC, thus linking the Harappans with both Sumerians and Egyptians, where cumin, anise and cinnamon were used for embalming by 2500 BC

By 1750 BC, the Harappan civilization had disappeared, probably due to floods and tectonic shifts, to be replaced by the Aryans who invaded via Hindu Kush by 1500 BC The Aryans had considerable contact with Babylon from whence the original flood legend arose to be adopted by both the Aryans and the Hebrews and several other civilizations.

The Aryans were descendants of Indo-Europeans from the Caspian Sea and Russian Steppes, who also went on to Greece, Asia Minor and Iran. They regarded the indigenous Dasas they found in the Indus Valley as the lowest form of life, seemingly mainly because they were darker skinned and flat-nosed and, more threateningly, 'cattle thieves'.

Aryan civilization revolved around the cow hence *gavishti*, literally 'to send for cows', came to mean to fight. As cattle were a measure of wealth, meat eating was taboo except on very special occasions. The caste system did not exist at this time and did not really take hold until the Dasas were positioned as 'non-persons'. In fact the Sanskrit word for caste *'varna'* means colour. Gradually their society developed into warriors and aristocracy, priests, cultivators and others. The staple diet was milk, ghee, vegetables, fruit and barley.

In civilization terms the coming of the Aryans was a partial step backwards as the Harappans had had script but the Aryans did not develop it until 700 BC In Southern India the megolithic cultures of the Madras, Kerala and Mysore areas arrived from Western Asia - first Negrita, then Proto Australoid, Mongoloid and then Mediterranean, associated with the Dravidians.

Rice was domesticated in West Bengal in the Ganges Delta around 3000 BC and was introduced into the Yangtze Basin area of China soon after via the Burma Road. There is evidence however, that rice farming was known at Ho-mu-tu in Huang He in the Yangtze Delta much earlier, with a division into short and long grain varieties, and evidence was recently discovered in a cave in Southeast Asia (Thailand) of rice dating back to 6000 BC

As the Aryans were entering India, the early Hsia Dynasty in China was giving way to the Shang Dynasty and Chinese farming was developing along the Yellow River with millet, foxtail, brown corn, pigs, dogs and fish. Before the Aryans arrived there is evidence of pepper being traded from India by 2000 BC but they introduced a culture based on cattle as a source of wealth with the cultivation of cereals by ox-drawn plough and feasting and drinking becoming important social occasions. In China, large farming villages were widespread and food included millet, animals and a few vegetables with boiling, roasting and steaming in use as cooking methods. By 3000 BC, cultivation was universal and social differentiations started to appear in larger villages. An emperor of the Shang Dynasty (1520-1030 BC) held food and its preparation in such high regard that over 2000 people were employed in the Imperial Kitchens and one of his cooks was elevated to the position of Prime Minister.

The Spread of Civilization

By 4300 BC the population in the Nile Valley had settled into two tribes, with allegiance to the serpent god in the north and Horus the falcon and Nekhebet the vulture goddess in the south, later combining to be ruled by the Pharaohs of the Old Kingdom between 3500-2700 BC. By 4000 BC raised bread was known, although leavened bread was not discovered until 400 BC. Flat breads had been a feature of the late Stone Age, becoming tortilla, Johnny-cake, chapati and pancake.

The Canaanites settled in what is now the Lebanon in 3000 BC. They later became known as the Phoenicians who, so influenced by the Egyptians and later the Assyrians, spread their culture throughout the known world. In 814 BC the adventurous Phoenicians colonised Carthage soon followed by Urtica in Northern Tunisia, Malta, Molys in Sicily, Cadiz, Mogador in Morocco, Nova in Sardinia and Ibiza. Around the time the Canaanites were entering Lebanon, winter squash, tomatoes, avocados, beans and corn were used as staples in Central America, potatoes in Peru and rice, coconuts and bananas in Asia.

The Sumerians appeared in Mesopotamia around 3500 BC and civilisation began to develop apace after cuniform writing was invented by them whilst Shen Nung assembled the first ever documentation on herbs in China. In Ur, in Mesopotamia, beer was brewed in 3000 BC and Gilgamesh, he of legend, ruled from 2700-2650 BC. Their typical diet was made up of cereals and vegetables, flavoured with watercress and mustard leaves.

Tablets with cuniform text dating back to 1700 BC have been found near Babylon containing early recipes for meat in sauce with bread - probably an offering to the god Marduk.

The great period of pyramid building in Egypt took place between 2680-2565 BC and rice was farmed in an area which ranged from Taiwan to Central India. In Britain, Silbury Hill dates back to 2700 BC and the enigmatic Stonehenge on Salisbury Plain to 2000 BC.

The Semetic ruler Sargon I (2335-2279 BC) united the ancient lands of Akkad and Sumer and even tried to conquer Cyprus. He showed the nomads another way of life and trade to India and Egypt was conducted. By 2200 BC, Semitic Amonites had settled around the village of Babylon, and it was here that Hammurabi (1799-1750 BC) created his kingdom and settled his nomadic tribe and produced the famous Code of Hammurbi, including laws on irrigation, navigation, agriculture and more.

Corn was ground by hand, bread leavened and baked in a small brick oven. Flat cakes were made and thrown against the side of the oven. Mesopotamia was on a downward spiral by 2070 BC when the Hittites attacked, introducing the horse.

Meanwhile, the Phoenicians were looking seawards due to the poor nature of their land. They went out to Africa, Greece, Sicily, France, Spain, and even Cornwall. They called Spain 'Shapan' leading to the name Espana today and the City of Cadiz, Gadir which was founded in 1100 BC even before Rome. They carried cinnamon and cassia to Greece and saffron as far as Cornwall.

Cinnamon and cassia came from Somalia and the Greeks, and later the Romans, imported pepper, cassia, cinnamon and ginger whilst growing caraway, cardamom, anise, mustard and fennel. Such was the mystery surrounding spices and the importance placed upon them that elaborate stories were made up to disguise their origins, many of these stories being reported by Herodotus around 450 BC.

By 2000 BC Crete was the centre of a remarkable civilisation, often called Minoan, which reached its zenith in 1600 BC when 80,000 people lived in the capital, Knossos. Cheese was well known in Egypt by 2300 BC and by 1200 BC 40 kinds of breads and pastries were available to the upper class. Ice cream was invented in China in around 2000 BC as a soft milk and rice concoction.

In India, the thriving civilisation in the Indus Valley was soon to be destroyed by floods and tectonic shifts (1750 BC), to be replaced by the Aryans from Russia and Turkistan, invading over the Hindu Kush. The main tribe, the Bharatra took 500 years to pass Delhi. But the caste system took hold and meat eating was gradually given up, due to the value placed on cattle by the Aryans and to lessons learned in the steaming hot, southern climate.

The Vedas provide most of the information on Indian history at this time with Rig Veda being written around 1000 BC followed by the Sama, Yajur and Atharva Vedas and the medical and method of living from the Ayurveda, whose teachings continue today. Such was the influence of Ayurvedic teaching, which included what, when and how to eat, that the texts were translated into Greek by Cridos in 300 BC and Tibetan and Chinese by AD 300.

Mahavira was born in the sixth centry BC and became an ascetic at the age of thirty in 510 BC to found Jainism, teaching an extreme form of '*ahimsa*'- the non harming of all life. More influential, however, was the enlightenment of Siddhartha Gautama – Buddha whose less radical teachings were adopted by Ashoka (269-232 BC) who became the first Buddhist Emperor in India and forbade the killing of all animals as a consequence.

Eating habits were not universal throughout the sub-continent, however, as the Kashmir Brahmins continued to pride themselves on their mutton and those in Bengal on their fish.

In China around 2000 BC, there were civilised societies in the north and Manchuria and by the Shang Dynasty, (1776 BC), food preparation and service was being ritualised and regulated to a complex formula with ale being very important in the process. At the time, Abraham lived in Ur on the Tigris and became the founder of Judaism, Islam and Christianity, as each can trace their origins back to him. By 1200 BC the Phoenicians from Tyre and Sidon had become great traders and by 1000 BC had invented the phonetic alphabet.

By 1400 BC the nomadic Hebrews had split into two factions, with some settling in Palestine with the Hittites and others settling in Egypt, from where, in 1262 BC, they were eventually repatriated after the Exodus led by Moses, who was a sanitary expert and chief lawgiver by profession, and who created most of the Jewish food codes.

From 5000 BC onwards the original crops of emmer, barley and einkorn were being grown in Greece, especially Crete, plus bread, wheat, lentils and beans plus sheep and goats. Similar developments occurred a little later in the Mediterranean Basin and from the Middle Danube to the Rhine.

In 1200 BC the Empire of Crete had broken up and people had begun to wander around the EasternMediterranean and set up cities in Greece and Asia Minor. One group may have been the Etruscans who settled in Umbria in Italy from Southern Anatolia. The Romans did not finally drive them out until 509 BC, nineteen years before Marathon.

In South America, pepper, bottle-gourd, pumpkin, common bean (Oaxaca), squash (Tehuaca), plants indigenous to the area and not introduced from Asia, were grown. Maize was cultivated in Peru between 1900 – 1600 BC and had spread as far as Colorado by 1000 BC.

The Greeks

The fabled Troy was founded by Neolithic settlers from Kum Tepe by the Dardanelles in 3,600 BC The Trojan Wars began in 1,250 BC and Troy finally fell in 1,180 BC to the Achaeans, (called Greeks by the Italians), who were great eaters, tellers of tales and adventurers. Soon they were replaced by the Dorians from the North, but soon after, the Greek civilisation stretched from Asia Minor to Crimea and Byzantium. The Greeks brought culinary sophistication to many regions and even the King of Sidon had a famous Greek cook, called Cadmos. The Greeks colonized Provence in 600 BC and Catalonia in 550 BC as well as from Calabria to Naples in Italy, and parts of Sicily and the Black Sea.

The Greek love of bread dates back to Minoan Crete 3,000 -1,100 BC and the first usable bread oven was invented at the time of Pericles in 500 BC During the time of Augustus in Rome in 30 BC there were as many as 329 bakeries in Rome all run by Greeks. The bread was originally based on olive oil as butter was considered the food of barbarians with fat or butter not being added until the Middle Ages.

The fabulous civilization based around Knossos declined between 1,400-1,375 BC and the Mycenae became the leaders of the Greeks. Meze was founded by Greeks around 300 BC named from the Turkish or Arab word describing nibbling when talking as was common amongst politicians.

The first Olympiad was held in 776 BC at the height of Greek civilisation, but the seeds of their successor were already being sown. At this time olive oil was the source of artificial light, having been passed on to the Greeks by the Phoenicians. Olive oil was supposed to have been discovered by Isis, the wife of Osiris, who was said to have taught the Egyptians how to cultivate the trees and produce the oil.

By 600 BC civilisation in China had reached an advanced level. Fire, building, farming, medicine and script had supposedly been discovered during the reign of The Three Sovereigns in around 2,850 BC, but now the Chinese had cotton, silk, beans, square buckets, hatchets and coloured robe. Normal meals were millet or rice plus cucumber, pumpkins, peaches, apricots, cherries, chestnuts and plums flavoured with onions, mustard and other herbs.

By 500 BC in the time of Pericles, Aeschylus, Sophocles and Euripides, Athens was the centre of learning with cooking schools and dining clubs. When the great library of Alexandria was burned by Caliph Omar I destroying 700,000 scrolls, several were valuable ancient Greek cookery books. Eating in Greece reached great heights during this period and around 500 BC one of the world's first cook books was written by Hesiod of the Epicureans and *Life of Luxury* by Archestrateus in 400 BC. Breakfast tended to be bread and wine, followed by a light lunch and an evening meal of eggs, fish, cheese, vegetables and, very occasionally, meat, with garlic and onion, olive oil and honey. Fruit was always eaten at the end of meals, along with rich wines diluted with water. Athens at the time was excellent for olives and vines. Marseilles and Southern Italy were known as Great Greece at this time.

The Persians and Macedonians

Cyrus of Persia conquered Lydia in 546 BC, only to be beaten back at Marathon. Xerxes tried again in 480BC, only to be beaten back by the Greek army under Sparta. By 467 BC, all of the Aegean was controlled by the Greek Confederacy. Athens tried for the Nile Delta in 448 BC, then Sicily and Great Greece in 415 BC, only to be beaten at Syracuse.

All this campaigning meant that the core Greek cuisine was being influenced by not only Persia, and Egypt but also other parts of Europe and was influencing them in turn. In 400 BC, the father of modern medicine, Hippocrates expounded his theory, *'Let food be your medicine and medicine your food.'*

In 359 BC, Philip became king of Macedonia. He had been educated in Greece and gradually controlled the Northern Aegean. Before he could invade Persia he was murdered and the next world force, his son, Alexander the Great, came to power in 336 BC. Alexander quickly subdued Greece, Asia Minor, Syria, Eastern Mediterranean and Egypt, then routed the last of the Persians near Nineveh in 333BC. He went on to conquer Bactria, Turkistan and the Punjab between 330-324 BC and, at the height of his glory, died in 323 BC, having influenced much of the known world.

Elsewhere in the world two deaths had great influence on the development of civilization in those areas and beyond; Buddha in 489 BC and Confucius in 479 BC.

Rice was introduced to Japan from China in 300 BC to be used as a form of tribute and taxation, uses which were maintained until the early twentieth century.

The World of Alexander the Great

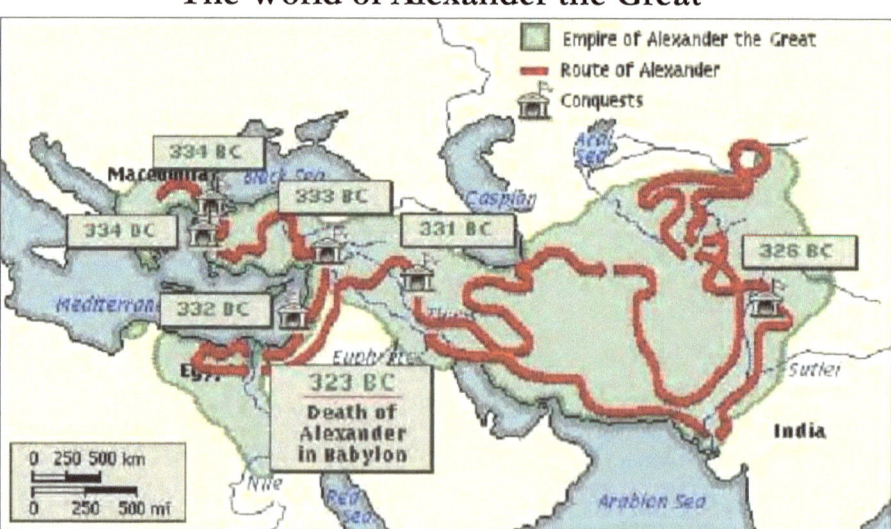

The Romans

The vacuum was filled by the growth of Rome, which had been founded in 700-800 BC. Rome was founded by Romulus, a descendant of the Trojan Aeneas in 753 BC according to legend (probably even earlier) but was taken over by the Etruscans in 616 BC. After the Romans recaptured the city in 509 BC, they had continued battles with the Etruscans until 390 BC and then with the Gallic forces attacking from the Milan area. A period of internal expansion then took place and by 326 BC they had captured Naples.

Conquests were started in 264 BC and they eventually defeated Hannibal of Carthage, a formidable foe, in 202 BC, then Spain, Sicily, North Africa, Greece, Macedonia, and all of the Mediterranean. Corinth was sacked by Rome in 146 BC. and Greece became the Eastern Roman Empire then the Byzantine Empire until 395 AD. The greatest Greek influence in the kitchen was when they were brought back home to Rome as house slaves. For the first time, the mistress of the house deserted her kitchen and gave it over to a Greek slave-chef who was well-versed in all Greek and Sicilian cookery. Dining refinement continued and most meals, by now, were served on pottery. Food was equally important in China, where it was central to family events and social transactions and no business deal was complete without a meal.

Despite battle reversals, Greece continued to refine its cultural activities. Euthydemus wrote his, '*On Vegetables*' in 150BC, but when the Romans sacked Corinth in 146 BC, and went on to control Greece until 395 AD, the influence of the Greek kitchen spread far and wide. Greek cooks were mainly responsible for introducing a diversity of breads to Rome. Plato wrote with disgust about the gluttony of the Sicilian Greeks and Petronius described huge, lavish, Roman feasts.

And so, the main planks of modern culinary activity were laid even before Jesus Christ had appeared, to become such an influence on the world stage. Religion had always had some influence on food usage, with ceremonial and dietary requirements, but with little overall effect. Even the

The Roman Empire

reverence of all animal life by Hindus, Buddhists and Jains only underlined a trend recognised by the invading Aryans centuries before. Islam was soon to follow the Jews in banning pork and shellfish, for very sound reasons and, more recently, Seventh Day Adventists banned the eating of meat. Although neither created any of the world's great cuisines or supplies of food produce, the two great influences of pre-history in terms of the spread of food information and products were firstly the Phoenicians and then Alexander the Great.

The Greeks supplied the great melting pot where many roads from around the world met and they in turn greatly influenced the Romans who were destined to conquer much of the world. It was Rome and later the Crusades that provided the greatest influences on the cuisines of the world in the early centuries of the last two millennia.

Chapter 3

A THOUSAND YEARS OF CONFLICT

The first thousand years   1 AD - 1000 AD

The last years of the century before the birth of Christ were ones of the expansion of the power of Rome over much of the known world. Rome proved to be the equal of Carthage in the Punic War and so Carthage turned its attention to Spain.

The Second Punic War started in 218 BC when Hannibal crossed the Alps and defeated the Romans in a series of battles. Fortunately for Rome, Hannibal was recalled to Africa to face Scipio only to be beaten himself at Zama in 202 BC This left Rome in control of the Western Mediterranean and they moved on to defeat Philip V of Macedonia 200-197 BC, then Syria, then Philip's son Perseus who was routed at Pydna in 168 BC Scipio finally destroyed the power of Carthage in 146 BC

This supremacy brought internal strife and when Sulla descended on Rome in 83 BC with 40,000 troops he set the precedent for rule by strength of arms. By the turn of the millennium Rome's agriculture was in decline and Africa became the source of its grain supply.

By 55 BC Pompey controlled Spain and Africa, Crassus controlled Syria and Caesar campaigned in Gaul where he briefly invaded Britain. The Senate elected Pompey sole consul in 52 BC on the death of Crassus and demanded the disbanding of Caesar's army in 49 BC Caesar and his legions marched on Rome and by 45 BC the Pompey cause was crushed and Caesar was declared dictator for life.

This did not prove to be for long as he was murdered in the following year and a struggle for power ensued culminating in the suicide of Antony and Cleopatra after the Battle of Actium in 31 BC leaving Octavian - later Augustus - undisputed ruler. The Augustian period saw the beginning of a cultural golden age that lasted until the death of Nero in 62 A.D. when lack of a hereditary Emperor resulted in the Roman world being split into four.

Claudius I completed the conquest of Britain 41 - 54 A.D. after they had been paying tribute to Rome for nearly one hundred years and London was founded in 50 A.D., later to be made capital in the ninth century by King Alfred.

Rome broke the Arab spice monopoly in 40 AD and by 92 AD was building special warehouses in Rome for pepper, such was its importance. They introduced paid chefs and many town houses had a large grill, vast preparation tables and complex masonry cookstoves. Fish sauce had originally come from Greece but was raised to an artform in Rome as confirmed by Apicius. Almost all dishes had a sauce or dressing and garum, the fish sauce, was in wide use.

In 40 AD, Apicius wrote the first great cookery book, '*De Re Coquinaria*', during the reign of Tiberius, and Rome spread its culture around much of the known world. The Greeks had advocated fruit as a dessert, but the Romans added vegetables and lettuce as hors d'oeuvres. Most products known today were in use before Christ was born, with only spinach, celery, rhubarb, cauliflower, broccoli and Brussels sprouts added later in the Mediterranean and yam, water chestnut, bamboo, eggplant, lemon, lime, orange, clove, mace and tarragon in Asia.

The new religion of Christianity had little international effect for the first two hundred years of its existence, being generally regarded as a strange offshoot of the Jewish religion. The gods of Rome had been the old Aryan gods linked with Greece. The intelligencia had no gods, so the gods of the East filled the vacuum in the first two centuries as Christianity quietly grew under the impetus provided by Paul.

The first such religion to become popular was the worship of Isis, wife of Osiris from Eqypt, followed by that of Mithras. Finally the worship of the Emperors themselves as gods took hold.

In 234 AD the last emperor of the Severus Dynasty was murdered and the Roman Empire descended into a period of constant civil war. The Christian Church was blamed for much of the breakdown and in 250 AD an edict outlawing the religion was issued leading to a period of great persecution.

The strife continued until the eventual emergence of Constantine as a power in the Roman Empire. He brought back the period of prosperity, and ended the persecution of the Christians by making it the official religion of the Empire.

In 330 AD he founded Constantinople as the new capital of the Roman Byzantine Empire as a bullwork against the barbarian hoards. Situated in northeast Algeria on the site of Cirta, the capital of Numidia, Constantinople stood firm until it became the centre of the Ottoman Empire in 1453 AD.

It soon became the centre of culture and the spice trade, attracting goods from all over the East including cloves and nutmeg from the Moluccas. The Arabs raided it constantly from 634 AD and it was Alexius I's appeal to the Pope in Rome for help that brought about the First Crusade 1096-99 AD.

In the fourth century, the first Christian World Council was held creating the 'Trinity' amongst other things and outside pressures on Rome began to appear.

In 408 AD Alaric the Visigoth attacked Rome and was famously paid 3,000 lb of pepper plus gold, silver, silks and furs to lift the blockade. It was all rather pointless as three years later he sacked the city anyway.

As Roman influence broke down, numerous challenges to its authority and culture arose and it was not until 451 AD that the next major force appeared in the shape of the fearful Attila and his Huns. As devastating as they were, the Huns had little effect on world cuisine, and little more of note occurred for many years and it brought the development of Western cuisines to a standstill. The only other notable contribution of Italy to world cuisine in this period was the first appearance of the pizza in Gaeta between Naples and Rome in 997 AD.

The Middle East

Rome held sway in Egypt from 30 BC to 641 AD and had considerable influence as a centre for cultural development.

Arabs enjoyed the monopoly of spice trading until 40 AD when Rome took over, and the Middle East had little influence on world affairs except as a spice supplier until 570 AD when Mohammed was born. In 622 AD he took his famous Hejira to Medina and eight years later, the religion of Islam was born to become a major power all over the Middle East and Africa.

In 711 AD the Moors took over Al Andalus coming from the spice routes, and brought cinnamon, nutmeg, pepper, aniseed, sesame, cumin, coriander, ginger and caraway with them. Spices spread throughout Europe and in England in 982 AD, King Aethelred II levied a special Christmas and Easter tax, payable in pepper, on German ships coming up the Thames to trade at London Bridge.

Ginger reached Britain by the tenth century after gaining great popularity in Germany a century before. Saffron started to be grown in Saffron Walden in Essex and elsewhere in Europe, caraway was found growing naturally.

The Far East

As the start of the Christian era dawned in the Middle East, China was experiencing the Hsin Dynasty 9-23 AD. Emperor Wang, a onetime courtier, abolished slavery and tried the uphill struggle of improving the lot of the peasants. The Hsin was replaced by the Han Dynasty 25-220 AD, which led to a period of strife as the government was torn by conflicting factions. It was under the Hans that the flour mill was first seen in China. Little of import emerged from China until the Sui Dynasty 589-618 AD, when a stronger government reunited the country, apart from the discovery of how to make matches by the ladies of the Royal Court in 577 AD.

The best period of the millennium for China however, was the rule of the Tang Dynasty 618-907 AD, when administration was centralized after a period of disunity. This was the golden age of poetry and culture when printing first started during the rule of Mung Huang 712-756 AD. The oldest known printed book is the Diamond Sutra dated 868 AD.

In Japan, meat eating and milk drinking were common until the late seventh century and only disappeared due to the teachings of Buddhism which first arrived in Japan from Korea in 500 AD. The result was a ban in the eighth century and the appearance of sushi. Soy sauce came from the Asian mainland in the eighth or ninth century but Japanese style soy sauce did not appear until the fifteenth century. Tea was introduced from China in the ninth century but popularity faded until it was re-introduced during the Zen Period in the twelfth century.

India

India was the wonderland in the West for the Chinese and in 61 AD the Emperor sent a mission to the sub-continent over the Himalayas which returned in 67 AD and Buddhism returned with it. India also had an early effect on the Roman Empire when, in 40 AD, a Greek named Hippolas discovered that the monsoon winds cut the voyage time to the land of spice considerably. Soon the Romans had broken the Arab monopoly bringing pepper from India and cinnamon from Ceylon.

By 335 AD, Samudra Gupta had risen to power in India, ruling until 375 AD, to become India's 'Napoleon'. But it was Chandragupta II who subjugated all of the sub-continent north of the Marmada River bringing 160 years of peace and prosperity and a resurgence of Hinduism.

In the fifth century the White Huns from central Asia invaded India and held sway until 565 AD. By

606 AD Harsha ruled in northern India and became the last main Hindu monarch. On his death the sub-continent dissolved into a series of warring states until the beginning of the eleventh century.

In 630 AD the new religion of Islam appeared and by 712 AD the Muslims had invaded Sind and their influence over the sub-continent of India and its cuisine started.

Another great influence on Indian cuisine was the arrival of a boatload of Parsees from Persia, fleeing the persecution of Islam in 745 AD. They landed at Gujarat and were allowed to settle there bringing Parsee food to the sub-continent.

The first millennium after the birth of Christ was one of perpetual war and strife throughout the 'civilized world'. Although Rome ensured their culture and cuisine spread throughout their Empire and periods of great prosperity were enjoyed in both China and India, the overall effect was to slow down the growth and spread of food styles and food stuffs the world over.

Chapter 4

MEDIEVAL TO MODERN

The last thousand years   1000 AD - 2000 AD

As the second millennium after the birth of Jesus dawned, it was once again religion that was taking centre stage, affecting people all over the civilized world. The spread of Islam moved on apace with conquests on many fronts, until the West finally became alarmed with the conquest of Syria and Palestine by the Seljuk Turks. Other followers of Islam were making regular incursions into the Christian Byzantine Empire, until Pope Urban II called for a 'Holy Crusade' in 1095.

The Crusades (1095 - 1270)

The First Crusade began assembling in 1096 amidst great enthusiasm and congregated in Constantinople which was hoping to regain territories lost to its Byzantine Empire in recent years. The Crusade was unique in the series in that it was one of disparate groups - knights and adventurers not Kings or Popes. It had the clear target in most minds of capturing Jerusalem which it achieved amidst tales of heroism and sadistic cruelty in 1099 and then much of the army dispersed, taking with it back to Europe, knowledge of many of the foods, herbs and spices of the East.

The event proved to be somewhat of a re-awakening for the Muslim powers which then experienced a period of re-unification under Imas-ad-In-Zangri who recaptured Edessa on the Euphrates in 1144.

The response from the West was the Second Crusade in 1145 which was brief and, in general terms, a failure. Zangri died in 1146 and the gradual emergence of the brilliant Saladin was noted when he took control of Egypt in 1169. In 1174 he became the Muslim ruler and regained Jerusalem in 1187.

This prompted the Third Crusade which is remembered in history for the involvement of Philip II of France, Frederick I (Barbarossa) and Richard I the Lionheart. They did not re-capture Jerusalem but achieved significant gains until Richard eventually left the Holy Land in 1192.

The Fourth Crusade, perhaps the most infamous, was called and led by Pope Innocent III in 1202 and was beset by transport and financial problems. The Venetians, who had undertaken to transport the armies but were not paid the agreed price, persuaded the Crusaders to attack and sack Constantinople, centre of the Christian Byzantine Empire in 1204, giving the Venetians control of the very considerable Byzantine trade.

Some historians claim Pope Innocent was horrified at this whilst others say he actively participated in it, but the result was an irrevocable rift between the Churches of the East and West and considerable commercial gain to Venice.

Another Crusade, largely in Western Europe, was fought 1208 - 1229 and yet another in 1217-1221 which attacked Egypt and achieved little. Frederick II started the next Crusade in 1227 but fell ill and incurred the wrath of the Pope who excommunicated him, but he still tried again in 1228. His style was to negotiate the return of Jerusalem which resulted in Pope Gregory declaring a Crusade against him.

The Muslims re-captured Jerusalem in 1244 resulting in yet another Crusade by Louis IX in 1248. The army was outmanoeuvred and flooded outside Cairo and surrendered in 1250. The last Crusade was declared in 1270 by Louis again but he reached no further than Tunisia before dying and ending a period that was highly significant in introducing the foods and cuisines of the East to Western kitchens.

Europe

In Europe the focus was on the invasion of England by the Normans, introducing new elements to a culture influenced by the Romans. The use of spices from the East became a status symbol by 1200 and the European preoccupation with the world of spice was born.

In Medieval times, dinner guests would select their food from 'chargers' full of food, which was then placed on large slices of bread, or 'trenchers', which were used as edible plates. These were often coloured and flavoured with parsley or saffron. Guests would arrive carrying their own knife and did not eat so much in quantity, but hospitality meant that an abundant choice should be made available. Menus were large and extensive, but small portions were deemed correct and tasting more important than gorging. Food painting and even sculpture also became important.

The use of spice in food meant money and power, with cinnamon the most popular, having been in use in wine dating back to the Anglo-Saxons and associated with Roman and Greek usage. Ginger was used for digestion, cloves for the sinews, mace for colic, nutmeg for colds.

The coming of William the Conquerer in 1066 was a watershed in English cuisine. He used dining to appeal to people of diverse stations and instituted three new major feast days. Christmas was celebrated at Gloucester with everyone invited, Easter at Winchester and Whitsun at Westminster. The real revolution, however, came in the time of Richard I the Lionheart.

The influence from France and from the returning Crusaders ensured a wide range of herbs and spices were added to those of Roman Britain and used in noble kitchens. Basil, borage, mallow, ditany, true love, fennel, ginger, cardamom, galingale, clove, sorrel, mustard seed, nutmeg, anise, mace, mint, peppercorn and cinnamon were all in use in medieval times.

Salt was considered so important it was stored in the Tower of London. The result was a highly spiced cuisine for the nobility and, apart from preserving and adding taste, spices were very much a sign of wealth. Frumenty was one of the staple dishes for the masses - wheat berries, long boiled in broth or milk, flavoured and sweetened.

During the reign of King John, standard mixes - *powder fort, powder douce and powder blanch* - were created and colour became highly prized. In 1357, Sauce Blanc was first recorded as the classic '*balsamella*', in Cesna, in Italy. As an interesting aside, the word '*garbage*' was in common use in this period, but meant animals innards or giblets, later thrown away, hence the association.

The alehouse first became popular in the thirteenth century and the first taverns opened in London in 1272. By 1309 there were 354. In feudal times a large manor had a mill for grinding, an oven for baking and gardens for growing. The feudal castle had ducks, pheasants, pigeons, geese, hens, partridges, fish, pork, beef, mutton, cabbage, turnips, carrots, onions, beans, peas, bread, cheese, butter, ale and wine.

The first celebrated chef came from France to work for Edward III (1327-1377). Guillaume Tirel, known as Taillevent, wrote one of the first major cookbooks called '*Le Viander*'.

A recipe from Taillevent, "Stewed Beef with Macrows" was blind taste-tested by a BBC Radio 4 dicussion panel against a modern curry dish and it was generally agreed that the medieval dish tasted very similar to a modern medium-strength curry.

Stewed Beef with Macrows

 1lb (450g) stewing beef – cubed
 1.5 pts (570ml) good beef stock
 1 carrot, sliced
 1 large onion, peeled and finely chopped
 1 tsp minced garlic
 2 tbsp fresh parsley, chopped
 Half tsp dried sage
 Half tsp white pepper
 2.5 inch cinnamon stick
 Half tsp black peppercorns
 Half tsp cloves
 2 blades mace
 Roughly ground in a pestle and mortar, then placed in a muslin bag or spice ball
 20 ml cider vinegar
 2 large slices brown bread broken up

Method

Simmer meat, onions, herbs, seasoning and all spices except for the saffron in the stock, skimming from time to time. After 1 hour of cooking take quarter pint (150ml) of the stock out of the pot and mix with the vinegar. Add the crumbled bread and allow to soak. When the meat is cooked, add the soaked bread and simmer until gravy is thickened. Add the steeped saffron and cook briefly until colour develops. Adjust seasoning to taste, sprinkle with fresh parsley and serve with macrows (similar to modern macaroni).

However it was left to the reign of Richard II (1377-1399) for the first English cookbook to be written - *The Forme of Cury* in 1390 with 196 recipes contributed by the Royal cooks, physicians and philosophers.

In France, the first cookbooks were '*The Little Treatise*' of 1306 and a Sion manuscript of the late thirteenth to early fourteenth century, nicknamed "Taillevent before Taillevent" as it formed much of the backbone of Taillevent's '*Le Viander*'.

It must also be noted that there was very little reference to sugar in these books as, up until contact with the Muslims from the eleventh century, sugar had only been used as a medicine. French cuisine was not, however, deemed to be the culinary peak of the era as a cookbook written by Muhammed ibn al-Hasan ibn Muhammed al-Karim al-Katab-al Baghdadi in 1226 in Bagdad, is generally considered to be far more varied and informative than the French works. Mesopotamia, however, where all of it started, had sunk almost to subsistence levels by the twelfth century with agriculture and cuisine development completely static.

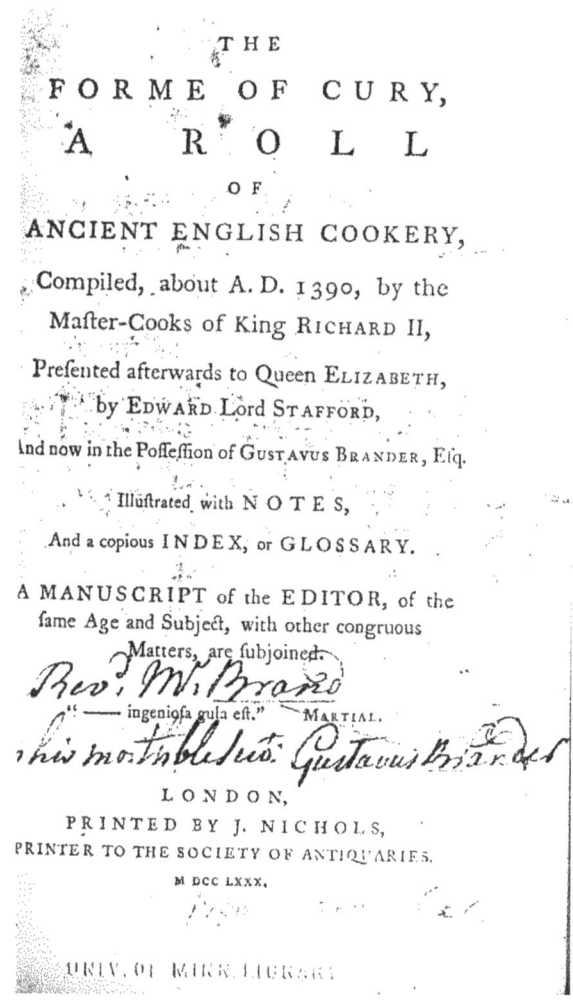

The first English cookbook to be written - *The Forme of Cury* – 1390

India

The second millennium was one of continued invasion for the Indian sub-continent. It started with the challenge for Khorasan in Samarind by Mahmoud Gahazmi (999-1030) who sent seventeen expeditions into India from Afghanistan. By 1025 he had annexed the Punjab and sacked many western cities.

The real founder of Muslim power, however, was Muhammed of Ghur in 1173. By 1206 AD Kutbuddin was Sultan of Delhi and the power was consolidated by Alauddin (1296-1316) who conquered the Deccan.

The next to invade were the Mongols under Tamerlane who invaded in 1398 and sacked Delhi. When he withdrew he left the last of the Tughluq, Mahmud (1399-1413) in power. It was left to Babur, a descendant of Tamerlane, to found the Mughal Dynasty that was to last from 1526-1761 and do so much for cuisine development.

Akbar, the son of Emperor Humayun who came to power at a very young age in 1542, was perhaps the greatest in the line adding Bengal to his territories and conquering Kashmir heralding a period of tolerance, but the dynasty peaked under his grandson Shah Jahan (1626-1658). It was the coming of the Muslim invader followed by the considerable Mughal influence that gave India much of the wide variety of cuisine that is enjoyed in the West today.

The East

Muslim and Mogul power were also the dual influences in the East during the first half of the second millennium. The plundering of Constantinople by the Crusaders in 1204 was the beginning of the end for the Byzantine Empire and by 1354 it had been overrun by the Ottomans, disappearing entirely by 1453.

Muhammed II captured Constantinople and much of Europe up to the Danube. Selim I conquered Syria, Palestine, Egypt and Arabia in 1517 and in 1529 Suleiman II conquered Hungary and besieged Vienna. It took until 1571 for the tide to turn when John of Austria defeated the Ottoman fleet at the Battle of Lepanto. The Ottoman Empire suffered continued wars throughout the seventeenth and eighteenth centuries culminating in a disastrous war with Russia (1768-1792).

China was shocked out of its complacency by the invasion of the Mongol Horde in 1206, led by Chenghis Khan, who captured Beijing in 1215 and held sway until his death in 1227. Between 1219 and 1222 Chenghis Khan and his Mongol horde invaded Iraq, Iran, Western Turkistan, Bukhoro, Samarkand then Peshawar and Lahore in India/Pakistan and finally on to Russia.

The famous Kublai Khan then swept to power, continuing their influence on China, eventually conquering the Sung Dynasty in the South and starting the Yuan Dynasty (1279-1368). Kublai Khan attracted visits by adventurers from all over the world including the Polo brothers who returned to Venice after a first visit to Kublai Khan's court in 1269 and then departed on a second trip taking son Marco Polo who did so much to tell the West about the marvels of the East when he returned to Venice.

It should be noted that one of these marvels was not the introduction of pasta to the West as legend maintains as it was known in Sicily in the twelfth century and is mentioned in documents from Genoa dated 1279 and Marco Polo did not return from his travels until 1295.

Japan enjoyed the Shogun Period from the twelfth to nineteenth century. The Hojo's, although never actually Shoguns, were weakened by continued attacks from the Mongols in 1274 and again in 1281. The Hojo were pushed out by Go-Daigo in 1333 and by Ashikaga who imposed strict fuedal control. The Tokugawa Shogunate (1603-1867) maintained the fuedal society and kept Japan isolated from international influence.

Very little meat was consumed in Japan up to the Meiji era (1869-1911 AD). An Elizabethan traveller recorded *"they delight not much in fleshe, but lyve for the most part with hearbes, fyshe, barley and rice"*.

The Exploration Years

The mid fifteenth century onwards saw the emergence of a series of adventurers and dreamers who either acted out of dreams of exotic, distant lands in the mystic East or were prompted by nationalism and commercial pressures.

Christopher Columbus (1451-1506) started his adventuring to Chios in the Aegean in the mid 1470s and in 1476 set out for England getting only as far as Lisbon where he settled for a while. In his first voyage of discovery seeking the Americas and Indies in 1492 he discovered San Salvador, Cuba and other islands where, amongst other things, the hot red pepper was discovered in Santa Domingo. In 1493 he discovered Domenico, Guadalupe, Antigua and Puerto Rico on his second voyage, finding paprika in Hispaniola. In 1498 he visited Trinidad then Venezuela and finally travelled down as far as Panama in 1506.

Amerigo Vespucci (1454-1512) explored the northern coast of South America from 1499-1500 and the Spanish and Portuguese interest in the New World was then at fever pitch. In 1499 Alonso de Ojeda discovered Curacao and in 1500 Vicente Yanez Pinza landed at Recife whilst Pedro Alvares Cabral claimed Brazil for Portugal.

The Aztecs, who had been in Mexico since the thirteenth century, had spread across Mesoamerica by the mid 1400s. The main religion was the worship of Quetzelcoatl, the plumed serpent, who was tricked and disgraced by another god Tezcatlipoca, and he left vowing to return, showing close parallels to the ancient Osiris legend.

Modern archeologists in Mexico have recently made discoveries that lead them to suggest that Roman sailors reached the Americas but this seems unlikely as neither chillis nor tomatoes appeared in Europe in Roman times although both would have been very popular if they had. If explorers did reach those shores in Roman times, it would seem they did not return to the Empire.

It was left to Hernan Cortes (1485-1547) to 'discover' South America when he sailed for Santa Domingo in 1504. In 1509 the Spanish found allspice in Jamaica and in 1518 Cortes launched his expedition to Mexico, launching his attack on the Aztecs in 1519. By 1565 Saint Augustine had been founded by the Spanish in Florida and Jamestown became the first English settlement in 1607. At the time of the arrival of Spain in the New World, there was no riding of animals but squash, beans, peas and corn were part of the normal diet. The consequences of this period for world cuisine cannot be over-emphasised, introducing many, previously unknown foodstuffs to Europe, not the least of which were the tomato and chilli.

The Portuguese were in Guinea-Bissau in Africa in the person of slave trader Nuno Tristao in 1446 but their most famous explorer was Vasco da Gama, who set out for India in 1497 and in 1498 landed in Calicut in the south and brought back cinnamon, cloves, ginger and pepper.

The Portuguese influence which led to a trade monopoly was strengthened between 1509 - 1515 under Dom Alfonso d'Alberqueque. It was the Portuguese who introduced or influenced so much of the Goan food which is so popular today, and such dishes as Vindaloo - nothing to with potatoes (aloo), but rather, based on the Portuguese words for wine and garlic.

It was the Portuguese who introduced chillies into Cochin and Calicut in 1501 and by 1543 three varieties were successfully being grown locally. So unfamiliar were the local people with chilli prior to the coming of the Portuguese that, for many years, it was known as Goan Pepper.

It was the Spanish who brought the tomato from Peru and Mexico to Spain from where it spread initially unsuccessfully, throughout the world whilst Portugal was responsible for taking the taro, potato, sweet potato and frying in batter (Tempura) to Japan in the sixteenth century as well as castera or kasutera (sponge cake) which was new to that country as they had no history of cake making with wheat flour.

As Spain and Portugal continued their exploration and exploitation of newly discovered countries, Holland, France and England looked on with envy and all three soon entered the fray. Under the influence of Elizabeth I in England, Sir Francis Drake (1540-1596) ranged as far as Valparaiso then San Francisco in 1578 and in 1579 visited the Moluccas and Java returning in 1580 with a rich cargo of spices. Sir Walter Raleigh (1554-1618) also travelled in search of riches and conquest for his Queen, visiting America in 1578 and Guyana in 1595.

The East India Companies

Following the example of Portugal, Denmark, England, France and Holland each encouraged private commerce to become involved in the riches the Indies had to offer. The first of these was the English East India Company founded in 1600 and arriving at Surat in 1608 and again in 1612, travelling to Japan in 1610 and 1611. English cooking at the time was heavy with cumin, caraway, ginger, pepper, cloves and nutmeg so the commercial opportunities of a cheap, ready supply were very obvious.

The Dutch East India Company travelled throughout China, Japan, India, Iran, Cape of Good Hope, Malaysia, Indonesia and Malabar reaching a peak in 1669 when they finally destroyed the Portuguese monopoly. The French were relatively late on the scene not being founded until 1664 but made their presence known at Surat in 1675 and ruled supreme at Pondicherry until 1761. Other voyages of exploration also went to Africa and the Mississippi area of America.

The last to enter the race were the Danish in 1729 but they were almost immediately broken by the British and had little influence. The appearance of the English East India Company at the court of Emperor Jahangir at Surat in 1612 heralded three hundred years of influence in the Indian sub-continent. The Portuguese attacked the people they saw as intruders but were defeated at sea and soon it was the turn of the Dutch to attack, only to be defeated by the end of the seventeenth century.

In 1633 the Company visited Orissa founding Madras (now Chennai) in 1639. Trading privileges were given for Bengal in 1651 and the British acquired Bombay (now Mumbai) from Portugal in 1661 and were in Calcutta by 1690.

This laid the whole of the Indian spice trade open to Britain and although the demand had been there since the times of the Crusades and even before, the new prices made them available to a much wider market.

The French provided a serious threat in 1746 when they seized Madras, not returning it until 1748. Hostilities continued from 1756-1763 as an extension of the Seven Years War in Europe. Britain won many victories the most important of which was Robert Clive's victory at Plassey making Britain the masters of Bengal with the French reduced to a few trading posts.

Europe

France had gradually taken over the mantle of cuisine leader of Europe. From 1400-1800 AD, much of the world ate mainly vegetables, with the exception of Europe, which enjoyed meat eating from the Middle Ages onwards due to a relatively low population density.

From the seventeenth century, the amount of meat eaten by the lower classes fell as the population increased, to be reversed in the middle of the nineteenth century as meat came from America and refrigeration was introduced. Luncheon only became recognised as a mid-day meal in the early nineteenth century. Before this was nuncheon, a snack between early breakfast and afternoon dinner, which gradually moved from around 3:00pm to 8:00pm. The characteristic meal in France in the Middle Ages was the feast, which changed to a collation in the sixteenth, the fête in the seventeenth and the intimate supper in the eighteenth century.

With the Renaissance in Europe, the French bean was an immediate success, but the tomato only took off initially in Italy. Corn and potato were seen mainly as foods for livestock or the poor. Salads became popular around 1700 and the French decreed the rule of fruit at the start of the meal and salad at the end. Vegetables became dishes, rather than garnish, from the seventeenth century, due to the fasting period of Lent, although this did not apply in England.

Much is made by some historians of the move by Catherine de Medici and her entourage to France as Queen in 1530 and they have even attributed the growth of French cuisine from this time on to the influence of her Italian cooks. Influence she certainly did have but there is little evidence to suggest it was of the kind popularly attributed to her.

She was just fourteen when she became Queen of France and had a very small entourage, most of whom were not even Italian. Catherine's main influence was on feasts and major gatherings. The style of cuisine throughout France showed no change in the 1530s and 40s but certainly did so after the two year tour of the country in 1564 when she introduced her son to the people of France and gave so many the opportunity to experience Court cuisine.

The evidence suggests it was left to Catherine's third son Henri III to introduce the fork to France after a trip to Venice. Even then the fork had the specific purpose of allowing those adopting the neck ruff to dine properly by spearing the food and putting it into their mouths from above, clear of the ruff. Knife, fork and spoon did not appear together until the sixteenth century and the earliest printed reference to them was in Scappi's cookbook of 1570.

Meanwhile, in China, which was reaching the height of its influence under the Manchu Dynasty (1644-1911), reaching out to Tibet, Mongolia, Burma, Korea, Vietnam and even Nepal, the humble chopsticks remained the eating implement as they had since the time of Confucius. It was he who argued that no weapon of agression should grace the dining table, thus ruling out knives as used elsewhere in the world.

Gradually, French cuisine developed with Francois Pierre de la Varenne developing the first real French sauces in the 1600s. Printing proved to be very important to this development as it gave access to the recipes of Greece and Rome. *Le Viander* was the first printed cookbook in 1490 followed by Apicius in 1498 and the *The Deipnosophists* by Athanaeus in 1514. It was not, however, until the late seventeenth century that French cuisine took on its present character.

London

Meanwhile, in London, the population had increased in the sixteenth century up to 250,000 with cookshops, inns and alehouses. Bread was still the staple and ten commercial bakeries were set up in 1516. The cookshops were the forerunners of the snack bar and restaurant and were located in Bread Street, Eastcheap and similar areas. Lavish meals were organised by the livery companies and the Dinner Book of the Draper's Company contained complete menus from 1564-1602. From small beginnings the City of London alone had 1000 alehouses by 1613.

The seventeenth century saw the change from medieval. Business was concluded in taverns and, later, coffee houses though poor people stayed with the cookshops and street hawkers. Luxury Eating Houses began to open, especially after the influx of Hughenots from France in 1680. Lunch remained the main meal but by 1660 it had moved to mid/late afternoon. The first hallmarked fork appeared in 1632 and 'ordinaries' opened with fixed price meals.

The first London coffee house opened in 1652 in St Michaels Alley, Cornhill and by the following year there were 63 in the City serving coffee from Turkey and the Middle East. It is for this reason that many establishments were called The Turks Head and tipping is said to have come from putting money in a box to ensure prompt service. During the seventeenth century punch was very popular containing arrack from Goa and in 1650 chocolate was introduced. Meanwhile, in America, Britain was faced with rebellion with the American Revolution 1775-1783.

Up to modern times

Continual wars saw the map of the world change on a regular basis as Imperialism grew, introducing an ever increasing array of cuisine influences to the older European nations.

In the Orient, Hong Kong became a British Dependency after the First Opium War in 1842, opening up the way for Chinese cuisine to travel to Britain and in 1853 Commodore Matthew Perry opened up the USA link with Japan which had been insular for so long.

In Europe Napoleon Bonaparte struck at British trade in Egypt when he attacked in 1798 but was defeated by Nelson. His army failed to take Syria but beat the Turks at Abi Qir in 1799 when he returned to seize power in France. He defeated the Austrians in 1800 and a worried Britain resumed the war in 1803. In 1806 Napoleon seized Naples and blockaded British goods before finally being beaten at Waterloo in 1815.

Elsewhere in the world the first horse-drawn omnibus was seen in 1828 and Antoine Careme was appointed cook to Tsar Alexander I of Russia and Baron de Rothschild. Henry Jones of Bristol produced the first self raising flour in 1845 and the first gas cooker was introduced in the 1850s and the electric cooker in the 1890s.

From 1853-56 Europe was rocked by the Crimean War followed by the American Civil War 1861-1865. By the mid nineteenth century the French had plunged themselves into the joys offered by food and its preparation and all the great houses in Europe and America boasted French chefs. And from 1870-1871 Russia besieged Paris and the Parisians starved whilst in 1875 Remington was introducing the typewriter and Alexander Graham Bell the telephone in 1876. Karl Benz revealed his three wheeled car in 1885. In America, Chili con Carne was first written about in The Camp and Fields in 1857 by S. Compton-Smith and in 1896 Chop Suey was supposedly created in New York by Li Hung-Chang.

In India, Britain had gained complete mastery from the other European powers with the last Nawab of Bengal being killed at Plassey in 1757. At this time India adopted the chop (although it became a round potato cake with stuffing), and the cutlet, consisting of meat, chicken or prawn pounded to a flat oval with the bone sticking out.

In 1838 Lea and Perrins launched Worcestershire Sauce, the recipe for which had been brought back from India in 1835 by Lord Marcus Sandys. Curry powder had been invented along the lines of garam masala long before in the seventeeth century and was very similar to *Kitchen pepper* which was noted in English recipes around 1682, including ginger, pepper, clove, nutmeg and cinnamon.

In 1809 Dean Mohamet (or Mahomed) from Patna in Bihar, India, opened the first 'Indian' restaurant dedicated to Indian cuisine. The Hindostanee Coffee House in George Street, London offered meat and vegetable dishes with Indian spices and seasoned rice. The restaurant was very ornate and costs were high such that he had to apply for bankruptcy in 1812.

By 1850 curry was well established. Queen Victoria, who had an Indian confidant, Abdul Karim, is said to have had a curry prepared every day by two Indian chefs in the event she had a visitor from India.

Abdul Karim became the Queen's favourite and most favoured servant, often being referred to as "her Munshi". He remained close to her during all her travels until she died in 1901 when he was allowed to walk with the funeral procession. He finally returned to Agra where he died at the age of 46 in 1909. During this century migrating Hindus took the curry to the West Indies creating the influences on Caribbean cuisine we see today.

As the nineteenth century progressed, unrest emerged throughout India resulting in the revolts by the Sikhs of Punjab in 1845 and 1846 causing 2,500 British casualities. They were eventually defeated in 1849 but this saw the beginning of disenchantment back in Britain with the sub-continent.

In 1857 the famous Sepoy Mutiny near Delhi began under the banner of Bahadur Shah II the last of the Mughal Emperors. Europeans were massacred and siege was laid to the British Residency in Lucknow. The uprising was put down in 1859 ending the final chapter of Mughal history in India and the British Government assumed control from the East India Company.

This aggression further alienated British public opinion which was heightened by the spread of Indian nationalism with acts of terrorism by a few and acts of repression by the British. In 1885 the India National Congress was founded to further fan the flames and by the early years of the new century British goods were being banned in India. Thus the love affair with all things Indian, particularly the food, which had been so obvious up to the mid nineteenth century, gave ground to the total influence of French cusine and virtual disappearance of spicy food.

Service à la Russe was introduced into England around 1850 from Russia via France, leading eventually to the three course meal of today. Each country developed a style to suit its own requirements.

Denmark had the *Smörrebrod* for lunch, (open sandwich), plus an evening meal with fruit or cake; an enormous breakfast was the habit in Norway with a sandwich for lunch and a two-course dinner; in Sweden, *smorgasbord* originated for the pooling of resources; in Finland, a simple breakfast was followed by a soup and a main course for lunch and a three-course dinner; Spain and Portugal enjoyed foods rather more sober and conservative, undisguised by sauces and dressings; North Africa kept alive the feasting ritual and great desserts; and in France, it depended upon where you lived as to whether you cooked in olive oil, goosefat or butter and used garlic, shallots or onions.

Restaurants were not important in France until after the Revolution and the earliest use of the word 'restaurant' was by Clement Marot in the early sixteenth century to refer to a group of fortifying meat broths. In 1765, however, a man named Boulanger set up a business to avoid the Guild monopoly on the sale of broths by offering '*restaurants*' - ragouts on his own premises on little marble tables without cloth with a choice of poached poultry with coarse salt, fresh eggs and broth. Restaurants had arrived, and one of Paris' three Michelin star restaurants still operating, Le Grand Vefours, opened by 1800.

Britain in the eighteenth century was a time of new money and flourishing commerce. Recipe books were published, eating houses flourished and Coffee Houses offered food. Chop Houses opened and beef was considered a sign of strength and prosperity. Even then weight was considered a problem and moderation recommended although the diet for the poor was still bread, cheese and pie. Inns became unisex but taverns remained men only.

The London Tavern, for instance, was known for its food and association with politics with John Wilkes as a regular customer. Chop Houses were popular and turtle was considered a high status food with those who could not afford it having mock-turtle made from calves head.

In 1830 Alexis Soyer was one of the many French chefs who came to Britain and his thinking influenced British dining for many years. The nineteenth century saw the arrival of restaurants and hotels in Britain with celebrity chefs such as Ude, Francatelli and Escoffier, who started the a la carte style of dining during his twenty years at the London Carlton from 1899.

Three establishments in Leicester Square in 1815 were described as 'French restaurants'. Concern about food adulteration led to the 1875 Sale of Food and Drugs Act with a great improvement in quality by 1880. Sandwiches became very popular and some eating houses started to specialise in fish and baked potato leading to the famous British fish and chip industry.

In 1851 the Great Exhibition helped people forget the tragedies of the Irish potato famine and poor corn harvests of 1845-1846 but it took until 1880 before women began to join men in restaurants. In 1860 the first recorded fish and chip shop was opened by John Lees in Oldham and from small beginnings numbers grew to 30,000 outlets in the early 1900s, falling back to the present day 8,500. In England and Wales, the 1871 census recorded an Italian population of 5,063 and by 1911 this number had risen to 20,389. The Italian community in London dates back to the eighteenth century and were originally mainly political refugees.

In 1900 Coca Cola came into Britain with Charles Candler after being introduced in America in 1886 at Jacobs Pharmacy in Atlanta and Britain was pre-occupied with the Boer War 1899-1902.

The War Years

The war years of the twentieth century completely reversed natural cuisine development with many on an almost starvation diet and most meals "bulked-out" to compensate for lack of meat and dairy produce. Few exotic foods or spices were available in Europe and vegetables predominated with bread, tea and potatoes.

J. Lyons & Co Ltd

J. Lyons & Co Ltd opened their first huge establishment in Coventry Street in 1907 and the Strand in London in 1912. Such was the success of their simple concept that Maison Lyons was opened near Marble Arch in 1933 seating 2000 people and employing 1000 staff but even at that it did not equal the 4000 seating at Coventry Street.

The cream of Britain's and Europe's men had been lost in the 1914-18 war and the depression of the twenties added to the misery but the Empire Exhibition at Wembley in 1924 put on a brave imperial face and did much to legitimise ethnic foods. The great exhibition boasted a Mughal palace (operated by the man who went on to open Veeraswamy in London), a Nigerian fortress, a Hong Kong street and even a Samoan house.

In 1927 Charles Lindbergh flew to Paris and in 1937 Xavier Marcel Boulestin became the first TV chef. The beginning of the Second World War put Britain back to subsistance eating and food rationing of bacon, ham, butter, sugar, cooking fat, meat, tea, cheese, jam, eggs and sweets was introduced in 1940. Lemons and oranges disappeared overnight and luxury fruits sold at amazing prices. Bananas also disappeared as did, strangely, onions and in 1941 melons were selling at £2 each. Just when people thought the hardships were over, bread rationing was introduced in 1946 until 1948. However, the Second World War did introduce an enforced understanding of the need for a nutritionally balanced diet.

The post war years gradually saw the return to restaurant dining, with groups like Berni (first one opened in Bristol selling steak, chips and peas) and Beefeater and a gradual international influence in the foods eaten in Britain. The Good Food Guide was established and Elizabeth David wrote her famous *'Book of Mediterranean Food & French Country Cooking'*. Wimpy opened in 1954 and by 1956 Britain boasted 3,000 self service stores as food shopping changed its style.

In the mid fifties the package tour began to show itself, becoming the accepted form of overseas holiday over the following ten years and the process of British people learning overseas cuisines at first hand began.

Immigration became an important factor as peoples from British interests all over the world arrived seeking a new life and bringing their culture and cuisines. Political changes in India with Partition into India and East and West Pakistan on August 15th, 1947 caused great upheavals as did the Independence of East Pakistan (originally Bengal) on 26th March 1971 to become Bangladesh.

Between 1951 and 1961 the number of Pakistanis in Britain grew from 5,000 to 24,000 - Indians from 38,800 to 81,400 - West Indians from 25,300 to 171,800 - East Asians from 12,000 to 29,600 and West African from 5,600 to 19,800.

Interest in food from the mysterious East was further heightened when Coronation Chicken, a spicy mixture including curry paste, red wine, apricot halves, mayonnaise and cream, was invented by Constance Spry and served at the Queen's Coronation lunch in 1953. This was followed by Vesta Instant Curries (beef & chicken) in the 1960s, often many peoples first introduction to Indian food.

Fast food appeared with Pizza Express starting in 1965 and McDonalds in 1974 and the 1960s saw a veritable feast of new foodstyles with ethnic food becoming very popular in some sections of the community. By 1966 the retail emphasis had moved from the self service store to the supermarket with 2,500 outlets available to the British public.

Only in the last twenty five years has the world become a global food market and, for the first time since agriculture started, some ten thousand years ago, people in the West can readily enjoy foods from all over the world, economically and of a high quality.

The culinary phenomenon of the second half of the twentieth century in Britain was the growth in ethnic restaurants and the booming retail market for ethnic foods. The phenomenon was heralded as an inexplicable occurance by many who had long considered British food to be bland and boring - that is until they dipped into history.

The Empire Exhibition at Wembley
(Photos courtesy of Pye's of Clitheroe)

Chapter 5

MEDIEVAL FOCUS

'Pease Pudding and a suck of Bacon'

The Medieval period was a time of great change in England and Europe. It saw social change, religious and economic change. It saw the change of a system built on feudalism to the start of a system based on capitalism. Many foreign foods, herbs and spices had been in England since the time of the Romans, but they had not filtered through to the general populace.

London had been burnt in AD 61 after the rebellion of Queen Boudica but in 100 AD it was rebuilt and by the 3rd century had some 30,000 inhabitants. The city slumped in importance on the departure of the Romans and was then sacked by the Danes in the 9th century. Alfred resettled it in 883 and by the time William the Conqueror arrived in 1066 it had become known as Lundontoun.

Old London Bridge was built for commerce across the Thames in 1209 and remained the only bridge until 1750. By 1400 there were only some 2.5 million people in England and when it became the capital under Edward III in the 14th century it was the only British city comparable in size with cities on the continent (around 50,000).

William the Conqueror provided the first impetus to major change when he used dining to appeal to people of diverse station, holding feasts in Gloucester at Christmas, Winchester, Easter and Westminster at Whitsun.

The second major impetus was the First Crusade 1096-1097 which, unlike other Crusades, was one of knights and adventurers who dispersed in 1099 spreading the foods, herbs and spices they had found in the East.

By 1200 spices had already become a status symbol although cinnamon had been used since Anglo Saxon times in wine and the Romans and Greeks had introduced ginger for digestion, cloves for sinews, mace for colic and nutmeg for colds. These two major forces caused England to open up from the feudal Dark Ages.

Henry FitzAilwyn became London's first mayor in 1193 after the community's recognition by John in 1191 who then went on to grant its first charter in 1215.

London was a hub of growing commerce, very crowded, full of rats, the water polluted and the streets strewn with mud, excrement and offal. There were regular fires and the Church, the major landowner, held sway.

The alehouse became popular in the 13th century and London had its first tavern in 1272. By 1309 there were 354. Many church sites were built by a growing number of factions. One such was the Hospital of St Mary Spital founded in 1197 for the sick, poor and pregnant mothers. It was refounded in 1235 and the Spitalfields Chapel and Charnel House built in 1391 dedicated to St Mary Magdalene and St Edmund.

In 1349 the Black Death reached London and wiped out one third of the populace acting as a natural break to growth. Life was hard and life expectancy low.

The rich and gentry lived a generally debauched, colourful existence, though short due to ill health. Edward III (1327-77) employed Guillaume Tirel (Taillevent) as his chef such was the interest in and importance of food amongst the upper classes and Tirel wrote *Le Viander*, one of the first major cookery books.

Noble kitchens had been influenced by returning Crusaders featuring basil, borage, mallow, dittany, true love, fennel, ginger, cardamom, galingale, cloves, sorrel, mustard seed, nutmeg, anise, mace, mint, peppercorns and cinnamon. Salt was considered so important it was kept in the Tower of London. The active day for both peasant and noble was sunrise to sunset.

Castle life consisted of a small breakfast of bread, cheese and wine then a large dinner taken between 10-12 and supper at sunset, once again with bread, cheese and a stew or soup (hence souper).

Wine was usually the drink of choice (England was the main consumer of wine from the Continent) plus mead and ale. Wassail (ale, honey and spices) was used for special occasions. They would have ducks, pheasants, pigeons, geese, hens, partridges, fish, pork, beef, mutton, cabbage, turnips, carrots, onions, beans, peas, bread, cheese, butter, ale and wine all available to them as required.

A large manor would also be quite self-sufficient with a mill for grinding, oven for baking and gardens for growing. Indeed, food was becoming such a status symbol that special spice powders (fort, douce, blanch) were introduced in the time of King John and in 1390 in the time of Richard II, the first English cookery book, *The Forme of Cury*, was produced with 196 recipes compiled by his chefs and others.

Throughout the Medieval period England developed under the impetus of war and trade which was most keenly felt in London. The Hundred Years War with France ran from 1337-1453 in a series of conflicts between the Capetions and Plantagenets. Crafts grew apace as did trade and in 1358 several cities in Germany formed the Hanseatic League to trade with England. They were given the name *'Easterlings'* from which our currency *'sterling'* derives.

The gentry were attracted to London from the country to 'make their fortune' which many did. One such was Richard (Dick) Whittington, son of a knight who came to London to sell cloth and velvets and became an Alderman in 1393 then Lord Mayor in 1397-1406 and again in 1419.

In 1400 the orange was first introduced to the West but it was not until 1492 that Columbus discovered red chilli peppers in Santa Domingo and even later that such things as tomatoes and turkey appeared.

The forerunners of the modern snack bar appeared on specialist streets in London such as Bread Street and Eastcheap and by 1516 there were ten commercial bakeries in London. The diet of nobility (including the Church) was rich and indulgent. The installation of Archbishop Neville of York in 1467 had 6,000 guests and required:

300 quarters of wheat	2,000 pigs
300 tuns ale	104 peacocks
100 tuns wine	13,500 other birds
1 pipe hippocras	500 stags
104 oxen	1,500 venison pies
6 wild bulls	1,000 sheep
304 calves	304 porkas
400 swans	608 pike and bream
2,000 geese	12 porpoises and seals
1,000 capons	13,000 dishes of jelly, tarts, sugared delicacies.

The gentry were, however, not the only ones to be attracted to London. In the early Medieval period England still operated under villeinage (serfdom) although it was often accepted that one who escaped to a city such as London and remained free for a year and a day was a freeman.

These found the streets not paved with gold but mud, excrement and offal. Indeed the cast-off innards and giblets often thrown out casually from the richer houses were called *'garbage'*, later to come to mean rubbish.

One of the many street cries *"Pease pudding and a suck of bacon"* came from the vendor selling slices of quite firm but nutritious pease pudding with a piece of bacon on a string which was yanked back out of the purchasers mouth once he or she had had their 'suck'.

The peasant's life was hard. Homes tended to be one room with a central stone hearth that served to provide lighting and heating. Where extra light was required, tallow candles were used making the rooms not only dark and dingy but smelly and smoke-filled. Washing was rare.

Their diet consisted of vegetables - often turnips - plus dark, rough, breads not fit for the nobility. In addition frumenty was very popular (wheat berries, long boiled in broth or sometimes milk, flavoured or sweetened) plus fish occasionally, cheese curds, small beer, ale and rarely, meat of an inferior type. Chickens were rarely eaten due to the importance of eggs.

The winter was particularly hard with food quite scarce (even the rich often turned to pigeons) but the working hours were shorter and physical demands less, apart from just trying to keep warm. The diet might be considered healthy, if on the meagre side (not much more than 1,000 kcals), today but for the unsanitary conditions they lived in.

Lifespan rarely extended beyond 30 and girls were married at 13 or 14. Death in childbirth was common. They still believed toothache was caused by a worm so the treatment was to hold a lighted candle to it and if all else failed, yank it. The treatment for wounds was soot or a hot poker.

The rich, despite their lavish diet, were even less healthy due to over-indulgence. They had scurvy, syphilis, tooth decay, heart problems, skin rashes, infections caused by rotting meat and lack of proper nutrition.

The first signs of real social change came in 1381 with the Peasants Revolt. The uprising came from a popular upswell of those who no longer wanted to be serfs or do labour services. They demanded an escape from villeinage and to pay 4 pence a year to rent the land they worked.

The general imbalance of nutrition for rich and peasant alike can be seen by a comparison with optimum nutrition levels today. An athlete in training needs some 5,000 kcal a day (or more depending on size and weight). The rich undoubtedly consumed more than this on a regular basis with little or no activity. An active male needs 2,900 kcals a day but with frumenty only providing 400 kcals a portion and a chunk of dark, rough bread just 215 kcals, it is unlikely the peasants ever reached the optimum level and paupers way below this.

The very popular *frumenty*

Chapter 6

HISTORY OF COFFEE HOUSES IN BRITAIN

Antony Wood writes in Athenae Oxonienses (1691) that the first coffee house opened in Oxford in 1651:-

"Jacob, a Jew, opened a Coffee house at the Angel, in the Parish of St Peter in the East, Oxon, and there it was by some, who delighted in the novelty, drank"

By 1652, at the time of the Restoration, the first coffee house was opened in London by Pasqua Rosee, a Ragusian man-servant, in St Michaels Alley, Cornhill. Quickly other coffee houses opened and they soon became a focus for the cultural ferment in England. In fact, coffee houses became such a popular forum for the intelligensia that they were dubbed 'penny universities,' a penny being the price of a cup of coffee.

A fateful decision made by the East India Company to import tea instead of coffee led to the demise of the Coffee House and England's 'Cafi Culture.' But for that event, coffee could have been the UK's national drink.

By 1663 it is recorded that there were 82 coffee houses in London and by 1700 there were 3,000. The popularity of these establishments led to certain opposition. For example 'The Women's Petition Against Coffee' was set up and it claimed in 1674 that coffee:-

> *... made men as unfruitful as the deserts whence the unhappy berry is said to be brought.*

In the following year King Charles II tried to rid London of its coffee houses with an edict:-

Whereas it is most apparent that the multitude of coffee houses of late years set up and kept within this kingdom, the dominion of Wales and the town of Berwick-upon-Tweed, and the great resort of idle and disaffected persons to them, have produced very evil and dangerous effects, as well as that many tradesmen and others do therein misspend much of their time, which might and probably would otherwise be employed in and about their lawful callings and affairs, but also for that in such houses, and by occasion of the meeting of such persons therein, many false, malicious, and scandalous reports are devised and spread abroad, to the deformation of his Majesty's government and to the disturbance of the peace and quiet of the realm, his Majesty has thought it fit and necessary that the said coffee houses be for the future put down and suppressed.

The edict went on to ban the sale of coffee, chocolate, sherbet and tea in coffee houses or private homes. The outcry was such that Charles decided to back off and no further mention was made of his edict.

Different coffee houses acted as the meeting place for different groups of people. In fact many people would give a particular coffee house as the address where they might be contacted. For example Child's Coffee House near Gresham College, was frequented by the clergy.

As a testament to the influence of these places, Lloyd's Coffee House, founded by Edward Lloyd of Tower Street had ship owners and merchants as customers and acted as a hub through which news about ships was passed. It moved to Lombard Street in 1692 and eventually moved into insurance and became Lloyd's of London.

The Grecian, as the name might suggest, attracted those interested in philosophy and other academic disciplines. Macaulay wrote:-

Those who wished to find a gentleman commonly asked, not whether he lived in Fleet Street or Chancery Lane, but whether he frequented the Grecian or the Rainbow.

The second coffee house mentioned in this quote is the Rainbow, the second oldest coffee house in London, opened by James Farr in Fleet Street in 1657. Another quote by one who frequented the Grecian is the following:-

While other parts of the town are amused with the present actions, we generally spend the evening at this table in inquiries into antiquity, and think anything news which gives us new knowledge.

In Inns and Taverns of Old London by Henry C Shelley one reads:-

Men of science as well as scholars gave liberal patronage to the Grecian. It was a common thing for meetings of the Royal Society to be continued in a social way at this coffee-house, the president, Sir Isaac Newton, being frequently of the parties. Hither, too, came Professor Halley, the great astronomer, to meet his friends on his weekly visit to London from Oxford.

Jonathan's Coffee House, in Exchange Alley, had merchants as customers and is now considered as having developed into the London Stock Exchange. Hooke and Wren were often in Jonathan's taking part in scientific discussions.

Slaughter's Coffee House in St Martin's Lane was established in 1692. It was famed as a centre for chess players but it was also a popular place for those seeking mathematical advice. Abraham de Moivre was considered the resident mathematician at Slaughter's. He would give advice on risk, or chance of loss as he called it.

Dating from 1802, the term café comes from the French 'café' (meaning 'coffee' or 'coffeehouse') and the Italian 'caffe' (also meaning 'coffee'.) In 1839 'caféteria' had been coined in American English from Mexican Spanish to indicate a coffee-store. But the café has been reinvented many times over the centuries.

From 1675, a thousand or so coffee houses flowered during the reigns of Charles II, Queen Anne and George I. By the 19th century however, coffee houses had become exclusive clubs as a prolific press and an efficient post and transport system undermined the function of the coffee houses as centres of communication.

Sometimes coffee houses were used for more formal educational activities such as lectures, but more commonly they provided a base for clubs and societies - including debating clubs. The first of these is supposed to have been based at Mile's Coffee House, at the sign of the Turk's Head in New Palace Yard in 1659.

William Lovett noted that around a quarter of the 2,000 London coffee houses had libraries - some of which had as many as 2,000 volumes. Coffee Houses also, traditionally, supplied newspapers for customers to read.

The Character of a Coffee-House

And if you see the great Morat
With shash on's head instead of hat,
Or any Sultan in his dress,
Or picture of a Sultaness,
Or John's admired curl'd pate,
Or th' great Mogul in's Chair of State,
Or Constantine the Grecian,
Who 14 years was th' only man
That made coffee for th' great Bashaw,
Although the man he never saw;
Of if you see a coffee-cup
Filled from a Turkish pot, hung up
Withing the clouds, and round it Pipes,
Wax candles, stoppers, these are types
And certain signs (with many more
Would be too long to write them ore'),
Which plainly do spectators tell
That in that house they coffee sell.

[Anonymous, 1665]

So far as is known the first coffee house in the Piazza (Covent Garden) was the Bedford, established at No. 14 in 1726. Coffee houses were soon increasing in number, probably because of the growth of custom from the patrons and hangers-on of the two neighbouring theatres. The Piazza Coffee House was in fact founded by the actor, Charles Macklin, in 1754. 'The Piazza: The Social Decline of the Piazza', Survey of London tells us:-

The earliest account of the existence of a coffee-house in the capital is found in a 1652 reference to a Ragusian man-servant known as Pasqua Rosee. Mr Rosee had been brought to England from Ottoman Smyrna by his former employer, Mr Daniel Edwards, a "Turkey merchant" (one who dealt in coffee and other such luxury items). After a falling out with his boss, Pasqua Rosee then teamed up and went into business with another employee of Mr Edwards', his old coachman. The two unlikely business partners proceeded to establish a coffee-house in Cornhill, known in some accounts as "The Turk's Head". It is claimed that this is how coffee first came to these sceptred isles, about 100 years after the first coffee-houses opened in Turkey. However, the Elizabethan essayist Francis Bacon, in his Historia Vitae et Mortis, which was published as early as 1605, warned the public against the dangerous properties of coffee and this implies that some contact at least had existed prior to the establishing of the actual coffee-house.

Up to 57 different "Turk's Head" coffee-houses were recorded in one form or other. We also find "The Jerusalem Coffee-house"; various types of the "Blackamoor" or "Ye Blackmore's Head"; "The Oriental Cigar Divan"; "The Saracen's Head" (of Dickens fame); "The Africa and Senegal Coffee-house"; "The Sultaness"; "The Sultan's Head"; "Solyman's Coffee House"; "Morat Ye Great", and many, many more examples can be found, among them the first Indian restaurant of London, "The Hindoostanee" of 1810.

The "Great Turk Coffee House" (also known as "Morat Ye Great") in Exchange Alley in 1662 is a case in point. Apparently, inside could be found a bust of "Sultan Almurath IV" himself, "the most detestable tyrant that ever ruled the Ottoman Empire". The customer could not only find coffee, tea and tobacco here, but also chocolate and a range of sherbets, which, according to the Mercurius Publicus (12-19 March 1662), were "made in Turkie; made of lemons, roses, and violets perfumed". Another chronicler of the time has suggested that "Morat" was actually the name of the proprietor himself.

Chapter 7

HISTORY OF THE ETHNIC RESTAURANT IN BRITAIN

Although the term 'restaurant' was originally used by Clermont Marot in the sixteenth century to describe a broth, it was not until the time of Boulanger in 1765 that it actually began to be used in its present context. Food catering establishments which may be described as restaurants, were known since the 12th century in Hangzhou, a cultural, political and economic centre during China's Song Dynasty. With a population of over 1 million people, a culture of hospitality and a paper currency, Hangzhou was ripe for the development of restaurants.

Probably growing out of the tea houses and taverns that catered to travellers, Hangzhou's restaurants blossomed into an industry catering to locals as well. Restaurants catered to different styles of cuisine, price brackets, and religious requirements. The earliest recorded commercial eating house is Ma Yung's Bucket Chicken House Chuin in Kaifung, China where dim sum was supposedly invented in 1153 AD.

According to the Guinness Book of Records, the Sobrino de Botin in Madrid, Spain is the oldest restaurant in existence today having opened in 1725. Ethnic restaurants in Britain are mainly a phenomenon of the twentieth century but the recipes and dishes themselves did appear on menus in Coffee Houses and Taverns over a hundred years earlier.

Indian

The history of Indian food in Britain is now over four hundred years old and not only has the cuisine undergone a great change in the United Kingdom but also in its native land. Apart from the reports of occasional explorers, the story really starts with the arrival in Surat of the English merchants of the East India Company in 1608 and then again and more successfully in 1612.

Soon lascars - seamen, mainly from Bengal - were helping to man British ships and despite The Navigation Act of 1660 stating that 75% of the crew of a British ship had to be British, a number began appearing in London throughout the century.

The first recorded case of an Indian being christened in Britain was bound up with British commercial adventures in South Asia. The baptism on 22 December 1616 at St Dionis Backchurch in the City of London, took place in the presence of governors of the East India Company. Many of the first Asian arrivals in Britain came as servants to returning East India Company agents.

By 1804 the number of lascars in London was quoted as 471 and yet by 1810 it had risen to over 1400, around 130 of which would die each year such was the poor condition of their circumstances. Concern about their plight led to the creation of The Society for the Protection of Asiatic Sailors in 1814 and in 1869 complaint was made to the India Office in London that there were upwards of 400 destitute Asians on the streets.

As the influence of the British in India grew, so did the interest in Indian food back in Britain, leading to the publishing of recipes and the commercial creation of curry powder in 1780. The first appearance of curry on a menu was at the Coffee House in Norris Street, Haymarket, London in 1773 but the first establishment dedicated to Indian cuisine was the Hindostanee Coffee House at 34 George Street, Portman Square, London in 1809 as recorded in *The Epicure's Almanack (The commemorative blue plaque, seen below, is actually at 102 George Street and dated 1810, the date the property was valued for rates)*.

It was opened by Dean Mahomet (or Mohamed/Mahomed) from Patna, Bihar, India, via Cork in Ireland. He appreciated the interest in all things Indian and offered a house "*for the Nobility and Gentry where they might enjoy the Hookha with real Chilm tobacco and Indian dishes of the highest perfection*". Decor was very Colonial, with bamboo chairs and picture-bedecked walls, and it proved to be well received. As with many 'coffee houses', however, it did not serve coffee, but was simply cashing in on a popular name of the time. Unfortunately, outgoings were greater than incomings and Mahomet had to file for bankruptcy in 1812, although the restaurant did carry on without him in some form until 1833.

Lascar desertion continued to be a big problem with many ending up on the streets whilst others became entertainers or sold herbs and spices as did the famous Dr Bokanby who sold herbs in London's Petticoat Lane in 1861.

As the twentieth century dawned, the only eating establishments offering Indian cuisine were specialist venues such as the restaurant at The East India United Services Club (founded 1866 in St James Square) and community meeting places for those who had jumped ship in London looking for a new life or, more often, been put ashore without any means of support. Some of these were *Vandary* (Indian chefs) who jumped ship to seek work in London's growing restaurant community but not enough to provide any real impetus for the cuisine.

The first recorded Indian restaurant of the 20th century was the Salut e Hind in Holborn in 1911 but the first to have any real influence was The Shafi opened by Mohammed Wayseem and Mohammed Rahim. Originally thought to have opened in 1920, new evidence from Roy Nolder shows it was actually in 1915. Coming from North India they opened their cafe in London's Gerrard Street (now the centre of London's Chinatown) and employed 4-5 ex seamen. It soon became a kind of community and Indian student centre. Indian students in the UK rose from 100 in 1880 to 1,800 by 1931.

ESTABLISHED 1915
THE OLDEST
INDIAN RESTAURANT IN EUROPE

With Compliments
Mr. & Mrs. L. K. ISHANI

18 GERRARD STREET
PICCADILLY - LONDON W.1
Off Shaftesbury Avenue
01 - 437 2354
FULLY LICENSED

A business card from the 1960s

Soon The Shafi was taken over by Dharam Lal Bodua and run by an English manager with employees such as Israil Miah and Gofur Miah who were later to run their own establishments. One of Dharam's great friends was Vir Bahadur from Delhi who opened his first restaurant in 1927 the Taj Mahal on Charing Cross Road then others in Argyll Street next to The Palladium and Percy Street and The Koh-i-noor in Rupert Street (pulled down in 1978) and was to have a major influence on the industry opening restaurants with his brothers outside London.

Following in her mother's footsteps, his eldest daughter Kashmirin, became his chef, and met an Indian prince, Yashwant Singh, Raja of Sumel, son of an official concubine of the Maharajah of Jaipur in the restaurant. They married in 1938 and lived in the fabulous Rambagh Palace before moving to Sumel House, Ajmer Road, Jaipur. Yashwant Singh had promised Vir Bahadur that he would only have one wife, a promise that he kept and the love match continued until they died within a year of each other some eight years ago (approx 2002).

By 1937 Vir Bahadur had changed his name to Krishna Vir (Sanskrit for Bahadur) and his son Chandra Vir, now resident in Toronto, Canada, remembers "As a child after the war, I remember that the restaurant had queues of customers and my father had to hire a doorman, all decked out in a uniform and turban." Chandra managed the restaurant for a few years in the 1960s.

Ayub Ali Master opened a Curry Cafe in Commercial Road, London in 1920s and then Shah Jalal a Coffee House at 76 Commecial Street. Later, he also started the Indian Seaman's Welfare league in 1943 and his coffee shop was often the first port of call for seamen seeking guidance.

These restaurants were, not surprisingly, mainly for Asians but in 1926/7 the first fashionable Indian restaurant opened when Edward Palmer opened Veeraswamy's Indian Restaurant in London's Regent Street where it still thrives today owned by Ranjit Mathrani and Namita Panjabi. Edward Palmer had been greatly encouraged by friends and acquaintances after his successful running of the Mughal Palace in The Empire Exhibition at Wembley a few years before and he brought staff from India and created a traditional atmosphere such that it became called *"The ex-Indian higher serviceman's curry club"*.

Many of the people from all over India who were later to become the backbone of the new *'curry'* restaurant industry, learned their trade at Veeraswamy. In 1935 Veeraswamy's was sold to Sir William

Steward, M.P., who ran the restaurant for 40 years. He travelled the world in order to source produce and was dubbed 'the curry king' by The Times. His other claim to fame is the introduction of curry in a can. It was at Veeraswamy that lager is first said to have been introduced into Indian restaurants during a visit by the Prince of Denmark.

Queen Victoria, shortly after the Prince Consort's death, arranged for her son to marry Princess Alexandra of Denmark, the beautiful eldest daughter of King Christian IX of Denmark. The couple wed at St. George's Chapel, Windsor on 10 March 1863. The Princess became Queen of England until her death in 1925. Prince Axel of Denmark first met Edward Palmer when visiting the Empire Exhibition at Wembley on May 2nd 1924.

Palmer ran the fantastic Mughal Pavilion at this early 'Disneyland' venture and the King and Queen of Denmark also visited on 24th and 27th June. Having heard of the opening of Veeraswamy's, the Prince visited and was enchanted so much that he made a present of a case of the royal beer, Carlsberg and gave orders for a case to be delivered each year. Many staff learned their trade at Veeraswamy's at that time so Carlsberg became the beer of choice as they moved around Britain opening their own establishments.

The name of the restaurant was later changed to The Veeraswamy during ownership by Sarova Hotels and to Veeraswamy under the present ownership. Meanwhile Sardar and Shamsher Bahadur had come from India to join their brother and opened The Taj Mahal, Brighton; Taj Mahal, Oxford; Taj Mahal Northampton; Kohinoor, Cambridge; Kohinoor, Manchester all before the outbreak of the Second World War and mainly staffed by ex-seamen.

Other establishments for the seamen, usually from the province of Sylhet, opened throughout the years between the wars, such as Abdul Rashim and Koni Khan's coffee shop serving curry and rice on Victoria Dock Road as early as 1920. Gradually the development of Indian restaurants spread outwards from London between the two Great Wars and many of the restaurants that have influenced those established today were created.

Amongst those in London pre 1939 were The Durbar on Percy Street owned by Asuk Mukerjee from Calcutta, and his compatriot from the same city Nogandro Goush who owned The Dilkush in Windmill Street. Asif Khan from Punjab had The Shalimar on Wardour Street and Jobbul Haque of Urrishi owned The Bengal India on Percy Street.

Abdul Gofur opened a café/shop at 120 Brick Lane as well as others in New Road and Commercial Road. Shirref's in Great Castle Street opened in 1935 and Halal, which still thrives today, opened in St Marks Street E1 in 1939.

Such was the influence of the Bahadur family that it was estimated that nearly all first generation East Pakistani, or what was to become Bangladeshi, restaurateurs learned their trade from the Bahadur brothers.

The early Indian restaurants had access to only a limited number of spices and oils. This led to a standard British curry flavour which became the basic taste. For Madras chicken curry there was more cayenne; for Malaysian chicken curry, one added pineapple. Bhuna gosht was a dry lamb dish, rogan gosht had onions and tomato on top. Pulao was rice stir fried with a basic curry, biryani was a pulao with raisins, fried onions and egg on top!

Above: The popular Shafi which opened in 1920

Below: Veeraswamy's as it was in 1927, the first really fashionable Indian restaurant in Britain.

Many cafes opened up around the seaports of Britain by ex seamen but they had great difficulty in obtaining the necessary rice and spices. During the Second World War the social focus shifted to The Gathor, a basement cafe at 36 Percy Street, London but soon after, Sanu Miah opened The Green Mask on Brompton Road, which became a centre for prominent East Pakistanis and their politicians.

Also in 1942-3 Mosrof Ali and Israil Miah opened The Anglo Asian at 146 Brompton Road, London and by 1957 Mosrof Ali also had The Durbar in Hereford Road. His last business was The Curry Garden Indian in 1975 before retiring in 1979.

Some of the restaurants that opened in the 50s & 60s

Ambala, Brick Lane E1	- 1965
Ambala, Gerrard Street	- 1965
Dilchad, Widegate Street E1	- 1962
Sweet & Spicy, Brick Lane E1	- 1969
Jomuna, Wilton Road SW1	- 1969
Tandoori of Chelsea, Fulham Rd SW3	- 1965
Maharani, Clapham High Street, SW4	- 1965
Noorjahan, Bina Gardens, SW5	- 1965
Star of India, Old Brompton Road, SW5	- 1954
Moti Mahal, Glendower Place, SW7	- 1956
Sonargaon, Brixton Road, SW9	- 1966
Nazims, Garratt Lane, SW18	- 1966
Agra, Whitfield Street, W1	- 1954
Amjadia, Picton Place, W1	- 1968
Anwars, Grafton Way, W1	- 1962
Gaylord, Mortimer Street, W1	- 1966
Everest, Craven Road, W2	- 1961
Ganges, Praed Street, W2	- 1965
Akash, Irving Street, WC2	- 1958
Punjab, Neal Street, WC2	- 1947
The India Club, The Strand, WC2	- 1950
Bombay, Oxford	- 1955

The 1950s saw a great influx of Punjabis in the Southall area due to the specialised employment policy of Woolf's Rubber Factory whose executive had personal experience of the excellence of Punjabi staff, and Bengalis continued to settle around the Tower Hamlets area. Until 1962 members of the Commonwealth were allowed to enter Britain freely but even thereafter many Asians came from Africa and a bigger group came from Kenya in 1968.

The fifties and sixties saw a rapid growth in Indian restaurant numbers in Britain, especially in London and the South East, where over 45% of Indian restaurants are still located. Gradually the Indian restaurant concept spread all over Britain, even though those running the restaurants were often not Indian at all. Until Bangladeshi Independence in 1971 at least three quarters of 'Indian' restaurants in Britain were Pakistani owned.

After 1971, the geographical differences became clear, with over half the restaurants owned and managed by Bangladeshis, most of who were from the one area of Sylhet. Once you reach Birmingham, however, the situation changes with the number of Bangladeshis decreasing and Pakistanis increasing. By the time you reach Bradford and Manchester, the restaurateurs are almost entirely Pakistani,

Kashmiri and North Indian and once you reach Glasgow the concentration is almost entirely Punjabi as it is in the Southall, Wembley region of London.

In Birmingham, Abdul Aziz opened a café/shop selling curry and rice in Steelhouse Lane in 1945 which became The Darjeeling, the first Indian in Birmingham, owned by Afrose Miah although some say it was The Shah Bag on Bristol Street owned by Abul Kalam Nozmul Islam who also owned Anuh Bag. The growth really got underway in the 1950's. The Aloka, originally called The Curry House, opened on Bristol Street in 1960 and Banu on Hagley Road in 1969.

Manchester started with the Bahadur brother's Kohinoor in Oxford Street, followed by Malik Bokth with The Everest, Nojir Uddin who opened Monzil and Lal Miah who opened The Orient. The first restaurant in Rusholme, the location of Manchester's modern day Curry Mile, opened in 1959. Rajdoot, long a favourite in Manchester, opened in 1966. Malik Miah Guri, manager at The Kohinoor, moved to Birmingham and opened The Shalimar at Dale End.

In Bradford, The Sweet Centre on Lumb Lane which opened in 1964 was one of the earliest after The Kashmir in Morley Street in 1958. When the owner of The Shafi in London, Mr Dharan died in 1963, Ahmed Kutub, who worked there, went to open his own restaurant in Newcastle and in the 1950s Rashid Ali moved from a café/shop in London's Drummond Street to Cardiff to open his own establishment. The first restaurant to open in the north was The Anglo Asian on Ocean Road, South Shields run by Syed Lukman Ali.

North of the border, the first record is of a restaurant opened in Glasgow by Dr Deb from Nawakhali before 1939 and since that time the management staff in most existing restaurants seem to have developed from just two original Punjabi style establishments giving rise to a great similarity of menu.

According to other pundits, however, the first modern curry shop opened in the city in 1954, although there had been cafes for seamen and others of Asian origin before this. The Taj Mahal was opened in Park Road by Sultan Ahmed Ansari. The great man died in 1995, having triggered the mushrooming effect that has created the Glasgow curry scene of today - that is unless you listen to the other stories that say the first was Green Gates in Bank Street in 1959!!

Whichever is correct, it was a time when you could have a feast for just over 3 shillings (15p today). The credentials of the Taj Mahal are confirmed by Ansari's daughter, Noreen, who remembers going to the restaurant after school. For his part, Nasim Ahmed, whose father Noor Mohammed started Green Gates and then went on to found the Shish Mahal dynasty, remembers 2 shilling (10p) curries and being pressed into service as a waiter and kitchen porter.

Menus were basic and people would set their own cutlery to encourage speedier service. Then the Shish Mahal opened in Gibson Street offering a very different scene, with dinner-jacketed waiters and flock wallpaper, soon to be followed by the Koh-i-Noor, opened by their cousin, Rasul Tahir. Unfortunately, once the curry centre of Glasgow, the influence of Gibson Street is no more. The Koh-i-Noor moved to its present incarnation in Charing Cross and the Shish Mahal to the premises that were originally occupied by Taj Mahal, Ansari having sold out after 30 years to move into the hotel business.

The cuisine moved up-market again with the Indian (as opposed to Pakistani) influence of Balbir Sumal's Ashoka in the 1980s, which eventually led to the development of The Harlequin Group by his one-time partner, Charan Gill. Although Glasgow celebrated 50 years of curry history in 2004, before they get carried away - would it be too impolitie to point out that Kushi's was opened in Edinburgh in 1947 by Kushi Mohammed from the Indus Valley - so which city was first, after all?

In the sixties and seventies, owners began to make serious money from the industry, with people such as Rajiv Ali, who became Chairman of the South East Bank in Bangladesh having found his fortune with a curry house on Whitechapel Road E1. Haji Abdul Razzah came to Britain with an early wave of immigrants and lived in Kentish Town in 1960. He returned to Bangladesh in 1985 and opened The Polash Hotel in Sylhet having made his fortune from chicken tikka masala.

The three main influences on the growth of Indian restaurants were firstly the growing affluence and cosmopolitan nature of the British public and secondly the introduction of the tandoor in the sixties.

The tandoor came, originally from the Middle East with the name deriving from the Babylonian word *'tinuru'* meaning fire. Hebrew and Arabic then made it *tannur* then *tandur* in Turkey, Central Asia and, finally Pakistan and India, who made it famous worldwide.

The first tandoor in India in a restaurant is said to have been in the Kashmiri Moti Mahal in New Delhi in 1948 and several restaurants have claimed to be the first to have a tandoor in Britain. Although several restaurants have claimed to be the first to have a tandoor in Britain, initial research suggested the man responsible was, in fact, Mahendra Kaul who started the excellent Gaylord group.

The other major influence was the continued growth of immigration to provide the people to staff the growing number of Indian restaurants. 360,000 Bangladeshis are forecast for the year 2050.

In 1960 there were just 500 Indian restaurants in Britain but by 1970 this had grown to 1,200. With the influx after Bangladesh Independence numbers grew rapidly to 3,000 in 1980 and by 2000 there were almost 8,000 Indian restaurants in Britain turning over more than £2 billion a year employing some 70,000 people as one of the major industries in the country.

By 2008 numbers had exceeded 9,000 with a turnover approaching £3.5bn. Chicken Tikka Masala, a British-Bangladeshi creation predating the relatively short-lived balti craze, has become so popular that it is available in a wide variety of forms ranging from crisps to pies and statistics show that 14.6% of all first choices in restaurants are for the dish which has no real recipe and can vary from hot to creamy and red to green.

The first to claim CTM's invention are descendents of Sultan Ahmed Ansari who owned The Taj Mahal in Glasgow in the 1950s but it is also claimed by Ali Ahmed Aslam who took over the restaurant from him and called it Shish Mahal circa 1970. Sheikh Abdul Khalique from Essex also claimed the creation of CTM as it was nicknamed for the first time by Colleen Grove in Spice-n-Easy Magazine in 1994, as have half a dozen other chefs and, according to folklore, it came about when gravy loving Brits wanted a sauce with their Chicken Tikka and Condensed Tomato Soup with added spices was used on the spur of the moment in a flash of commercially motivated creation.

In 1982, Taj International Hotels flew in the face of advice and opened The Bombay Brasserie in Courtfield Road SW7 under Adi Modi and changed the entire Indian restaurant scene by setting a new benchmark for quality. Many of the previous owners and chefs had learned their trade 'hands on' but now a new class of chef was to appear backed by years of training in Taj and Oberoi management colleges in India.

Soon London boasted several top class establishments such as Namita Panjabi's Chutney Mary, Amin Ali's The Red Fort, Tamarind, La Port des Indes, Cafe Lazeez, Cyrus Todiwala's Cafe Spice Namaste, Chor Bizarre, Andy Varma's Vama and more recently, Rasoi Vineet Bhatia, Amaya, Zaika, Benares and Quilon. Enam Ali of Le Raj was one of the early pace setters for Bangaldeshi restaurants as well as being one of the founder members of The Guild of Bangladeshi Restaurateurs, created to serve the community alongside the Bangladesh Caterers Association, first started in 1960. He also started the very successful British Curry Awards in 2005.

In 1984 Pat Chapman created The Curry Club and *Good Curry Guide* to publicise the cuisine and bring pressure to bear on supermarkets to stock both ingredients and chilled/frozen meals and was followed by the first edition of our own *Real Curry Restaurant Guide* in 1988/9 which covered over 6,000 Indian restaurants followed by the *Best in Britain Awards (BIBA)* and *National Curry Week*.

Entrepreneurs such as Kirit and Meena Pathak of Pataks, G.K. Noon of Noon Products and Perween Warsi of S&A Foods identified the gaps in the retail market accompanied by rice brands Tilda, Veetee and Westmill and Indian lagers Kingfisher, Cobra and Lal Toofan, such that the Indian sector has for some years been seen as one of the fastest growing food and drink sectors in Britain. More chapters of the story are yet to unfold as the cuisine moves upmarket, establishments become ever more refined, chefs become more adventurous and demand continues to grow.

Chinese

The first wave of Chinese immigrants, who arrived in the second half of the 19th Century, came after China's defeat in the Opium Wars and, as with the lascars, were mainly seamen. They jumped ship in Britain and settled in the port cities of Liverpool, Cardiff and London and as the new century dawned, the movement away from the docks to the cities into first laundries then catering began. The earliest arrivals were often associated with the East India Company and settled in the East End of London in general and Limehouse Causeway in particular by the 1880s.

The Chinese from Shanghai settled around Pennyfields, Amoy Place and Ming Street in Poplar whilst those from Canton and Southern China gravitated towards Gill Street and Limehouse Causeway. By 1913 there were thirty shops and cafes for Chinese people in Pennyfield and Limehouse Causeway although this 'mini boom' was to decline rapidly by the 1930's as shipping slumped.

After World War Two, the thousands of sailors taken on for the duration were laid off and repatriated to China. Some contrived to stay in the UK, by whatever means. There was also a small community of diplomatic and business exiles who preferred not to go back to China after the Communist Party came to power in 1949.

But the turmoil in China caused by war stimulated a much larger wave of migration from Hong Kong and the New Territories. The 1951 census recorded 12,523 Chinese people in the UK, a figure which rose to 38,750 in 1961 and just over 96,000 in 1971.

By the 1950's the Chinese community began to focus on Soho in London for the theatre trade and when diplomatic relations standardised in 1950, several Mandarin speaking former diplomats opened Peking-style restaurants. The famous Kenneth Lo, whose grandfather was a Chinese Ambassador to

London and knighted by Queen Victoria, became one such, starting as a low level diplomat and opening three top class restaurants after writing numerous Chinese cookery books.

This movement continued and by the 1960's Soho had become London's Chinatown and the flow outward to the suburbs and elsewhere started where costs were much cheaper. The first Chinese restaurant in London was opened (probably in 1907) by Charlie Cheung in Limehouse in the East End but, more importantly, a year later, by Chung Koon, a former ship's chef on the Red Funnel Line who had settled in London and married an English girl. He opened the very smart Maxim's in Soho in 1908 which served Cantonese food of which the favourite dish was 'jarjow', pork in a sweet and sour sauce. Soon after, he opened The Cathay in Glasshouse Street which eventually became a Japanese establishment in 1996 which Koon would have hated.

By the 1930s there were three Chinese restaurants operating in Soho catering for the West End theatre crowds. A few years later Choys opened and still operates restaurants in Kings Road, Chelsea and London SW19.

In Manchester, the first Chinese restaurant to open was Ping Hong in Moseley Street in 1948 only to close a couple of years later. The first in Sheffield was The Rickshaw around 1957 followed by Zing Va in 1959 and the first in Huddersfield was the Rice Bowl in 1957. The first vessel to arrive in Liverpool from China was in 1834 so it is not surprising that there were at least five restaurants opened in Pitt Street soon after the First World War.

However, there were fewer than 5,000 Chinese in Britain up until the War and it was not until after the Second World War that Chinese food gained any real popularity fostered by American servicemen taking English girls to The Cathay supported by returning British servicemen with a taste for Oriental food acquired during overseas postings. It is said that even General de Gaulle had to seek out The Cathay to get away from an Anglo-Saxon diet.

Chung Koon's son John was born in 1926 and took over The Cathay in 1957. He opened the first real up-market Chinese restaurant, Lotus House in 1958. Such was the demand for his food that John Koon then did the un-heard of and launched the first ever Chinese takeaway in London's Queensway and followed it up according to legend, by convincing Billy Butlin to open a Chinese kitchen in every Butlins Holiday Camp with a simple menu of Chicken Chop Suey and Chips.

The Chinese quickly adopted the takeaway principle as well as the British love for fish and chips and soon most small villages and towns had their Chinese takeaway which doubled as a fish and chip shop.

Britain had no history of colonial contact in China and Japan except for Hong Kong, so much of the post war influence was from America until the Commonwealth Immigration Act in 1962 introduced the 'voucher system'. The breakthrough came in 1951 when the British government finally recognised Mao's communist regime leaving the diplomats of the defunct Nationalist government with a dilemma. They could not return to China but also needed new jobs and catering was a way out - Embassy kitchens had chefs and the diplomats were resourceful.

The boom in demand in Britain for dining out was fuelled by the new-found consumer wealth in the Middle Class and coincided with a post war boom in Chinese immigration rising to 38,750 by 1961. Chinese food spread all over Britain until today there are over 7,600 outlets turning over some £2 billion a year and the Chinese population has grown to 157,000.

It wasn't until the late 1950s and the arrival of the Hong Kong Emporium on London's Rupert Street that better ingredients became available in Britain. In 1963 the now communist Chinese Embassy once again gave the business a boost when a group of Chinese restaurateurs managed to convince the ambassador's chef, a Mr Kuo from Beijing, to defect. They set him up with his own restaurant, the Kuo Yuan in North West London, and it soon became a huge hit, not least because he was serving the first Pekinese dishes Britain had ever seen, including Peking Duck.

In the south, Choy's in Kings Road, London SW3 was one of the pioneers, opening in 1937 and Old Friends in Commercial Road, E14 opened in the 1950's followed by Good Friends in Salmon Lane E14 in 1962 and Young Friends E14 in the late 1960's. Poon & Co in WC2 also opened in the late 1960's and Empire Palace in Chelmsford in Essex dates back to 1963.

In 1968, a hair salon designer called Michael Chow opened Mr Chow in Knightsbridge, soon frequented by the likes of Mick Jagger, Marlene Dietrich and the Beatles, and Chinese food was finally established as a staple of British life.

In the Midlands and North, The New Happy Gathering in Station Street was the first Cantonese to open in Birmingham in 1970 and Ping On in Deanhaugh Street is the oldest Chinese restaurant in Edinburgh followed by The Rendezvous in 1956. There could have been a new surge of immigration from Hong Kong in 1997 when it was handed back to China, with 50,000 families being entitled to move to Britain but the influx was minimal, although a considerable flow of investment funds was evident.

Today there is a huge range of Chinese restaurants for the public to enjoy from the simple Hong Kong style that has been successful for so many years, to Soho's oldest restaurant, Christine Yau's Yming and the smart, modern restaurants opening in Britain's cities such as Kai in London's Mayfair.

Each major city has its Chinatown, particularly London, Glasgow and Manchester, where people flock to enjoy Peking, Cantonese, Szechuan, Hunan and even Fukien food in quite often huge establishments with massive menus. In the restaurant sector growth is somewhat static as we move further into the third millennium, after poor publicity over MSG and lack of innovation within the industry due to its tie in with fish and chips and cheap takeaway but in the retail sector demand continues to grow apace and the 'all you can eat' Chinese buffet sector continues to be very popular.

Thai

There were only some 5,000 Thai people in Britain in 1996 so it is not surprising that the cuisine has not swamped the market despite its rapid growth in popularity. One of the main reasons for growth in interest in Thai cuisine has been the growing numbers of British tourists going to Thailand which grew to 102,209 in 1986 and further to 300,000 by 1996.

The first Thai restaurant in London was The Bangkok in Bute Street SW7 which opened in 1967 followed by The Siam in St Albans Grove off Kensington High Street in 1970 and the owner Mudita Karnasuta, then opened Busabong in Fulham Road and Loy Krathong in Newcastle plus Thai Orchid in Northumberland, all since sold. Her daughter and an important figure in the Thai community, Mini Chutrakul-Gosling then opened Busabong Too and Busabong Tree alongside the River Thames and sold the former to her mother who opened The Hamilton Arms in 1991.

S&P Thai followed in Fulham Road in 1973 but the real boom came in the eighties. Saigon in Frith Street W1 opened in 1984 and the benchmark for quality and success came with the opening of The Blue Elephant in Fulham Broadway SW5 in 1986. Mantanah Thai opened in SE25 in 1988 as did Tamnag Thai on West Hill SE19 followed by Sang Thai in Glentworth Street NW1 in 1989.

Today there are over 600 Thai restaurants throughout Britain and numbers are growing healthily, especially in public houses, which have been quick to recognise the attractions of the simple, healthy cuisine. Thai restaurants such as Blue Elephant and Yum Yum Thai in Stoke Newington are now considered amongst the top restaurants in London showing how far the cuisine has come in just over thirty years.

Other Asian Influences

Japanese presence in Britain dates from after the Second World War and there has been very little demand for Japanese cuisine by other than the Japanese community and tourists until the last decade of the twentieth century. Many Japanese people who now live in London came in the 1980s as Japanese companies spread into Europe. But there have been Japanese people living in Britain since the 1860s following the Meiji Restoration and the reopening of Japan's borders.

The first recorded Japanese visitors to Britain were sailors, arriving in 1614 and perhaps even earlier in 1587. Today over 55,000 Japanese people live in London.

The first Japanese restaurant to open was in 1967 when Akiko Kuzusaka founded Hiroko in London. The Ajimura in Shelton Street WC2 and Tsukuba WC2 followed in 1972, Kiku in Mayfair in 1978 and Ikeda also in Mayfair in 1978 and Mitsukoshi in Lower Regent Street in 1985 and the first Benihana at Swiss Cottage in 1986 and even forty years later there are still only 300 or so.

The 1991 Census showed there to be just 25,000 Japanese in Britain and most of these live around London giving rise to a figure of 83% of Japanese restaurants being located in London and the South East. Interest in Japanese food has grown considerably in the last fifteen years bringing the appearance of new restaurants in other cities around Britain but the numbers are likely to remain small. Sushi and Ramen (noodle) Bars are the latest trend to appear with the first Wagamama noodle bar opening in 1992.

Malaysian/Indonesian cuisine has been available in London for well over thirty years but, once again, the numbers are very small - some 100 outlets, 71% of which are in London - based on a population of just 10,000. Satay House first opened in London in 1973 and Melati in Peter Street W1 in 1979. Raffles in Kenilworth claims to be one of the first Colonial Malaysian restaurants in Britain, but with the recent openings of such up-market restaurants as Awana in London and Suka in Berners Street, Malaysian cuisine is on the move.

Vietnamese cuisine is a relative newcomer to Britain and was boosted by the 20,000 refugees from Vietnam after the fall of Saigon in 1975 and the US troop withdrawal. The population has settled down to around 14,000 now, 54% of whom live in London and 77% of the 30 restaurants are in London and the South East. The earliest restaurants were simple affairs but the range now goes from the basic to up-market establishments such as Saigon Saigon in Hammersmith. Thanh Binh in North London boasts of having the same chef since 1990 and Pho opened in Clerkenwell in June 2005 as London's first Vietnamese street food restaurant to offer yet another dimension.

Korean restaurants have blossomed in the past ten years or so due to the presence of a considerable Korean community working in Britain, mainly in the electronics and computer-allied industries. Since immigration restrictions were relaxed in 1989, the British Korean population has grown rapidly to around 30,000, and most of them - some say as many as 20,000 - live in New Malden. Ran opened in Soho in 1987 and Kaya in Mayfair in 1983.

There are presently 40 Korean restaurants in Britain but almost all of these (91%) are in London and the South East. New Malden just outside London was the first settling place for the Korean community and several restaurants appeared from 1991 onwards to service it including the very popular Asadal owned by the Park family, which then made the transformation to central London in Holborn.

Italian

The Italian community, dating back to the eighteenth century, settled around Clerkenwell and Holborn in London and were mainly educated political refugees. The first restaurant we know of was run by Joseph Moretti who was born in Venice in 1773. He ran an 'Italian Eating House, just off Leicester Square from 1803-1805 according to his great grandson Colin. Moretti married Jane Bargmann in 1799.

John Baptiste Pagliano, born in Piedmont in 1764, came to England in 1774 where he was employed as a cook to the Venetian Ambassador. He then established an hotel in St Martins Street called Newton's (1799) and later owned The Sabloniere in Leicester Suare which was renowned for its catering. He married Sarah Bargmann in 1798 and the family continued to run it until 1845. By 1881 there were 3,500 Italians in London and by 1901 the number had risen dramatically to 11,000.

Excerpt from Epicures Almanack (1815) pp 152-155 (courtesy of Colin Moretti)

Pagliano's

A few doors from Brunet's Hotel, there is a large establishment rendered conspicuous by the following label in staring capitals, SABLONIÈRE, which inscription is an obvious absurdity. La Sablonière is the name of the once famous cook in Paris, whose performances on the spit, gridiron, and kitchen dresser, were so much admired, that his rivals and followers, by way of obtaining a share of his custom, used to announce that they gave dinners à la Sablonière. Such was the announcement here! But some John Bull of a house-painter retrenched the article at the expense of propriety, and for the sake of brevity. This house is now kept by Signor Pagliano, who is himself, perhaps as good a cook as the noted La Sablonière. Make the experiment, and you will at all events find his establishment the most excellent and reasonable house for getting a good dinner either in the French, English, or Italian style. Mr Pagliano has another and a cheaper house near at hand in St Martins Street which house was the very identical residence of our great Sir Isaac Newton. His observatory is still to be seen on the roof. One of our coadjutors, by way of experiment – did penance here (as the Spaniards say when they make a feast of a dinner) by bill of fare, at the following moderate expense. It is one of the heaviest charges made against John Bull that when he intends to fare well, he cannot help crying out "roast beef". We caution him, that when at this or any other house, he sees announced in the bill of fare, a stewed lion, or a roasted owl, he do hold his tongue, preserve every muscle in his jolly countenance undistorted, lift not for his bushy eye-brows, but quietly order up some of the lion or owl. He will find either dish excellent fare; the one is like hare and the other like partridge as gold is like to gold. But he must not say aught for or against the game-lairs or poachers; he must use his teeth and hold his tongue; he must not say as Pistol1 did, and as he sometimes used to do, when bad news annoyed him, "eat; and eat; and swear".

Pizza

The Italian-American Historical Society once stated that pizza was brought back to Rome by legionnaires stationed in Palestine in the first century BC. The soldiers had grown tired of the local, unleavened bread and spiced it up with cheese and olive oil. So goes the argument that pizza's true ancestor is the matzoh. The world's first pizzeria was the Port'Alba, which opened in Naples in 1830. It cooked its pizzas in an oven lined with Vesuvian lava. The Port'Alba became a haunt for artists and writers, and the poet Salvatore di Giacomo wrote several poems about pizza from one of its tables.

The restaurant now called the Antica Pizzeria Brandi, just off the trendy Via Chiaia, was founded in 1780 by Pietro Colicchio, who had neither sons nor daughters, so he left it to Enrico Brandi, who left it to Maria Brandi, who married Rafaele Esposito, who sold it to Vincenzo Pagnani, who turned it over to his son, Eduardo Pagnani; it was here that pizza got its modern look in 1889 when a treat was prepared for Queen Margherita and taken to the nearby royal palace. It was also the first known pizza delivery.

To give the pizza a patriotic appearance, Rafaele Esposito used the colours of the new Italian flag: tomato sauce for the red; basil for the green; and for the white, a key ingredient - mozzarella di bufala. The Queen loved the pizza, and an international delicacy was born. Even as Rafaele Esposito was concocting a pizza fit for a queen, his countrymen were flocking to America, and they took pizza with them. In 1905, Gennaro Lombardi opened the first American pizzeria at 53½ Spring St. in New York. But pizza was considered foreign food and could be found only in Italian neighborhoods. When World War II sent great waves of Americans to Italy, GIs with names such as Kelly and Schwartz got their first taste of pizza. It was love at first bite, and, when they returned, pizza became a national obsession.

Immigration

Although most Italian immigrants at this time were not catering orientated, there was obviously an interest in Italian cuisine as several entries were noted in PO London Directory in 1851 including Charles Gatti Pastrycook, Luigi Previtali, Italian Hotel, 15 Arundel Street, V Guardetti, Secretary Italian Club of the Culinary Art in St Martins Street. Bertolini's at 32 St Martins Lane is noted in Cruchlys London 1865 and Solferino at 7 Rupert Street in Routledge's Popular Guide 1873.

One of the early Italian connections with catering came when Swiss Italian Carlo Gatti started selling ice cream in London in 1850. His product rapidly became famous and he died a millionaire in 1870. Over one hundred years later the frozen ice cream industry is worth over £2.6 billion a year. Pursuing the catering connection Terroni & Son opened in Clerkenwell Road in 1890 and G. Gazzano & Son in Farringdon Road in 1901.

A restaurant since 1880, 45 Dean Street Soho is perhaps most famously remembered as Gennaro's. Here such luminaries as the Kings of Greece, Yugoslavia and Siam dined alongside Caruso and Dame Nellie Melba. Up until his death Gennaro would greet his guests at the door to present each female diner with a red rose.

With Gennaro's death, though it remained an Italian restaurant, 45 Dean Street fell in to disrepair, and there was little proof of its glamorous past when The Groucho Club purchased the site in 1984. An early cafe restaurant, which doubled as a delicatessen, was Salvo Jure which opened in Brushfield Street E1 in 1859 near the Spitalfield Market.

From the 1890s onwards a new grouping of Italian immigrants began to settle around Soho in London following the hotel and restaurant trades. The Italian Society of Mutual Aid for Hotel and Restaurant Employees was actually set up in 1886 in Gerrard Street, now centre of London's Chinatown. Many of these new immigrants worked in London's restaurants and then started their own restaurant as did the four Bertorelli brothers who created Bertorelli's in Charlotte Street in 1912.

The Contis, Rossis, Sidolis, Basinis, Gazzis, Servinis and so on come from the plains of northern Emilia-Romagna. Much of the Italian population of South Wales and elsewhere in the UK hales from Bardi in Emilia-Romagna over a century ago, having forsaken their poverty-stricken homeland for Britain's 'gold-lined' streets. The Bernis (later famous for Berni Inns), the Rabaiottis, the Sidolis and the Bracchis as well. Indeed, 'bracchi' is still a generic name in Wales for a café.

By 1911 there were 12,000 Italians in London which had fallen to 11,000 by 1921 after the First World War. Gradually Italian restaurants became fashionable such as Leoni's Quo Vadis in Dean Street, Bertorelli's and Quaglino's. In 1934 Pizza Paradiso opened in Store Street WC1 followed by Ristorante Italiano in Curzon Street W1 in 1936.

The Second World War was a major setback for the industry as Britain went to war with Germany and Italy. The Second World War proved a tricky time for the UK's Italian community. Churchill's instruction to imprison every Italian male between the ages of 16 and 70 as an enemy alien ("Collar the lot!" he famously said, after Mussolini joined forces with Hitler in June 1940) created general panic and considerable antipathy. By 1951 there were still only 10,000 Italians in London.

Gradually they became accepted as part of London's cosmopolitan life again and Italian restaurants boomed, pushing out of London all over Britain. By 1971 there were 30,000 Italians in London and many more thousands all over the country, most of whom were still involved in the catering industry. By 1998 there were some 5,000 Italian restaurants in Britain, 2,900 of which were pasta or pizza establishments and the balance full service restaurants, with an annual turnover approaching £1 billion.

Italian restaurants responded to the British middle class boom in the 60s & 70s

La Fontana, London SW1	- 1964	Da Renato, Bristol	- 1971
Verbanella, London SW3	- 1966	Casa Italia, Southport	- 1978
Verbanella, London W1	- 1962	Casalingo, Brighton	- 1972
Paradiso e Inferno, London WC2	- 1966	Ristorante Roma, Newcastle	- 1965
Conca D'Oro, London WC1	- 1964	Da Corrado, Shirley, Birmingham	- 1965
Mario e Franco's Tiberia, Queen Street	- 1962	Pizzeria Giovanni, Sheffield	- 1973
Concordia, London W2	- 1970	Poldino's, Aberdeen	- 1977
La Lupa, London W2	- 1967	Caprice, Edinburgh	- 1967
Da Pappino, Windsor	- 1962		

Charlotte Street W1 is the site of the original Bertorelli's founded over 90 years ago (1912) by the Bertorelli family

The Spaghetti House first opened in 1955 in London - First San Rocco restaurant opened in 1971 in Manchester - Birmingham's oldest Italian is La Galleria, which opened in 1977 Newcastle-upon-Tyne's first Italian opened in 1965. Pasqualino Fulgenzi is still at the helm at the Roma, in Collingwood Street - Salvos in Leeds opened 1976.

The pasta market alone in 1997 was worth £571 million and major chains have grown up such as Pizza Hut, Bella Pasta and, more recently, ASK, Its, and Est Est Est with every sign that growth will continue fuelled by Spanish and Portuguese moving into what they see as a profitable sector.

Greek & Turkish

There was a Greek community in Greek Street, London as long ago as 1677 so Greek cuisine is notexactly new to Britain. The influx of Cypriots started in the 1920s and 1930s and they began opening restaurants after the Second World War. Greek Cypriots tended to settle in Hackney, Palmers Green, Islington and Haringey and Turkish Cypriots in Stoke Newington. Greek Cypriots appeared in Soho in the 1930s then Camden Town after the war and then Fulham by the mid 1960s. The main influx of Turkish Cypriots was in the 1960s and by 1971 the Greek Cypriot community had turned its attention to Wood Green, Palmers Green and Turnpike Lane.

Only around one third of the 550 or so Greek restaurants in Britain are in London, most of these being in North and West London. Some 40% of the 150 or so Turkish restaurants are in the capital with a heavy concentration in North London. Turkish cuisine is also well represented in Scotland. One of the earliest Greek restaurants was not in London at all but Georges in St Michael Street, Southampton in 1940, slightly pre-dated by The White Tower in London's West End in 1939. Kalamaras in London W2 opened in 1966 and remains popular today; Andreas started in Charlotte Street in 1960 and the cuisine moved up-market with the opening of The Real Greek in Hoxton in 1999.

Many of the earliest Turkish restaurants grew up in the Stoke Newington area where the earliest community was located. The most successful of the Turkish restaurants was the Efes Group which started in 1974 in London and moved to several locations throughout the country, Husayin Oser's Sofra Group and the Tas Group in London.

Tex Mex/Afro-Caribbean

Tex Mex is a modern, Texas influenced version of traditional Mexican cuisine based around staples such as the tortilla, enchiladas, tacos and tostados but introducing chilli con carne, burritos, fajitas and chimichangas. The introduction of Tex Mex and Mexican cuisine came from the American servicemen and the tourists since the Second World War and the present popularity of all this group of cuisines has been very much influenced by travel. There are some 380 Tex Mex/Caribbean restaurants in Britain turning over some £300 million a year.

Whilst public demand for Tex Mex, Mexican and Caribbean food grew in the last decade of the last millennium, the growth of good class restaurants was slow to respond. The retail sector was the first to respond to the demand but the quality of the restaurants in the sector is now improving rapidly. Tex Mex in Edinburgh was first opened in July 1984 and was the first Mexican Restaurant outside London. It prospered for 16 years with branch restaurants in Glasgow and Edinburgh. Inexpensive groups such as Chiquito and the new Chimichanga chain, have done a lot to popularise Tex/Mex and Mexican cuisine.

Creole and Cajun cuisines, which also derive from the Southern States of America, particularly the Mississippi Delta around Louisiana, are very much centred around fresh, local produce and have never developed to any great extent overseas. Creoles are the descendents of seventeenth century European settlers whilst Cajuns were French-Canadians who dashed southwards when the British became dominant in Canada. Creole food has French flair plus the Spanish love of strong seasonings and both Cajun and Creole have absorbed the influence of the African slaves bringing okra, black-eyed peas and beans.

Afro-Caribbean cuisine started with the peaceful Arawaks who first settled the area then the war-like Caribs from South America, who brought allspice, cassava and chillies. The African slaves provided the next influence plus an input from the colonial powers - Captain Bligh introduced the West African tree that ackees come from - and finally the Hindus from India in the nineteenth century bringing their own curry. In the 1951 Census there were only 27,218 people of Caribbean birth or born of West Indian parents but this figure had boomed to 548,070 by 1971. Since that time numbers have remained reasonably static although numbers actually born in the Caribbean have actually fallen 40,000.

The biggest country of origin was Jamaica who tended to settle in Clapham and Brixton. The Barbadian community went for Notting Hill and Guyanese, Tottenham and Wood Green. The restaurant community for Afro-Caribbean cuisine has been slow to develop but the signs of real growth are definitely there. Initial growth was, as with most ethnic cuisines, in London but there are now restaurants all over the country. UK Mama, opened in 1985 in Sheffield, was the first Afro-Caribbean restaurant in the history of Yorkshire. The Hummingbird in Finsbury Park, was one of the capital's first Caribbean restaurants.

Other Ethnic Styles

Britain in general and London in particular is a melting pot for cuisines from all over the world such that London can presently lay claim to being the restaurant capital of the world. Spanish cuisine is particularly well represented with over 200 restaurants, 50% of which are in London. The lavish Spanish Club opened in Cavendish Square W1 as long ago as 1920 and Don Pepe in Frampton Street NW8 claims to have led the 'tapas' craze when they opened in 1974 and the La Tasca group is very successful.

There is a very good selection of top class Lebanese restaurants in London and elsewhere in the UK, as well as Portuguese (the Nando's Group), Russian, Brazilian, Moroccan, Egyptian and even Ethiopian and most of the ethnic cuisines of the world are represented to differing degrees in Britain's capital.

Cajun speciality - Louisiana Crawfish

Chapter 8

DEAN MAHOMED

FIRST MAN OF CURRY

Sake Dean Mahomed's remarkable career in Britain, where he lived for nearly three-quarters of a century, gives us unique insights into how one early Indian migrant managed to find a place for himself and his family, first in Georgian Ireland and then in England.

Born in 1759 in Patna, Bihar, Dean Mahomed, came from an elite Muslim family, being related to the Nawabs of Bengal and Bihar, his ancestors having risen in the administrative service of the Mughal emperors. In 1769, aged 11, when his father died prematurely, Mahomed fulfilled his early ambition to enter a 'military life' when he joined Godfrey Baker, an Irish Cadet, as a camp follower. Mahomed rose rapidly, first to the position of Market Master in 1781, then jemedar (ensign) and finally subedar (captain). Such rapid promotion reflects Baker's patronage, whose own fortunes had risen too. As part of Baker's battalion, Mahomed saw action and he took part in several of the battles (e.g., against Cheyt Singh) that extended the Company's domination over India, a process completed during Mahomed's own lifetime.

In 1782, Mahomed resigned from the Army to accompany Captain Baker, who was dismissed from active service, to Ireland. At the age of 25, in September 1784, Mahomed arrived at Dartmouth to start a new life in Britain.

For the first several years Mahomed lived in Ireland with the Baker family, in a prosperous part of Cork on the South Mall. Mahomed's life in Cork is not well documented except for a brief account from Abu Talib Khan's visit to the Baker household in December 1799, during which he met Mahomed. We learn that Mahomed was sent to school to learn English, where he met a young woman 'known to be fair and beautiful', the daughter of 'a family of rank of Cork', with whom he eloped to another town, returning to Cork after their marriage in 1786. This was Jane Daly.

According to Abu Talib Khan, the Mahomeds had 'several beautiful children ... a separate house and wealth'; Mahomed had published a book, giving an account of himself and the customs of India. From the account of Abu Talib Khan there is no doubting that Mahomed had retained the patronage of the Baker clan for this unusual relationship.

In 1794 Mahomed's book *The Travels of Dean Mahomet*, written as a series of letters to an imaginary friend, was published in Cork. It is the first book to be written and published in English by an Indian. As an historical document, it provides a valuable 'Indian voice', describing India's conquest, which Mahomed witnessed as a member of the Company's army, in a version different from existing European accounts. Mahomed also describes the physical landscape of India - its cities and towns, as well as Indian society - and Muslim life as an insider, giving us an Indian perspective to set alongside contemporary European accounts.

Around 1807-8 Mahomed arrived in London with wife Jane and ten year old son William. The birth of his daughter Amelia in August 1808 locates Mahomed in London's Portman Square, a fashionable area and a haunt of India-returned nabobs. Here, Mahomed first found employment with a rich nabob, Sir Basil Cochrane, who had set up a vapour bath establishment in his huge mansion in Portman Square. Mahomed is said to have added an Indian treatment, 'shampooing' (champi) or therapeutic massage, to Cochrane's vapour bath, a treatment that would later make Mahomed famous in Brighton under the name 'Sake Dean Mahomed'. However he was given little acknowledgement at the time so he embarked on a different independent career: as proprietor of the Hindoostanee Coffee-House.

The Coffee-House, was established in 1809 at 34 George Street, Portman Square just behind Cochrane's house. Aimed at Anglo-Indians, Mahomed offered them *"the enjoyment of Hookha, with 'real chilm tobacco"*, and Indian dishes *"in the highest perfection, and allowed by the greatest epicures to be unequalled to any curries ever made in England, in a setting decorated with Indian and Oriental scenes"*. Mahomed, unfortunately, over-reached himself by too rapid an expansion despite taking John Spencer on as partner: his 'purse' was not *"strong enough to stand the slow test of public encouragement"*, and he was forced to declare bankruptcy in the London Gazette in 1812.

Having fallen on hard times, with Henry Edwin born 1810 and Deen in 1812, Mahomed advertised for a situation as a butler or valet in 1813, adding that he had *"no objection to town or country"* in order to increase his employability. His son William, aged 16 and a postman in London, could not have earned enough to support the family. Around 1814 Mahomed arrived in Brighton as a 'shampooing surgeon' at the Devonshire Place bath-house, possibly as a result of his advertisement. The date can be inferred from two sources: a testimonial from a grateful patient, dated 10 November 1814, and the baptism record from March 1815 of his daughter Rosanna.

Here Mahomed set up his own distinctive establishment: the Indian Vapour Baths and Shampooing Establishment. As with the Hindoostanee Coffee-House, he found a new way to cultural entrepreneurship, trading on his Indian-ness, and emphasising the Indian qualities of his Medicated Vapour Bath with the use of special Indian oils in shampooing and herbs for the bath *"brought expressly from India"*. Mahomed claimed that he introduced shampooing to Britain, that his treatment was more powerful and *"superior"* to other remedies for rheumatic aches and pains, that he alone, *"a native of India"*, possessed *"to an eminent degree"* the art of shampooing.

At Mahomed's Baths patients first lay in a steaming, aromatic herbal bath; having sweated freely, they were then placed in a kind of flannel tent with sleeves. They were then massaged vigorously by someone outside the tent, whose arms alone penetrated the flannel walls. Soon he was claiming to have served thousands of visitors.

Cases Cured, a book of letters from grateful patients, was published in 1820, according to Mahomed at *"the pressing desire"* of the nobility and gentry. In the vestibule of his establishments were *"hung ... crutches of former martyrs of rheumatism, lumbago or sciatica"*, said to have been cured by Mahomed's *"vigourous and scientific shampooing"*.

He kept visitors books (separate ones for men and women) for patients' comments. Each new edition of his book *Shampooing, or Benefits Resulting From the Use of the Indian Medicated Vapour Bath, As introduced Into This Country*, by S.D. Mahomed (A native of India), first published in 1822, carried the names of patients successfully cured and glowing notices from them.It largely consisting of descriptions of successful cures for asthma, paralysis, rheumatism, sciatica and loss of voice, reached a third edition in 1838. Mahomed attempted to demonstrate that what in India was regarded as *"a restorative luxury"*, in England worked as a *"most surprising and powerful remedy"* for many diseases.

Re-inventing himself, Mahomed edited out his period in Cork and London. He advanced his birth by ten years to 1749 and provided himself with medical training, claiming that he had been *"educated to the profession of, and served in the Company's services as a surgeon"*, a claim that is dubious and unproven. Mahomed's Baths became famous, meriting a mention in Brighton guidebooks and newspapers in both Brighton and London.

He moved to Brighton with his family and soon created Mahomed's Bath House

According to one gushing notice, Mahomed's Baths were *"daily thronged, not only with the ailing but the hale ... the powerful efficacy of [the Baths] ... have brought foreigners to him from all quarters of the world."* Indeed, the visitors' books bear testimony to how well the Baths were patronised. His patients from among the nobility and gentry included Lords Castlereagh, Canning and Reay, and Lady Cornwallis and Sir Robert Peel. Mahomed's highest achievement was to be appointed Shampooing Surgeon to King George IV, an appointment continued under William IV.

Mahomed opened a second establishment in London, at 7 Ryder Street, St James's, managed by his son Horatio. Mahomed's Baths remained among the noted institutions of Brighton and Mahomed himself one of its local celebrities, long remembered driving to the Races *"gorgeous in Eastern costume, with his pretty wife by his side, and a dagger in his girdle"*. A kind-hearted and benevolent man, in his prosperous days he was said to have *"a heart and hand ready to relieve the wants of others"*. As a public figure patronised by royalty, Mahomed often loyally illuminated his Baths with gas lights to mark royal occasions. From 1841, as a Brighton citizen, he was on the register of voters.

Mahomed retired from active work in 1834, aged 75, handing over to his son Arthur. With Queen Victoria's accession to the throne in 1837, Brighton lost its favoured place and Mahomed his prominence. A financial blow in 1841 spelled the end of Mahomed's Baths. He died in February 1851, his wife Jane preceding him in December 1850. He was buried in St Nicholas' churchyard in Brighton and his tombstone says he was 102 years old!!

Chapter 9

ORIGINS OF CURRY

Is it really English?

Most people in the world today know what a curry is - or at least think they do. In Britain the term *'curry'* has come to mean almost any Indian dish, whilst most people from the sub-continent would say it is not a word they use, but if they did it would mean a meat, vegetable or fish dish with spicy sauce and rice or bread.

The earliest known recipe for meat in spicy sauce with bread appeared on tablets found near Babylon in Mesopotamia, written in cuniform text as discovered by the Sumerians, and dated around 1700 BC, probably as an offering to the god Marduk.

The origin of the word itself is the stuff of legends, but most pundits have settled on the origins being the Tamil word *'kari'* meaning spiced sauce. In his excellent *Oxford Companion to Food*, Alan Davidson quotes this as a fact and supports it with reference to the accounts from a Dutch traveller in 1598 referring to a dish called *'Carriel'*. He also refers to a Portuguese cookery book from the seventeenth century called *Atre do Cozinha*, with chilli-based curry powder called *'caril'*.

In her *50 Great Curries of India*, Camellia Panjabi says the word today simply means 'gravy'. She also goes for the Tamil word *'kaari or kaaree'* as the origin, but with some reservations, noting that in the north, where the English first landed in 1608 then 1612, a gravy dish is called *'khadi'*. Pat Chapman of Curry Club fame offers several possibilities: *'karahi or karai (Hindi)'* from the wok-shaped cooking dish, or perhaps *'kari'* from the Tamil or *'Turkuri'* a seasonal sauce or stew.

The one thing all the experts seem to agree on is that the word originates from India and was adapted and adopted by the British Raj. On closer inspection, however, there is just as much evidence to suggest that this could be a misconception and the word, if not the dish, was English all along.

In the time of Richard I there was a revolution in English cooking. In the better-off kitchens, cooks were regularly using ginger, cinnamon, nutmeg, cloves, galingale, cubebs, coriander, cumin, cardamom and aniseed, resulting in highly spiced cooking very similar to India. They also had a *'powder fort'*, *'powder douce'* and *'powder blanch'*.

Then, in Richard II's reign (1377-1399) the first real English cookery book was written. Richard employed 200 cooks and they, plus others including philosophers, produced a work with 196 recipes in 1390 called *The Forme of Cury* followed by *Curye on Inglish: English Culinary Manuscripts of the Fourteenth-Century*. *'Cury'* being the Old English word for cooking derived from the French *'cuire'* - to cook, boil, grill - hence *cuisine*. In the preface it says:

'forme of cury was compiled of the chef maistes cokes of kyng Richard the Secunde kyng of nglond aftir the conquest; the which was accounted the best and ryallest vyand of alle csten ynges: and it was compiled by assent and avysement of

maisters and phisik and of philosophie that dwellid in his court. First it techith a man to make commune pottages and commune meetis for howshold, as they shold be made, craftly and holsomly, Aftirward it techith for to make curious potages and meetes and sotiltees for alle maner of states, bothe hye and lowe. And the techyng of the forme of making of potages and of meetes, bothe flesh and of fissh, buth y sette here by noumbre and by ordre".

In his book *Manners and Meals in Olden Times* (1868) F.J.Furnell noted a passage from a fifteenth century treatise (*John Russells Boke of Nurture 1460-1470*) against nouvelle cuisine well before the English merchants visited India:

'Cooks with peire newe conceytes,
choppynge, stampynge and gryndynge
Many new curies alle day pey ar contryvynge and fyndynge
pat provotethe pe peple to perelles of passage prouz peyne soore pyndynge
and prouz nice excesse of such receytes of pe life to make a endynge.'

("Cooks are always inventing new dishes that tempt people and endanger their lives")

So when the English merchants landed at Surat in 1608 and 1612, then Calcutta 1633, Madras 1640 and Bombay 1668, the word '*cury*' had been part of the English language for well over two hundred years. In fact, it was noted that the meal from Emperor Jahangir's kitchens of dumpukht fowl stewed in butter with spices, almond and raisins served to those merchants in 1612, was very similar to a recipe for English Chicken Pie in a popular cookery book of the time, *The English Huswife, Containing the Inward and Outward Virtues Which Ought to Be in a Complete Woman* first published in London in 1615 by Gervase Markham.

Indeed many spices had been in Europe for hundreds of years by then, after the conquests of the Romans in 40 AD and the taking of Al Andulus by the Moors in 711 AD, bringing to Europe the culinary treasures of the spice routes.

Many supporters of the Tamil word *kari* as the basis for curry, use the definition from the excellent Hobson-Jobson Anglo English Dictionary, first published in 1886. The book quotes a passage from the *Mahavanso* (c A.D. 477) which says *"he partook of rice dressed in butter with its full accompaniment of curries."* The important thing, however, is the note that this is Turnour's translation of the original *Pali* which used the word "*supa*" not the word curry.

Indeed Hobson - Jobson even accepts that there is a possibility that *"the kind of curry used by Europeans and Mohommedans is not of purely Indian origin, but has come down from the spiced cookery of medieval Europe and Western Asia."*

Whatever the truth, '*curry*' was rapidly adopted in Britain. In 1747 Hannah Glasse produced the first known printed recipe for modern '*currey*' in *Glasse's Art of Cookery* and by 1773 at least one London Coffee House had curry on the menu. Hannah Glasse was born and raised in Hexham and had an idyllic country upbringing before moving to London and producing her recipe for *Currey the Indian Way* with Northumberland game and just two spices, pepper and coriander seeds, making it like an aromatic stew.

Hannah married a soldier of fortune, John Glasse, at the age of 16 and moved to London where they fell on hard times. She started on her book in 1746 to make ends meet and offered advice on everything from roasting to preserving and was a huge success. Despite the success she went bankrupt and ended up in debtor's prison from where she was released in 1757.

Hannah Glasse's Recipe for Currey the Indian Way

Two fowls or rabbits, cut into small pieces, three or four small onions, peeled and cut very small. 30 peppercorns, large spoonful of rice, coriander seeds browned over the fire in a cler shovel and beaten to a powder, tea-spoonful of salt, fresh butter, pint of water.

Mix all well together with the meat, put all together in a saucepan or stew pan with a pint of water, let it stew softly till the meat is enough, then put in a piece of fresh butter, about as big as a large walnut, shake it well together, and when it is smooth and of a fine thickness, dish it up and send it to table; the sauce is too thick, add a little more water before it is done, and more salt if it wants it. You are to observe that the sauce must be pretty thick.

Thus Britain's love affair with India was solidified (growing from up to 15% of UK imports being from India in the 1720s) with the total rule of the East India Company effectively starting in 1757 with the conquest of Bengal after the Battle of Plessey until 1858 when the British Crown took over following the Indian Rebellion of 1857.

Another very popular cookery book writer of the period, Elizabeth Raffald (1733 - 1781) also included a recipe for curry in her *The Experienced English Housekeeper* first published in 1769. She was the housekeeper at Arley Hall in Cheshire and dedicated the book, which became a favourite of Queen Victoria, to Lady Elizabeth Warburton.

In 1791 Stephana Malcom, the granddaughter of the Laird of Craig included a curry recipe she called Chicken Topperfield plus Currypowder, Chutnies and Mulligatawny soup as recorded in *In The Lairds Kitchen, Three Hundred Years of Food in Scotland*. Around the same time the word "*consumer*" began to appear which, conversely, was not originally an English word, as one might think, but derived from '*Khansaman*', the title of the house steward – the chief table servant and purchaser as well as provider of all food in Anglo-Indian households.

In the 1780s the first commercial curry powder appeared. A notice in the Morning Post Newspaper in 1784 quoted the introduction of curry powder by Solander from the East Indies. It was "*only to be had at Sorlie's Perfumery Warehouse 23 Piccadilly*" and said to be "*exceedingly pleasant and healthful*".

However, curry recipes really came to the fore when a complete chapter on Anglo-Indian recipes was included by editor Emma Roberts (died 1840) in the 64th edition of Maria Rundell's *A New System of Domestic Cookery* published after her death in 1841. In 1846 its fame was assured when William Makepeace Thackeray wrote a '*Poem to Curry*' in his *Kitchen Melodies*.

Curry

Three pounds of veal my darling girl prepares,
And chops it nicely into little squares;

Five onions next prures the little minx
(The biggest are the best, her Samiwel thinks),
And Epping butter nearly half a pound,
And stews them in a pan until they're brown'd.

What's next my dexterous little girl will do?
She pops the meat into the savoury stew,

With curry-powder table-spoonfuls three,
And milk a pint (the richest that may be),

And, when the dish has stewed for half an hour,
A lemon's ready juice she'll o'er it pour.

Then, bless her! Then she gives the luscious pot
A very gentle boil - and serves quite hot.

PS - Beef, mutton, rabbit, if you wish,
Lobsters, or prawns, or any kind fish,

Are fit to make a CURRY. 'Tis, when done,
A dish for Emperors to feed upon

In the same year Charles Elme Francatelli, chief cook and maitre d'hotel to Queen Victoria included a recipe for *Indian Curry Sauce* in his *The Modern Cook*, based on Cook's or Bruce's meat curry paste.

In 1861 it was Mrs Beeton's turn in her *Book of Household Management* where she included no less than fourteen curry recipes, including Dr Kitchener's Recipe for India Curry Powder. Even Charles Ranhofer, chef at Delmonico's (1862-98) wrote in *The Epicurean*:

"Curry - the best comes from India. An imitation is made of one ounce of coriander seeds, two ounces of cayenne, a quarter ounce of cardamom seeds, one ounce salt, two ounces turmeric, one ounce ginger, half an ounce of mace and a third of an ounce of saffron".

The development of the curry industry in Britain has been peculiarly Anglo-Asian such that many people brandish 'authenticity' as if it were the Holy Grail. According to Camellia Panjabi: "*Ninety nine per cent of Indians do not have a tandoor and so neither Tandoori Chicken nor Naan are part of India's middle class cuisine. This is even so in the Punjab, although some villages have communal tandoors where rotis can be baked. Ninety five per cent of Indians don't know what a vindaloo, jhal farezi or, for that matter, a Madras curry is".*

Since the opening of The Bombay Brasserie in London in 1982 there has been a growing group of highly trained chefs offering the classic Indian dishes, but the backbone of the British industry has consisted largely of self taught chefs who have been clever enough to adapt to market requirements resulting in the Balti craze and the, now world famous, Chicken Tikka Masala amongst others.

'*Curry*' has not looked back since and was recently named the British National dish after a major opinion poll by Gallup. It is interesting to note that the Portuguese, Dutch and even the French were in India long before or concurrently with the English and yet it was Britain that readily adopted curry, not the others. Perhaps it was because England had had a tradition of 'cury' all along!

From top row, left to right: Turmeric, Cumin, Red Chili Powder, Dry Whole Chili, Coriander, Mustard Seeds, Garam Masala, Fenugreek Seeds

Chapter 10

IS IT OR ISN'T IT?
The Chicken Tikka Masala Story

- Marks & Spenser once claimed to sell 18 tonnes a week of the stuff -

- 23 million portions a year are sold in Indian restaurants -

- Many schools and charities in Sylhet, Bangladesh are run by proceeds from its sales -

- Chef Iftekar Haris from Newport, Gwent once wrote a musical in praise of it -

Organisers of National Curry Week claim that if all the portions sold in one year in UK were stacked they would constitute a tikka tower 2,770 times taller than the Greenwich Millennium Dome (now 02 Arena). Yet in an article in The Daily Telegraph in November 1999, journalist Amit Roy referred to it as, "*a dish which does not exist in Indian cuisine*". So the question is:

'is it a genuine Indian dish or isn't it?'

The name of this enigma? - Chicken Tikka Masala of course. The flagship dish of Britain's acclaimed 'national cuisine' boasting a huge 14.6% of the sales of the almost half a million curries consumed, on average, in the restaurants and homes of the United Kingdom every day of the year. Chicken Tikka Masala, or CTM as it was affectionately dubbed by food writer Colleen Grove in 'Spice n Easy Magazine' in November 1994, is one of those culinary fables that lends a touch of intrigue and excitement to an already exotic cuisine.

Amit Roy was quite correct to observe that the dish does not hail from India and that it was specifically created to appeal to the British palate by some very astute restaurateurs. This much is not in doubt but when one moves on to the history of the dish, fact becomes fiction and depends on just who one talks to.

No 'Indian' chef seems to have produced any real evidence that he or she first invented the dish and it is commonly thought that its invention came about almost by accident. Journalist Peter Grove and restaurateur Iqbal Wahhab created an urban legend when they claimed as a joke that it was created when a Bangladeshi chef produced a dish of traditional Chicken Tikka only to be asked "*where's my gravy?*" The response was, supposedly, a can of Campbell's cream of tomato soup and a few spices and the 'masala' element was born.

Top food writer Charles Campion refers to CTM as "*a dish invented in London in the Seventies so that the ignorant could have gravy with their chicken tikka*". Several chefs have made claim to the invention of CTM but none with any firm evidence or witness support so the mystery will have to remain. The descendents of Sultan Ahmed Ansari, who owned the Taj Mahal in Glasgow claim with absolute conviction that he invented it in the late 1950s although this competes with numerous other similar claims of invention. The tandoor, which boosted tikka sales, had not even arrived in Britain at that time, having only been introduced for the first time to the Indian restaurant, Moti Mahal in New Delhi in 1948.

Other claimants for the invention of CTM include Zaeemuddin Ahmad, a chef at Delhi's Karim Hotel, which was established by the last chef of the last Mughal emperor Bahadur Shah Zafar, who says the recipe had been passed down through the generations in his family.

"Chicken tikka masala is an authentic Mughlai recipe prepared by our forefathers who were royal chefs in the Mughal period. Mughals were avid trekkers and used to spend months altogether in jungles and far off places. They liked roasted form of chickens with spices," he said.

Rahul Verma, Delhi's most authoritative expert on street food, said he first tasted the dish in 1971 and that its origins were in Punjab. "*It's basically a Punjabi dish not more than 40-50 years old and must be an accidental discovery which has had periodical improvisations,*" he said.

Alternatively another claim says Chicken Tikka Masala was invented by a famous Bengali music composer, Moslehuddin, when working in the restaurant trade in the city of Birmingham, in a restaurant called the Houseboat in the mid 1970's.

The story goes that he was unable to find long term employment in the UK and had to work in the restaurant trade. While there he could not let go of his creativity and decided to try out several new dishes that would get a positive response from his clientele. In one such creation he took chicken tikka cooked in a clay oven and mixed it with chicken curry, making it milder than normal by adding liquid from yogurt and tomato puree or sauce. He got such a positive reaction from this dish that he refined it further and had it placed as a permanent item on the menu.

It wasn't long before other restaurants in Birmingham, of which there were many, started to copy the menu item. Regulars at the "Houseboat" and later at the "Rajdoot", the "Shah" on Broad street and then at "Mosley's" on Broad street, which were all restaurants where Moslehuddin offered Chicken Tikka Masala in the 1970s and 1980s, continued to demand the succulent dish according to his wife Nahid Niazi.

Whatever the various claims, the Moti Mahal can be seen as the true origins of CTM in its basic form of Butter Chicken. Lala Kundan Lal Gujral first set up in Peshawar in 1920 but came to Delhi in 1947 to set up Moti Mahal. He worked with a local man to produce the first restaurant version of the tandoor and invented tandoori spice mix for tandoori chicken - *ground coriander seeds, black pepper and mild red pepper.*

Called Murg Makhani in Hindi, Butter Chicken originated in the 1950s at the Moti Mahal restaurant in Old Delhi. Famed for its Tandoori Chicken, the cooks there used to recycle the leftover chicken juices in the marinade trays by adding butter and tomato. This sauce was then tossed around with the tandoor-cooked chicken pieces and presto - Butter Chicken was ready! The leftover dish appealed to Delhites and was quickly lapped up by the rest of the world.

RECIPE FOR KEBAB BUTTER MASALA (Courtesy Monish Gujral of Moti Mahal)

Ingredients for the Kebabs

Minced lamb- 500 gm
Egg, beaten- 1
Onion, finely chopped- 1
Green chillies, finely chopped- 2
Red chilli powder- 5 tsp
Ginger, chopped- 1tsp
Garam masala- 5 tsp
Salt to taste
Green coriander chopped- 2 tsp
Lemon cut into wedges-1

Method used in cooking Kebabs

Combine all ingredients except last two in a bowl. Divide the mixture equally in 16 balls. Skewer each ball and with wet hands make 2" long kebabs with the skewer. Put the skewers in the tandoor or preheated conventional oven pre set at 350 deg for 7-8 minutes. Take them, out brush them with oil, turn them over and cook again. Remove from skewers and keep aside. These also can be served as a snack – arranged on a platter garnished with chopped coriander and lemon wedges

Ingredients for the Masala

Refined oil- 2 tbsp
Onion chopped- 1
Ginger-garlic paste 2 tbsp
Cumin powder- 1 tsp
Coriander powder- 1 tsp
Turmeric powder- 1tsp
Red chilli powder- 2 tsp
Garam masala- 1 tsp

Salt to taste
Green chilli sliced- 2
Tomato puree – 300 ml
Lemon juice- 15ml
Butter-50gm
Fresh double cream- 100 ml
Green coriander chopped- 1 tbsp

Method for the masala

Heat the oil in the wok. Add onions and sauté till golden brown. Stir in ginger garlic paste. Add spices and salt. Now add the seekh kebabs and stir for 3-4 minutes. Add green chillies, tomato puree and lemon juice and stir for few minutes. Now add butter. As the butter melts add cream and remove from fire. Serve hot, garnished with chopped coriander.

So impressed was India's first Prime Minister Jawaharlal Nehru by Kundal Lal's dishes that Moti Mahal became a permanent fixture in all his state banquets. Legend has it that when former Soviet premier Nikita Kruschev was asked what he liked about India, he replied, *"Taj Mahal and Moti Mahal"*. When the

Shah of Iran came on a state visit to India, the Indian Education Minister Maulana Azad told him that coming to Delhi without eating at Moti Mahal was like going to Agra and not seeing the Taj Mahal.

Kundan Lal Gujral

After Nehru, his daughter and then Prime Minister Indira Gandhi continued the relationship with Moti Mahal. So fascinated was she by the food that at the wedding of her younger son Sanjay Gandhi, Moti Mahal specialties dominated the dinner. Kundan Lal Gujral, a larger-than-life figure whom people still remember for his immaculate Pathani suits, handlebar moustache, love for good whisky and the favours he dispensed because of his proximity to Indira Gandhi, would personally serve his guests. His wife would begin each day grinding the masalas, a closely guarded secret that went into the signature dishes. His grandson Monish has revived the fortunes of Moti Mahal in recent years and now boasts a group with 72 outlets.

An advertisement in a programme for the London Palladium promoting Cinderella starring Cliff Richard in 1966 by The Gaylord in Mortimer Street featured what was thought to be the first tandoor dishes in Britain. Mahendra Kaul, now involved with Chor Bizarre and Viceroy Brasserie in London, sent 'the tandoor' to the USA for the World's Fair a few years earlier before loaning it and his staff to an unamed restaurant of a friend in the United Kingdom who was on hard times, before installing it in The Gaylord.

However, information from archived documents at the famous Veeraswamy in London show the tandoor was in use at the restaurant as early as 1959, some ten years before it became widely known in Britain.

Top restaurateur Amin Ali, owner of The Red Fort in London's Soho remembers serving CTM when he first arrived in London in 1974. A lowly waiter at the time he remembers wondering just what the dish was.

Certainly one family to have tangible benefits from the success of CTM is that of Sheik Abdul Khalique who owns The Polash in Shoeburyness which opened in 1979. His father, Haji Abdul Razzah, returned to Bangladesh in 1985 having made sufficient profit to build The Polash Hotel in Sylhet and a Mosque; The Polash Sheba Charitable Trust was added after his death. The family firmly claim their fortunes are largely down to CTM, the mysterious Indian/British hybrid.

CTM was introduced to Waitrose by G.K.Noon in 1983 when he was still in the United States and by the end of the Millennium it was generally acknowledged as the most popular single dish in

Britain.

"Chicken tikka masala is now Britain's true national dish, not only because it is the most popular, but because it is a perfect illustration of the way Britain absorbs and adapts external influences. Chicken tikka is an Indian dish. The masala sauce was added to satisfy the desire of British people to have their meat served in gravy"

Foreign Secretary Robin Cook, April 2001

For something that is so popular with the public and with the restaurateurs who make their living from it, Chicken Tikka Masala is very much a Cinderella of culinary creations. Very few recipes for CTM appear in the plethora of Indian Cuisine cookbooks that have appeared over the last twenty years and Alan Davidson's *Oxford Companion to Food* does not even consider it deserving of a listing. Indeed, such are the passions it generates in the industry, that many top chefs originally refused to cook or serve it due to its complete 'lack of authenticity'.

However, exist it does and demanded it is, so just what is Chicken Tikka Masala? Tikkas are the bite-sized chunks you cut chicken into and these are marinated and cooked in the tandoor. The masala part is where things become difficult. Masala means spices but no exact recipe for these seems to exist. CTM can be yellow, red, brownish or even green and can be very creamy, a little creamy, chilli hot or quite mild. In restaurants it tends to be a creamy sauce - not too hot; a bit tomatoey; very smooth and, all too often, quite sweet and very red (although food colouring has now been replaced by natural ingredients such as beetroot). In supermarkets, once you have by-passed the masses of CTM pizzas, filled pancakes, kievs, pies, microwave rolls and so on, you come to the chilled and frozen ready meals which range from mild onion gravy to saffron cream to velvety vermillion.

Created on the spur of the moment under pressure it may have been but, as a culinary concept, the basic dish, if not the name, already existed – the cuniform text found on tablets in Mesopotamia in 1700BC.

The North Indian dishes Murg Masalla and Murgh Makhni have been part of the Indian chef's repertoire for many years. *The Bombay Palace Cookbook* by Stendahl in 1985 listed a recipe for Palace Murgh Kari including yoghurt, tomato paste and heavy cream and Niru Gupta's *Everyday Indian* (1995) lists Murgh Rasedar, which includes most of the required ingredients, including cream, tomatoes and onions.

The shape of things to come may have been a recipe for Shahi Chicken Masala in Mrs Balbir Singh's *Indian Cookery* published in 1961.

Mridula Baljekar is one of the few cookery writers to have included CTM in her bestselling *Complete Indian Cookbook* (1993) including food colouring and tomato puree as well as double cream and almonds. Chef Mohammed Moneer introduced yet another ingredient with half a cup of coconut milk instead of cream.

It seems that the ingredients generally include yoghurt, tomatoes, cream and spices as well as the chicken pieces and if you have found a version that suits you then stick to it. The "Spice n Easy" article in 1993 endeavoured to produce the definitive recipe from forty eight versions on offer where the only common denominator was the chicken, and came up with a 'standard' version.

Chicken Tikka Masala was most certainly invented in Britain, probably by a Bangaldeshi chef, based on Butter Chicken and is so popular it is even being served in some hotel restaurants in India and Bangladesh and around the world. It does not come from the Raj or the kitchens of the Moghul Emperors, but millions of people enjoy it every year and perhaps that is all the pedigree it needs!

Best in Britain Awards (BIBA)

Chef Manzoor Ahmed of Tabaq Restaurant South Clapham, London (now closed)

Chicken Tikka Masala of the Year 2002 - Recipe

Ingredients

- 1lb large diced boneles chicken breast
- 1 oz garlic
- 1 oz ginger
- 4 tbs fresh natural yoghurt
- 2 small fresh green chillies
- 1 tsp salt
- 1 tbs lemon juice
- 1 tsp coriander powder
- 1 tsp cumin powder
- 1 tbs red paprika
- 4-5 fresh green coriander

Method - Grind fresh green chillies, fresh coriander, garlic and ginger with 2-3 tbs water until a thick paste is formed. Marinate the chicken in the paste then add the salt and yoghurt. Next add the lemon juice, cumin, coriander powder and red paprika and mix thoroughly. Leave chicken to marinate in the paste overnight.

Sauce

- 4 oz chopped onions
- 3 oz ghee
- 1 oz ground garlic
- 1 oz ground ginger
- 3 oz yoghurt
- ½ tsp cumin powder
- 2 tbs desicated coconut
- 4 oz fresh single cream
- 2 medium tomatoes (liquidised)
- ½ tsp salt
- ½ tsp chilli powder
- ½ tsp coriander powder
- pinch dried methi

Method - Take marinated chicken and cook on skewers in tandoor or 10-12 minutes under a grill on a moderate high heat. Fry onions in the ghee. Add tomatoes and yoghurt and mix on low/moderate heat. Add cumin powder, chilli powder, coriander powder, salt, desiccated coconut, dried methi and fresh single cream and mix thoroughly. Water may be added if more liquid is required. Add cooked pieces or chicken to the sauce and mix well. Leave to simmer on low heat. Transfer to serving dish, garnish with a little single cream and sprinkle liberally with fresh coriander and garam masala.

Traditional Butter Chicken

Chapter 11

ON THE TRAIL OF THE TANDOOR

It was there at the dawn of civilisation

The Punjab in India is known by many today as the 'home of the tandoor', a cooking method that has become known all over the world as the popularity of 'curry' has spread. Its history, however, actually goes back to the dawn of civilisation from where it spread from Arab countries to India and finally, the West.

The tandoor in its simplest form is a large clay jar with an opening at the bottom for adding and removing fuel. It was used for bread baking where the dough was slapped onto the vertical wall to bake quickly by radiant heat and convection. It was usually made of good clay and shredded coir rope and, once complete, a paste of mustard oil, jaggery, yoghurt and ground spinach was rubbed on the inside to harden it up.

In Afghanistan, the tandoor was usually built into the ground. Most homes were too poor to have their own so they prepared their own dough and took it to the tandoor bakery *(the nanwaee)* to be baked. A long notched stick called a *chobe khat* kept note of the number of breads baked for a household each day and was totalled each week for payment.

The word tandoor came originally from the Middle East with the name deriving from the Babylonian word *'tinuru'* from the Semitic word *nar* meaning fire. Hebrew and Arabic then made it *tannur* then *tandur* in Turkey, Central Asia and, finally Pakistan and India, who made it famous worldwide. Understandably, many people assume the tandoor to be native to India as evidence exists of early tandoors around 3000 BC.

The first evidence comes from early farming settlements of the time such as Umm Bubaghiyeh on the plains between the Rivers Tigris and Euphrates. It is here that the world's first major civilization, the Sumerians, they of the legendary King-Hero Gilgamesh, appeared, introducing advances that were to shape the world.

Metal worked tools had been known in several areas since 5000 BC and pottery from Iran to the East Mediterraean Basin since 6000BC and Sumer built up the infrastructure of civilzation including cuniform writing by 3500 BC in Eridu. The Sumerians of Mesopotamia cultivated dates and, later, cereals as the land improved. Sheep and cattle were kept and donkeys ridden. They were the earliest people to use the wheel and, gradually, city states grew up and trade spread as far as India.

India was first populated 250,000 years ago but the first major civilization was the Harappans, who occupied the Indus Valley where Baluchistan was a farming community from 3500 BC By 3000 BC turmeric, cardamom, pepper and mustard were harvested in India. The Harappans, who occupied Harappa and Mohenjodero in the Indus Valley, were of mixed stock, somewhat larger in stature than either the Sumerians or Egyptians denying theories that they were an extension of those communities. They had club wheat, barley, sheep and goats from the Iranian Plateau and cotton from Southern Arabia or North East Africa but were held back by their reliance on flood waters due to general lack of knowledge of irrigation.

The Tandoor as it is today complete with naan

Sumer had trade links with the Indus Valley via the Hindu Kush by 3000 BC introducing the tandoor amongst many other things and by sea from 2500 BC, thus linking the Harappans with both Sumerians and Egyptians, where cumin, anise and cinnamon were used for embalming by 2500 BC.

Lala Kundan Lal Gujral first set up in Peshawar in 1920 but came to Delhi in 1947 to set up Moti Mahal. He worked with a local man to produce the first restaurant version of the tandoor a year later and, indeed, Ranjit Mathrani of Chutney Mary and Veeraswamy remembers eating tandoori food there in 1951 at the tender age of eight. Today the modern Moti Mahal is a very successful group run by the great man's grandson Monish Gujral.

The original tandoor at Moti Mahal looked like this

As perhaps expected, several restaurants have claimed to be the first to have a tandoor in Britain. Initial research suggested the man responsible was, in fact, Mahendra Kaul who started the excellent Gaylord group and it was The Gaylord in Mortimer Street who advertised it in a Palladium Theatre programme in 1966. Mr Kaul had taken the tandoor to America for the Worlds Fair in 1964 then loaned it and his staff to the Kwality in Whitfield Street, London that no longer exists, before starting the Gaylord. He is still a partner in Chor Bizarre in London making him one of the most experienced people still working in the industry.

Recently viewed archived documents at Veeraswamy indicate, however, a tandoor in use much earlier, in 1959 and so, this famous restaurant seems to have been responsible for the earliest introduction of tandoori style dishes to the UK, although it would be some ten years and more before the tandoor became widely used in Britain. If you had visited Veerawamy's, as it was then called, in December 1959, you could have enjoyed Chicken Tandoori (allow 15-20 minutes) for the princely sum of ten shillings and sixpence.

Nowadays the tandoor is in use all over Britain and wherever the Indian restaurant industry thrives, as well as in its countries of origin, commercial tandoors now have cemented brick walls and large commercial units of iron. Many Pakistani and Kashmiri restaurants in Britain continue to use the tandoor for breads only, preferring to grill their kebabs whilst others have expanded the uses of the versatile tandoor to give that special flavour to meat and fish.

One mystery still remains. Who introduced the word 'Tandoori' into restaurant names in Britain such that in the year 2002, a large percentage of 'Indian' restaurants still used the word in their restaurant name? It certainly wasn't either of the two pioneers Veeraswamy or Gaylord, as they are not known as 'Tandoori' restaurants, so who was the first? Any suggestions?

Chapter 12

THE 'CURRIFICATION' OF THE WORLD

Although the ancestral home of 'curry' is the Indian sub-continent, the cuisine has become one of the widest food styles enjoyed in the world and has spread with a variety of amendments and innovations to many countries the world over.

Foremost amongst its fans are the people of Great Britain who have adopted curry as their 'national dish' with over 9,000 restaurants and the creation of British/Asian dishes such as chicken tikka masala and balti. Although Britain is probably the curry centre of the world on a - per head of population - reckoning it also exists in many other places and is enjoyed for its variations and peculiarities.

Bengal/Bihar

Originally inhabited by Dravidians and other ethnic groups, and later, further settled by the Aryans during the Gupta era, Bengal fell under the sway of various Muslim rulers from the early thirteenth century onwards, and was then ruled by the British for two centuries. Bengali cuisine includes many curries that are little known to the outside world and are known for their spiciness.

The growth of Bengali cuisine has been very much shaped by the influence of Hindu widows whose life largely revolved around the kitchen. Since widows were banned 'impassioning' condiments such as onion or garlic, many traditional Bengali recipes don't use them

Authentic Bengali recipes are difficult to find outside Bengali kitchens, although certain dishes are popular, such as jhalfrezi and prawn malai curry. Seafood and fresh fish are a great favourite with Bengalis, and a dazzling array of curries have been devised to accompany them. Mustard seeds and mustard oil are added to many recipes, so are poppy seeds, and these are flavours highly specific to the Bengali curries.

Much of Bihari cuisine resembles North Indian cuisine except for the use of mustard oil. Dairy products are consumed frequently throughout the year, with common foods including yoghurt known as dahi and also buttermilk known as mattha, ghee, lassi and butter. Bihari cuisine is predominantly vegetarian. Biharis are quite famous for their Bihari kebabs, a typical Bihari non-vegetarian dish. This dish is traditionally made from mutton and is eaten with roti, paratha or boiled rice.

Punjab/Kashmir

Punjabi cuisine is characterized by a profusion of dairy products in the form of malai (cream), paneer (cottage cheese) and curds. Punjabi cuisine is mainly based upon wheat, masalas (spice blends), pure desi ghee, with liberal amounts of butter and cream.

There are certain dishes that are exclusive to Punjab, such as maha di dal and saron da saag (sarson ka saag). The main masala in a Punjabi dish consists of onion, garlic and ginger. Many of the most popular elements of Anglo-Indian cuisine - such as tandoor, naan, pakoras and vegetable dishes with paneer - derive from the Punjab.

Although chicken is a favourite with non-vegetarians, fish is also considered a delicacy, especially in the Amritsar region, which is also known for its kulcha, baked bread made of refined flour. The earliest references to the region's food are found in the Vedas, which document the lives of the Aryans in the Punjab over 6,000 years ago.

Kashmiri cuisine is famous for its multi-course wazwan. The most notable ingredient in Kashmir cuisine is mutton, of which there are over 30 varieties.

South India

Andhra Pradesh, one of the four states of Southern India, has its own cuisine. The main dish of Andhra/Telugu cuisine is called "Koora" in Telugu, taken with hot rice and ghee. It could be made of a vegetable, a combination of vegetables or meat and vegetable. It could be wet (koora, pulusu or gojju) or dry (vaepudu). There are numerous types of recipes with various combinations of spices and in various proportions.

The second course is any liquid/soup type taken with rice and ghee. It could be made with just vegetables, "rasam"/"chaaru" or vegetable and dal, called pappu and sambar or butter milk and vegetable, called "majjiga pulusu" and many more.

The last course is rice with either curd or buttermilk. It is believed that this soothes the effect of spices and helps digestion. Hyderabad cuisine (a city in Andhra Pradesh) has a direct influence from the kitchens of the Nizams, who were the rulers that settled in Southern India in the early 18th century. The Hyderabadi cuisine is the amalgamation of varied cooking techniques and meats, combined with vibrant spices and ingredients.

One of India's finest foods, the biryani or rice with meats and brinjal (or eggplant) or baghare baiganis are originally the gems of Hyderabadi cooking.

Malayali curries of Kerala typically contain shredded coconut paste or coconut milk, curry leaves, and various spices. Mustard seeds are used in almost every dish along with onions, curry leaves and sliced red chillies fried in hot oil. Rice is the staple food and accompanies many of the foods that are served such as appam, masala dosa, idiyappam, parotta, puttu, iddali. The sadya is customarily served on a banana leaf.

Tamil cuisine's distinctive flavour and aroma is achieved by a blend and combination of spices, including curry leaves, tamarind, coriander, ginger, garlic, chili, pepper, cinnamon, cloves, cardamom, cumin, fennel or anise seeds, fenugreek seeds, nutmeg, coconut, turmeric root or powder, and rosewater. Lentils, vegetables and dairy products are essential accompaniments, and are often served with rice.

Assam/Nagaland

Rice is a part of all meals in Assam. The number of varieties of rice found in the region has led to speculation that the grain was first domesticated in the Assam/Yunnan region. Fish is very important second only to rice in Assam and the most popular dish from Assam, the *tenga*, is an indispensable part of a proper meal. The Assamese meat and fish dish is characterised by a low amount of spices and oil, higher quantity of ginger, norosingho paat (curry leaves) and lemon juice.

Naga cuisine, of Nagaland, is known for exotic meats but simple and flavourful ingredients and use of mustard oil. The meat and fish used are often smoked, dried or fermented. It is famous for use of dried bamboo shoots and for being the only state in India for its consumption of dog meat. Zutho is a special rice beer. Other North East Indian cuisines rarely experienced outside the sub-continent are Arunachali, Manipuri, Meghalayan, Mizoram, Sikkamese and Tripuri.

Bangladesh

Bangladeshi food is best known for its rich, spicy flavours and alluring aroma. Dessert recipes from Bangladesh are sweet and milky, an absolutely melt-in-your-mouth experience. Bangladeshi cuisine has considerable regional variations. These include lots of Bengali cuisine but are known more for their original spicyness compared to Indian Bengali Cuisine.

The heavy use of coconut milk is refined to the district of Khulna and Kommilla. A staple across the country is rice, fish and the use of mustard oil. Tea is grown in the hilly region around Sylhet and the drink is popular throughout Bangladesh.

The most important spices in Bangladeshi cuisine are garlic, ginger, coriander, cumin, turmeric and chilli. In sweet dishes, cardamom and cinnamon are amongst the natural flavours. Hilsa, very tasty but full of small bones, is the most popular of all fish, and is available in the rainy season.

Pakistan

A favourite Pakistani curry is karahi, either mutton or chicken cooked in a dry sauce. Lahori karahi incorporates garlic, spices and vinegar. Peshawari karahi is a simple dish made with just meat, salt, tomatoes and coriander. Specialties include kababs, dhals, quormah, tikkas and nihari. Meat plays a more dominant role in Pakistani food, compared to other South Asian cuisines the most popular being beef, goat, lamb, and chicken. Curries, with or without meat, combined with local vegetables such as bitter gourd, cauliflower, eggplant, okra, cabbage, potatoes, rutabaga, saag is one of the most common and often cooked for everyday eating and drinking. Chili powder, turmeric, garlic, paprika, cumin seed, bay leaf, coriander, cardamom, cloves, ginger and saffron are amongst the many herbs and spices widely used.

Dips are very commonly used in Pakistan with every meal. The most popular types are raita and chutneys. Raita is a soothing dip made of yogurt, whereas chutney is hotter and spicer and is preferred by the more daring.

Nepal

Indian, Chinese and Tibetan flavours and aromas can easily be detected in Nepalese meals. Whilst Nepalese cuisine is somewhat basic, it certainly does not lack in flavour, making extensive use of spices and flavourings such as ginger, garlic, coriander, pepper, cumin, chilies, cilantro, mustard oil, ghee and occasionally yak butter. The staple diet of Nepal's population is dal (lentils), bhat (rice) and tarkari (curried vegetables).

Newars are an ethnic group originally living in the Kathmandu Valley, now also in bazaar towns elsewhere in the hills (Himalayan foothills, up to about 10,000'/3,000m) with widespread use of water buffalo meat regarded as Newari pizza. Chatamari is a flat bread made from rice flour with or without toppings (meat, vegetables, eggs, sugar). It is highly savoured by the tourists who consider it as a good and healthy substitute to pizza. *Masu* is spiced or curried meat (usually chicken, mutton, buffalo or pork) with gravy. Served with rice, it is a main course dish, very popular in Nepal.

Sri Lanka

Sri Lankan cuisine mostly consists of rice and curry meals, and revolves heavily around chillies, spices, vegetables, and seafood. The most famous dish is the coconut sambol, made of ground coconut mixed with chillies, dried Maldive fish and lime juice. This is ground to a paste and eaten with rice, as it gives zest to the meal and is believed to increase appetite. Sri Lankans eat "*mallung*", chopped leaves mixed with grated coconut and red onions. Coconut milk is found in most Sri Lankan dishes to give the cuisine its unique flavour.

Sri Lankan food is generally spicy. There are three main types of curry: White, Red and Black. White curries are, mild, based on coconut milk and are very liquid. Red curries contain a large amount of chilli powder or ground red chillies with a few other spices. Black curries are dark in colour which is achieved by the roasting of the spices until they are a deep brown and are the most typical curries eaten in Sri Lanka.

Indonesia

In Indonesia, gulai and kari (North Sumatra) or kare (*kare*, a Javanese term for curry) are based on curry. They are often highly localised and reflect the meat and vegetables available. They can therefore employ a variety of meats (chicken, beef, water buffalo and goat as in the flavoursome gulai kambing), seafood (prawn, crab, mussel, clam, squid, etc), fish or vegetable dishes in a spiced sauce. They use local ingredients such as chilli peppers, kaffir lime leaves, lemon grass, galangal, Indonesian bay leaves or salam leaves, candlenuts, turmeric, shrimp paste (terasi), cumin, coriander seed and coconut milk.

One popular curry is rendang from West Sumatran cuisine, not Malaysia as is claimed in many British restaurants. Although it is originally from Sumatra and Indonesia it became very popular among Malays in Malaysia and Singapore. Authentic rendang uses water buffalo slow-cooked in thick coconut milk over a number of hours to tenderise and flavour the meat. In Aceh, curries use daun salam koja or daun kari (curry leaves). Opor Ayam is another kind of curry.

Rendang is the most famous dish and is considered a "dry" curry, which means the sauce is simmered down to a minimum. Typical Malaysian curry includes cumin, coconut, coriander, fennel, red chillies, shrimp paste, turmeric, lemongrass, garlic, onion, salt, and nuts. In Indonesia, curry paste is often made with coconut, soured fish, limes, peanuts, onions, caraway, chillies, nutmeg, cloves, turmeric, ginger, and poppy seeds.

Malaysia

Being at the crossroad of ancient trade routes has left a unique mark on Malaysian cuisine. Practically everything on the Asian menu can be found here, and the local fare is also a reflection of its multi-cultural, multi-ethnic heritage. While curry may have initially found its way to Malaysian shores via the

Indian population, it has since become a staple among the Malays and Chinese too. Malaysian curries differ from state to state, even within similar ethnic groupings as they are influenced by the many factors, be it cultural, religious, agricultural or economical.

Malaysian curries typically use curry powders rich in turmeric, coconut milk, shallots, ginger, belacan (shrimp paste), chillies, and garlic. Tamarind is also often used. Rendang is another form of curry consumed in Malaysia, although it is drier and contains mostly meat and more coconut milk than a conventional Malaysian curry. All sorts of things are curried in Malaysia, including goat, chicken, shrimp, cuttlefish, fish, fish head, aubergine, eggs, and mixed vegetables.

So rich and different are the flavours, that today Malaysian-themed restaurants are mushrooming globally from Canada to Australia, and Malaysian curry powders too are now much sought-after internationally.

One of the most popular kinds of food by the Indian Muslims is called nasi kandar (white rice or biryani rice served with other dishes of curry and either with chicken, fish, beef, or mutton and usually with pickled vegetables too. It is usually accompanied by some papadums).

Thailand

In Thai cuisine, curries are meat, fish or vegetable dishes in a spiced sauce. They use local ingredients such as chili peppers, kaffir lime leaves, lemon grass, galangal and coconut milk, and tend to be more aromatic than Indian curries as a result.

Curries are often described by colour; red curries use red chillis while green curries use green chillies. Yellow curries are more similar to Indian curries, with their use of turmeric and cumin. Yellow curries in Thailand usually don't contain potatoes except in southern style cooking, however, Thai restaurants abroad usually have them. Yellow curry is also called gaeng curry (by various spellings), of which a word-for-word translation would be "soup curry".

Thai curries also include, massaman curry, gold curry, panang, jungle curry, khao soi. Curry Laksa: a noodle dish served in curry, blends boiled chicken, cockles, tofu and bean sprouts for a surprisingly good treat.

Cambodia

Chicken Samla is one of the most popular dishes in Cambodia. It's a soupy curry that's more aromatic and less spicy than curries found in other parts of Southeast Asia. It uses a substantial amount of fresh ginger and lemongrass for flavour and fragrance. It is served over rice to soak up the sauce. Other popular curries are massaman beef and Cambodian style pork and butternut squash curry.

Curry paste is called kroeung and it is usually made from lemon grass, galangal, rhizome, turmeric, zest of kaffir lime, garlic and shallot. These seven herbs are the basis for almost every kroeung. Kroeung comes in three colours, green, yellow and red, depending on the ingredients used. Red kroeung receives its deep colour from a type of chilli pod which contributes very little flavour to the kroeung. The green kroeung uses more leaf than stalk of the lemon grass, giving it the green colour. And the yellow kroeung uses stalk of lemon grass only, it is the basis for a famous sour soup called samla machou kroeung.

Burma (Myanmar)

If one were to cross Indian and Chinese food, and the result were successful, it would describe Burmese curry with its many dimensions of flavour. Burmese chicken curry is a Punjabi-style chicken dish - but without tomatoes or peppers - but instead: coconut milk and besan (gram flour) with a dash of Thai fish sauce at the finish.

China

Curry is frequently used in Southern China to lend flavour to seafood, vegetable and noodle dishes. Chinese curries are light and aromatic and typically consist of green peppers, chicken, beef, fish, lamb, or other meats, onions, chunks of potatoes, and a variety of other ingredients plus spices in a spicy yellow curry sauce, and topped over steamed rice. White pepper, soy sauce, hot sauce, and/or hot chili oil may be applied to the sauce to enhance the flavour of the curry.

The most common Chinese variety of curry sauce is usually sold in powder form. It seems to have derived from a Singaporean and Malaysian variety, countries which also introduced the satay sauce to the Chinese. Chinese curry is popular in North America, and there are many different varieties of Chinese curry, depending on each restaurant. Unlike other Asian curries, which usually have a thicker consistency, Chinese curry can often be watery in nature.

Japan

Japanese curry is one of the most popular dishes in Japan, where people eat it 62 times a year according to a survey. It is usually thicker, sweeter, and not as hot as its Indian equivalent. It is usually eaten as karē raisu - curry, rice and often pickled vegetables, served on the same plate and eaten with a spoon, a common lunchtime canteen dish.

Curry was introduced to Japan by the British in the Meiji era (1869–1913). Kenjiro Yamakawa was supposedly the first Japanese to be introduced to curry onboard a ship to the USA in 1871. Ginza Fugetsudo restaurant in 1877 listed curry and rice at "8 sen" while noodles cost just "1 sen". Its spread across the country is commonly attributed to its use in the Japanese Army and Navy which adopted it extensively as convenient field and naval canteen cooking, allowing even conscripts from the remotest countryside to experience the dish.

The recipe for curry & rice was said to be invented in 1912 featuring onions, carrots and potatoes. Sometimes grated apples or honey are added for additional sweetness and other vegetables are sometimes used instead. Japanese curry powder was introduced in 1930. Sometimes the curry-rice is topped with breaded pork cutlet (tonkatsu); this is called katsu-karē ("cutlet curry"). Korokke (potato croquettes) are also a common topping. Apart from with rice, karē udon (thick noodles in curry flavoured soup) and karē-pan ("curry bread" — deep fried battered bread with curry in the middle) are also popular.

South Africa

South Africans – and especially those living in Durban – have a particular fondness for curry, as the metropolis is home to the largest Indian population outside of India in any city in the world.

The first Malay people in South Africa were brought as slaves from what is today Indonesia. As a result of the influence of the Malay and West Asians from the Indian sub-continent who came later, many curry (or kerrie) dishes are popular in South Africa such as the Cape Malay curry. The first group of Malaysian state prisoners landed on the shores of South Africa from Java and the neighbouring Indonesian islands in the late 1600s.

Many more followed in the years 1727 until 1749. Not only did this proud and attractive people bring with them the Moslem faith and fine architecture, they also brought with them a unique cookery style, introducing exciting mixtures of pungent spices that has had a heady influence on traditional South African cuisine. Indeed, the Malay-Portuguese words such as bobotie (a curried ground beef and egg custard dish), sosatie (kebabs marinated in a curry mixture) and bredie (slowly cooked stews rich in meat, tomatoes and spices) are integral in their cookery vocabulary.

There is some discussion as to the origin of the popular street food called bunny chow which broadly consists of curry ladled into a scooped-out loaf of bread. A theory is that bunny chow originated as a means for the (mostly Indian) labourers to take lunch onto the sugar cane plantations of Kwa-Zulu Natal in the days before disposable containers. Legend also has it that the simple recipe was invented as a response to apartheid. During racial segregation in South Africa, seats in Durban's curry houses were reserved for white people. Hungry customers of other races were largely forced into getting take-outs. And so the bunny chow was born. It was easy to take away and even easier to eat just with the hands. Still others maintain that it was a South African family of Indian origin, the Bhanias, who invented the bunny chow. It is said the way the food was served, right there on the putting green, eliminated the golfers' need for knives and forks and still satisfied their appetite for good curry. The meal became known, as "Bhania chow," which later became "bunny chow," as this was "easier to pronounce." Take your choice.

The curry used in a bunny chow varies according to taste - chicken, lamb, beef or vegetable are all popular, and the level of heat varies (beware - Durbanites like theirs HOT!). The bread component of a bunny chow may be a whole, half or quarter white loaf, and the scooped out centre (known as the virgin) is replaced on top of the curry before serving. The virgin is then dipped into the gravy and eaten as an appetiser – the ultimate street food. Bobotie with yellow rice is one of the most famous Cape Dutch dishes. It originates from the 17th century, when the Dutch used the Cape Colony in South Africa as a halfway station to the richer colonies in Asia.

Caribbean

Hindus came from India in the nineteenth century bringing their own curry to add to the spicy cuisine originally brought to the Caribbean by the Arawaks.

Pork Colombo is a Creole curry from Martinique and Guadeloupe. Its origins lie with the Sri Lankans, who were taken to the French West Indies to work on the sugar plantations and brought curry powder with them. On the islands, Colombo' is now a general term for a curried meat or seafood stew. The many spices used in Caribbean cooking include bay leaves, chillies, cinnamon bark, garlic, ginger, lemon, mace, nutmeg, onion, oregano, pimento, scotch bonnet peppers, sugar, thyme, coconut, lime, tamarind, and vanilla. Goat meat is very popular throughout the Caribbean and particularly in Jamaica and curry goat may be the most common method of preparation. Goat is quite delicious; it has a flavour similar to lamb, but is considerably milder. Grace brand and Jamaican Country Style are two prepared local curry blends that work well and are tasty.

Ethiopia

Ethiopian food is similar to Indian food in many ways - specially their split lentil dish which is similar to dal curry or parippu curry and their chicken and beef entrees which are similar to Keralan cuisine's chicken roast and beef ularthiyathu respectively. They have an appetizer called sambosa which is similar to the Indian samosa. You can either choose a beef or lentil filling.

Doro Wat is a thick, heavily spiced stew with chicken pieces and a boiled egg. Wat is virtually the Ethiopian version of an Indian curry and can be based on any vegetables or meat except pork. Berbère is the traditional Ethiopian seasoning for lentils and beans and is excellent for flavouring meats. Used as a dry rub or mixed with a little water to make into a curry paste. It is great as a seasoning for vegetables, whole grains, legumes and sauces.

East Africa

Whilst curry can be found all over Africa, its popularity is particularly notable in East Africa where the British and the Indians both brought their foods with them, like Indian spiced vegetable curries, lentil soups, chapattis and a variety of pickles. Just before the British and the Indians, the Portuguese had introduced techniques of roasting and marinating, and also use of spices, turning the quite bland diet into aromatic stewed dishes.

The Portuguese also brought from their Asian colonies fruits like the orange, lemon and lime. From their colonies in the New World, Portuguese brought exotic items like chilies, peppers, maize, tomatoes, pineapple, bananas, and the domestic pig – now, all common elements of East African food. With the combined British, Indian & Portuguese influences, East African curry dishes can often be quite hot with highly enjoyable layers of taste.

Germany

The Currywurst Museum, which opened in 2009, celebrates the iconic dish, nicknamed the "poor man's steak", 800 million of which are consumed every year in Germany -- a staggering 1,500 sausages per minute.

Despite its name, it is not actually the sausage that is curried. The secret of currywurst's acquired taste stems from the sauce - a simple but unforgettable melange of pureed tomato sprinkled with curry powder. Former US president George W. Bush reputedly once turned up his nose at it, but currywurst was ex-chancellor Gerhard Schroeder's favourite dish and Volkswagen sells more currywurst in its canteens than it does Golf cars so we are told.

Currywurst has been a firm favourite in Germany for 60 years although there are doubts about its origins. The curry and tomato sauce-flavoured sausage is its most celebrated snack supposedly from Berlin. Berliners insist a bored sausage seller, Herta Heuwer, created the currywurst on a drizzly September 4, 1949, less than four months after the end of the Western Allies' Berlin Airlift. Lacking clients, so the story goes, Heuwer mixed up a dash of American ketchup, a pinch of British curry sauce, a few spices and a drop of Worcester sauce and hey presto: currywurst sauce was born.

Recently Hamburg claimed currywurst for their own, with the Currywurst Club Hamburg even going so far as to accuse Berlin of re-writing the history books. Nearly a billion currywurst are believed to be consumed in Germany every year. A new study suggests that 80% of Germans regard the currywurst as central to their diet.

Australia

Modern Australian cuisines have been heavily influenced by its Asian and South-East Asian neighbours, particularly Chinese, Japanese, Thai and Vietnamese, and by the many waves of immigrants from there, and all parts of the world. Curry is increasingly popular in Australia partly due to Indian immigration and partly to the demands of the British ex pat community.

Recently, Michael Nash, Hobart's leading marine heritage expert, traced Australia's trade with India back to 1791, when a government store ship, Sydney Cove, was sent to Calcutta in British India for additional food supplies. While returning with a cargo including rice, sugar, tobacco, salted meat, soap, candles, textiles, leather wear and livestock, the ship sank off the coast of Tasmania in 1797.

India is always considered to be the home of curry (the dish) even though England may have supplied the name. However, curry as we know it today, nearly always includes chilli and tomatoes and neither were known in the sub-continent 400 years ago. It is a cuisine that welcomes adaptation and innovation and, as such, has been influenced by other cuisines and cultures all over the world to the great benefit of the international curry lover and thus may be considered as the first truly global cuisine.

Chapter 13

COMPENDIUM OF FOOD TERMS

INDIAN

Avial
Name Origins: South India

History: According to legend, a 16th century king ordered his kitchen to provide a feast for subjects for 30 days – stocks only being held for 29 of them. On the 30th day the chef realised the oil was gone except a few drops and only bits and pieces of vegetables were left from which he created avial. Avial is an essential part of the Onasadhya. A Sadhya is a big feast and could be associated with festivals like Onam, marriages, birthdays and the like.

Preparation: Avial is an important dish of Keralan Cuisine. Avial is a semi dry preparation of all sorts of vegetables. The vegetables that can be used for avial include beans, carrots, drumsticks, peas, yams, gourds, pumpkins and so on. Other main ingredients to flavour and season this avial are coconut paste, curry leaves and coconut oil which give a very unique aroma to this dish. The uniqueness of avial is that this tasty dish is usually made of all the leftover vegetables.

Balti
Name Origins: According to Hobson Jobson the word derives from 'balte' the Hindi word for pail or bucket (for slops, water or 'unsavoury' matter) which is the same as the Portuguese and Spanish word 'balte' for pail or bucket. Others say it derives from Baltistan, a remote area in Kasmiri Pakistan and that it is named after the thick flat-bottomed steel or iron pot in which it is both cooked and served.

History: Balti is another of those British Indian dishes with an almost legendary, unproven background. Despite the very interesting ideas of many pundits, there is no evidence it is a highly developed cuisine from either Baltistan or from Mirpur in Northern Pakistan. The name 'balti' for food has nothing to do with an ethnic group living in India and Pakistan who are also called Balti.

These Balti people are Tibetan Muslims. Balti staple cusine includes cha-phe (tsampa), Ladakhi salt tea (balti cha), marzan (cooked dough and yak butter); thsodma (greens) and chuli-chhu (apricot juice). Cereals are planted in late spring and at lands with elevations not above 2,500m, particularly along the Indus (Sengge Chhu) and Shyok River.

It is more likely that the balti as a style of food originated in the Sparkhill area of Birmingham in the late 1960's and grew to prominence in the 1970s. One Dr. M.A. Qureshi is often credited as the pioneer of balti dishes in the UK and claims (without any known supporting evidence) that the balti was originated by Indian soldiers who wore tin hats in the WW1 and would heat whatever food was available on the move in the cup-shaped headgear.

As far back as the early 1960s, Dr. Qureshi owned a coffee house on Cleveland Road in Balsall Heath Birmingham, which had a loyal following of his countrymen ready to try his original and authentic dishes and take cooking lessons at his house on Court Road, Balsall Heath. It is possible that many of the contemporary establishments were influenced by him.

Loyd Grossman, under whose name a line of British curry sauces is marketed, claims on his Balti sauce jar that the term comes from a word for "hubcap," since Indian truckers would cook their Balti in a hubcap – this also seems to be unverified.

Preparation: Balti is somewhat similar to the Punjabi karahi except for the inclusion of onions. Balti involves the fast cooking of marinated meat and spices over a high flame. Vegetables, such as spinach, potato, mushroom or aubergine may be added to chicken, beef, fish or prawns. Vegetarian versions of balti are also prepared. The cooking and serving method ensures that the flavours of all the spices are retained. Normally the balti is served with large naan bread; pieces of which are torn off by hand and used to scoop up the hot curry sauce from the pot. Side dishes and starters usually include onion bhajis, samosas, poppadums and creamy dips.

Restaurant: Balti is entirely a restaurant-created dish and the restaurant experience varies from the often serious offerings in the restaurants of Birmingham's Balti Triangle to others all over the UK who do not appear to know just what a balti is meant to be. As with chicken tikka masala, balti would have been unrecognisable in the Indian sub-continent until re-introduced from Britain.

Bhuna

Name Origins: From Urdu bhunna 'to be fried' - The act of browning - a cooking process where spices are gently fried in oil to bring out their flavour.

History: Introduced after 1869 when Bombay became the Gateway to India and Suez was opened bringing in the Chinese, woks and stir fry. When the Nawabs were exiled to Bengal, their royal cooks and Masalchi influenced the creation of Bhuna.

Preparation: Bhuna means 'dry cooking' in a little oil and its own juices and is excellent for rolling into wraps or bread. Similar to French 'reduction' – often needing to keep a cup of water to hand in case of scorching. The dish "bhuna" is fried for a long time with ground and whole spices over high heat and is an extension of that process where meat is added to the spices and then cooked in its own juices which results in deep strong flavours but very little sauce. This style of cooking gives a wonderfully rich and aromatic flavour to a dish.

Restaurant: The restaurant bhuna is a well spiced curry with a thick sauce. It is often garnished with fried green peppers and shredded onions, usually medium hot. A combination of onion, garlic, ginger and spices fried together in a shallow pan until golden brown to fully release their flavours. These are stirred constantly to prevent any burning or sticking. Bhuna dishes like chicken bhuna, lamb bhuna and vegetable bhuna are very popular in Anglo-Indian cuisine.

Biryani

Name Origins: The name is derived from the Persian (Farsi) word beryā(n) which means "fried" or "roasted".

History: One legend has it that Timor the Lame brought it down from Kazakhstan via Afghanistan to Northern India. According to another legend, Mumtaz Mahal (she who sleeps in Taj Mahal) concocted this dish as a "complete meal" to feed the army. Yet others say the dish really originated in West Asia. The Nomads would bury an earthen pot full of meat, rice and spices in a pit, eventually the pot was dug up and there was the Biryani.

Most likely it is a combination of all these and the Biryani was developed as a way of providing quick nourishment to the troops. Biryani, a mainly North Indian dish, was brought to Hyderabad by the invading Mughal army of Aurangazeb under the command of Khaja Abid, the father of the first Nizam of Hyderabad. Apparently, Biryani was meant to be a sort of ready-to-eat food for the soldiers during time of war.

During the Mogul empire, Lucknow was known as Awadh, giving rise to Awadhi Biryani. In 1856, the British deposed Nawab Wajid Ali Shah in Calcutta, giving rise to Calcutta Biryani. Aurangzeb installed Nizam-ul-mulk as the Asfa Jahi ruler of Hyderabad, as well as a 'Nawab of Arcot' to oversee Aaru Kaadu region south of Hyderabad. These moves gave rise to Hyderabadi Biryani and Arcot Biryani. The Biryani spread to Mysore by Tipu Sultan of Carnatic. Needless to say it was a royal dish for Nawabs and Nizams. They hired vegetarian Hindus as bookkeepers leading to the development of Tahiri Biryani.

Historians claim that the earlier Nawabs of Punjab wore a matching turban for each variety of biryani. The Nizam's kitchen boasted 49 kinds, which included biryanis made from fish, quail, shrimp, deer and hare.

Preparation: In an earthen pot called a Haandi, the rice and meat are layered; the bottom and top layer are always rice and cooked dum style. Traditionally, the leg of goat was used to make Biryani. There are up to 49 different varieties of biryani in the sub-continent 26 of which are found regularly.

The Sindhi variant of biryani is very popular in Pakistani cuisine and biryanis of all types are eaten in all parts of Pakistan. Another popular form of biryani is the Awadhi biryani. Malabar chicken biryani is very popular in Kerala. Tehri is the name given to the vegetarian version of the dish and is very popular in Indian and Pakistani homes. In Bangladesh, Tehri refers to Biryani prepared by adding the meat to the rice, as opposed to traditional Biryani where the rice is added to the meat.

Kacchi biryani is prepared with raw meat, which is marinated in curd and then cooked along with the rice by sealing the haandi (vessel) with a layer of dough, and is cooked on a dum - steaming over coal, or the baking process.

The accompanying sauce is redolent of mace, ittar and kewra. Saffron and cardamom are also used. In the Indian restaurant, however, all the dishes are made to order and the chef has to find a way of preparing the biryani in a short space of time. So the restaurant biryani is often just pilau rice stir fried with chicken or lamb which has been cooked as an extra dry bhuna.

Restaurants: Many restaurant biryanis are mild and usually garnished with almonds and sultanas and accompanied by a mixed vegetable curry to add a little juiciness to the rice.

Breads

Chapatti (Chapati) – Chapati historically is mentioned in *Ain-i-Akbari*, a 16th century document, by Mughal Emperor, Akbar's vizier, Abu'l-Fazl ibn Mubarak.

Chapatis are made from a dough consisting of atta flour (whole grain durum wheat), water, and salt. The dough is rolled out into discs of approximately 14 cm in diameter with a rolling pin. It is then heated on both sides on a very hot, dry tawa or frying pan Often, the finished chapatis are smeared with ghee (clarified butter). **Phulka** are small chapattis; **roti** are chapattis prepared with maize flour.

In Gujarat, chapatis which are toasted so that they are crisp are known as **khakra.** Khakra may be spread with chutney and other ingredients, and is a popular breakfast food. **Puris**, or pooris, are chapatis fried in oil so that they are crispy, and puris often form large bubbles as well. Since they are fried, puris should be eaten hot.

Paratha - Parathas originated in Peshawar and then spread all over the former northern parts of India. A specially prepared thick, unleavened bread made with wheat flour and home made ghee. Butter is also used as an alternative. It is normally shallow fried on a 'tawa', a thick, cast iron skillet. There are many different varieties of paratha served in UK Indian restaurants. Lacha paratha is a layered plain paratha that is crispier and flakier. You can have paratha's stuffed with potatoes, vegetables, keema (minced lamb), eggs or any other stuffing that you prefer. In Northern India, parathas are eaten at breakfast with pickle, home made ghee or a saag made from green mustard leaves.

Naan - Hindi nān, bread, from Farsi, ultimately from Old Persian nagna. The first recorded mention of naan can be found in the notes of Amir Khusrau (1300 AD) as naan-e-tunuk (light bread) and naan-e-tanuri (cooked in a tandoor oven) at the imperial court in Delhi. The word is believed to have originated in Central Asia within the Persian speaking nations of Afghanistan, Uzbekistan, Iran, and Tajikistan, the word naan literally meaning "bread."

Naan is cooked in a tandoor, or clay oven stuffed with a filling: for example, keema naan is stuffed with a minced meat mixture (usually lamb or mutton); Another variation is peshwari or peshawari naan. Peshawari naan and Kashmiri naan are filled with a mixture of nuts and raisins; aloo naan is stuffed with potatoes. A typical naan recipe involves mixing white flour with salt, a yeast culture, and enough yoghurt to make a smooth, elastic dough.

Poppadom (pappadam – South India) From Tamil pappaṭam. Made from lentil, chickpea, black gram or rice flour. The dough is shaped into a thin, round flat bread and then dried (traditionally in the sun) and can be cooked by deep-frying, roasting over an open flame, and toasting. In Bengali cuisine poppadoms are served after the main course but in Britain they are served as an appetiser. The average British restaurant curry fan consumes one and a half poppadoms per meal.

Luchi – A deep-fried, crisp, fluffy flatbread made of wheat flour that is typical of Bengali cuisine. In order to make luchis, a dough is prepared by mixing fine maida flour with water and a spoonful of ghee, which is then divided into small balls. These balls are flattened and individually deep-fried in cooking oil or ghee. A typical luchi will measure 4-5 inches in diameter. A luchi that is stuffed is called kochuri; kochuri stuffed with mashed peas (koraishutir kochuri) is one notable variety.

Kulcha – A north Indian Punjabi bread, usually eaten with chole. It is typically made with Maida flour. Amritsar is well known for its Amritsari kulchas more than any other city in the state. Flour dough, mashed potatoes, onion (optional) and lots of spices are rolled into a flat round bread and baked in an earthen clay oven. After it is golden brown it is rubbed with butter and then eaten with spicy chole (chickpea curry).

Cafreal

Name Origins: Goa via Africa

History: Chicken Cafreal, originated as Galinha (Frango) Piri-piri, a grilled bush dish from Mozambique. When the Portuguese came into contact with this, several changes were made to the dish when it was brought to another Portuguese colony, Goa. It is claimed to be named after the African soldiers or Kaffirs in Mozambique.

Chicken tikka marinated the Goan, Portuguese way redolent with the flavours of garlic, lime juice with fresh coriander and mint amongst others and olive oil. The classical cafreal was simply crumbled garlic with olive oil and lots of lime juice. The Goan version naturally had to add fresh green chilli and coriander to it as well.

Preparation: Today, the dish is made by marinating pieces of chicken in a paste made of spices, chilies, garlic and ginger and lemon juice and then deep-fried or shallow fried until dry. The result is a rather dry but spicy dish. This is the equivalent of Portuguese-style grilled chicken and the sauce it is marinated in tastes a lot like the famous Portuguese Peri-peri sauce.

Chettinad

Name Origins: Chettinad is a region of the Sivaganga district of southern Tamil Nadu state.

History: Based on a community of bankers and businessmen (Chettiars) who travelled to China and elsewhere. In 1077 the Chola King Kulottunja sent an embassy of 72 merchants to the Chinese court, hence the introduction of star anise. The cuisine had its origin in a small village called Nedungudi, about 600 km south of Chennai.

Preparation: The dishes are hot and pungent with fresh ground masalas, and often topped with a boiled egg. poppy seeds, coconut, fennel seeds, cinnamon, cardamom, cloves, turmeric powder, garam masala, onion, ginger, garlic, star anise, red chilli powder, tomatoes, curry leaves, coriander. chicken chettinad, pepper chicken, fish varuval etc.

Restaurants: One of the newer, regional dishes that is increasingly popular in the more adventurous restaurants in Britain for those with a spicier palate.

Chicken Tikka Masala

Name Origins: Unconfirmed. Probably of British/Bangladeshi origin and was, until recently, unknown in India. CTM used as an abbreviated version first coined by food writer Colleen Grove in 'Spice N'Easy' Magazine.

History: Chicken Tikka Masala was most certainly invented in Britain, probably by a Bangaldeshi chef, and is so popular it is even being served in some hotel restaurants in India and Bangladesh.

The tandoor, which boosted tikka sales, was introduced by Moti Mahal in New Delhi in 1948. In fact this can be seen as the birth of CTM in its original form of butter chicken. Lala Kundan Lal Gujral first set up in Peshawar in 1920 but came to Delhi in 1947 to set up Moti Mahal. He worked with a local man to produce the first restaurant version of the tandoor and invented tandoori spice mix for tandoori chicken -ground coriander seeds, black pepper and mild red pepper. Called murg makhani in Hindi, butter chicken originated in the 1950s at the Moti Mahal restaurant in Old Delhi. Famed for its tandoori chicken, the cooks there used to recycle the leftover chicken juices in the marinade trays by adding butter and tomato. This sauce was then tossed around with the tandoor- cooked chicken pieces and presto - butter chicken was ready! The leftover dish appealed to Delhites and was quickly lapped up by the rest of the world.

Top restaurateur Amin Ali, owner of The Red Fort and Soho Spice in London's Soho remembers serving CTM when he first arrived in London in 1974. A lowly waiter at the time he remembers wondering just what the dish was.

Top food writer Charles Campion refers to CTM as *"a dish invented in London in the Seventies so that the ignorant could have gravy with their chicken tikka"*. Several chefs have made claim to the invention of CTM but none with any evidence or witness support so the mystery will have to remain. The descendents of Sultan Ahmed Ansari, who owned the Taj Mahal in Glasgow claim he invented it in the late 1950s.

The cross-cultural popularity of the dish in the United Kingdom led former Labour foreign secretary Robin Cook to proclaim it as "Britain's true national dish". Urban legend has it that chicken tikka masala was actually created in the U K in the 1960s when a diner in a restaurant demanded some spicy gravy on the dry chicken dish served to him. The chef was at his wits end and improvised by adding a tin of Campbell's tomato soup, yogurt and some spices to the dry chicken dish. This was relished by the diner who enjoyed it and the first chicken tikka masala was born.

Preparation: The perfect chicken tikka masala should be rich and creamy in a lush red sauce with a hint of coconut, the meat should be tender and slightly smoky from the tandoor with beautiful aromas coming from the dish. There is no definitive recipe for chicken tikka masala and is very much a case of personal preference.

Restaurant: The chicken tikka masala experience can vary in heat, colour and even texture depending on the chef. The colour can be radioactive red, to a quieter red, brown and even green. It is normally quite a mild, creamy dish but some chefs like to introduce a chilli tang. It remains the most popular single dish requested in Indian restaurants accounting for up to 15% of all orders.

Dhansak

Name Origins: Dhansak is a Parsi dish traditionally served on Sundays and very popular with the Parsi community around Mumbai. It is a hot, sweet and sour dish offered at feasts and made of mutton, lentils, vegetables, spices, cumin seeds, ginger, garlic etc. Dhan means grain or rice and sak means vegetables.

History: In order to escape persecution at the hands of the Muslims in Iran, a small group of Zoroastrians left their ancestral town of Paras and set sail for India. Known as Parsis, according to legend, this group on reaching Sanjan, on the Gujarat coast, asked the local king Jadi Rana, for asylum.

Before getting permission, they were asked to prove how they wouldn't be a burden on the local people. The leader of the group stirred some sugar into a bowl of milk which was filled to the brim. When the sugar dissolved, the priest told the Rana, *"The bowl of milk represents your people, the sugar represents us. Just like the sugar gets absorbed in the milk and sweetens it without spilling, we, too, will assimilate with your people and sweeten their life without disturbing it."*

The Rana was taken aback with the Parsi's reply. He gave them asylum but laid down five conditions. These were:

- The esoteric and exoteric doctrines and practices of the religion should be explained.
- They should forsake their native language for the local one. Hence, their mother tongue is Gujarati.
- Parsi women would only wear what the local women wore. Parsi women wear sarees, wrapped in the Gujarati style even today.
- Eating beef would not be permitted. Most Parsis do not eat beef even today.
- They would not convert the locals to the Zoroastrian faith and should perform their religious ceremonies where the local population couldn't witness it.

Preparation: Dhansak is one of the most popular dishes in the UK and offers a wonderful mix of textures and flavours. When made by a Parsi chef and offered, as is traditional, with brown rice and kachumbar salad it is one of the most exciting dishes on the menu. The meat is traditionally mutton and there are different types of lentils such as masoor, or mung, urad and toovar dhal. The sweetness comes from red pumpkin and the sourness from fresh dill. Other ingredients include aubergine, fenugreek, onions, cloves, Kashmiri red chilli powder, turmeric and tamarind pulp.

Restaurant: Chicken Dhansak is the most famous version in most restaurants and is usually not served with brown rice or salad but conventional rice and side dishes. The dish served in Indian restaurants today is based on the addition of a lentil puree to the cooking process. It is described as a sweet and sour curry with a lentil sauce. The serving varies from restaurant to restaurant, but often expect a pineapple ring or some other fruit to be included in the curry for added sweetness plus sugar and very rarely will you find the required red pumpkin.

Dopiaza

Name Origins: The name dopiaza is from the Hindi for two, do, and onions, piaz. The name means double or twice onions and hence is somewhat confusing. Some chefs take the meaning to be double onions compared with meat and others, twice onions' with onions added at two different stages both fried and boiled. Very popular in Hyderabad and Andrah Pradesh.

History: Legend has it that Mullah Do Paiza, a courtier and advisor of Mugal Emperor Akbar, discovered this dish when accidentally doubling the amount of onion in the dish he was cooking. One of the Navratans (nine jewels) of the Court, it is said he could *"conjure up culinary delights using only two onions"*.

Preparation: Usually contains one large onion or two medium plus garlic, yoghurt, turmeric, red chilli powder, cumin coriander, bay plus cardamom, cloves, cinnamon and peppercorns for the garam masala. No water is used in cooking this dish and it is usually of medium heat with a thickish sauce.

Restaurant: Most restaurant versions of the dish today, fry small pieces of sliced onions first in a thick curry sauce with green peppers and chopped tomatoes and then add larger chunks of onions towards the end of the cooking. With the less subtle versions you can find chunks of raw onion added to the dish before presentation.

Dum Pukht

Name Origins: Dumpukht is derived from Persian meaning 'air-cooked' or 'baked. "DUM" means to "breathe in" and "PUKHT" means "to cook".

History: This is a slow-cooking method dating back to early sixteenth century and used in Akbar's kitchens and first mentioned in writing in 1590 according to Hobson Jobson. Dum cooking was introduced to India by the Mughals.

The cuisine was popular at the time of Nawab Asaf-ud-Daulah, the erstwhile ruler of the State of Awadh. The State was hit by a famine and unemployment was high. Nawab Asaf-ud-Daulah decreed the never ending construction of a giant edifice, the Bara Imambara, creating unceasing employment. By royal decree too, arrangements were made to provide food. Enormous containers were filled with rice, meat, vegetables and spices, and sealed. Hot charcoal was placed on top and fires lit beneath, while slow cooking ensured food was available day or night. The result was extraordinary, for when

the containers were unsealed; the splendid aromas attracted even the royal attention. The "dummed" cuisine was then perfected for the royal table. Exotic dishes were evolved, in which flavours and fragrances intermingled, with exquisite results.

Preparation: Slow Oven means cooking on a very low flame, mostly in sealed containers, allowing the meats to cook, as far as possible, in their own juices and bone-marrow. Fewer spices are used than in traditional Indian cooking, with fresh spices and herbs for flavouring.

In some cases, cooking dough is spread over the container, like a lid, to seal the foods. Its famous recipes include Dum Chicken Biryani, Hyderabadi Mutton Biryani, Nihari Gosht, Dal Bukhara, Mirch ka Salan, etc. This cuisine is popular in Pakistan, Punjab, Kashmir and UP in India.

Garam Masala

Name Origins: Urdu - a basic blend of ground spices used alone or with other seasonings. Garam masala varies region by region and even by town or village. Some of the best known are:

Punjabi Masala — toasts whole spices and grinds coriander seeds, bay leaves, cumin seeds, cloves, cardamom seeds, black peppercorns and cinnamon sticks.

Bangala Masala — not toasted, cloves, cardamom seeds, cinnamon sticks.

Rajasthani Masala — finishing spice, black peppercorns, black cumin seeds, cloves, cardamom seeds, bay leaves, mint leaves, Kashmiri chile, ground ginger, ground nutmeg, ground mace, ground cinnamon.

Maharashtrian Masala — raw peanuts, white sesame seeds, coriander seeds, cumin seeds, Thai chilies, nutmeg, mace, unsweetened coconut.

Kashmiri Masala — cumin seeds, cinnamon sticks, fennel seeds, black peppercorns, ground ginger, black cumin seeds, cloves, ground nutmeg, mace, black cardamom pods

Balti Masala — fennel seeds, coriander seeds, cumin seeds, mustard seeds, cloves, cardamom seeds, nigella seeds, bay leaves, cinnamon sticks, cayenne, nutmeg.

Kolhapuri Masala — red Thai chilies, unsweetened coconut, white sesame seeds, coriander seeds, cumin seeds, black peppercorns, mustard seeds, fenugreek seeds, mace, bay leaves, oil, ground Kashmiri chiles.

Sambhar Masala — curry leaves, red Thai chilies, chana dal, coriander seeds, cumin seeds, fenugreek seeds, mustard seeds, white poppy seeds, cinnamon sticks, sesame oil.

Chaat Masala — cumin seeds, dried pomegranate seeds, black peppercorns, mango powder, black salt, sea salt.

Haandi

Name Origins: Unknown

History: Originated in Lahore in Pakistan. Supposedly introduced to the UK by Manzoor Ahmed of Tabaq Restaurant in London (now closed). Haandi is an Indian pot that has a bottom like a wok and then has a narrow opening on the top. Slow cooking in steam or in seasoned moist flavourings are its special attributes. The cooking is done in a thick bottomed pan so that the food does not stick or burn; the lid helps retain the aroma and flavour. Both bhunao and dum are aspects of Haandi cooking.

Jardaloo

Name Origins: Parsee (apricot)

History: A Parsee celebration dish with lamb or chicken cooked with Hunza or Afghan apricots, ginger, cloves, cinnamon, cardamom, red chilli powder, cumin, wine vinegar, sugar, pepper and garam masa

Jalfrezi

Name Origins: (many alternative spellings such as jhal frezi, zalfrezi) The name is said to come indirectly from Bengali jhāl, spicy food, and Urdu parhezī, suitable for a diet. Rather than originating as the name of a dish, it is actually a style of cooking.

History: Said to have originated in Pakistan or Eastern India perhaps encouraged by non Indians based on the Chinese stir fry style of cooking. The literal meaning of the word Jalfrezi is "hot-fry" and entered the English language at the time of the British Raj in India. Colonial households employed Indian cooks who would use the jalfrezi method of cooking to heat up cold roasted meat and potatoes.

Preparation: Marinated pieces of meat or vegetables are stir fried in oil and spices to produce a dry, thick sauce. It is cooked with green chillies, with the result that a jalfrezi can range in heat from a medium dish to a very hot one. Other main ingredients include peppers, onion and tomato.

Restaurant: Jalfrezi has become one of the standard curry house dishes in Indian and Bangladeshi restaurants in the UK slotting in, in spice heat terms, between Madras and Vindaloo.

Karahi

Name Origins: The actual meaning of korai, karai or karahi is an Indian cooking pot made from cast iron, very similar to a wok. Origins are from the Pakistani Frontier region. Karahi is the 'Urdu' word for the pan in which this dish, with fresh garlic, ginger, tomatoes, onions, chillies and coriander is prepared.

History: A Karahi (karai) is a type of thick, circular, and deep vessel (similar in shape to a Chinese Wok) used in Pakistani and Indian cooking. Karahi are traditionally made out of cast iron. Karahi or kadai (also spelled "kadhi," "kadahi," or "kadhai") is a kind of dish cooked in a Karahi. Dishes in India are often presented "kadai fresh," like Kadai Chicken, and Kadai Paneer, where the dish is served with a miniature kadai and hot coals underneath it to give the impression of being hot from the stove.

Preparation: Karahi is a stir fry dish with similarities to balti. Both meat and vegetarian versions are popular and ingredients vary considerably according to the cook.

Restaurants: Karahi has been a popular dish with many diners since its introduction onto the menu's of Indian restaurants long before a balti was ever thought of. A dish with large pieces of onion, capsicums and tomatoes with herbs and spices, often served in a sizzling karahi at the table. Chicken, lamb or king prawns are usually the preferred meat used to cook the karahi but vegetable karahi's are also very popular.

Kedgeree

Name Origins : A dish consisting of flaked fish, usually smoked haddock but sometimes salmon, boiled rice, eggs and butter. Said to be adapted from Indian dish Kichri or Kichdi, a popular comfort food.

History: *The Scottish Kitchen* by Christopher Trotter has traced the origins for the kedgeree recipe to books by the Malcolms dating back to the year 1790 and many suggest Scottish troops during the Raj introduced the dish into India where it was adapted by local chefs.

The Indian dish Kichri or Kichari existed well before this (first mentioned in 1340) so whether they introduced it to the Scots or the other way round is impossible to say. In Victorian times kedgeree was a typical breakfast dish in Britain.

Preparation: Most recipes now contain light curry powder and or turmeric, coriander leaves (cilantro) or parsley to accompany the rice, boiled egg, butter, peppercorns, small onion, bay leaf and haddock. Sometimes cream or yogurt are stirred into the rice after cooking to make the dish richer.

Restaurants: Raj dishes such as mulligatawny and kedgeree are rarely found in Indian restaurants in Britain (with some very tasty exceptions) and tend to be produced more in the home

Korma

Name Origins: Hindi & Urdu gormā, of Turkic origin; akin to Turkish kavurma fried meat, from kavur- to fry, roast.

History: A Muslim court dish originated in the 16th - 19th century from Persia. Emperor Shahjehan used to have all white banquets on full moon nights at the Agra Fort. – white carpets, cushions and flowers with guests in white and white food. Shahi (Royal) Korma is said to have been perfected for the mainly toothless Nawabs of Oudh in Lucknow.

Preparation: Korma is a greatly mis-understood curry. Korma is "slow cooking or braising" rather than meaning a mild curry as it has become accepted in Britain. It can be very mild or rather fiery depending on which part of the country the recipe originated. Northern kormas generally have rich ingredients like saffron, nuts, nut pastes, khoya (full fat dried milk), cream, etc.

Moglai korma originates from the north of India, and is cooked with almonds, cashews, yoghurt in a creamy base, and with cardamoms and saffron to give it added flavour and aroma. Kashmir Korma originates from the Kashmir region of Pakistan/India, and uses all the same ingredients as the Moglai Korma but with dried fruits also being used in the cooking proccess.

The South Indian korma is quite different to the Moglai and Kashmir korma as fresh coconut or coconut milk is added along with fennel seeds, and unlike the other kormas this one is slightly spicier as cayenne powder is added. A Korma (quorma, qorma) is a very popular dish throughout India and even Pakistan and Afghanistan and varies from mild to a strong medium spice heat.

Restaurant: These days the Korma you get served in your local Indian is a very mild, creamy rich dish, cooked slowly on low heat with coconuts, cinnamon, cloves, nutmeg and double cream and often recommended for "curry virgins". Shahi Korma can be very rich and quite sweet but is very popular with those being introduced to Indian cuisine. Originally almonds were used but often now includes cashews plus poppy seeds, yoghurt, bay, onions, green chillis, cardamom, ginger, cloves, nutmeg and mace.

Madras

Name Origins: The dish gets its name from the city of Madras in South India, now known as Chennai.

History: Madras curry is one of those dishes peculiar to the British Indian restaurant industry and has come to be one of the standard dishes offered and enjoyed over the past 50 years. It is said to originate in the south of India and according to legend an Englishman named Sharwood was dining with the Maharaja of Madras, who mentioned to him the shop kept by a famous master maker of curry powder called Vencatachellum.

The Englishman visited it and obtained the secret of this curry powder, a mixture of saffron, tumeric, cumin, Kerala coriander and a selection of Orissa chillies, all of which were roasted then ground to make a masala, which came to be called Madras.

Preparation: Madras is a medium hot dish which originates from the Indian restaurants of Britain. In actual fact there is no such dish as Madras in India, and because it is a restaurant invention rather than a traditional Indian recipe, the characteristics of a Madras dish can change from restaurant to restaurant.

Restaurant: Your typical Madras dish will be cooked in a hot curry sauce, with tomatoes, lemon juice and with hot chilli powder. The Madras can be hot or really hot and red or brown - it can be just a version of a plain curry or very rich in tomatoes.

The curry house Madras is a restaurant invention which started life as simply a 'hotted up' version of the standard restaurant curry. The dish is a fairly hot curry sauce, red or brown in colour and with heavy use of chilli powder and can be vegetarian or meat.

Pasanda

Name Origins: In Hindi and Urdu, the words 'pasand' or 'pasanda' mean 'like' or 'liked' or 'to like' depending upon the verb it is used with. Therefore a Pasanda dish (often Badam (almond) Pasanda) is taken as meaning that the dish is to everyone's liking; children, beginner, meat eaters and old hands alike.

History: Pasanda is supposedly of North Indian and Pakistani origins dating back to as early as the Moghul era, where it was a favourite of the Emperors of the time. This is a mild dish, traditionally made with thinly sliced strips of boneless chicken or lamb fillets, marinated in aromatic spices.

Preparation: Pasanda is commonly, but mistakenly, taken to mean the style of sauce (usually very rich) in which this dish is presented. The term "pasanda" actually refers to the manner of preparing meat for cooking by beating it and cutting into strips. It is of a creamy consistency, lamb being marinated in a mix of yoghurt, ground almonds, onion, ginger and garlic.

Restaurant: Pasanda is a special preparation of ground almonds, cream and selected spices. This dish is mild to medium, flavoured with cardamoms, cinnamon and spices and it is not very hot. It is a favourite among the people who enjoy a milder experience and is highly recommended for people with mild palates. It is best enjoyed with rice or naan.

Pathia

Name Origins: A dish of Persian origins (Pathia, Patea), possibly Parsee (fish in dark vinegar sauce), although others say East and even Southern Indian.

Preparation: A sweet and sour, quite hot dish. Often lemon is used for the sour taste, and either other fruits, or the shameless use of sugar provides sweetness. It should be an exotic balance of sweet and sour.

It is hot, garnished with onion, green pepper and a touch of almond, in a thick sauce with chicken or lamb, generally similar to a Madras with lemon juice and tomato purée.

Restaurants: Started as a starter using mainly prawns but is now offered as a maincourse dish with prawn, chicken or lamb and often garnished with tomato pieces.

Prawn Balchao

Name Origins: Originated in Macao

History: Brought to Goa by the Portuguese, Balchão originated in Macao, where it is called Balichao.

Preparation: Prawn Balchão is another Goan favourite. Balchao is a method of cooking either fish or prawns in a dark red and tangy sauce. Balchao is almost like pickling and can be made days in advance without reheating. The traditional Balchao uses a paste made from dried shrimp known as 'galmbo' in Konkani spices. This paste is added to fresh prawns, onion, spices and oil to prepare a prawn balchao. Balchao is often bottled and eaten as an accompaniment in meals. But many people leave out the dried shrimp paste as this lends a fairly strong fishy flavour to the dish.

Raan

Name Origins: Indian whole leg of lamb.

History: Sikandri Raan was first known to have been prepared for Alexander of Macedonia's wedding feast when he married Roxanne, daughter of Oxyrates, a king of the Hindu Kush region, which Alexander (or Sikander) had just conquered. The leg of lamb preparation was also eaten at the battlefield banquet held to celebrate the now legendary friendship of the great conqueror with King Porus of Takshila.

Preparation: Leg of lamb marinated in yogurt-based masala. Ingredients can include almonds, onions, chillies, garlic, ginger, cloves, cardamom, cinnamon, black peppercorns, cumin seeds, coriander seeds, cayenne peppers, garam masala, yoghurt.

Restaurants: There was a time when you would have to book 48 hours ahead for a Raan in a restaurant but nowadays much quicker versions (though possibly not as succulent) are on offer.

Rezala

Name Origins: West Bengal.

History: Bengali. Originated in the kitchens of a Mogul ruler who lived near Calcutta.

Preparation: Traditionally made with mutton chops or goat. A curry made by simmering a wide variety of ingredients in flavoured yogurt. It has to be cooked on low heat with constant stirring to prevent the yogurt from splitting.

Ingredients include yoghurt, onion, garlic, cardamom, cinnamon, clove, peppercorn, Keora water, sour curd, green chilli, chicken, goat or lamb.

Restaurants: A popular dish found in most Bangladeshi restaurants in Britain. Medium spiced with a rich sauce and, although not a traditional favourite, chicken rezala is very popular.

Rogon Josh

Name Origins: (sometimes called Rogon Ghost) a Kashmiri dish. There is some dispute as to meaning. Camellia Panjabi says Rogan = fat and josh = heat (intensity). Others say it means red meat and was called Rogon Ghost originally. Another definition states that Rogan in Persian means clarified butter and Josh means hot and passionate. Cinnamon Club chef Vivek Singh states it actually means 'red juice' and its redness does not come from colouring, red chillies or tomatoes but from the bark of a Kashmiri tree called rattan jyoth.

History: The history of modern Kashmiri cuisine can be traced back to the fifteenth century invasion of India by Timur, and the migration of 1700 skilled woodcarvers, weavers, architects, calligraphers and cooks from Samarkand to the valley of Kashmir. The descendants of these cooks, the Wazas, are the master chefs of Kashmir.

The Mughals who brought the best of cuisine and arts with them, are the originators of this recipe. To escape the heat of Delhi and Central India, the Mughals went frequently to Kashmir which was once considered as the 'Switzerland of the East'. They took the recipe with them. Kashmir with a Hindu king and an Islamic population welcomed the Mughals, their art, literature and food. The Rogan Josh with a few modifications came to be known later as 'Kashmiri Rogan Josh'. Rogan Josh was a favourite of Jawaharlal Nehru and Indira Gandhi being Kashmiris.

Preparation: Rogan Josh is meat (traditionally mutton) cooked in clarified butter at intense heat. – cooked in its own fat with large black cardamoms and cloves. Recipes vary widely across different regions and traditions, but all include lamb or goat, oil or ghee (clarified butter), and a mixture of spices. These may include paprika for its red colour or crushed beetroot, aniseed, cloves, cumin, cinnamon, and many others. Many variations have ginger, garlic, and yoghurt, and some also use tomatoes. The Kashmiri Pandits use asafoetida (hing) and fennel seeds instead of garlic and onions and some achieve the deep red colour from the liberal use of dried red Kashmiri chillies.

Restaurants: Rogan Josh is one of the most popular dishes in restaurants throughout Britain but versions of the dish vary widely. The dish is usually medium hot and the redness comes from chopped tomatoes and red peppers (although some amazingly still use colouring). Many restaurants now also offer Rogan Chicken and even prawn but lamb remains the most popular.

Sorpotel

Name Origins: The word Sorpotel is said to be derived from the konkani word Soro which means Alcohol/Liquor. A party dish from the Christians of Goa.

History: Sorpatel, Sarapatel adapted from Portuguese dish sarabulho served at Christmas and on feast days

Preparation: Pork, pork liver & heart, kidneys, red chillis, black peppercorns, garlic, ginger, cumin, cloves, cinnamon, vinegar, oil, coconut feni, green chillies, onions. Sorpotel, like balchao, keeps for several days, and is actually considered to taste better if left for three to four days before being reheated. The meats are first parboiled, then diced and sauteed before being cooked in a spicy and vinegary sauce. Sorpotel is often accompanied by "sanna" - a spongy, white, and slightly sweet steamed rice and coconut bread.

Tawa

Name Origins: (Tava) Unknown

History: A tawa is a round, thick iron griddle, it is also slightly concave in the centre. It is used when very high temperatures are needed and mostly for Indian unleavened breads called chappati or rotis. It is also used for cooking some unique dishes which require fast cooking with the outer rim used to keep the dish warm. Popular in street food especially Pau-Bhaji which is a typical tawa dish and needs to be constantly stirred to avoid burning, and is served straight out of the tawa and eaten immediately on sour dough bread.

Thali

Name Origins: Hindi meaning plate. A thali is a selection of different dishes, usually served in small bowls on a round tray. The Thali is set with a number of small bowls (katoris in Hindi) containing all sorts of vegetarian and non-vegetarian foods. Rice, bread (like chapatis), pickles, chutneys and a dessert are also usually included.

Preparation: Thali dining is more a style than a dish. The content varies very much from region to region. For instance the Gujarati thali will have farsans (Gujarati vegetarian canapes), vegetables, dals, chapatis (rotis), rice, salads and pickles. In the south the emphasis shifts to rice delicacies as well as vegetables.

Restaurants: Most restaurants in Britain feature a vegetarian or meat based Thali in their menus and they are very popular.

Tikka

Name Origins: Hindi/Urdu - a piece of meat, such as a cutlet – Persian for 'bits', 'pieces'.

History: Originated in the Punjab region of Pakistan and India, possibly among the Hindkowans of the city of Peshawar. Tikka became very popular in British/Asian cuisine with the introduction of the tandoor, leading to the creation of Britain's 'favourite dish' chicken tikka masala. The dish is also known and eaten in Afghanistan, though the Afghan version is less spicy in comparison with the Indian version.

Preparation: Usually boneless pieces of chicken, lamb, duck, king prawn or vegetables marinated in a special mixture of tandoori red spices and yoghurt. The Punjabi version, though, is barbecued on red-hot coal and does not always contain boneless pieces. The pieces are regularly brushed with ghee (fat), which gives its taste, while being continuously fanned. It is typically eaten with a green coriander & tamarind chutney, served with onion rings and lemons.

Restaurant: Chicken tikka is one of the most popular starters in Indian restaurants in UK. The pieces of chicken are presented hot and red from the tandoor but since the pressure to omit food colouring, many restaurants present the dish in its natural, non-red, state.

Vindaloo

Name Origins: Derivative of the Portuguese "vinha d'alhos", and also called Vindalho or Vindallo meaning wine/vinegar of garlic

History: Portuguese sailors introduced vindaloo to India as they carried on board their ships barrels of pork preserved in wine or vinegar and garlic to provide sustenance on their long journeys.

Britons have known about this hot curry dish at least since 1888, when W. H. Dawe explained it in *The Wife's Help to Indian Cookery*, published in London: "*Vindaloo or Bindaloo--A Portuguese Karhi.... The best Vindaloo is prepared in mustard-oil.... Beef and pork, or duck can be made into this excellent curry.*"

Portuguese sailors brought their garlic-flavoured vinegar stew to Goa, which, from 1510 to 1961, was a Portuguese colony on the southwestern coast of India. The Goans spiced up the recipe and the name, making it vindaloo in their Konkani language, a member of the Indo-Iranian branch of the Indo-European language family. The English tongue has only vindaloo from Konkani.

Preparation: The traditional Portuguese dish was made with pork preserved in red wine or red wine vinegar, and stewed with garlic and only included chili pepper after it was discovered it in South America. In Goa, where wine was less easy to come by, vinegar was substituted, and local spices were added (the Portuguese dish was not spicy). Goan vindaloo is sweet-and-sour pork, the vinegar derived from tapping the high branches of the coconut palm tree to give it that special taste rather than the lip-searing dish found in some UK restaurants.

Restaurant: Vindaloo is a mainstay of the "Indian" menu in the UK and is the classic 'hot' dish, so much so that it has even inspired songs when in 1998 Fat Les recorded "Vindaloo" for the FIFA football World Cup. Restaurants often serve this dish with chicken or lamb and also often mistakenly mixed with potatoes. Traditional vindaloos do not include potatoes, the discrepancy arising from misinterpretation of the name because the word "aloo" means "potato" in Hindi. Hence the restaurant definition tends to be *"very hot with potato in spicy sauce"*.

The vindaloo you are likely to get served in your local restaurant or take-away is just a much hotter version of a normal madras style dish, although some chefs have interpreted the "aloo" part of vindaloo, as meaning potato and have introduced diced potato in the dish.

A typical vindaloo contains a whole range of spices including: garlic, vinegar, chillies, coriander, cumin, onions, ginger, peppercorns and tomatoes. It is the favourite 'macho' dish of British Indian restaurants.

Xacuti

Name Origins: The name is supposedly derived from "Xac Ku Tic" or "Xaque Ku Tik" meaning that the dish is very spicy

History: Xacuti used to be prepared only of game meat, and it was always the men who prepared it after returning from hunting.

Preparation: A curry prepared in Goa with quite complex spicing, including white poppy seeds and large dried red chillies and has its origins in Portuguese cooking. It has lots of earthy spices like nutmeg, coriander, turmeric, chilies, ginger and cloves. Additionally tamarind and lemon juice make for a pungent curry.

MEXICAN

Real Mexican food is quite unlike the dishes found in most Mexican and Tex-Mex restaurants in countries outside Mexico and can be very exciting in quality terms rather than the quantity emphasis of some Tex/Mex.

Achiote

A paste or powder for culinary use, mainly as a colour: it is known as "achiote," "annatto," "bijol," or "pimentão doce." It is a main ingredient in the Yucatecan spice mixture recado rojo, or "achiote paste." Achiote Paste is made from thousands of slightly bitter, earthy flavoured, red annatto seeds. Ground into a paste, achiote is a distinctly coloured and flavoured mainstay.

In the West it used to colour confectionery, butter, smoked fish and cheeses like Cheshire, Leicester, Edam and Muenster. The Mayan Indians of Central America used the bright dye as war paint.

Chalupas

A tostada platter in Mexican cuisine. It is a specialty of south-central Mexico, such as the states of Puebla, Guerrero and Oaxaca. It is made by pressing a thin layer of masa dough around the outside of a small mold and deep frying to produce a crisp shallow corn cup. It is filled with various ingredients such as shredded chicken, pork, chopped onion, chipotle pepper, sour cream, cheese, red salsa, and green salsa. Chalupa means boat or launch in Spanish.

Chimichanga

The dish is prepared by folding a flour tortilla into a rectangular package and filling it with a wide range of ingredients, most commonly beans, rice, cheese, ground beef, shredded beef, or shredded chicken. It is then deep-fried and may be accompanied with salsa, guacamole, sour cream or cheese. The origins of the dish are disputed, the earliest claim being from 1922 in Tucson, Arizona.

Enchilada

A corn tortilla rolled around a filling and covered with a chili pepper sauce. Enchiladas can be filled with a variety of ingredients, including meat, cheese, beans, potatoes, vegetables, seafood or combinations. This Mexican dish is a filled tortilla with a variety of fillings such as shredded chicken, beef, vegetables or beans, then covered with a sauce and some grated cheese. The filled tortillas are then baked in the oven until cooked and the cheese is melted and golden.

Fajita

The word fajita originally referred to a particular cut of beef – the tough skirt steak. In traditional fashion the strips of fajita beef would have been eaten by Mexican ranch workers wrapped in a tortilla with hot sauce and guacamole if avocados were to hand. In the late 1970s a restaurateur in San Antonio, Texas opened the Mi Senor restaurant with a menu featuring the first restaurant selection of fajitas using stir fry strips of beef, chicken, prawns and pork, far removed from the original humble Mexican fare. The meat is often cooked with onions and bell peppers and wrapped in a flour or corn tortilla. Popular condiments are shredded lettuce, sour cream, guacamole, salsa, pico de gallo, cheese, and tomato.

Frijoles

Refried beans, traditionally prepared with pinto beans, but many other varieties of bean can be used, such as black or red beans. Frijoles refritos can appear on a Mexican table three times a day: with breakfast eggs, after the main meat course at midday (the largest meal), or with the evening's tacos. They are used to spread on tostadas, in burritos, in enchiladas, on tacos, on nachos, or just by themselves.

Guacamole

Of Aztec origin, it was originally valued for its high fat and vitamin content. Guacamole was originally made by mashing the avocado with a mortar and pestle and adding tomatoes and salt. Ripe avocados, onions, lime, and salt are common to most recipes with lime or lemon juice added for flavour, and to slow the enzyme causing browning.

Other common ingredients include minced tomatoes, black pepper, chili pepper, garlic, cumin, and cilantro. Traditional Mexican ingredients include avocados, minced tomatoes and white onions, fresh coriander, lime, garlic, salt and pepper

Mole

It is the generic name for several sauces used in Mexican cuisine. Mole poblano, whose name comes from the Mexican state of Puebla is the mole that most people in the U.S. think of when they think of mole. Mole poblano is prepared with dried chili peppers (commonly ancho, pasilla, mulato and chipotle), ground nuts and/or seeds (almonds, indigenous peanuts, and/or sesame seeds), spices, Mexican chocolate (cacao ground with sugar and cinnamon and occasionally nuts), salt, and a variety of other ingredients including charred avocado leaves, onions, and garlic.

Dried seasonings such as ground oregano are also used. In order to provide a rich thickness to the sauce, bread crumbs or crackers are added to the mix. There are eight other well-known moles with differing ingredients. Chicken Mole is the national dish of Mexico. Standard Mexican mole usually includes vegetable oil, onion, finely chopped, good quality cocoa powder, ground cumin, dried coriander, garlic, minced tin chopped tomatoes, diced jalapeño chillies.

Pipian

Pipián sauce is a piquant Mexican seed sauce traditionally served over roast chicken or enchiladas. It is part of a larger family of ground sauces known as moles, and it has a very distinctive, nutty, earthy flavour. Pipian is a grand and quite ancient dish of Mexican cuisine. Recipes vary but include pumpkin, masa harina, garlic and dry red chillies.

Other recipes call for toasted sesame seeds, blanched almonds, garlic and jalapeno chillies. Green Pipian includes tomatillos, lettuce, garlic, onions, cilantro, radish and avocado leaves, epazote, cumin, chillies, pumpkin seeds and peanuts.

Quesadillas

A fast-food item in Mexican cuisine, which involves cooking ingredients, most importantly cheese, inside a corn, wheat or flour tortilla or a wrapping of masa (cornmeal dough). The word comes from Spanish, and literally means "little cheesy thing".

Originally, in most regions (especially the central region) of Mexico, a quesadilla was a circle of uncooked corn masa folded in half and filled with cheese, then warmed up until the cheese has melted.

However, variations include the use of wheat flour tortillas, especially in the northeast part of Mexico, which are more like cheese tacos found in the U.S. Wheat dough is used in place of corn masa in pastes, a preparation typical of the Mexican city of Pachuca, Hidalgo. Wheat tortillas are also used to make a gringa, which is a cross of a taco al pastor and a quesadilla. Quesadillas can be stuffed with ingredients other than just cheese.

Mexican Quesadillas   Serves 6

Prep Time: 10 mins
Cook Time: 15 mins

Ingredients:

- 6 soft wheat tortillas
- 2 jalopeno chillis in brine, drained and finely chopped
- 200-250g Applewood smoked - flavoured cheese, grated
- 3 spring onions, finely chopped
- 25g butter

Method:

1. Place 3 of the wheat tortillas on a clean work surface.
2. In a bowl, mix together the cheese, spring onions and chilli.
3. Divide the cheese mixture over the three tortillas. Top with the other three tortillas and press down to flatten.
4. Heat a little of the butter in a frying pan. Add a tortilla and cook for 5 mins, pressing down on the top of the tortilla. Turn the tortilla over and cook the second side until crisp.
5. Remove from the pan and cut into wedges. Repeat with the remaining tortillas.

TIP: To create very runny cheese, pop the cooked quesadillas in the microwave for a minute or so.

Salsa

Salsa has been America's favourite condiment since 2000—supplanting ketchup. The chile has been domesticated since about 5200 BC., and tomatoes since 3000 BC both in Central America. The two were combined into a condiment, which the Conquistadors named "salsa," or sauce. The spicy sauce gave name to a hot and spicy late 20th century dance related to the mambo...but that's just the tail end of the story. In 1494, Dr. Diego Álvarez Chanca brought the first chiles to Spain, after traveling to the West Indies on Columbus' second voyage. He wrote of their medicinal effect. In 1529, Bernardino de Sahagún arrived and began to document Aztec culture, which included foods (and salsa).

Aztecs combined tomatoes with chiles and ground squash seeds and consumed them mainly as a condiment with seafood, turkey and venison. This combination was named salsa in 1571 by Alonso de Molina, a Spanish priest and missionary (c. 1510-1584) who was taken by his parents to Santo Domingo, and went onto Mexico in 1523, after the conquest, where he learnt the Aztec language, Nahuatl.

In 1807, the first bottled hot sauces, made with cayenne chiles, appeared in Massachusetts. In 1941, Henry Tanklage formed La Victoria Sales Company to market a new La Victoria salsa line. He introduced red and green taco and enchilada sauces, the first salsa hot sauces in the U.S. He took over the entire La Victoria operation in 1946, which manufactures ten different hot sauces now covering the entire salsa spectrum, including Green Chili Salsa and Red Salsa jalapeño. Salsa is low in calories and contains little or no fat. Tomatoes, chiles and coriander contain vitamins A and C; tomatoes also have potassium.

Tamales

From Nahuatl, tamalli is a traditional indigenous Latin American food consisting of steam-cooked corn dough with or without a filling. The corn meal dough made from hominy (called masa), or a masa mix such as Maseca, usually filled with sweet or savoury filling, wrapped in plant leaves or corn husks, and cooked, usually by steaming. Masa is made of dried white corn, cal (slaked lime) and water.

Tamales are a gastronomic heritage from the ancient Indians of Mesoamerica, for whom tamales were a main dish. Tamales wrapped in corn husks were the featured dish eaten at celebratory banquets. They made tamales stuffed with snails, game, boiled fruit, broad beans and fish with chile sauce. Nowadays the filling in the tamales depends largely on the region.

Tostadas

The tostada was created when tortillas went stale but were still fresh enough to eat. Not wanting to waste old tortillas, which was one of the staple foods of the Mexican people, beans, rice, meat, cheese and vegetables were spread onto the tortillas like an "open faced" taco. This invention became very popular and people soon began to fry fresh tortillas to recreate the dish. Tostadas nowadays are like flat tacos that are usually made by layering frijoles (refried beans) on top of a fried, flat corn tortilla and then adding a variety of different toppings, like meat, lettuce, guacamole, cheese and salsa.

MIDDLE EASTERN

Couscous
This is a Berber dish consisting of spherical granules made by rolling and shaping moistened semolina wheat and then coating them with finely ground wheat flour. Couscous has been a staple food for over 1,000 years in Morocco, Algeria, Tunisia, Libya and Egypt. Traditional couscous requires considerable preparation time and is usually steamed. The name is possibly derived from the classical Arabic word kaskasah, meaning "to grind" or "to pound".

Couscous is traditionally served under a meat or vegetable stew. It can also be eaten alone, flavoured or plain, warm or cold, as a dessert or a side dish. It has also become another "designer" ingredient in many European countries as well as South America and the United States.

Falafel
Falafel is made from fava beans or chickpeas or a combination of the two rolled into balls. Originally said to be an Egyptian dish well over 1,000 years ago though other countries claim it. Israel claims falafel as its national food (it is mentioned in the Bible) whilst Palestinians complain that falafel was stolen from them. Falafel balls may also be eaten alone as a snack or served as part of a mezze or served in pita bread with salad. Lebanese falafel often use a combination of fava beans and chickpeas, while in Egypt, it is traditional to use just fava beans. They are very nutritious and include both high-quality protein and vegetables.

Fattoosh
Fattoosh is a tangy, very popular Lebanese salad. It is prepared with fresh ba'leh or purslane (mache), tomatoes, green onions, mint, sumak, and also leftover pita bread.

Harissa
A North African hot red sauce or paste made from chili peppers (often smoked or dried) and garlic, often with coriander and caraway or cumin and served with olive oil. Important in Tunisian cuisine as well as in Morocco, Algeria and Libya. There is also a special variety flavoured with roses. Often served with couscous.

Hummus
Also spelled hamos, houmous, hommos, hommus, hummos, hummous or humus). It's a Levantine Arab (and traditional Greek) dip or

spread made from cooked, mashed chickpeas, blended with tahini, olive oil, lemon juice, salt and garlic. Serve one type of hummus or a variety with hot pita bread wedges, pita chips or fresh veggies sticks (carrot, sliced peppers & celery are delicious). Chickpeas are a good source of cholesterol-lowering fibre, in addition to lowering cholesterol, chickpeas high fibre content prevents blood sugar levels from rising too rapidly after a meal.

Kibbe
Kibbeh is one of the most characteristic foods of Levantine cuisine particularly in the area of Aleppo, but also in the rest of the Levant (Syria, Lebanon, Palestine, Israel, Jordan), the surrounding regions (Iraq, Turkey, Cyprus (koupes or koubes), the Arabian Peninsula, Armenia) and as far afield as Brazil, Colombia, and the Dominican Republic. Torpedo-shaped bulgur shells stuffed with a filling based on spiced minced lamb and fried till brown – know in the War as "Syrian torpedoes".

Mezze
A selection of appetizers or small dishes often served with a beverage, like anise-flavoured liqueurs such as arak, ouzo, or raki. Whilst they sometimes resemble tapas, mezze (meze, mazza) are not an appetiser opener, as starters are not part of the Arabic eating concept. A mezze table would probably consist of an entire meal. Said by some to come from the Italian word mezzano, meaning middle, but this is discounted by others. Popular throughout Middle East, Turkey and Greece.

Moussaka
Originated in the Balkans and Middle East but most famous in Greece, consisting of sautéed eggplant and tomato, usually with minced meat. The Greek version, which is the best-known outside the region, includes layers of meat and eggplant topped with a white sauce and baked. Turkish musakka, unlike the Greek version, is not layered. Instead, it is prepared with sautéed eggplants, green peppers, tomatoes, onions, and minced meat. Greek version possibly introduced by Tselementes in the 1920s. Food historians say it is descended from the Arabian dish maghmuna or musakhkhan and a very similar dish appears in a 13th century Arabic cookbook

Pita
A round, brown, wheat flatbread made with yeast often known as Syrian bread. Similar to other double-layered flat or pocket breads, pita is traditional in many Middle Eastern and Mediterranean cuisines. Pita is used to scoop sauces or dips such as hummus and to wrap kebabs, gyros or falafel in the manner of sandwiches. Pita originated in Egypt and the Middle East centuries ago.

Tabbouleh
A popular salad dish in most Middle Eastern countries. Primary ingredients are bulgur, finely chopped parsley, mint, tomato, scallion, and other herbs with lemon juice, olive oil and various seasonings, generally including black

pepper and sometimes cinnamon and allspice. Often used as part of mezze. Tabbouleh is popular in Brazil, USA, the Levant and in the Dominican Republic. The name is from a Levantine Arabic word meaning literally "little spicy."

Tahini
Tahini is a paste of ground sesame seeds used in cooking. Tahini is a major component of hummus bi tahini and other Middle Eastern foods. Tahini is a thick dip, made of raw tahini which is a sesame paste. It is eaten with hummus, all sorts of salads, burgers and meat, and goes wonderfully with many kinds of casseroles.

Taramasalata
Greek – a dip often served as a mezze dish - it is traditionally made from *taramas*, the salted and cured roe of the cod or the carp, though blends based on other forms of fish roe, particularly cod, have become more common. The roe is mixed with either bread crumbs or mashed potato, and lemon juice, vinegar and olive oil.

Sambusak
A traditional Jewish pastry for Hannukah and the Sabbath. Flaky sesame-seed crusted pastries are filled with a savoury beef or cheese mixture. It is an Arabic version of the Indian samosa.

From top row, left to right: Dried Curry Leaves, Ajwain, Dried Fenugreek Leaves, Saffron

ORIENTAL

Anhui

Most ingredients in Anhui cuisine, such as pangolin, stone frog, mushroom, bayberry, tea leaves, bamboo shoots, dates, games, etc., are from mountain areas. Anhui cuisine chefs pay more attention to the taste, colour of dishes and the temperature to cook them, and are good at braising and stewing. Generally the food is slightly spicy and salty. Popular dishes include stewed soft shell turtle with ham, Huangshan braised pigeon, steamed stone frog, steamed rock partridge, stewed fish belly in brown sauce, bamboo shoots cooked with sausage and dried mushroom. Anhui Cuisine places importance on its ingredients rather than its seasonings and can be greasy and salty.

Cantonese

Southern China - Cantonese cuisine is not generally spicy-hot or highly seasoned and is the best known Chinese cuisine outside China. As most residents originate from the Guangdong province where Guangzhou (Canton) is located, Hong Kong is the world capital for this style of cooking. The sub-tropical region boasts ingredients such as pineapple, coconut, peanuts, sugar cane, plus plenty of fish and seafood from the coast.

We also have the Cantonese to thank for dim sum, literally meaning "touch your heart" - the custom of feasting on a varied assortment of pastries and dumplings that originated in China's teahouses. The most popular dim sum items are: 'ha gau' (shrimp dumpling), 'siu mai' (prawn and pork dumpling), 'pai gwat' (steamed spareribs), 'chun guen' (spring rolls), 'cha siu pau' (steamed barbecued pork buns), and 'cheung fun' (steamed rice flour rolls with barbecue pork, beef, or shrimp).

Cantonese cuisine incorporates almost all edible meats, including organ meats, chicken feet, duck and duck tongues, snakes, and snails. Steaming and stir-frying is the most favoured cooking method. Spring onion, sugar, salt, soy sauce, rice wine, corn starch, vinegar, sesame oil, and other oils suffice to enhance flavour in most Cantonese cooking. Sauces include: Hoisin, Oyster, Plum, sweet and sour, Black bean, Fermented bean, and Shrimp paste.

Chop Suey

Meaning 'mixed pieces', it is an American-Chinese dish consisting of meats (often chicken, fish beef, shrimp or pork), cooked quickly with vegetables such as bean sprouts, cabbage, and celery and bound in a starch-thickened sauce. Invented in America by Chinese immigrants and first appeared in an American publication in 1898, described as *"A Hash of Pork, with Celery, Onions, Bean Sprouts, etc."* May have come from "za sui", an old Chinese dish with cooked entrails. Legend has it that, while he was visiting New York City, Chinese ambassador Li Hung Chang's cooks invented the dish for his American guests at a dinner on August 29, 1896 though there is no evidence for this.

Chow Mein

A generic Chinese term for a dish of stir-fried noodles, of which there are many varieties. The term chow mein is derived from the Taishan dialect of the Chinese. Chow mein is generally made of soft noodles, however Hong Kong-style chow mein is made from thin crispy noodles.

The dish migrated to America with Chinese immigrants in the mid-19th century where meat and vegetables were added. The Taishan dialect of Chinese was the dialect spoken by the first Chinese immigrants from Taishan to America. The dish is one of the most popular 'Chinese' dishes in the West

Crispy Duck

Crispy aromatic duck is a variant of Peking Duck that originated from the Chinese community in the United Kingdom in the latter half of the 20th century. The meat is served with pancakes, finely chopped cucumber and spring onions and hoisin sauce The meat has less fat, but is drier and crispier compared to that of Peking Duck.

The origin of the Peking Duck dates back to before the Ming Dynasty, about 600 years ago. Cooks from all over China traveled to Beijing to cook for the Emperor. It was a prestigious occupation as only the best chefs could enter the palace kitchens. Many of the recipes for such foods of the Emperor were later smuggled out of the kitchen and onto the streets of Beijing.

With the eventual fall of the Ching dynasty in 1911, court chefs who left the Forbidden City set up restaurants around Beijing and brought Peking Duck and other delicious dishes to the masses. Ducks bred specially for the dish are slaughtered after 65 days and seasoned before being roasted in a closed or hung oven. The first restaurant specialising in Peking Duck, Bianyifang, was established in the Xianyukou, Qianmen area of Beijing in 1416.

Dim Sum

The name for a Chinese cuisine which involves a wide range of light dishes served alongside Chinese

tea (Yum Cha). Traditional dim sum includes various types of steamed buns such as cha siu baau, dumplings and rice noodle rolls (cheong fun), which contain a range of ingredients, including beef, chicken, pork, prawns and vegetarian options. Typical items are Shrimp Dumpling, Chiu-chao style dumplings, Potsticker, Shaomai, Cha siu baau, Rice noodle rolls, Spare ribs, Sou, Steamed meatball.

Fujian

The native cooking style of the province of Fujian, China. Fujian style cuisine is known to be light but flavourful, soft, and tender, with particular emphasis on umami taste, known in Chinese cooking as xiānwèi.

Unique seasoning from the province and its regions include shrimp oil, shrimp paste, sugar, Shacha sauce, and preserved apricot.

Fujian cuisine emphasizes seafood and mountain delicacies and the most characteristic aspect of Fujian cuisine is that its dishes are often served in soup. Cutting is important in the Fujian cuisine. Most famous dishes are Buddha-jumping-over-the-wall, edible bird's nest, cuttlefish, and sturgeon.

Hakka

The cooking style of the Hakka people, who are primarily found in south eastern China. Also well known in India where the version is really more Indian-Chinese cuisine (or Chindian) with dishes such as Chilli Chicken and Manchurian Chow Mein. Famous authentic Hakka dishes include Dung Gong Yam Guk Gai - Salt baked chicken, Noh Mi Ap - Duck stuffed with rice, Beef ball soup, Yong Tau Foo and Kiu nyuk. Pork is by far the most favoured meat of the Hakkas, with belly bacon being the preferred cut.

Huaiyang

Huaiyang cuisine tends to have a sweet side to it and, in contrast to that of Sichuan cuisine, is almost never spicy. Huaiyang cuisine is characterized by stewing, braising, and steaming over a low fire for a long time. Famous dishes cooked this way are chicken braised with chestnuts, pork steamed in lotus leaf, duck stewed with eight treasures, meatballs with crab meat in Yangzhou style, and butterfly sea cucumber (sea cucumber cut into butterfly shapes and cooked with flavourings). The cuisine is also well-known for utilizing its famous Chinkiang vinegar

Hunan

The cuisine of the Xiang River region, Dongting Lake and western Hunan Province and is well known for its hot spicy flavour, fresh aroma and deep colour. The cooking skills of Hunan cuisine reached a high standard as early as the Western Han Dynasty, 2,100 years ago. Common cooking techniques include stewing, frying, pot-roasting, braising, and smoking with liberal use of chilli peppers, shallots and garlic. Often spicier by pure chili content than Sichuan cuisine, and contains a larger variety of fresh ingredients, whilst tending to be oilier. It is said that Hunan cuisine is the most pleasing to the eye of all Chinese cuisines, classic examples being Hunan spicy beef with vegetables, Crispy duck and Garlic-Fried String Beans.

Jiangsu

Jiangsu dishes taste fresh, light and mellow. Typical courses of Jiangsu cuisine are Jinling salted dried duck (Nanjing's most famous dish), crystal meat (pork heals in a bright, brown sauce), clear crab shell meatballs (pork meatballs in crab shell powder, fatty, yet fresh), Yangzhou steamed Jerky strips (dried tofu, chicken, ham and pea leaves), triple combo duck, dried duck, and Farewell My Concubine (soft-shelled turtle stewed with many other ingredients such as chicken, mushroomsand wine). Using fish and crustaceans as the main ingredients, it stresses freshness. Its high carving techniques are delicate, of which the melon carving technique is especially well known.

Shandong

Shandong cuisine consists of two major styles: Jiaodong style characterized by seafood cooking, with light tastes and Jinan style famed for its soup and utilizing soups in its dishes. Shandong cuisine remains rooted in its ancient traditions. Most notable is the staggering array of seafood, including scallops, prawns, clams, sea cucumbers, and squid. Shandong's most famous dish is the "sweet and sour carp". A truly authentic "sweet and sour carp" must come from the Yellow River. Condiments such as sauce paste, fistulous onion and garlic are freely used, so Shandong dishes usually taste pungent. Dezhou stewed chicken is known throughout the country; the chicken is so well cooked that the meat easily separates from the bone although the shape of the chicken is preserved.

Sichuan (Szechwan)

Western China - a well-balanced Sichuan dish should feature the full range of salty, sweet, sour and hot chilli flavours. Hot pepper, an important flavouring in Sichuan cuisine, was introduced into China only 200 to 300 years ago. The local Sichuan pepper (used alone and as an ingredient of Chinese five-spice powder) is peppery, but more numbing than burning.

Some well-known Szechuan dishes include Kung Pao chicken and Twice Cooked Pork. Typical flavourings include soy sauce from Zhongba, cooking vinegar from Baoning, special vinegar from Sanhui, fermented soy beans from Tongchuan, hot pickled mustard tubers from Fuling, chili sauce from Chongqing, thick, broad – bean sauce from Pixian, and well salt from Zigong.

Sichuan cuisine tends to use quick – frying, quick stir – frying, dry – braising, and dry – stewing. Sichuan cuisine also has many delicious snacks and desserts, such as Bangbang chicken, chicken with sesame paste, lantern shadow beef, husband and wife's pork lung slices, steamed beef, noodles with chili sauce, and rice dumplings stuffed with sesame paste. Although many Sichuan dishes live up to their spicy reputation, often ignored are the large percentage of recipes that use little or no spice at all, including recipes such as "tea smoked duck".

Wonton

A noodle-dough dumpling filled typically with spiced minced pork or other ground meat, usually boiled in soup or fried and eaten as a side dish. Each region of China has its own variations of wonton (small filled dumpling parcels), and examples include Beijing, Sichuan, Hubei, Jiangnan, Jiangxi, Guangdong (Cantonese), Fujian, etc. Shrimp filled in Cantonese, minced meat in Shanghai, chāo shǒu in Sichuan

Zhejiang

Zhejiang style is not greasy, having instead a fresh and soft flavour with a mellow fragrance. There is use of bamboo shoots, poultry and freshwater fish and seafood, with emphasis on freshness and salty dishes. Zhejiang cuisine specializes in quick-frying, stir-frying, deep-frying, simmering and steaming, obtaining the natural flavour and taste. Typical dishes include Hangzhou roast chicken (commonly known as Beggar's chicken), Dongpo pork, west lake fish in vinegar sauce, and Songsao Shredded Fishsoup.

THAI

An important principle of Thai food is a balance of five flavours - spicy, salty, sweet, sour and bitter.

Gai Pad Khring
Thai Ginger Chicken contains fried chicken and different vegetables such as peppers and onions, but other meats may be used. The most important ingredient is the sliced ginger which gives the dish a very characteristic taste.

Green Curry (Gaeng Khiew-waan)
Originating in Asia, green curry paste has been changed to suit the taste of every adoptive palate. When Siam opened up to trade during the Ayutthaya period the Indian and Moorish peoples were said to have added milk and cream and later, coconut milk, to a basic paste of coriander seed and roots, cumin, peppercorns, lemongrass, lime, garlic, shallots and shrimp. The dish is green through the use of green chilli peppers. Green curry, like all curry blends, varies in composition and flavour, depending on the cook. A basic green curry includes green chillis, onion, coriander, lime juice and rind, lemongrass, garlic, soy sauce, cumin and ginger. The dish has citrus undertones and can be mild or hot

Khao Pad
One of the most common dishes in Thailand - Fried rice, Thai style - usually with chicken, beef, shrimp, pork, crab or coconut or pineapple or vegetarian. Khao Pad Naem is with sausage and Khao Pad Gai with chicken, Poo with crab and Moo with pork. Differs from Chinese stir fried rice due to use of Jasmine rice.

Massaman Curry (Gaeng Massaman)
A Thai dish that is Muslim in origin using Portuguese spicing. The name Massaman is thought to be derived from the word "Musulman", the older form of the word "Muslim". The dish is a blend of traditional Thai and Indian curries and usually contains coconut milk, roasted peanuts, potatoes, bay leaves, cardamom pods, cinnamon, palm sugar, fish sauce, and tamarind sauce and is commonly made with beef.

Pad Thai
A dish of stir-fried rice noodles with eggs, fish sauce, tamarind juice, red chilli pepper, plus any combination of bean sprouts, shrimp, chicken, or tofu, garnished with crushed peanuts and coriander. Pad Thai is one of Thailand's national dishes. Although the dish has been around for centuries (possibly of Chinese origins) - it is thought to have been brought to the ancient Thai capital of Ayutthaya by Vietnamese traders – it was first made popular as a national dish by Luang Phibunsongkhram when he was prime minister during the 1930s and 1940s. This dish uses the combination of sweet, sour and salty to great effect and the contrast of textures is also important

Red Curry (Gaeng Phet)

A popular Thai dish named from the red chilli pepper based on coconut milk heated with red curry paste and fish sauce. Red curry dishes may include ingredients such as kaffir lime leaves or peel, Thai eggplant, coconut milk, bamboo shoots, Thai basil, and some sort of meat such as chicken, beef, pork, shrimp, or duck. Thai Red Curry is often compared to the Indian Sambar.

Tom Yam Goong

This hot and sour prawn soup is perhaps one of the most famous dishes in Thai cuisine. Tom yum is characterized by its distinct hot and sour flavours, with fragrant herbs generously used. The basic broth is made of stock and fresh ingredients such as lemon grass, kaffir lime leaves, galangal, shallots, lime juice, fish sauce, tamarind, slices of ginger and crushed chili peppers with prawns (goong). Tom Yam Gai uses chicken instead. Often called the signature dish of Thailand.

From top row, left to right: cinnamon, cloves, black cardamom, bay leaves, black pepper, ground dried ginger, green cardamom, asafetida

INDONESIAN / MALAYSIAN

As a multi-national region, Indonesian/Malaysian cuisine reflects the influences of China and India and numerous other regions to create a truly diverse cuisine. As well as dishes originating in the region, the area offers a rich array of dishes originating in India but with a Malaysian influence such as Thosai, Idli and Mamak, a special Malaysian style for Indian Muslims or China such as Bakkwa, Bak Kut Teh and the steamed bub Pao.

Beef Rendang
Often seen as the Indonesian version of an Indian curry. Contains thinly sliced beef, turmeric, lemongrass, galangal, kaffir lime leaves, hot red chillies, garlic, ginger and coconut milk. Originated from the Minangkabau ethnic group of Indonesia. The dish is slow cooked so that the meat absorbs all the spices and becomes very tender and very tasty. Given stronger exposure in the West, this dish has been signalled as one that could become extremely popular.

Laksa
A popular spicy noodle soup from the Peranakan culture also known as Baba and Nyonya, which is a merger of Chinese, Indian and Malay elements found in Malaysia and Singapore. Curry Laksa, a coconut based curry soup, is one of the most popular versions. Assam or Penang Laksa is a sour fish based soup and there are many other variations.

Nasi Goreng
Literally means "fried rice". Main ingredients for the plain nasi goreng include pre-cooked rice, soy sauce, garlic, shallot and some spring onions for garnishing. In restaurants, it is often served as a main meal with additional items such as fried egg, fried chicken, satay, vegetables, and kerupuk (prawn crackers).

Rijsttafel
The rice table, that was actually an invention of the Dutch, back in colonial times, is very well known. It consists of many (forty is not an unusual number) side dishes served in small portions, accompanied by rice prepared in several different ways, a bit like an exotic buffet. Dishes include fried rice (nasi goreng), satay and maybe some of the Indonesian soups (soto).

Satay
The national dish of Malaysia. Pieces of chicken, goat, mutton, beef, pork or fish on skewers from the midrib of the coconut leaf, although bamboo skewers are often used. These are grilled or barbecued over a wood or charcoal fire, then served with various spicy seasonings, usually satay sauce. Probably originated in Java.

JAPANESE

Japanese cuisine is based on combining staple foods, typically rice or noodles, with a soup, and okazu - dishes made from fish, meat, vegetable, tofu and the like, designed to add flavour to the staple food. These are typically flavoured with dashi, miso, and soy sauce and are usually low in fat and high in salt.

Kare Raisu
Cooked rice with a curry sauce. It can be served with additional toppings such as tonkatsu. Curry is not a native Japanese dish, but has been used in Japan for over a century and is very popular.

Ramen
Ramen are Chinese style noodles prepared in a soup with various toppings. Ramen is one of the many popular dishes originally introduced from China but have become completely Japanized over time. Other noodle dishes are Udon (wheat flour), Soba (buckwheat flour), and Yakisoba (fried).

Sashimi
Means "pierced body". Very fresh raw seafood, sliced into thin pieces and served with only a dipping sauce (soy sauce with wasabi paste or other condiments such as grated fresh ginger, or ponzu), depending on the fish, and simple garnishes such as shiso and shredded daikon radish.

Shabu Shabu
Shabu-shabu is a Japanese style meat fondue or hot pot. Thinly sliced meat, along with vegetables, mushrooms and tofu is dipped into a hot soup and then into ponzu vinegar or a sesame sauce before being eaten. More savoury and less sweet than sukiyaki.

Sukiyaki
A nabe dish prepared in a hot pot with thinly sliced meat, vegetables, mushrooms, tofu and shirataki (konyaku noodles). The pieces of food are dipped into a raw egg before eaten. Often prepared steamboat style.

Sushi

Sushi is perhaps the most famous Japanese food in the world. In Japanese cuisine, sushi indicates dishes that use sushi rice, which is seasoned with a sweet vinegar mixture.

Varieties include Nigirizushi (hand-formed sushi), Makizushi (rolled sushi), Oshizushi (pressed sushi), Inarizushi (stuffed sushi), Chirashizushi (scattered sushi), and Narezushi (matured sushi).

The sushi is often wrapped in Nori (seaweed) topped with fish.

Tempura
Tempura is deep fried vegetable or seafood. The light batter is made of cold water and wheat flour. Eggs, baking soda or baking powder, starch, oil, and/or spices may also be added. Tempura was introduced to Japan in the mid-sixteenth century by early Portuguese missionaries and traders.

Teppanyaki
A style of Japanese cuisine using an iron griddle (teppan). More popular with foreigners than Japanese and very popular in the USA due to the antics of the chefs cooking in front of you. Made famous by the Benihana restaurant chain which opened its first restaurant in New York in 1964. Usually includes beef, shrimp, scallops, lobster, and chicken and is often enjoyed with sake.

Yakitori
Yakitori is grilled chicken speared on sticks. All different parts of the chicken, thighs, skin, liver, etc. can be used for yakitori. Ingredients include soy sauce, honey, sake and green onion. Somewhat like Malaysian satay.

Teppanyaki

Chapter 14

EXOTIC FOODS, HERBS & SPICES
A – Z

Allspice (*Pimenta dioica, Pimenta officinalis, Jamaica Pepper*)

Despite its common name, Allspice, thought up in the late 17th century to describe its taste - a mixture of cinnamon, cloves, nutmeg and pepper - it is really just one spice. The dried, unripe berry of a tropical tree of the myrtle family, native to Central America and West Indies, grown exclusively in the Western hemisphere, having resisted various efforts at production elsewhere in the world. The trees are fairly productive, though, being very easy to grow and each tree remaining productive for around 100 years.

Discovered by the Spanish in Mexico at the beginning of the 16th century and in use in London by 1601, the spice quickly found favour for use in pickles, marinades, sausages, fish preserves, cakes and puddings. Pimento seeds were also used by the Aztecs to flavour their chocolate preparations. The ripe berries are very similar in appearance to peppercorns and most of the world's supply of the spice comes from Jamaica, hence its alternative name, *Jamaica Pepper*, and the variation on the Spanish word, *pimienta* (pepper) in its Latin botanical name. The green berries are hand-picked before reaching ripeness and sun-dried to a reddish-brown colour for about 10 days before being cleaned ready for shipping.

Medicinal: Its main active volatile oil is eugenol, which is also the principal flavouring in cloves and an extract of allspice oils has been used for its digestive and slightly narcotic properties. Perhaps the most unusual use of this spice in a medicinal role is by Russian soldiers during the Napoleonic Wars; in order to prevent chillblains, they placed allspice berries in their boots. Nutritionally 1tsp of ground allspice weighs 2g contains fats, carbohydrates, fibre, sodium, protein, vitamin A, vitamin C and Iron and contains 7 kcals.

Almond (*Prunus dulcis (Sweet), Prunus amygdalus (Bitter), Badam*)

The almond originated in the Near East, then spread throughout the Mediterranean, where it is grown alongside the olive, both ideal crops in rocky, poor ground. According to the Bible, Aaron's rod, chosen to sprout by God, thus indicating his choice of the House of Levi as his priests, was made from almond wood, although it was the Greeks who were thought to have cultivated it first and who gave it the name, *amygdalon*, from which its Latin botanical specific name is derived. Almond seeds have been found in the Neolithic layer below the Palace of Knossos in Crete and evidence of the early use of wild almonds by Man has been found at several sites in Greece. The ancient Romans, who called it *nux Graeca*, the Greek nut, may have introduced the tree to Britain, although it is grown here for the blossom rather than the nut, due to its intolerance to high winds and frosts. The Phoenicians probably were most responsible for its wider distribution, taking it both to Spain and France, where it is thought to have been under cultivation as far back as the 8th century BC.

The almond has long been a symbol of luxury and wealth, being pounded up with sugar, colourings and flavourings to make confectionery, comfits and celebration cake coverings in the form of marchpane, or marzipan, as it became known when our main supply came from Germany. Almonds also form the basis for French Nougat and Spanish Turon, and in Italy, sugar-coated and gilded almonds are given as a symbolic gift on special occasions, such as weddings or religious festivals. The almond was used extensively in Medieval cookery, especially in displaying the wealth or status of the host, making the nut an important commodity for many years.

Elizabethan cookery used a lot of almond milk, that is almonds pounded up with water, in dishes such as blancmanges, and herbalists still use this for helping cradle cap in infants and gastric problems in adults.

Almond oil is used in massage, both as a carrier for aromatherapy fragrances and to alleviate eczema, and ground almonds make a very good cleansing and softening facial scrub.

Medicinal: The almond kernel is rich in monounsaturated fatty acids, which reduce bad cholesterol levels and also in vitamin E, a powerful antioxidant, which research has shown may prevent the accumulation of plaque in arteries and the formation of cancer cells. They are also a good source of minerals, such as potassium, magnesium, iron and phosphates.

Its real mineral strength, however, is as a non-dairy source of calcium, vital for the production of strong bones and teeth and the regulation of heart beat and blood pressure. One ounce provides approximately 10% of the adult RDA at 240mg per 100g of drupe flesh - very good news indeed for vegans.

Could almonds also be a prospective ingredient in that elusive Elixir of Life - perhaps? A major study, involving 26,000 members of the Seventh Day Adventist Church in the USA, showed that those who ate almonds, peanuts and walnuts at least six times a week had a lifespan, on average, 7 years longer than that of the general population and a much lower rate of heart attack. As with every Dr Jekyll, however, there is the inevitable Mr Hyde lurking in the wings. The almond, especially the bitter variety, contains the glucoside amygdalin which, with enzyme reaction, breaks down into glucose, benzoic acid and hydrocyanic acid, becoming poisonous in large quantities.

Almost all the seeds of the genus Prunus, (apricot, cherry, nectarine, peach, plum), contain amygdalin and should be treated with caution. Even the lovely sweet almond has its drawbacks: almonds are also very rich in oil, yielding just over half their weight in fats and just 100g, flesh only, is a dieter's nightmare at a whopping great 612 calories!

Aniseed (*Pimpinella anisum - Sweet cumin*)

Aniseed was cultivated by all the ancient civilisations; Egyptians, Romans and Greeks. It is referred to by Theophrastus and Pliny as *ánison*, the source of its modern Latin specific name *anisum*. The Romans grew it, mainly in Tuscany, for both culinary and medicinal purposes. The seeds contain the volatile oil, anethole, found also in the unrelated star anise and liquorice, which is a digestive. The Greek physician, Hippocrates prescribed aniseed for coughs and as a mild expectorant in the 5th century BC.

Aniseed was a very important ingredient, probably for those same digestive properties, in Mustaceum, a spicy cake eaten at the end of very elaborate feasts by the Romans, and which is thought by some to have been the earliest ancestor of the modern wedding cake. In northern India too, aniseed is commonly used as a digestive. Together with fennel, it is a main ingredient in paan, a seed, lime and betel leaf preparation designed to sweeten the breath, settle the stomach and prevent flatulence after rich meals (particularly Indian).

Medicinal: In 1597, John Gerard, the herbalist advised: *"Anise helpeth the yeoxing or hicket (hiccups)."* and modern herbalists still recommend aniseed tea, taken warm with honey for not only hiccups, but diarrhoea, colic, asthma, and with fennel added to ease bronchial catarrh. 1 tsp of aniseed weighs 2g is 8 kcalories and contains fats, carbohydrates, sodium, proteins and iron.

Apricots (*Prunus armeniaca*)

Despite its botanical specific name, which would, on first glance, seem to place its origins in the Caucasus, the apricot actually originated in Northern China, probably the Tien-Shan region; the Assyrian and Babylonian name for it was *armanu*, which probably explains the armeniaca in its botanical name, rather than being any kind of geographical reference. Archaeologists believe that it may have been cultivated initially around 2200BC, and in the great orchards of Mesopotamia, before spreading westwards through Persia and Asia Minor.

Its use was spread by the Arabs, great lovers of fruit, who have long used *mishmish*, as they call it, along with other dried fruits in their dishes - especially, of course, in Mishmishiya, a traditional lamb and dried apricot stew. In Persia it was given the name *Zard-alu*, or yellow plum, a name which lives on today in the Parsee Indian dish of Jardaloo. The common name, apricot, is derived from the Roman name for the fruit, *praecocium*, or precocious, given for the quickness of its ripening.

It seems to be generally agreed that the apricot was brought to England in 1524 by Thomas Walk, gardener to Henry VIII and was known throughout the Tudor and Elizabethan periods as the *apricock*. There are those who argue, however, that this must have been a re-introduction of the fruit, and that it must originally have been brought to our shores by the Romans, who prized it and, according to Pliny, were willing to pay handsome sums for it when it first appeared in Rome. One very strong argument against this theory may be that, as Britain was a far-flung and one of the least favoured of Rome dominions, the transport of such luxury items would have come quite far down the provisions list.

Apicius, whose recipes seem to reflect ingredients used by the very highest strata within his society included a recipe for shoulder of pork with apricots in his collection. William Turner dubbed it "an hasty peach tree" in 1548 and by 1597 Gerard, the famous herbalist, noted that he had been able to grow the tree in his garden in Holborn. Nowadays serious 'foodies' insist that the best dried apricots are the sun-dried Hunza variety, which come from the eponymous small kingdom in north-western Kashmir, and which are reputed to be responsible for the extreme longevity of the Hunza people.

Chinese healers believe that apricots make a potent energy tonic and that they can also be used in the diet to suppress coughs and relieve asthma. Ironically, because of the sulphur dioxide that is sometimes used in drying, modern medical advice is for asthmatics to steer well clear of dried apricots, as the sulphites can trigger asthmatic attacks.

Nutritionally, the apricot is a little powerhouse. It is full of beta-carotene, the vegetable form of vitamin A - just three small, fresh apricots contain 2,770IU of beta-carotene, more than 50% of the Recommended Daily Allowance (RDA), for just 50 calories. The drying process only makes the fruit even more nutritious, although it does boost its calories content: 75g of dried apricots is equal to 165 kcalories.

To balance this, however, the same amount contains a whole day's supply of beta-carotene - nearly 100 times the amount of vitamin A found in other fruit. It is also a good source of boron, potassium and an impressive 20% of RDA for iron, which is essential in the formation of red blood cells and in fighting fatigue. In fact, dried apricot, along with other dried fruits, are recommended for those on a vegetarian or vegan diet as an important source of non-animal iron. Beta-carotene is a powerful anti-oxidant, which prevents plaque deposits building up in the arteries. Boron is now thought to help in the prevention of osteoporosis, by helping post-menopausal women retain their oestrogen, which helps in the absorption of calcium. Potassium helps to maintain body fluid balance, normalising blood pressure and heart function.

Dried apricots are also higher in fibre than fresh, the soluble fibre helping to relieve chronic constipation, irritable bowel syndrome, diverticulitis and disorders of the gut. Both types contain no sodium or fats. In addition to all the nutrients found in the fruit, apricot is also low on the Glycaemic Index - the scale invented to help in the treatment of diabetes, which is used to measure the rate at which blood sugar levels rise when a particular carbohydrate bearing food is ingested. Low level GI foods are more complex and hence digested more slowly, ensuring a longer feeling of satiety, longer term energy maintenance and keeping blood sugar levels constant. Fresh apricots have a GI of 57 and dried 30.

No accident, then, that dried apricots were a natural choice for NASA when choosing compact, lightweight, high-output foods for their astronauts.

Fresh apricots too, also have their darker side; their kernels contain prussic acid, cumulatively poisonous, which hasn't stopped Man, ever contrary by nature, roasting out the poison and turning them into alcoholic beverages, such as the eau de noyeaux liqueur.

Asafoetida (*Ferula asafoetida, Ferula gummosa, Ferula narthaex, Felura scorodosoma – Hing*)

One of the more important members of the Umbelliferae family, which includes parsley, fennel, carrot, cumin, coriander and caraway, amongst many others. Cultivated by the Babylonians, Greek and Romans, Asafoetida is now grown throughout western Asia, from Iran to Kashmir. Native to Afghanistan and Iran, where it is often eaten whole as a vegetable and meat tenderiser. The plant faintly resembles Cow Parsley; thick-ribbed stems with feathery-fine, laciniate, almost dill-like leaves.

The main attraction for the Indian cook, however, is the sap which is produced in its stems and roots. In the early summer, these parts of the plant are cut to produce a thick, milky, malodorous fluid, which quickly congeals to a brownish-orange resin on contact with the air. It is this resin, sold both in lump and ground form, which is used as a spice in cooking and in the cosmetic industry. This last use is its most surprising, given its very smelly properties. Its specific name is derived from two words, the Persian *aze*, mastic, and the Latin *foetida*, stinking.

The ancient Romans were particularly partial to it, despite the smell. They knew it as *Laser, lasertum* or *Laserpitum*. Their celebrated gourmet/gourmand and early food writer, Apicius used it extensively - especially in his own version of '*Lamb Curry*' - (Roast Lamb flavoured with a spice mix of black pepper, spikenard, ginger, parsley). It was, of course, very expensive and he advised storing it in a jar of pine nuts, using the nuts, which absorb the flavour, and keeping the resin to flavour more nuts.

The Romans brought it even further west, where it was adopted, mainly by the apothecaries in the monasteries for use in their lotions, potions and tinctures, the only place where such practices could be safely carried out without the danger of being accused of practising witchcraft. Perhaps it was the fact that it was named by these god-fearing monks, (or perhaps we English are just basically a coarse and unromantic lot - which we refuse to believe!), led to its local name here being Devil's Dung!

Its legendary digestive properties make it an essential ingredient in traditional Indian vegetarian cooking where a lot of the basic foodstuffs come from that notoriously difficult-to-digest group of food-stuffs, the pulses, lentils and beans. The Brahmin and Jain sects in particular find it a useful flavouring as, when cooked, especially by frying in oil, it loses the 'fetid' quality and takes on a garlicky-onion flavour, making it a perfect substitute for those allia, specifically forbidden them under their dietary laws. It is not surprising, then, that Ayurveda, the study of the life forces which originated in the region most strongly linked with those cultures, has a great deal to say about the benefits of Asafoetida.

Medicinal: It is said to be a digestive, disinfectant, antispasmodic, mildly diuretic, a stimulant for glandular secretion, an improver of circulation and particularly useful for strengthening the nerves. Another industrial product is a resinoid, a tincture using alcoholic extraction. Steam distillation removes the notorious smell, leaving a product ideal for use in perfumery which has excellent fixative properties - so important for a perfume's staying power.

As with most exotic ingredients, Asafoetida is one of those anonymous stars of modern life, being consumed on a virtual daily basis by people who have never heard its name even uttered. How? Well, in 1835, one Lord Marcus Sandys, a former governor of Bengal returned to England with a recipe for a certain liquor that he felt he could not possible live without in his retirement 'back in Blighty'. He took it to two local chemists in Worcester - a Mr Lea and Mr Perrins, to be exact. The two chemists made double the quantity, found it to be appalling stuff and hid the surplus away in their cellars.

A year or so later, however, further investigation during a spring-clean revealed a very different product indeed. Over a century-and-a-half later, Worcestershire Sauce is used world-wide in dishes, ranging from Cantonese stir-fries to Spaghetti Bolognese, Lancashire Hot-Pots to Hashis Parmentier (Shepherd's Pie to you and me). And, although the exact ingredients are still kept a closely guarded secret, even in this day and age of extensive food labelling, what is one of the mysterious essential ingredients? Why, good old Devil's Dung, of course!

Aubergine (*Solanum melongena – Brinjal*)

Aubergine is a member of the botanical family, Solanaceae, the Nightshades. It is believed to be a native of India, its name being derived, via the Persian *badingen*, Arabic *al-badinjam* and Spanish *albadingena*, all taken originally from the Sanskrit name, *vatingana*, meaning an anti-flatulent vegetable.

The Italian *melanzana* and Greek *melitzana* are both derived from its Roman name *mala insana*, madness apple. The West Indians call it the '*Brown Jolly*', taking the Indian brinjal even further along the phililogical evolutionary timeline. Yet another name, the eggplant, now extensively for all varieties in North America, was originally used to described the small, white, egg-shaped variety which is still enjoyed pickled, *en escabeche*, in Spain, where they were initially introduced by their Moorish invaders.

Western Europeans were very slow to realise the plant's food potential, however, and refused to grow it for any other reason than ornamental. The Spanish and Portuguese, however, knew better and their colonists exported it to the New World, where it thrived and became popular. Like its cousins, the chili pepper and tomato, the aubergine is one of the foods currently being investigated by scientists for its potential as a cancer combatant. They have found that the solanaceae vegetables contain certain phytochemicals that have been shown to block cancer formation.

Aubergine contains terpenes, thought to prevent oxidative cell damage that can cause certain types of tumours by deactivating the steroidal hormones that promote their growth. Aubergine also contains potassium, which helps to normalise blood pressure levels, reducing the risk of heart attack and stroke and, when not cooked in oil, which it soaks up alarmingly, is extremely low in calories at just 15 per 100g portion.

Avocado (*Persea drymifolia, Persea americana - Butter-fruit, alligator pear*)

Excavations of Mayan and Aztec burial grounds have indicated that this member of the laurel family, related to cinnamon, camphor and sassafras, may have been grown by Man over 8,000 years ago. Avocado was a mainstay of the Central American diet for centuries and its modern, common name is a product of the attempts of early explorers to reproduce its original Aztec name, *ahuacatl*.

The Spanish transplanted it to Jamaica and in 1692 Sir Hans Sloane listed it in his catalogue of Jamaican flora as the *alligator pear-tree*, probably because of the similarity of its skin to alligator hide. The avocado has had a fairly unremarkable journey through history, being neither pretty nor fiery enough, to command instant culinary success.

The reaction to its introduction into Bengal in the late 19th century was less than rapturous, with the authors of one publication of the day commenting that, "*had it been worth eating it would have come long before*." and dismissing it as being so tasteless that it would need liberal amounts of salt and pepper to make it as tasty even as marrow!

Despite its critics, the avocado travelled and gained fans amongst those willing to try it and now it is grown in most tropical countries around the world: Australasia, South Africa, West Indies, California, Florida, Hawaii, the Phillipines, the Mediterranean and Israel joining the original suppliers in South America. As with all acquired tastes, however, the avocado grew on us, and gradually, we are coming to realise the value and versatility of this fruit. It makes a non-combative partner when simply split and filled with a delicate seafood; mixes well with other, stronger flavours or crisper textures as a filling or salad; mashes with spices and other fruits and vegetables for use as a dip or sauce; grills beautifully when sliced and layered with cheese and mushrooms; and makes an excellent and unusual garnish to soups, cubed and added just before serving.

Other names for avocado, such as *midshipman's butter*, *butter-pear* and *butter fruit* also bear testament to its long-time use as a spread and as a substitute for dairy spreads. Ironically, the nick- name that probably suits the avocado best of all, is one that doesn't seem to have stuck - *the lady pear*. No, not because of any resemblance to the figure of a woman, but because, of all the fruits, the avocado is, perhaps, one of the most female-friendly in the plant kingdom.

Medicinal: Avocado is a rich source of vitamin E which is thought to help relieve irregular periods, the symptoms of pre-menstrual syndrome, menstrual pain and, as a powerful anti-oxidant, is thought to protect against the ageing process, preventing oxidation within body and skin cells. It may also be linked to female fertility: the scientists who discovered vitamin E initially called it *tocopherol*, Greek for 'bring forth children', after they discovered that a lack of the vitamin in laboratory rats brought about infertility in the animals. All this good news for the goose, though, doesn't mean that the gander has been forgotten. Men, too can benefit. The same anti-oxidant power of vitamin E protects against cancer and helps to prevent the coagulation of the blood which can lead to heart attacks and strokes.

Vitamin E also promotes white blood cell activity, especially in the production of T-cells which are the white cells which fight infections. The avocado used to be regarded as fattening because of the quite high fat content (25% in an average fruit). Most of this, as with palm and olive oils, is in the form of monounsaturated fats which help to lower the LDL, or bad, cholesterol levels in the body. 100g of avocado flesh equals around 190 kcalories and contains 19.5g of fats. It also contains protein, carbohydrate, fibre, calcium, iron, sodium, a good amount of potassium, beta-carotene (vitamin A), Thiamin (vitamin B1), folic acid, and vitamin C.

Bamboo Shoots (*Bambusa sp.*)
Bamboo is one of the most versatile and widely used plants, being used for purposes as diverse as house and bridge building to cups, hats, baskets and even food.

Part of the Gramineae, or grass, family, there are about 480 species of bamboo in all. The young shoots are sliced and used in Oriental cooking. The shoots are a good source of magnesium, which is necessary in the development of bones and teeth and producing chemical energy in body cells. 100g of bamboo shoots equal a mere 27 kcalories and also contain water, protein, a slight trace of fats, carbohydrate, calcium, a little bit of iron and a quite good 10% of the recommended daily allowance for zinc. It also contains carotene (vitamin A), vitamin B1, vitamin B2, niacin, vitamin C and some folic acid.

Banana (*Musa sapientum, musa paradisiacal*)
References to banana cultivation in India go back to at least 5000BC and in Hindu tradition it is known as '*the forbidden fruit*'. Indeed, some even think that it was more likely to have been the banana, not the apple, which was Eden's forbidden fruit of the tree of knowledge of good and evil. This theme is taken further with two of the species specific names both reflecting the knowledge theme; *musa sapientum* (dessert) 'sages' banana' and *musa paradisiaca* (plantain) 'banana of paradise'. The name *musa* is from the Sanskrit, *Moca*, via its Arabic counterpart, *mauz*.

Chinese banana cultivation is thought to have started in around AD 200, with the fruit reaching Africa during the 1st modern millennium, then to the Mediterranean and Phillipines around 1,000 years ago and the Canary Islands by the early 15th century. It is officially recorded that the plant was taken westwards by Friar Tomas de Berlanga, (later Bishop of Panama), in 1516, to Santo Domingo, although remains found in early Peruvian tombs may provide evidence of earlier arrivals via trans-Pacific migration.

Their appearance in England caused quite a stir and a bunch of bananas was displayed as a public attraction and novelty at Johnson's Herbalry in the City of London in 1627. It wasn't until 1878, when Fyffe, Hudson & Co started shipping supplies from the Canary Islands, that any signifant quantities reached our shore. As synonymous as Fyffe's became with the banana in this country, however, it was actually the shipping magnate, Sir Alfred Jones, who was largely responsible for the greatest growth in banana imports. He ensured that his ships carried bananas in any spare cargo space and even hired costermongers and barrows to ensure that they were sold immediately upon unloading, before they could over-ripen.

So London and Liverpool, whose docks Sir Alfred's ships came into, were the first cities in England to be introduced to the banana. Further boosts to banana imports came in 1900 when there was a decline in the importation of cochineal from the Canaries and bananas were substituted, further aided in 1901 with the introduction of the new refrigerated ships which meant that the cargo would ripen more slowly.

Banana cargoes became almost an obsession with the British, and, from the mid-19th century until the outbreak of the Second World War, arrivals were reported in the daily national newspapers such as the Times.

Banan is the Arabic word for 'finger', and was probably assigned to the fruit more for its finger-shape than for the fact that it is, indeed, Mother Nature's perfect finger food. Healthy, filling, no core, no pips and conveniently wrapped in a disposable and biodegradable skin which is also, happily a great aid to eating the fruit cleanly and hygienically.

It's not just the fruit of the banana, however, which can be used. The banana flower is eaten in many Asian countries; boiled, sliced and used in dishes such as salads, curries or as a vegetable accompaniment. The leaves, too, serve many purposes in the tropics; providing a convenient wrapping medium for foodstuffs; plates and platters; cups and bowls for fruits and desserts; containers for snack foods; linings for cooking pots and utensils; and as a way of wrapping foods such as fish or rice for steaming.

There are hundreds of varieties of banana, although we mainly see the fairly straight, yellow dessert types of the Cavendish family in this country. However, the Red, with its soft, orange flesh and pear-drop flavour, the small ovoid Apple, whose flavour is, as its name would suggest, very apple-like, and the cooking Plantain varieties are starting to appear in major supermarket chains and specialist retailers.

In 1994, Eurocrats in Brussels, never having heard the old Music Hall ditty 'I've never seen a straight banana', actually introduced legislation detailing the ideal specifications for a banana destined for import into the community: the Euro-banana should be 14cm (5½ inches) long by 2.5cm (1 inch) and should 'not be abnormally curved'. All this with a straight face! The banana is not just a pretty fruit that the kids can use as a toy gun in their packed lunches, though.

Looks aside, it has actually been described as the 'perfect' food by many a food writer and nutritionist. One famous American professor of nutrition, Earl Mindell, has been quoted as saying that if he was ever stranded on a desert island, the two things he would need to survive would be a banana tree and water!

Medicinal: Chinese medicine recommends eating one or two soft bananas morning and night on an empty stomach to relieve constipation; and, apparently, water which has had banana peel boiled in it makes an effective hangover cure. Traditional Oriental medical practitioners also recommend bananas to treat hypertension and to prevent gastric ulcers.

The sugars in ripe bananas take 45-60 minutes to be absorbed by the body, giving a sustained release of energy. Which is why bananas are often the chosen energy snack for athletes and why the tennis players at Wimbledon get through 91kg (2001b) of bananas per day during the Open Championship fortnight. The soluble fibre in ripe bananas is good for both constipation and diarrhoea but, ironically, unripe bananas contain resistant starches, which have not yet been converted to sugars, and which cannot be digested in the small intestine, leading to them fermenting in the large intestine and causing wind.

High in potassium, the average banana contains 451 mg - a full quarter of the recommended daily allowance (RDA). Potassium is essential to body fluid balance. This can prevent cramps and is important for normal blood pressure and heart function, a very useful weapon in the prevention of heart attacks and stroke. In a recent study, patients being treated for high blood pressure who were put on a high potassium diet, were able to either dramatically reduce or even eliminate their medication. Also, it has been found that those taking diuretics, especially for the treatment of high blood pressure, or people who have been suffering from chronic diarrhoea, should eat a banana or two a day in order to replace the potassium which is literally washed away through their system.

Bananas are also a good source of vitamin B6, providing more than 25% of the daily requirement, together with about 15% of a non-smokers requirement for vitamin C. Vitamin B6 is a natural immune system booster and helps the body to convert and use proteins and fats and, with the vitamin C, a powerful antioxidant, helps to fight infections.Investigations are still under way on the effects of bananas on the lining of the stomach.

There have been claims that they stimulate cell and mucous production, thus thickening and strengthening the surface, helping to heal existing ulcers and staving off new ones. Apparently, the jury is still out on this, though it is generally agreed that a banana will act as an antacid and counter indigestion and heartburn, and that a ripe banana is one of the few foodstuffs least likely to trigger an allergic reaction. *And all for just 95 kcalories!*

On the 'feelgood factor' side, the fruit releases dopamine and seratonin, two chemicals hugely enjoyed by the brain, a fact which led a hopeful few in the 1960s, (when experimentation in such things seemed to be at a peak), to try smoking dried banana skins.

A recent innovation in household stores and catalogues has been the wooden or metal banana tree which, at first glance may seem a silly idea, but actually is the best way to keep the ethylene gas, which causes fruit to ripen, from spoiling the other fruit in your bowl. On the other hand, this process can be turned to advantage when a hard avocado or bowl of home-grown, green tomatoes need to be ripened speedily.

Basil (*Ocimum sanctum, ocimum basilicum – Tulsi*)

Basil (*ocimum sanctum*) is the only member of the mint family which is native to India, where it was called *arjaka* in the ancient language, Sanskrit. Its Latin botanical names are derived from the Greek *okimon*, 'fragrant lipped' and *basilikan*, 'Royal'.

Feelings about Basil have been mixed throughout history, the herb having been variously associated with death, religious ritual, medicine, fertility, erotica, and even as being responsible for the breeding of scorpions. It is probably for this reason, following homeopathic logic of like treats ilke, that it was recommended at one time for the treatment of scorpion stings and snakebites. The ancients, although holding mixed feelings about the herbs, even swore oaths on it in courts of law.

Culpeper, who combined astrology with herbalism, assigned it to the ruling planet Mars, associated with the sign of Scorpio. It has been used in European magic lore to attract love, wealth, protection, in love spells and incenses for purification and exorcism rites. It was also believed in some country communities that carrying basil in the pocket would attract wealth and was rubbed directly onto the skin to serve as a simple perfume.

Ocimum sanctum is sacred to the Hindu god, Vishnu and his avatar, Krishna and is placed on temple and house altars for its peppery, carnation-like scent. Another traditional Hindu custom was to place a sprig of basil on the dead before burial to ensure safe passage to the next world.

Medicinal: Ayurvedic practitioners recommend a decoction of European basil, (*O. basilicium*), for coughs and colds and prescribe a paste made from the leaves mixed with crushed black peppercorns for malarial fever. The juice, expressed from the leaves, is used as a gargle for pharyngitis, as eardrops, and to treat skin complaints and insect bites.

Unani Tibb, the medical and dietetics system started by Avicenna in the 10th century, states that the European basil is useful in the treatment of flatulence, bad eyesight, melancholy, rheumatism and influenza.

Bush basil, which grows in South America is also revered in a similar way, being sacred to the Haitian love goddess, Erzulie. European herbalists have also long used the crushed leaves externally for eye problems and to ease arthritis and internally for nerves, headaches and faintness. It contains rhymol, eugenol and camphor, making its essential oil an ideal ingredient for soaps, perfumes, mouthwashes and toothpastes, and it was the camphor especially for which it was once used mixed with snuff, in powdered form, to clear the head.

These oils are called monoterpenes; simple lipids which do not contain fatty acids and which have been found to be potent antioxidants, helping to protect against heart disease and cancers. Nutritionally, 100g of fresh basil leaf contains 29.09 kcalories, 033g fats, 5.08g carbohydrate, 4.44g fibre, 2.9mg sodium, 1.20g protein, 781iu vitamin A, 15.30mg vitamin C and 3.5mg iron.

Bay (*Laurus nobilis*)

The 'noble laurel', bay, a native of the Mediterranean and Asia Minor, has been used extensively since

 ancient times for medicinal, culinary and even magical purposes. Two main explanations for the origin of its botanical name have been put forward, both of which seem to bear merit: from the Celtic, *laur,* meaning green; from the Latin *laudo,* honour or praise. The specific name, *nobilis*, is the Latin for noble.

It is a key herb in mythology, ancient Greek especially: Apollo, the sun god, tried to force himself upon Daphne, a river nymph. In a desperate attempt to escape, she called upon the Earth Mother, Gaia, for help. Just as Apollo's arms wound around her, Daphne disappeared and a bay laurel sprang up in her place. This moved Apollo so much that he immediately pronounced the tree sacred and took to wearing a crown made from its leaves. His temple at Delphi, the site of the famous Delphic Oracle, was thatched with a bay-leaf roof in order to protect the Oracle, who could be vulnerable in times of trance - a trance which could even have been aided by chewing the leaves of the laurel, which has slightly narcotic powers.

These protective powers carry through into the folklore and myth of a lot of societies. Bay is said to protect against thunder and lightning; it is said that no bay tree has ever been struck by lightning. It was also said to have been protection against witches and evil spirits and small bay trees were traditionally grown by the entrances of homes to keep these malevolents 'at bay'. Consequently, superstition holds that when a bay tree dies, it is a bad omen indeed.

Bay was also seen as a boost to athletic prowess, possibly because of its links with Apollo, and early victors in the original Olympic Games were awarded crowns made from laurel leaves. Even today, 'laureate' is used to refer to someone who has reached the very top of their discipline, as in Poet Laureate and, when someone is being warned not to let their standards slip, they are very often reminded 'not to sit on their laurels', or, in other words, rely on past glory. Herbal magic uses it to ward off negativity and one of its uses is as a trigger for meaningful and inspirational dreams - a young maiden will dream of the man she will marry if she pins five leaves to the pillow she sleeps upon!

Medicinal: In medicine, it has been used for inducing abortions, countering the effects of snakebite, urinary tract problems, indigestion and flatulence. Externally, bay leaf oil is used to help rheumatism.

Many cuisines use bay extensively - it is one of the basic herbs used in the French bouquet garni. Bay is used to flavour sauces, stocks and cooking waters and is used when cooking pulses to help guard against flatulence. Indian cooks often refer to bay leaf, but this is frequently the leaf of the cassia tree, *cinnamomum aromaticum*, which is interchangeable in most Asian recipes. Again, even in the kitchen, its protective powers were relied upon as bay leaves were traditionally placed in flour bins to deter weevils. One teaspoonful of bay weighs 2g and is 8.11 kcalories. The leaf contains fats, carbohydrate, fibre, sodium, protein, vitamin A, vitamin C and iron.

Beet *(Beta maritima, beta vulgaris)*

Quite a large family which includes *Swiss chard, seakale beet, mangelwurzel, leaf beet, sugar beet and spinach beet*. The leaves of these plants have been eaten by Man since prehistory and are native to a large area ranging from the British Isles to India.

Archaeologists believe that their earliest origins may have been in the Mediterranean, and varieties are still to be found growing wild as far as Iran. The roots were being eaten by about 300BC, although many cultures saw these primarily as medicinal for many centuries. Theophrastus referred to the beet in his writings, as did Pliny, who referred to their use in salads, and Apicius, the great Roman gourmet and cookery writer, included it in his viridian, or greens, for broth.

The red beet was introduced to Britain in the 17th century, our common beets all having been a lighter, yellow colour to this point, much to the delight of Gerard, who saw it as an excellent addition to salads.

In 1590 the French botanist Olivier de Serres extracted sugar syrup from the roots of one of the members of the beta vulgaris group, but it wasn't until around 1800, when Frederick the Great of Prussia lent his support to German chemist, Karl Franz Achard, that the beet was taken seriously as a source of sugar and a small factory was set up. Twelve years later, during the Napoleonic wars, Napoleon himself ordered full scale production of sugar from beets to replace the cane sugar which was no longer available to France. Not without difficulties, the industry grew until beet was the major source of sugar in Northern Europe.

Medicinal: The nutritional pros for beets are that the anthocyanins which give the vegetable its colour - the purple pigment, betacyanin with yellow pigment, betaxanthin, are what give the beet its vivid redness - are antioxidant and can help to protect against cancer. The same properties also make beet a good blood cleanser and immune booster, further backed up by its vitamin A and vitamin C content. The colourants are very stable, making it the most reliable and one of the safest plant-based colourings.

It also contains iron, safeguarding against anaemia and the leaves are rich in folates, also known as folic acid, which is used to help prevent birth defects. In addition, the leaves also contain xeaxanthin and lutein, which are thought to protect against macular degeneration, a common cause of blindness in the elderly and which are also powerful anti-carginogens. On the down side, the oxalic acid in dark green leaf vegetables such as beet leaf can hinder the absorption of calcium, bad news for those in the deficiency risk groups, such as post-menopausal women.

100g of beet contains 47 kcalories, composed of fats, carbohydrate, fibre, sodium, protein vitamin A, vitamin C, iron and manganese. 100g of beet leaf equals 23 kcalories made up of fats, carbohydrate, fibre sodium, protein, a good deal of vitamin A, vitamin C, iron and manganese.

Black Pepper (*Piper nigrum - Kali mirchi*)

The Keralans call black pepper '*the King of Spices*' and it certainly has occupied the 'top-slot' in the history of Man's obsession with spices and condiments for centuries. Greek and Roman courtesans used a mixture of black pepper and myrrh, mixed with equal quantities of two scents named *Cyprus* and *Egyptian* as a love potion.

Pliny (1st century AD) refers to the spice, complaining about its high price and that white pepper cost twice that of black. In AD 408, Alaric the Goth demanded 3,000lb (1,360kg) of black pepper as part of his ransom for Rome. The Romans paid over the pepper, which Alaric more than thankfully accepted before sacking the city anyway in AD 410!

The statutes of Ethelred (978-1016), provide the earliest reference to a pepper trade in England, stipulating that 'Esterlings' who brought their ships up the River Thames to Billingsgate should pay a toll at Christmas and Easter, together with 10lb of pepper.

One of the oldest guilds in the City of London is the Guild of Pepperers, who were fined for not having a Royal Licence in 1180, and were registered as *Grosserii*, or wholesalers, in 1328. Not surprisingly, it is from this word that the modern 'grocer' is derived.

The term 'peppercorn rent', nowadays tending to denote a nominal fee, actually started off meaning that such a contract was taken very seriously indeed, based on the cost of a given weight of peppercorns per year, which were very expensive and seen as a more stable form of currency than money.

European nobles found it indispensible during the Middle Ages, using it both as a seasoning and a preservative. It's value grew to at least equal that of silver or gold and in 1204, the Venetians, who were supposed to transport the Fourth Crusade against Muslim Egypt, persuaded the penniless crusaders to loot the Christian city of Constantinople instead, wresting control of the spice trade for Venice in payment.

It was the quest for a new source of pepper, second only to the desire to find gold, which fuelled the enthusiasm of the great explorers of the Renaissance. In 1498, Portugal's Vasco da Gama landed at Calicut on the Malabar coast and offered beads and baubles in trade for pepper and other spices. The king was offended at such a mediocre offer, refused, and Da Gama promised to return with gold. He did indeed return five years later, with 10 warships, and showered Calicut with lead, not gold.

Again, as with all spices, pepper has been imbued with magical qualities: pepper, caraway and fennel seeds were said to keep away evil forces when worn in a pouch around the neck and peppercorns were mixed with salt and scattered around homes to keep out negative influences.

The peppercorns are the fruit of a climbing plant which are left to varying states of ripeness and treated in different ways to obtain the black, green and white pepper spices. Black pepper is obtained from fruits which are picked just before reaching full ripeness, fermented and then spread out in the sun to dry; white from ripe fruit, picked when scarlet, before being soaked, the endocarp removed for fermentation; green pepper by pickling unripe fruits to prevent them darkening. It is the pungent alkeloid, *piperine* which gives the bite to peppercorns, and although white pepper has more *piperine*, it has less of the aromatic principles found in black pepper.

Other members of the Piper family are *P. longum*, used in India; *P. betle*, also an Indian native, whose leaves are wrapped around betel seeds and the juice of the gambier as a digestive and breath sweetener; *P. Cubeba* from Malaysia, which was very popular in this country during Medieval times; *P. retroflexum* from Indonesia; *P. guineense*, also known as Guinea or Benin pepper, a milder relative from West Africa.

Red pepper, also known as false pepper or Peruvian pepper, is obtained from a different family of plants entirely, *Schinus molle*, an evergreen of Central American origin. They are used in Peru for making vinegar and alcoholic drinks. *Xanthoxylum piperitum*, also called Japanese Prickly Ash, whose orange berries are used to make the Japanese pepper-spice, *sansho*, hit the headlines recently as a 'cure' for grey hair. Dr Ohji Ifuku and his team of researchers at the cosmetics firm, Shiseido, found that extract of *sansho* can reactivate the pigment cells, or melanocytes, which give hair its colour and which stop reproducing as the body ages.

Medicinal: Ayurveda, the healing doctrine which grew up in the home of pepper, naturally sees the spice as extremely beneficial to health. It is regarded as being dry, therapeutically heating and a digestive. It sharpens the appetite and stimulates the production of gastric juices and helps to expel excess wind. The essential oil is secreted by the lungs, so aiding in the treatment of pharyngitis and tonsilitis, and the recommended application is to take powdered pepper mixed with honey three times a day. A pinch of powdered black pepper, stirred into hot, sweetened milk is also used in Ayurveda to cure sore throats and headcolds. Pastes of black pepper are used for rheumatism and skin diseases and a hot dedoction of black pepper is used as an effective mouthwash to ease toothache. Its ability to promote sweating is also capitalised upon - a mixture of pepper, ginger and honey is prescribed for malarial fever.

Unnani Tibb, the doctrine founded by Avicenna 1,000 years ago also values pepper as a medicine, and prescribing it internally for fever, colic and indigestion, and as a remedy for throat and gum infections and externally for rheumatism. One teaspoon of ground black pepper weighs 2.1g and has an energy value of 5 kcalories. It contains carbohydrate, protein, vitamin A, vitamins B1 and B2, niacin, sodium, phosphorous, potassium, calcium, iron, magnesium, copper, zinc and selenium.

Caraway (*Carum cari*)

Probably the oldest herb known to Man, it has been in use since earliest times. Seeds have been found in the Swiss Mesolithic excavations dating back more than 8,000 years and caraway is mentioned in ancient texts such as the Bible. It is unsure where it acquired its name, different sources indicating either *karon* from the Greek, or an ancient Arabic word for 'seed'.

The whole plant is edible and, in this country during the Middle Ages, the root was boiled and eaten as a vegetable and the leaves chopped and used in soups, broths and salads. In Elizabethan England caraway seed cakes, breads and biscuits were common and a tradition grew up whereby farm labourers were given caraway cakes after wheat sowing. This was probably linked to the folklore superstition that the seed was supposed to inspire loyalty and fidelity.

Caraway seeds would be fed to livestock and poultry to prevent them wandering, woven into collars around their necks and caraway cakes would be placed in dovecotes and pigeon-lofts to ensure their return. There was even a popular belief that anything containing caraway was protected from theft - even to the extent to believing that the culprit would be imprisoned at the scene until discovered - meant that it was secreted into many unexpected places, from treasure chests to husbands' shirt-hems! Caraway was always included in village love potions.

The flavouring is still very popular in Germany and Austria, where it is used in cakes, breads, sauerkraut, kummel and Munster cheese. Medicinally, caraway has been a long-standing remedy for indigestion. The seeds were infused to make teas, cordials and to make digestive sweets or 'comfits'. Nicholas Culpeper, the herbalist and astrologer author of The English Physitian,

(1652), wrote *"The powder of the seed* (caraway) *put into a poultice taketh away black and blue spots of blows and bruises."* However, approbation has not always been widespread. Ogden Nash, for example, obviously wasn't impressed:

> *The Abbé Voltaire, alias Arouet,*
> *Never denounced the seed of the caraway;*
> *Sufficient proof, if proof we need,*
> *That he never bit into a caraway seed.'*
> The Caraway Seed

Ayurveda lists caraway as warming and incorporates it into infusions with its cousins, aniseed and fennel, for chest and stomach complaints, used as an expectorant and for relief of flatulence. Unani Tibb, too, mentions its use for these purposes in addition to treating nausea and toothache. Modern European herbalists recommend using caraway to stimulate the appetite, relieve indigestion and to ease menstrual cramps. One tsp caraway seeds weigh 2g and contain 2 kcalories, fats, carbohydrates, fibre, sodium, protein, vitamin A and iron.

Cardamom (*Elettaria cardamomum, - elaichi*)

The first recorded use of cardamom appears in Ayurvedic texts from around 4th century BC as a cure for urinary tract infections and as a weight loss aid, and the ancient Greeks were already trading the spice by that time. It also gained an early reputation as an aphrodisiac and accordingly, Nicholas Culpeper assigned it the astrological ruler Venus in his work, *The English Physician*, published in 1652 - even though it is actually a member of the same family as ginger, which is ruled by Mars. In herbalist witchcraft, the essential oil of cardamom is used in magic for love and lust!

Cardamom grows wild in the southern Indian tropical mountain forests and it is now cultivated in India, Thailand, and Central America. However, it is generally agreed that the best cardamom comes from its native Cardamom Hills of Kerala, where it is known as *elettari*, altered to *elaichi* in other parts of India, hence its Latin generic name, and over 2,500 tons are exported from India annually.

This rush-like shrub, which grows to around 2m (over 6 ft) produces the small greenish-brown fruit pods. Trilocular, nut-sized capsules, containing 4-8 seeds each, which are dried in the semi-ripe capsules and have an aromatic odour and a sweetish, warm, pungent taste. Around 5% of these are bleached white and fumed with hydrogen peroxide, although many people feel that this detracts from their quality. A further 10% are shucked for their seeds, and, although convenient, this becomes an expensive way of buying cardamom, as 10lb of pods yields just 6oz of seeds. This places it third in the 'expensive spice' pecking order, below saffron and vanilla.

Medicinal: Unani Tibb, the ancient Persian medicine and dietetic regime, recommends cardamom for all stomach disorders, as a heart stimulant, a tonic, an aphrodisiac, and as a condiment.

From Persia, too, comes the ancient recipe for regaining an errant husband. Apparently, wronged wives were advised to place cardamom, cloves and cinnamon in a jar, over which she was to recite a passage from the Koran seven times backwards. The jar was then to be filled with rosewater and left to steep.

The water was then used to soak the husband's shirt, together with a piece of paper bearing his name and the names of four angels. The mixture was then heated over a fire and, as the mixture boiled, the husband's affections would return.

An essential Indian food ingredient and a traditional Arabian coffee flavouring, cardamom is used as a breath sweetener, and to stimulate appetite and to relieve flatulence in aromatherapy. One tsp of ground spice = 6 cals, and the spice contains vitamin Bl, B2, niacin, trace sodium, phosphorous, potassium, calcium, iron, magnesium and zinc.

Carrot (*Daucus carota, v. sativa – Gajja*)

A native of Afghanistan, early varieties were a purple, dark red or black colour and were cultivated from early times. Remains of early carrots have been found at excavations of early Swiss lake dwellings and it was cultivated in the Mediterranean region many years BC. The plant was listed as being among those in the famous gardens of King Merodach-Baladan of Babylon in the 8th century BC, but in the herb category, suggesting that the root was probably discounted at that stage. The exact lineage is difficult to trace as it was often confused with its close relative, the parsnip, by early horticulturists.

The earliest written evidence of the carrot comes from Ibn al-Awam, an Arab writer living in Andalusia in Spain during their Moorish occupation, who described two varieties; one purple and another, less flavour-some yellowy-green variety, both of which were used as a vegetable and in salads.

The carrot arrived in France and the Low Countries in the 14th century and finally reached Britain in the 15th century. A pale yellow strain appeared in the 16th century, having had the dark purple anthocyanin colouring bred out by the Dutch, and which became very popular. The now familiar orange variety, developed by the Dutch breeders, appeared in the 17th century.

Carrots, like beets, contain sugars and were investigated as a source of refined sugar, but proved to be inferior to beets. It is this sweet quality, however, that has seen their use in sweet preparations since the Middle Ages in carrot cake, Christmas puddings and jams. On the Indian subContinent, too, this quality has been utilised, and the carrot has been a successful and very popular ingredient to make dishes for the sweet-toothed, such as halwa.

Medicinal: They have gained a place in the 'superfood' category for their beta-carotene content. Beta-carotene is the vegetable pre-cursor to vitamin A, and just one raw carrot provides twice the recommended daily allowance for an adult. The beta-carotene is converted into vitamin A by the body and is excellent for eyes, skin and mucous membranes and is a powerful anti-oxidant which has been shown to protect against cancers, cataracts, coronary disease and stroke.

Another derivative of vitamin A, *retinoic acid*, already used in cosmetic face and anti-wrinkle creams, have been found to stop tumour cells multiplying by accelerating them through their reproductive stage, thus preventing growth. Tests carried out on eight children at the Royal Victoria Infirmary in Newcastle, all suffering from neuroblastoma, a rare cancer which attacks the nerve tissues, found that the cells matured more quickly when exposed to retinoic acid, dying off when it was withdrawn.

The vegetable is also fibre-rich, especially in *calcium pectate*, a soluble fibre that has been shown to actually reduce bad cholesterol levels.

Carrots are also a good source of boron, the trace mineral which is believed to be important in helping to reduce the risk of osteoporosis, when taken with a good supply of calcium and magnesium, and in promoting strong bones and efficient brain functioning. Other minerals are sulphur, which fights infections and skin disorders, and potassium and magnesium which also help to keep heart, teeth and bones healthy.

Cooked carrots are rated at 49 in the Glycaemic Index, the scale invented to help in the treatment of diabetes, and which is used to measure the rate at which blood sugar levels rise when a particular carbohydrate bearing food is ingested. Lower level GI foods, (those below 50 are seen as best), are more complex and hence digested more slowly, ensuring a longer feeling of satiety, longer term energy maintenance and keeping blood sugar levels constant. Bugs Bunny knows his stuff - all in all, a dieter's dream at just 40 calories for one large, raw carrot.

Cauliflower *(Brassica oleracae – Gobi)*

A member of the cabbage family, the French dubbed it *chou de Chypre*, (Cyprus cabbage), as it was introduced to Western Europe from Cyprus in the late 16th and early 17th centuries. It is known to have been grown by the Arabs during the Middle Ages.

The white inflorescence is a sterile flowering structure, the lack of colour being managed by keeping it covered during growth, avoiding exposure to the sun to prevent the formation of chlorophyll.

Mark Twain, writing in Pudd'nhead Wilson's Calendar, made the observation that, *"Cauliflower is nothing but a cabbage with a college education."* Maybe, if he'd known how good it was for him, he may have afforded it a little more respect. As with all the cruciferous vegetables, people who include a high number of the family in their diet, such as cabbage, broccoli, Brussels sprouts etc, have been found to have a lower incidence of cancer than those who do not.

Medicinal: Recent studies have also found that they contain a compound called *sulphurophane*, which may stimulate cancer-fighting enzymes in the body.

Cauliflower also contains vitamin C, potassium (essential for the maintenance of normal body fluid balance and the regulation of heart function and blood pressure), fibre and essential minerals, and a 100g serving equals a mere 30 kcalories.

Chilli *(Capsicum frutescens, capsicum annuum – Mirch)*

'*In fourteen hundred and ninety two, Columbus sailed the ocean blue ....*' Whether this Spanish-funded Italian, who accidentally discovered the 'New World' whilst sailing west looking for an easier route to the rich, spice redolent cities of Asia, was actually the first to do so, is probably less important than the impact that this voyage had on the rest of the world and, in particular, Europe.

Never before had there been such a wealth of new resources, virtually laid at the feet of the European nations. The '*Columbian Exchange*' gave the 'Old World' new wealth, drugs, foods and the Chilli pepper.

One of the main reasons for Columbus' trip had been to find a new source of supply of the '*King of Spices*', pepper, so, imagine his delight when one of the plants he discovered actually produced a pepper, albeit a strange variety. A Peter Martyr, writing in September 1493, was one of the first to report that Christopher Columbus had brought back to Spain "... *peppers more pungent than that from Caucasus.*"

The native Americans had, of course been using them for a long time and archaeological evidence has been found that chillies were gathered from around 7500 BC and cultivated over 3,000 BC, predating the ancesters of the Mayans, the Olmecs, by about 1,000 years. The Mayans, whose civilisation occupied the area between the two Americas - now known as Guatemala, Mexico and Belize, used chillies medicinally for stomach disorders.

Some suggest that the fact that its seeds are encased in a fleshy pod or capsule gave it its botanical genus name, *capiscum*. Others say that its root is from the Greek for 'I bite' - *Kapto*. Either explanation would seem to have its merits. The common names are easier to track down: Cayenne is named after the capital of French Guyana; chilli is an altered form of Chile, after the country - it is still spelt this way in the United States; and piment and pimento from the Spanish word for pepper, *pimiento*.

Southern Europe quickly embraced this fiery little fruit. Pungent and jewel-coloured, it soon became a favourite of the Portuguese, and Vasco da Gama felt it to be indispensable enough to take with him on his marathon trip to India in 1498, thus, apparently, starting one of the most successful relationships in cookery: Indian food and the chilli.

The plant, in all its varieties, flourished and found favour in tropical India, and its cultivation and use travelled northwards to the nomadic Mongolians, through China, where it became a firm favourite in Szechuan, to come back, full circle, via the Turks, who, at war with the Portuguese, returned the sweeter, milder variety, Paprika, which became such an important part of the cuisine of the Austro-Hungarian Empire.

Paprika, or pimento, is a member of the smoother, milder capsicum annuum branch of the family, which also includes the bell pepper, *C. annuum var. grossum*. The capsicum arrived in Hungary in 1699 and only became an indispensable ingredient in their Gulyas (goulash), in the 18th century. This now famous dish was originally a meat and onion stew, developed by Magyar shepherds, and carried by them in containers made from sheep stomachs as they followed their flocks, dating from the 9th century.

Today, the chilli, is the most popular spice in the world. Used all over the Indian sub-continent, it is popular in Southeast Asia, Szechuan in China, Central America and the USA, where, usually in its liquid, Tabasco, form, it is central to the Creole, Cajun and Texan kitchens. Amazingly, Tabasco sauce, made from the eponymous chilli which is one of the hottest of the species, was invented 120 years ago by an Irish immigrant family, the McIlhennys, at Avery Island in Louisiana.

Southern Europe too, has embraced the chilli: Portugal, Spain, especially the Basques, and the Italian regions of Abruzzi and Basilicata use it to very good effect. European Gypsies were fond of peppers and used them in their love charms. The fruits, like caraway, cumin and dill were also seen in folklore to inspire fidelity and it was believed that two red peppers, tied together and placed under the marital pillow, would prevent a partner straying. It would seem that only the French have resisted its fiery charm, although, modern French chefs, such as Raymond Blanc, are increasingly exploring its use in their creations.

There are more than 1,600 varieties of this little plant, whose relatives include the tomato, the potato and deadly nightshade. Two hundred of these are grown in Mexico alone.

The heat of the chilli can be affected by the climate and soil where it is grown and by its ripeness and a test exists, to determine the level of heat in a chilli, called the Scoville Scale (founded by German chemist Wilbur Scoville prior to the 1920's). As a guide, the hottest on the scale was the *habanero* (up to 500,000 units) until the *naga jolokia or Tezpur* was found recently in Assam (850,000 units) followed by even hotter versions such as the *Dorset Naga* (900,000 units) and the latest over 1 million units. The mildest is the large, sweet bell pepper (0 units). The popular *jalapeno* is about 5,000 units.

The heat is caused by a chemical, the alkaloid *capsaicin*, found in its largest concentrations in the white placental central core which holds the seeds and in the seeds themselves. *Capsaicin* is its magic ingredient, both for the 'bite' and medicinally. It encourages the flow of gastric juices, which is why some people find their mouths water at the mere mention of chilli, and promotes regular peristalsis movement, further aiding digestion and preventing flatulence. Scientists have managed to find five capsaicinoid components, three of which give a 'rapid bite' and two a long, low intensity on tongue and mid-palate, the ratios of which vary from type to type and account for the differences in pungency and 'burn' sensation.

One of the components of chilli, *capsidicin*, is a natural antibiotic, and it has been found to posses antibacterial and antifungal properties and has been used since ancient times as a powerful pain killer: *Capsaicin* ointment is available to help relieve arthritis and inflamed joints. Researchers at Harvard Medical School discovered that the active ingredient in hot peppers, *capsaicin*, carries out its action by binding to a receptor - a protein that sits on the surface of a neuron or nerve cell. Drugs that bind to the protein may be capable of blocking the activation of pain sensing nerve cells or neurons.

Ironically, it seems to be the very pain produced by the alkaloid which helps to produce the pain killing effect: *Capsaicin* stimulates certain nerve endings to manufacture the chemical which transmits the sensation of pain through the nervous system, *Substance P*, until the cells are depleted, temporarily blocking the pain signals to the brain. It is also this process that produces the morphine-like effect of chilli, stimulating the release of endorphins in the brain and, perhaps, reinforcing the addictive effect, leading to chilli-based foods such as curry being referred to as '*sex on a plate*' by some. It is not soluble in water and its stinging pungency can only be countered by casein, a protein found in milk and its by-products such as cheese, which is why lassi is such a good foil to an Indian meal.

Capsaicin also has an affinity for fat, explaining why drinking more water after a spicy mouthful simply spreads the burning whereas absorbing the spice with another food is more effective. However, chilli is not just a pretty sting. Nutritionally, it is high in vitamin A and a source of vitamins B1, B2, niacin, sodium, phosphorous, potassium, calcium, iron, magnesium and zinc and, by weight, capsicum peppers contain between 6 to 9 times the amount of vitamin C than a tomato.

Medicinal: This is good news indeed in these carcinogenophobic times, as both vitamins A and C are powerful antioxidants, believed to protect against various forms of cancer and cardiovascular disease. Other research has found that it can also help combat heart attacks and strokes, as it appears to extend blood coagulation time, preventing harmful blood clots, and that it may also help to cut triglycerides and decrease bad cholesterol levels, when used in conjunction with a diet low in saturated fats.

Cinnamon *(Cinnamomum zeylanicum, cinnamomum aromaticum, cinnamomum cassia, Ceylon cinnamon, Dalchini, Chinese cinnamon, cassia, Dalchini cassia)*

Archaeologists have found evidence that cinnamon was used in Egypt as long ago as 3000 BC; employed in culinary, ritual and preservative roles, being one of the constituents in their embalming mixtures.

Cinnamomum zeyanicum, Ceylon cinnamon or *dalchini*, is, as its Latin specific name suggests, a native of Sri Lanka, and is the inner bark of the tree's branches, sun-dried after stripping, into tight, tan-coloured fragrant quills. It made quite an early appearance in Europe, brought by the spice caravans of Arab traders, and gained such popularity that, as a commodity, it was second in importance only to pepper during the Middle Ages.

The Portuguese seized and occupied Sri Lanka, then known as Ceylon, in the mid-16th century in order to control the supply of the spice, and were succeeded by the Dutch, who, in 1770, began large scale cultivation on the island.

Its close relative, *Cinnamomum cassia*, *cassia* or *dalchini cassia*, is Chinese in origin and is darker and rougher in appearance, with a less subtle flavour. Galen, the 2nd century Greek physician, advised that double the weight should be used if substituting cassia for 'true' cinnamon.

In ancient China, cassia, or *Kwei*, was thought to be the Tree of Life, 10,000ft high, flourishing since the beginning of time in Paradise, the beautiful garden situated at the source of the Yellow River. The legend said that whoever managed to enter the garden and eat the fruit of the tree would live in eternal bliss.

Medicinal: The leaves, *(tej pattar)* are also used for cooking and medicinal purposes, being good for the relief of colic and diarrhoea, and they are used in the manufacture of perfumery. Ayurveda and Unani Tibb both recommend cinnamon to aid digestion and to combat diarrhoea and nausea. Culpeper, the 17th century astrologer and herbalist gives the Sun as its ruling astral body, thus associating cinnamon with warmth, power and strength. In European folk medicine, it was said to be stimulating, was thought to raise spirituality and awareness and was used in 'magic' incenses to attract money, healing, protection, love and lust.

More recently, clinical studies at the United States' Drug Administration's Human Nutrition Centre have shown that cinnamon greatly enhances the ability of insulin to metabolise glucose and that it helps to control blood sugar levels. Some diabetics have reported that eating about ¼ tsp of ground cinnamon daily has had a beneficial effect on their blood sugar levels. This, happily, has a knock-on effect which also benefits non-diabetics, in that this same action helps the prevention of coronary artery disease and high blood pressure.

Nutritionally, both types have basically the same structure, although cassia contains more of the essential oil, cinnamic aldehyde, containing between 1-4%, as against the ½ - 1½ % content in Ceylon cinnamon. One teaspoon of the ground spice weighs 2.3g, packs 6 kcals of energy, and contains vitamins A, Bl, B2, niacin, vitamin C, sodium, phosphorous, potassium, iron, magnesium, selenium, zinc and a high level of calcium.

Citrus Fruit

The citrus family are thought to date back around 20 million years and are natives of East Asia and Australasia. The name citrus is derived from the Greek word for the lemon, *kitron*.

Nutritionally, all the family are valuable and have been used medicinally since the earliest time. Modern research backs this up; they contain *limonene*, a citrus oil which has been shown to reduce the growth of mammary tumours in laboratory animals. Citrus fruits also contain flavonoids, antioxidants which may prevent the spread of cancer tissue and phenolics which help the body to produce natural agents which help to detoxify carcinogens.

The whole family are also rich in vitamin C, a powerful antioxidant, which may help prevent heart disease and strokes by preventing the oxidation of LDL cholesterol which leads to plaque deposits forming on artery walls. Vitamin C also helps in the absorption of iron and is essential for the formation of collagen, necessary for cell and body tissue growth and virus resistance, helping to boost the immune system.

Bergamot - *Citrus bergamia*. Originally made an appearance in Italy from around 1600 as an ornamental tree and is now cultivated for its essence which is used in cosmetic and perfume manufacture and, notably for scenting Earl Grey tea. Its common name is a derivation of the name of a city in Asia Minor, Pergamum. Its main area of cultivation is the coastal region of Calabria in Italy, where 90% of the world's crop is produced.

Citron - *Citrus medica*. As its specific name suggests, the citron has been grown since the earliest times for its medicinal qualities, and is mentioned in a religious work, the *Vajasaneyi Samhita*, which dates back to before 800 BC. It was known to the Babylonians, where the exiled Jewish community came into contact with the fruit. They took it back to Palestine where, known as the *Ertog*, it became important in the Feast of the Tabernacles. The religious connection is strong in China too. A variety of citron which grows there has very defined ridges which looks like clasped hands, earning it the name *fo shu kan*, Buddha's hand. It is associated with happiness and sometimes used in temple offerings.

In India, the citron came to be associated with wealth and *Kuvera*, the god of affluence, is always depicted with a fruit in his hand. Brought to Europe by Alexander the Great in the 3rd century BC, it was seen in early medicine as a cure-all and was even credited with being able to counter the effects of poisoning. In folk medicine it has been traditionally used for insect bites, skin trouble and to ease muscular aches and spasms. The fruit has a thick rind which is used for making candied fruit and the essential oil is used, in conjunction with the oils obtained from the bergamot and the lemon, in perfumery, especially in the production of Eau de Cologne. It can also be used in a culinary role: in soft drinks, pickles and sauces, but is usually only used in candied form nowadays.

Grapefruit - *Citrus paradisi*. A variety of the citrus family which is a hybrid, formed from a cross between the pomelo (*citrus decumana*) and the sweet orange and gained its name because it grows in grape-like clusters on the tree. It was recognised as a separate species by around 1830 but did not enjoy a great deal of popularity in this country until the 1920's when it became the fashion to start a meal with it, a trend introduced by the Americans.

Medicinal: Chinese medicine recommends grapefruit to ease indigestion and heartburn during pregnancy and to counter the effects of over-indulgence in alcohol. A rich source of vitamin C, just half a grapefruit provides half the daily requirement for an adult non-smoker and the pectin in the white membrane is a useful source of soluble fibre which may help to lower blood cholesterol levels. Pink or ruby grapefruit are slightly higher in vitamin C levels and, like the tomato, contain lycopenes which, it is thought, may offer protection against cervical, pancreatic, bladder and prostate cancer.

Lemon - *Citrus medica v. limon*. Thought to have originated from northeast India, the lemon was taken both to the West and the East by Arab traders and with it the Persian name for the fruit, *Limun*, itself from a similar word in Hindustani, which has only been slightly altered by others, with even the Chinese using *Li mung*. Cultivation spread throughout the Mediterranean region by the time of the Crusades, eventually reaching Genoa by the mid-15th century and the Azores, an early source of lemons for the English, by the end of that century.

The Elizabethan horticulturist, John Gerard, made it clear that he regarded the lemon as non-edible, being prized more for its fragrance to freshen clothes. One reason, perhaps, could have been the expense. When it reached the kitchen, it was used quite sparingly; the rind in one recipe, the juice in another as a luxury replacement for vinegar.

In the 17th century, Pepys mentions lemonade, which also enjoyed some success as a street drink, *acquacedrata*, in Italy at the same time. But in England, although some of the grander estates and houses produced hothouse lemons, it and the fruit remained a luxury until the shipping boom in the second half of the 19th century.

Medicinal: Like its precursor, the citron, the lemon has always been seen as invaluable. The Chinese use it as a cough reliever and as a useful dietary supplement during pregnancy. Ayurveda recommends the juice, mixed with a pinch of salt to fight nausea, vomiting and digestive disorders; or mixed with honey and black pepper to cure hiccups and heartburn. Unani Tibb prescribes it internally for soothing inflammations, dental caries, vomiting, rheumatism, headache, colds, coughs, sore throat and externally as a hair rinse, facial astringent and for sunburn, warts and corns.

In Europe too the lemon has been a traditional cure, taken with honey, for colds and sore throats and is used as a base in many proprietary brands of cold cures and cough syrups. Herbalists also use lemon juice to balance the system, to expel threadworms and to remedy sluggishness in the liver and bowel. Externally, the juice is used to ease chapped skin, broken capillaries, to cure warts and ringworm and as an anti-fungal. One lemon contains half the recommended daily intake of vitamin C for a non-smoker and is a good source of limonene, shown to combat tumour growth in laboratory animals, and terpenes, which control the production of cholesterol.

Lime - *Citrus aurantifolia*. The smallest of the citrus family, the lime gained fame after the Naval Surgeon, James Lind, produced his *Treatise on Scurvy* in 1754, advocating the use of the fruit, together with its cousins, in naval rations to prevent the disease, which is caused by a vitamin C deficiency. However, it was not until 1795, a year after his death, that Lord Hood added it to sea rations, earning the sailors and, eventually all Britons, the 'Limey' tag in America. However, the Dutch had already discovered the same benefits some 200 years earlier, when they introduced a mixture of lime and lemon juice for use on their longer sea voyages, the lemon being richer in vitamin C than the lime.

Ayurveda recommends lime as a gastric stimulant; to relieve flatulence, nausea and cramps; to cool for fever and sunstroke; in bringing chronic diarrhoea under control.

Orange - *Citrus aurantium, citrus, sinensis, citrus amara*. A native of China, where the sweeter, mandarin varieties (*citrus sinensis*) have been enjoyed for millennia, being mentioned in texts as far back as 2400 BC. Its common name comes to us from the ancient Sanskrit, *naranga*, via the Arabic, *naranj*. It had reached India by AD 100, when it appeared in a medical text there, the *Charaka Samhita* and the sour (*citrus aurantium*), or Seville orange reached southern Italy by the 11th century but, ironically, didn't arrive at Seville until around a century after that! By the 15th century it had reached Western Europe, but mainly as an ornamental and spice tree. A spate of orangerys appeared, the fruit being used for its perfume and as a base for the pomander, a spice-studded citrus fruit carried to guard against infection, first carried in the country by Cardinal Wolsey at the court of Henry VIII.

The **sweet orange**, *citrus sinensis*, was brought to Europe from Ceylon by the Portuguese and, in around the mid-16th century, even sweeter varieties were introduced direct from China which gained favour in the orangerys of England. By the late 19th century, the Christmas stocking filler *citrus recticulata*, mandarin orange first arrived from China.

Folklore magic associates the orange with Leo and Sagittarius and it is ruled by the Sun. The orange was seen as a power source; used for lending energy and optimism in decision making and used in magic to heighten psychic awareness and to boost love, luck and for guidance in divination. Herbal medicine uses the orange to combat digestive upsets, poor appetite and constipation and externally as a tonic for tired and dry skin. In aromatherapy the essential oil is used to counter depression and anxiety.

One medium-sized orange provides one whole day's requirement of vitamin C for a healthy non-smoking adult and is a useful source of thaimin (vitamin B1), folic acid and pectin, a type of soluble dietary fibre which may reduce blood cholesterol levels.

Cloves *(Eugenia carophyllata, Eugenia aromatica)*

History leaves enigmatic messages for future generations to puzzle over. Nursery rhymes, for example, the satirical popular songs of their day, still hold clues to past events and personalities: "*Ring-a-ring-a-roses*" is actually a description of the onset of The Black Death; "*Georgy Porgey*", with his womanising tendencies, was a characature of the Prince Regent, destined to become George IV; and "*Peter Piper*", who picked a peck of pickled peppers was a real person, one very aptly named Pierre Poivre, a French Diplomat and Governor of Mauritius, and his famous peppers were actually cloves and nutmegs.

Cloves are the dried, unopened flowers of a tropical evergreen tree which was once grown only in the Moluccas. Arab spice merchants guarded the secret of their origin for centuries, as they took them, Eastwards first to China, where, during the Han Dynasty (approx. 300 BC) it was mandatory to chew a clove before entering the presence of a royal personage, and then West to ancient Rome, where they acquired their common name, *clavus* - 'nail', due to their stud-like shape.

Cloves only travelled more widely after the Venetians entered the spice trade from around 1500. Then the Moluccas were discovered by the Dutch, who, in order to keep prices high, decreed that cloves could only be cultivated on the island of Amboina and ordered all the trees on the other islands destroyed. This distressed the Moluccans because it was their custom to plant a clove tree to celebrate the birth of a child and believed that the fates of tree and child were intertwined. This monopoly also incensed the other European powers with interests in the area - notably the French and Portuguese - and the whole issue became a source of open hostility.

Then along came good old Pierre Poivre, the Peter Piper of the rhyme, who smuggled clove and nutmeg seedlings back to Mauritius, thus breaking the hold of the Dutch on those spices. After that, a succession of smugglers, including the Sultan of Zanzibar in 1800 and the British in the mid-19th century, managed to break the Dutch monopoly.

The anthropologist, George Frazer noted in his work, *The Golden Bough*, that the trees on the Moluccan Islands were treated very much like pregnant women: no-one was allowed to make a violent or sudden noise near them or to carry light or fire past them at night. It was even forbidden for a man to approach a tree wearing a hat! The theory was that the tree should be kept from any source of distress which may scare it into dropping the fruit early. Apparently, another tradition, was that clove trees were only planted in the dark of the moon.

Trees are first harvested after five years, each plant producing, on average, 3kg (71b) of flower buds annually. The flower buds, initially pale green, turn dark green. They are not allowed to open as they would lose their pungency and fragrance. The buds are then immersed for a few seconds in boiling water and then, stalk removed, left to dry, usually in the sun. It is possible to get two crops a year from each tree, although only one is taken to prevent damage to the trees.

More than just a nice taste to add to apple pie, the pungent main constituent of cloves is *eugenol*, which takes its name from the generic name, *Eugenia*, commemorating Prince Eugene of Savoy (1663-1736), Austrian statesman, field-marshal and patron of the sciences.

Although the bud contains the highest percentage of this volatile oil, other parts of the plant, such as discarded young shoots and leaves, are distilled to produce the essential oil. More than 10kg (221b) of essence comes from a single plant and is used as the base for synthetic vanilla, soaps, perfumes, toothpastes, mouthwash and medicines.

European witches have used the spice in spells invoking protection, money and love since the Middle Ages, and by European tradition, taken with colonists to North America, cloves were carried in a small pouch by the bereaved as a source of comfort.

Culpeper assigned it the ruling house of Jupiter, associated with Sagittarius. Herbal practitioners still recommend cloves for their antiseptic properties, as an anaesthetic, to ease toothache, indigestion, nausea and bad breath.

Cloves have excellent preservative powers and are widely used in pickles and chutneys, and the traditional clove and orange pomanders, first carried in this country by Cardinal Wolsey in the 16th century, not only sweeten the air, but also repel moths.

Medicinal: Antiseptic, stimulant, stomachic and digestive, anti-infectant cloves are effective against coli bacilli, streptococci, staphylococci, pneumococci and as an antimycolic, and are used in dentistry for their antiseptic and analgesic properties. Oh, yes, and they're very good in apple pies, too!

One teaspoonful of ground cloves is equal, on average, to 2.1g, 7 kcals and contains vitamins A, Bl, B2, niacin, vitamin C, sodium, phosphorous, potassium, calcium, iron, magnesium and zinc.

Chocolate (Cocoa) *(Theobroma cacao)*.

Cacoa is a small, broadleaf evergreen, native to the rainforests of southern America, originating in the Amazon and Orinoco basins of Ecuador and Brazil, which has been cultivated since prehistory. It is thought that the first people to realise the potential of chocolate were the Olmecs, the first highly developed civilisation in Mesoamerica, and the builders of colossal stone heads in southern Veracruz and Tabasco at the beginning of the 1st millennium BC.

Cocoa beans were very important in the successive societies that inhabited Central and South America, being regarded by the Maya as *'the food of the gods'*, hence the botanical name, *theobroma*. The importance of cocoa and its role in the ritual-driven Maya society can be seen in the very detailed depictions left in the tombs of their nobility, excavated at Copán in the Honduran uplands. Archaeologists have found vessels containing carbonised cocoa remains in vessels which bear the glyph *ka-ka-wa* (cocoa), with directions on how to mix the foaming brew, spiced and tinted with red achiote, perhaps so it resembled more closely the blood which was central to their religious rites.

Chocolate was also used in burial rites and in the chac ritual which they performed in the hope of appeasing their gods and be granted rainfall. Teams from Cornell University and the University of California at Berkeley have found evidence of a village which was continuously inhabited over a 3,000 year span, from 2000 BC – AD 1000, attributing chocolate as the key to the success and longevity of the community.

Ironically, another researcher, Dr David Lentz of the New York Botanical Garden, may have found evidence that it was the over-cultivation of the crop, leading to a decline in rainfall and also deforestation, which may have caused the sudden collapse of the Maya society at the turn of the 9th century. Much of the early history of cocoa, and of the everyday lives of the Maya, has been uncovered over the last twenty years at a site dubbed 'the Pompeii of the Americas', Cerén, a Maya village which was buried in ash and lava after a volcanic eruption in AD 590.

Cocoa beans were also used as a form of currency, a fact which was revealed to Columbus and his crew in 1502, when they witnessed the panic-stricken efforts of Maya to recover spilt beans. Seventeen years later Cortes described a banquet held by the Aztec ruler, Montezuma II, at which he counted 50 great dishes made of cocoa.

Montezuma was reputed to have loved chocolate and one story says that he would drink from a golden goblet of frothy and 'invigorating' chocolate before visiting one of his wives. Another story reports that he would drink up to 50 goblets in one day. This would lead one to assume that perhaps he had a lot of wives and hence needed a lot of invigoration!

The Spanish mixed the ground, roasted beans and moulded them into cakes, much as the natives had shown them, opting for a sweeter combination of sugar and cinnamon, preferring it to the original spicy and savoury concoction. The cakes would then be exported and reconstituted with water to make a cold drink. They and the Portuguese managed to guard the secret of the chocolate for about a hundred years, so well in fact that Dutch pirates, having captured a chocolate boat, were so disgusted by what they regarded as a spoiled cargo that they threw the whole shipment overboard.

The rest of Europe finally got in on the act in the 17th century and in 1657 the first advertisements appeared for the sale of chocolate at London chocolate houses. It remained a very expensive luxury until the Industrial Revolution introduced the first machines and chocolate factories.

A Dutch company, Van Houten revolutionised the chocolate industry, taking out a patent in 1828 for the method of extracting a large proportion of the fat - cocoa butter - from the ground beans, leaving a water soluble powder behind. This led to the production of cocoa powder, drinking chocolate and eating chocolate, which contains a large amount of cocoa butter. In 1876 a Swiss company produced the first milk chocolate, introducing the world to a new addictive substance.

During the 19th century the Quakers exploited this, seeing chocolate as a better alternative to the evils of alcohol, setting up companies like Cadburys, founded in 1828, in order to process cocoa products and wean the masses away from the demon drink.

Medicinal: Nutritionally, cocoa is rich in carbohydrates, vegetable oil, protein, vitamin E, calcium magnesium, iron and phosphorous and has formed an essential part of survival kits for adventurers, ranging from boy scouts to astronauts. It also contains phenolic compounds which act as antioxidants which may help reduce the risk of heart disease and stroke.

Chocolate also contains the stimulants theobromine and caffeine which help to sharpen the brain and body performance, as well as a natural antidepressant. The addiction to dessert chocolate is probably more to the sugar content than any naturally occurring component, mass produced confectionery chocolate bars being very high in saturated fats and sugars. However, we may be preaching to the converted here, as recent figures show that we now spend £3 billion per year on chocolate.

The most nutritious chocolate is the fine dark types which contain at least 50% cocoa solids. It is also lower in sugar and, unfortunately, more likely to trigger migraines in those prone to attacks. 100g of an average milk chocolate gives 529 kcalories energy, 8.4g protein, 59.4g carbohydrate, 30g fat and minimal amount of fibre. 100g unsweetened cocoa powder gives 391 kcalories energy, fats 12.7g, (of which 7.11g is saturated) 50.20g carbohydrate, 5.20g fibre, 717mg sodium, 19.20g protein 20 IU vitamin A and 10.7mg iron.

Coconut *(cocos nucifera - Coconut palm)*

The coconut is a tropical palm which grows to heights of up to 25 metres. Written about and depicted since earliest times, it is probably the most important of the cultivated palms, with every part of the plant being used in some form or another.

In Sri Lanka, a major exporter of coconuts, it is said that the coconut has 99 uses; in Kerala, in southern India, it is known as 'God's gift to God's own Country'; in some other parts of India, it is known as *'the tree of heaven'*; and the Sanskrit name for the coconut palm translates as *'a tree which furnishes all the necessities of life'*.

A palm starts to yield nuts from between 6-10 years from planting and can continue to be fruitful for up to one hundred years. Each tree has around 30 leaves and produces 12 new leaves each year to replace a similar number that die off. Conveniently, a new leaf is born each month and with each leaf, a flower which, after 12 months produces between 5-10 mature oval nuts, about 30cm long. The flowers also yield a sweet juice which, when boiled down, produces a dark-brown, caramel-flavoured sugar called *jaggery*. If left to ferment, which takes only a matter of hours, this becomes an alcoholic drink known as toddy which, in turn, can then be distilled further to make a very potent and, in some places, quite popular spirit called arrak. The leaves themselves are used to make thatching, mats, fans, screens and baskets, and the top bud, or 'palm cabbage' is considered a culinary delicacy, as is the central part of a young palm's stem.

The husks are used as organic fertiliser, can be turned into a fuel for the manufacture of bricks and are a traditional source of domestic fuel in the regions where the palms are grown. The husk fibre, coir, is used to make rope, cord and matting. The hard brown shells are turned into charcoal, then into activated carbon for use in water and gas purification filters and in battery manufacture. The inner brown skin and imperfect coconuts are smoked and dried to make copra, which is used to produce coconut oil, is used in cooking and in the production of soaps, candles, cosmetics and hair preparations. Even the root, which possesses mildly narcotic properties, is sometimes chewed. Inside each coconut is the natural 'milk', a sweet-tasting opaque liquid which can be used as a drink or marinade. 200ml of this natural coconut milk contains about 57 kcalories, around 12g carbohydrate, 0.7g protein and less than 0.55g fat. Coconut flesh, however, contains 351 kcalories per 100g and is cholesterol-free.

Medicinal: The total fat content of the same amount of coconut is 36g, 86% of which are saturated fats, making it one of only two vegetable oils high in saturated fats, (the other being palm oil), although recent research indicates that it may not be the 'harmful' type found in animal and dairy produce and may even help to reduce 'bad' cholesterol levels. It is a good source of fibre, containing just over 7% and potassium, which works with sodium to regulate the body's water balance and ensure normal heart rhythm and is essential for the normal functioning of nerves and muscles. Low potassium intake has been associated with palpitations and high blood pressure. Ayurveda, the ancient study of life and maintenance of its natural harmony, regards coconut milk as cooling, a mild laxative diuretic, and good for heartburn, kidney diseases, an recommends it as an ideal remedy for fever, nausea and cardiac weaknesses.

The flesh itself is one of the major ingredients in south Indian cookery and is used fresh; in shredded and dried (desiccated) form; liquidised and set into solid blocks, which is marketed as creamed coconut; liquidised and mixed with water and used as coconut milk or cream to thicken and add a nutty sweetness to a dish. Southern Indians use coconut not only as an ingredient in its own right, but also as a spice, either ground with other spices and flavourings to form a base Masala, often for non-vegetarian dishes, or fried lightly as a tempering and added as a final 'blessing' to a finished dish. To ring the changes even further, sometimes the coconut is lightly roasted first to add a deeper, nuttier taste. Even plain, steamed rice can benefit from the addition of a little coconut in any one of its various forms.

However, it's not just Asian cooking that can profit from the addition of a little coconut cream. Used instead of cream in a sauce for chicken, fish or light meats, or added as a swirl in a soup, it can add a certain extra dimension to traditional European dishes. It is even good in bread making, adding a sweet, creamy flavour.

Added just before the end of cooking, it is also a good, natural thickener for stews and casseroles, and when added to a stir-fry, it can provide an instant, rich-tasting sauce - which can even be given a further zing with a squeeze of lime juice. Coconut cream can even be used as an instant dip by just adding a little flavouring, such as a little chilli with a few popped black mustard seeds. Then, of course, there are the obvious dessert uses: coconut crème caramel; coconut brulée; syllabub; mousse; soufflé; trifle; rice pudding; swirled into a pouring custard or sauce; made into an ice cream, parfait or kulfi; pancake batters; added to marscapone cheese for an interesting alternative to custard.

Naturally, such an important food attracts superstition, one of these being in southern India that coconuts should not be cracked after sundown, but that breaking one open at a special occasion will bring luck, being used rather like the ceremonial cutting of a ribbon at some events.

Coffee *(Coffea arabica, coffea canephora (robusta), coffea stenophylla)*

Coffee belongs to the family of 'Whoeverthoughtofthatfirst?' After all, it does take a leap or two to take the bitter berries of a small evergreen tree and turn it into a beverage, the demand for which has ensured a position in the World commodities market which is second only to oil.

Legend attributes the first step to an Ethiopian goatherder named Kaldi in around the year AD 850: noticing that his goats started to act a little strangely, frolicking and dancing around, after eating the berries of a certain tree, he tried them himself and was thrilled to find that they evoked a feeling of exhilaration and well-being. Monks from a nearby monastery, noticing Kaldi's antics, came and tried the berries too, and, finding that they were able to stay alert throughout their night-time prayers, spread the use of the berries throughout religious communities as a non-alcoholic stimulant.

Its name is derived from the Arabic *qahwah*, originally a poetic word for wine, and its Turkish form, kahveh was gradually turned into the various European forms: café; caffé; kaffee; coffee. Cultivated from around the middle of the 6th century, it was treated as a medicine initially, and the earliest written record of it was in a work by the Arabian physician, Rhazes in the 10th century. The beans were eaten whole at first, then a fermented 'wine' made from the pulp appeared, followed by the precursor of our present day decoction in around 10th century. Roasting the beans before use was introduced in the 13th century, and by the end of the 15th century, coffee had reached the whole of Islam, taken to the outer reaches of the empire by traders and pilgrims returning from Mecca.

Coffee houses were opened where men could gather, talk, socialise and discuss business and politics. The first is thought to have appeared in Constaninople in the mid-16th century and reports started filtering through to Europe of, "*a drink enjoyed in that city called coffa, made of the seed of the coava*". Unfortunately, other entertainments began to be offered too: dancing, music, singing and gambling. All frowned upon by Islam, also, the Imams realised that, despite not being an alcoholic beverage, coffee certainly was a stimulant and began to regard it with a good deal of suspicion. It didn't help either, that their mosque attendances seemed to be falling off whilst the coffee houses were filling up. Coffee, and the places where people gathered to enjoy it, started to be seen by the 'Establishment' as being subversive.

In 1656 the Ottoman Grand Vizir Koprili prohibited coffee, decreeing that the punishment for a first violation should be a cudgelling and for the second that the perpertrator should be sewn into a leather bag and thrown into the Bosphorous. Dutch traders were the first to bring coffee to Europe. In 1616 the first stolen plant arrived in Holland and by the end of that century, the Netherlands East India Company had established plantations in their colonies in Indonesia and Ceylon.

Strangely, Oxford claims the first coffee house to be opened in England was by Jacob, a Turkish Jew. In 1652, Pasqua Rosée opened the first public coffee house in St Michael's Alley, in the City of London. Rosée invited potential clients to come and meet each other and enjoy the new beverage which, "*quickens the spirits, and makes the heart lightsome*". London took to the coffee houses, and such establishments as Jonathon's, Button's, Lloyds and Will's became the meeting place for all professions within the City. Lloyd's Coffee House, in Tower Street, became the place where the owners and insurers of commercial ships and their cargoes would meet in order to conduct business. Eventually, Lloyds Coffee House became the now famous insurance exchange, Lloyd's of London.

Throughout Europe the great coffee house phenomenon spread like wildfire - much to the chagrin of the more genteel female populace. In 1674 *The Women's Petition against Coffee* was published. An anonymous pamphlet, it claimed that coffee made men, "*Trifle away their time, scald their chops, and spend all their money, all for a little base, black, thick, nasty, bitter, stinking, nauseaous puddle of water.*"

Across the Channel too ladies were finding their gentlemen-folk's preoccupation with this tarry drink more than a little mystifying, even to the extent of accusing coffee of reducing their menfolk's libido. Their cause was more than happily backed by the wine merchants, seeing the growth in demand for this new drink as a serious competitor, and in 1695, a medical report was published by the École de Médecine in Paris, which warned that a regular intake of coffee would deprive men of their generative powers.

However, despite such heavyweight opposition, the French persevered, their coffee houses evolving into the fashionable cafés which were to attract the patronage of some of the greatest names in Art in years to come. The fate of the English coffee houses was to be much more respectable for, as with Lloyds, most of the establishments which had caused so much early concern, developed into gentlemen's clubs, exchanges and banks.

The ladies of Germany didn't appear to agree with their European sisters and the drink was so popular that Johann Sebastian Bach composed his Kaffee-Kantate, gently mocking the drinking habits of the coffee-mad ladies of Leipzig.

In Italy, the clergy joined forces against what they described as, *"a drink from Satan's followers"*. They petitioned Pope Clement VIII, arguing that, as Islam had forbidden wine, the drink used in Holy Communion, Satan had to be behind this new evil from the East. Pope Clement, having demanded a taste first, replied that it was a shame to let the infidels have exclusive use of such a delicious drink and compromised by baptising it, explaining to the irate priests that he had thus cheated the Devil. In Venice, the Council of Ten tried to close down their city's caffés, reasoning that they were dens of iniquity, although they can't have been very successful as one of the most famous, Florian's, is still going strong today.

Frederick the Great of Prussia was so enraged at the amount of money being spent on 'foreign' coffee, and so leaving the state, that he issued a declaration that his people must drink beer instead. In 1781 he was to go even further, banning the roasting of coffee by any but the nobility, and then only that supplied by the State monopoly, hiring professional 'sniffers' to track down any illegal stashes.

Coffee was taken to South America by a young French naval officer, Gabriel Mathieu de Clieu, who, having enjoyed the Paris coffee houses, obtained a seedling and, against all the odds, including a bad sea-trip and an irate fellow passenger, managed to plant it in his gardens in the French colony of Martinique. This one plant was destined to be the rootstock for all the estates in the West Indies and South America.

Britain finally started its cultivation in 1730, in Jamaica, but only introduced it into India over a hundred years later in 1840, where their main focus had been the cultivation of tea.

Brazil, too, whose name was eventually to become synonymous with coffee, came late into the picture. The story goes that a young Brazilian officer caught the eye of the wife of the Governor of French Guiana on a visit in 1727. To show her admiration she presented the young man with a bouquet of flowers, within which was hidden a coffee plant. The plant duly arrived in neighbouring Brazil and, with the help of Roman Catholic missionaries, cultivation was spread throughout that country. In the 19th century a terrible leaf disease hit the plantations in Asia, giving Brazil the impetus required to shoot to the top of the production table, a position which it still holds today, supplying more than half the world's coffee.

The area that consumes more coffee than anyone else in the world is, surprisingly, not the United States, but Scandinavia, where they get through an amazing 612 cups per person, per year - the average in Britain is a mere 34 cups per head.

Coffea arabica is the most widely grown variety, growing above a height of 3,000ft (900m), between the tropics of Cancer and Capricorn. Coffee plantations start production after their third year, productivity increasing up to their fifteenth year then falling off. The plant produces ripe fruits several times during the year, with both blossoms and berries alongside each other, at varying stages of maturity, on the same tree. This means that constant picking is required, each tree producing roughly 2lb of green berries per year.

The substance in coffee which Kaldi and his dancing goats found so invigorating was, of course, *caffeine*, the alkaloid which gives coffee its kick and aroma, and which is also found, in smaller quantities, in tea and chocolate. Researchers at Oxford University have also found that it may play a part in speeding up the pain-killing effect of the drug, *ibuprofen*. Patients who had surgery for impacted molars were given 100mg or 200mg of caffeine with their ibuprofen and it was found that they had significantly more relief an hour or so later than those who had received ibuprofen alone.

Medicinal: *Caffeine* also stimulates the heart and central nervous system, enhances mental performance, stimulates the production of digestive juices in the stomach, aiding digestion and also dilates the air passages in the lungs. Both ordinary and decaffeinated coffee contain antioxidants which can protect against ageing, cancer and heart disease, but strong coffee which has been made by methods such as cafetière has been shown to raise blood cholesterol levels. Unfortunately, the caffeine in coffee, (and tea), also acts as a diuretic, causing the body to lose water and flush away valuable minerals such as calcium. High caffeine intakes have also been associated with osteoporosis, which is a major cause of the weakening of bones in post-menopausal women. It is also addictive, and in high amounts can cause tremors, sweating and palpitations. Sudden withdrawal, however, can cause severe headaches, lethargy and irritability.

One teaspoon of instant coffee has an energy value of 2 kcalories, 190ml (average cup) of freshly ground coffee provides 4 kcalories.

Coriander *(Coriandrum sativum, - Dhania, Chinese parsley, Cilantro)*

Coriander is one of the oldest known herbs used by Man. A flavouring and medicine for over 3,000 years, it has been well documented through the ages, from ancient Sanskrit text, to the Ebers Papyrus and even the Book of Exodus in the Old Testament, where its seed was likened to the *manna* provided by God. *Manna* is probably the secretion left by a certain type of insect on twigs of tamarisk which is still gathered today by the Bedouin. It is gathered early, before ants can get to it and it is said that one man can collect at least 4lb each morning. The same substance is also found in Persia where it is mixed with honey and flour and made into cakes.

Coriander's Latin, and hence European, name is derived from the Greek word, *koris*, meaning bug, as the plant was perceived to posses an insect-like smell, reminiscent of that given off by bed bugs. The plant is a member of the Umbelliferae family, hailing originally from North Africa, and was brought into Western Europe by the taste-loving Ancient Romans.

Despite its supposed 'nasty' smell, the herb's leaf has been used extensively in Mediterranean, Chinese and Southeast Asian cooking since the earliest times. It was extremely popular during Elizabethan times, especially in sallets, and is now currently enjoying a revival, thinly disguised as 'discovery', primarily with the current interest in the 'Mediterranean Diet', seen to be a powerful weapon in the modern quest for the 'perfect diet'.

The small round, light brown seeds, sweet and spicy, with a hint of citron, are a feature of North African, Indian and Indonesian cooking. In Europe, they have traditionally been used to flavour breads, cakes and liqueurs, and, of course, are an indispensable pickling spice at harvest-time. In large quantities, coriander leaf has a slightly narcotic effect and it was this that earned it the early European tag of '*dizzycorn*', after observing its effects on grazing animals that had strayed into patches of the herb. Perhaps this same attribute went some way in endowing the plant with aphrodisiac qualities. It was regularly used in love potions in the Middle Ages and is mentioned in the 1001 Arabian Nights as a 'love herb'.

In European love potions, it was mixed with dill and was said to fill whoever drank it with desire, especially if the coriander had been picked in the last quarter of the moon. The seeds were also burned in incense, put into sweet dishes and carried in 'love sachets'. The Ancient Chinese believed that eating coriander brought immortality.

In 17th century Paris an amazing 'cure-all' liqueur was produced using coriander - *Eau de canes*, which was used both as a tonic and as a perfumed toilet water. In folklore and country witchcraft, its astrological ruler is Mars, and it has been used in 'magical' rites for healing and love.

Medicinal: In herbal healing, its powers in aiding the digestion, when used internally, have long been recognised, easing colic and flatulence and it was once used in proprietary brands of infant colic water. Its inner cleansing powers don't stop there, though, as both seeds and leaves are used both to strengthen the urinary tract and help in the treatment of urinary tract infections. Externally, the essential oil of the coriander seed is used in therapeutic massage to ease rheumatism and swollen joints. Nutritionally, 1 teaspoonful of coriander seed is equal to 1.8g in weight, it also releases 5kcalories of energy and contains vitamins B1 and B2, niacin, sodium, phosphorous, calcium, iron, magnesium and zinc.

As with most of the so-called 'curry spices', coriander is quite a good anti-oxidant, in both seed and leaf form, able to help in countering high blood pressure, aiding in the regulation of heart action and body fluid levels, as well as in combating the formation of the free radicals which are believed to trigger cancers.

Cucumber *(Cucumis sativus)*

Cucumber is one of the oldest plants known to man and one with which he has enjoyed an almost constant love-hate relationship. It is a native of southern India and cultivated for the last 4,000 years or so.

The Children of Israel bemoaned their lot after leaving Mount Sinai, declaring that they missed the cucumber which they had eaten so freely in the land of Egypt (Numbers, 11:5). Isaiah (1:8), on the other hand, seems to see it in a different light, likening the daughter of Zion to '*a lodge in a cucumber field, like a besieged city.*'

The Greek and Roman cultures were apparently very fond of the cucumber, Theophrastus mentioning three varieties which were grown in Greece during his time, and Apicius uses them as a patina, or paste, in salads and as a vegetable. The Emperor Tiberius was fond of them and insisted on having them, home grown, in moveable frames.

They came to France in the 9th century, taking their time to get across the Channel, reaching us in around the mid-14th century and where, for at least five centuries, they were regarded with a great deal of suspicion. The Columbian Exchange, meanwhile, saw the cucumber travelling the Atlantic, with Columbus taking the cucumber to Haiti on his trip of 1494. The vegetable can hardly have been a surprise to the New World, as several members of the same family, *Curcubita*; pumpkin, squash and pattypan were already well established as food crops.

John Gerard, author of *Herball*, or *General Historie of Plantes* in 1597 saw the healing potential in cucumber and recommended eating a pottage, or soup, made with cucumber and oatmeal three times a day, to combat a fiery and pimply complexion, to be accompanied by a treatment using a facewash, the principle constituent of which was cucumber.

Culpeper, who intertwined his herbalism with astrology, assigned the cucumber to the moon - cooling and healing and herballists, even now recommend a slice of cucumber to take away the initial sting, and bring down the skin temperature, after a minor burn.

As an object of culinary desire, however, it was making less of an impact. A sixteenth century axiom reflected the opinion of a great many that cucumber could be positively fatal: "*Raw cucumber makes the churchyards prosperous.*" They didn't receive any better press by the time of Boswell. In his The Journal of a Tour to the Hebrides, with Samuel Johnson, LL.D., James Boswell reflects upon the cucumber: "*it has been a common saying of physicians in England, that a cucumber should be well sliced, and dressed with pepper and vinegar, and then thrown out, as good for nothing.*"

Ironically, the English, who still maintained until quite recently that the cucumber was tasteless and indigestible, placed the cucumber at the very core of that very English institution, 'High Tea'. Sliced ultra-thinly, settling like gauze between barely buttered leaves of crustless bread they provide the centrepiece, even now, of such famous gatherings as the Buckingham Palace garden parties.

Medicinal: Ayurveda sees cucumber, called *soukas* in Sanskrit, as cooling, and many a spicy Indian meal has benefited from the foil of sliced cucumber, nestling in a cooling yoghurt, as a natural foil to the more piquant spicing. The seeds are also used in Ayurveda to expel tapeworm. Unani Tibb recommends it for kidney and heart problems and credits it with being able to dissolve the uric acid accumulations which lead to kidney and bladder stones.

Cucumber is, botanically: a berry; a simple fleshy fruit, enclosing a seed (or seeds), not having a separate, peelable skin. It contains sterols, mainly in the skin, which have been shown to lower bad cholesterol when tested on laboratory animals.

Cumin *(Cumninum cyminum, - Jeera)*

This member of the *umbelliferae* family has been cultivated in the Mediterranean region since prehistory, and the Greeks set up an early trade in the spice with Egypt, where it probably originated. Well preserved seeds have been found in the tombs of the Pharaohs and it is mentioned in the early texts of the region: The *Ebers Papyrus*; The *Old and New Testaments*; and *Historia Naturalis*, part of the great encyclopaedia compiled by Pliny the Elder in the 1st Century.

Probably the earliest evidence of the seed's use in Western Europe has been on the west coast of France where archaeologists have discovered that the native Celts there were rather fond of fish baked in cumin.

In Eastern medicine, cumin was used by the ancient hakims in virtually all their compound formulae, as it was believed that the spice was one of the few substances which would pass through the digestive process virtually unscathed, to release its properties directly at the site of the liver. In the Eastern holistic medical systems of Ayurveda and Tibb, cumin is used as a digestive, to aid in easing stomach cramps and colic and it was also used for this purpose in Norman monasteries in around the 8th century AD.

Both the Ancient Greek and Roman cultures regarded cumin seeds as a symbol of miserliness and greed, and the first century Roman Emperor, Antoninus Pius, was nicknamed 'The Cumin' because of his parsimonious nature.

Nicholas Culpeper, the herbalist who combined botany and astrology in his 1652 work, *The English Physician*, saw cumin as more positive and strengthening, assigning the planet Mars as its ruler. All across Medieval Europe, cumin was regarded in common lore as being able to safeguard against infidelity. It was used in love potions to keep a lover faithful and, in Germany, a bride would carry cumin, dill and salt in her pocket during her marriage ceremony to ensure a faithful and long marriage. The Germans also associated cumin with security, believing that anything containing it would be safe from theft, and baked it into loaves of bread to prevent it being stolen by wood spirits.

Other linked traditions existed throughout northern Europe. In one such custom, a young man, leaving his home to join the army, would share a glass of cumin-flavoured wine with his sweetheart, then would take with him a cumin-flavoured loaf, baked by the girl, to ensure his safe return.

Cumin, like all other herbs and spices, has been used throughout history in the practice of folk magic, where it is used principally as an ingredient in incense when preparing for protection, exorcism of evil, fidelity and to combat theft. Its culinary uses are many, and cumin is a popular flavouring spice world-wide.

The seeds, roughly 5mm long, ridged like those of its cousin, caraway, have a warm, strong aroma and a slightly bitter taste. Most of the recipes from the Indian subContinent relies on a mixture of cumin and coriander seeds as a basis for their spicing, and the northern yoghurt drinks and preparations invariably have a sprinkling of cumin to add that little extra touch. It is used extensively in Middle Eastern food, in dishes such as *Kibbeh* (fried meatballs); Northern European foods such as sauerkraut, sausages, stews, breads, biscuits, cheese and alcoholic drinks; Mexican *Chorizo* (spicy sausages), spiced sauces such as *Mole* and *Chile* are flavoured with it.

Medicinal: As with many of the other 'curry' spices, this combination of antioxidants may be helpful in combating many of the 'modern' diseases such as stroke, high blood pressure and cancers: Vitamin C and the carotenoid, vitamin A, are powerful antioxidants, preventing the formation of the free radicals which cause cell damage that can lead to ageing, cancer and a raised level of LDL or 'bad' cholesterol levels; vitamin B1 (Thiamin), which helps in the proper metabolism of foods; minerals like potassium, which helps the body to regulate body fluids, heart rhythm, and aid in the maintenance of normal blood pressure rates. Nutritionally, 1tsp of ground seed weighs around 2.1g, giving an energy value of 8 kcalories and contains vitamins A, B1, B2, niacin, Vitamin C, sodium, phosphorous, potassium, calcium, iron and zinc.

Curry Leaves *(Murraya koenigii - kari patta)*
Small, shiny, dark green leaves of a small tree which belongs to the citrus family. The tree is found wild

in much of South Asia and the leaves are used as a herb to flavour food in the Southern and Western coastal regions of India in particular. Fragrant and unique in flavour, they can be fried with the initial spicing preparation or added at the very last stage for a fuller impact.

100g raw curry leaves contain 88 kcalories, 9.7g protein, 1.7g fat, 7.7g carbohydrate, 811mg calcium, 3.1mg iron, 6000μg carotene 0.08mg vitamin B1, 0.21mg vitamin B2, 2.3mg niacin, 12mg vitamin C

Dates *(Phoenix dactylifera)*

The date has grown abundantly in the 'Fertile Crescent' in North Africa and Middle East since prehistoric times and was to become a staple for the peoples of the region. Cultivation goes back to at least 3000 BC and, without the date palm, the Bedouin of North Africa could not exist.

The fruit, eaten with bread and camel milk forms the basis of their diet; the scooped out trunks are used for irrigation; the palm fronds for building enclosures and fuel; the leaflets for making mats and baskets; the fibre for wadding and mattress stuffing; the sap for wine-making.

Use of the date palm was recorded on Assyrian and Babylonian monuments and in their texts, and in the text of *Shu-Sin*, dated at around 2050 BC, 3rd Dynasty of Ur, there is a mention of large date plantations. Date stones have been found at excavations in Northwest India, which have been estimated to have been from around 2500 BC.

The Ancient Egyptians used them fresh, fried or pressed and formed into cakes. The Romans, too, were extremely fond of dates, which they used as a sweetener, stuffed as 'sweetmeats', and made into pastes and sauces to accompany meats and fish. Dates had reached China by the Tang Dynasty (AD 618-907), taken by traders from Persia. As a basic food of the region, the date is mentioned a lot in the Bible and the Koran credits the date with having sustained Mary throughout her labour when she delivered Christ.

The date palm is extremely hardy, and is able to grow in sandy soil at temperatures in excess of 50°C. It is a very reliable producer, the female trees first coming to fruit when four years old and can continue for 70 years or more, growing to heights of around 30m (100ft), although producers tend to cut down trees when they exceed 15m (50ft) and reaching the fruit, which grows at the very top, becomes difficult.

The fruits are oval, grooved and yellow in colour, and hang down between the fronds in bunches of around 40, each strand bearing some 30 dates. With 4-5 bunches ripening at a time, and average yield for a tree is around 50kg (100lb) fruit per annum, although a good tree can produce two or even three times that amount.

Ayurveda classifies the date as being sweet; an energy giving food which is mildly laxative and which is said to encourage sperm production.

A large proportion of the harvest is allowed to ripen to the *tamer* stage, and sometimes sun-dried before being packed and shipped. Traditional uses are as a hand-held fruit, date syrup, dibbs, which is used in making date bread, *legaimat* (doughnut cake) and *mahmer* (sweet rice). The dates are also processed to make preserves and the countries of origin are continually researching to find new food products. One such is a weaning food called tamrina which has been developed in Iraq.

Nutritionally, 100g of dates gives 270 kcalories energy and contain protein, fats, carbohydrates in the form of sugar, fibre, calcium, iron, sodium, vitamin A and vitamin B1 (thiamin).

Dill *(Anethum graveolens)*

A member of the umbelliferae family, dill probably originated in the eastern Mediterranean and was then given a wider influence by the Ancient Romans. Its specific name, *graveolens*, is a description of its 'heavy' scent, the generic name already having been used for it by the Ancient Romans. It is has been in use since antiquity; well-known to the Ancient Egyptians, Greeks, Romans, Persians and Indians.

Introduced into Europe during the Middle Ages, it quickly became most popular in Scandinavia, where it is now an almost indispensable flavouring. Some sources believe that this is where it got its common name, from *dilla*, an Old Norse word meaning 'to lull'. This is undoubtedly a reference to its calming qualities, which have taken the major role in the herb's use over the centuries.

Dill contains a volatile oil which calms and settles the stomach, easing colic and flatulence and was a principle ingredient in gripe water preparations for infants and it also enjoys a reputation for encouraging milk flow in nursing mothers. Herbalists also use it to relieve spasms and convulsions and to stimulate menstrual flow.

Dill seeds were once known as 'Meeting House Seeds' in this country, as they were chewed during very long church sermons to stave off hunger pains and to still audibly rumbling stomachs. In country magic, a bath scented with dill seeds was believed to draw your lover to you and, although supposedly used by witches, dill seed was also said to hamper them, protecting the bearer from evil, it was also with this belief that sachets containing the seeds were placed in the cradles of new-born infants.

Dill leaves are delicate and lacy with a sharp, slightly sweet tang that tends to disappear with drying. Traditionally used with fish and vegetable salads in Western Europe, dill has a wider use in Scandinavia and Poland, where it is used rather like parsley or chives in this country, flavouring soured cream, sauces, pickled fish and vegetables. The dill plant, complete with its ripe seeds, is a classic ingredient in pickled gherkins

In the East, however, dill really comes into its own, especially in Parsee cooking, here it can be used to such stunning effect with shellfish and lobster, and to perfectly complement the lentils and vegetables in their classic dish, Dhansak.

Nutritionally, 100g fresh dill gives 28.48 kcalories energy and contains carbohydrate, fibre, sodium, protein and iron. One tsp dill seeds equals 13.6 kcalories and contains fat, carbohydrate, fibre, sodium, protein and iron.

Eggs *("A hen is only an egg's way of making another egg." Samuel Butler (1835-1902))*

Which came first, the chicken or the egg? Samuel Butler obviously thought he had the age-old riddle worked out. But he may have had a point: eggs have existed since the evolution of sexual reproduction in multi-celled organisms around 1 billion years ago; birds first appeared 150 million years ago; *Gallus domesticus*, the hen whose eggs we most commonly use, is a relative latecomer, only arriving on the scene some 4,500 years ago.

The ancestors of the hen lived in the jungles of Southeast Asia and India and were probably initially bred for use in cockfighting, one of the world's oldest 'sports', which dates back to at least the 5th century BC in India. The bird has also been used since earliest times as a means of divination and as a valuable sacrificial offering with which to appease a god.

Food use, for both flesh and eggs, would probably have followed quite quickly and, as each female chick is born bearing 5,000 eggs, 200-250 of which will be laid during her lifetime, the bird would have been regarded as a better source than most other species. A pheasant, for example, only lays between 60-80 and a goose a mere 20-30.

The egg is, of course, the perfect fertility symbol and it has been used in spring rituals since prehistoric times. Egg-rolling at Easter, for example, pre-dates Christianity by many centuries and was originally part of the spring rites, performed to transfer the eggs' fertility to the soil, thus ensuring a good harvest. The Christian faith added a further spiritual layer to the practice, attempting also to squash the pagan associations in the process, by explaining the practice as being a re-enactment of the rolling away of the stone which had sealed Christ in His tomb, allowing Him to rise again and save mankind.

The Romans loved eggs and Apicius, the Delia Smith of his day, gave instructions on how to boil and fry eggs and even included a recipe for an early type of custard.

La Ménagier de Paris and *The Forme of Cury*, cookbooks from the 14th century, include recipes for omelettes and custards which are very similar to the modern versions. The Victorians developed a craze for chicken breeding afte an exotic variety – the *cochin* – appeared from China and hundreds of new breeds then appeared in a very short space of time.

Industrialisation brought even more changes: birds born in incubators, fed on a diet of chemicals, living in cramped cages which caused deformities and with egg production forced up to between 250-290 eggs per bird. However, pressure from modern consumer groups seems to have started to take effect, with more and more 'free range' and organic eggs appearing on supermarket shelves. Eggs received a bad press during the salmonella crisis, but the slow change in farming methods and a public awareness of when eggs can be a risk, have helped to ease many minds.

They were also attacked for being high in fat and cholesterol. In fact, an average egg contains only about 6g fat, about 7% of the average person's daily intake and 65% of this fat is the 'healthy' unsaturated fat. As to the cholesterol, studies have shown that, as long as the whole diet is low in saturated fats, the dietary cholesterol in eggs has very little effect on blood cholesterol levels.

Eggs are rich in lecithin which is good for the nerves and metabolism and are rich in protein. 100g boiled hen's egg contains 75% water and gives 147 kcalories energy. The same weight also provides 12.5g protein, 10.8g fats, 3.1g saturated fatty acids, 57mg calcium, 1.9mg iron, 140mg sodium, 190μg vitamin A, 0.07mg vitamin B1 (thamin).

Fennel *(Foeniculum vulgare, Foeniculum dulce, - saunf)*

The Latin name is derived from the phrase meaning 'little hay', *(foenum - hay)*, describing its very fine, strand-like leaves. The original wild, bitter fennel, *(vulgare)*, is thought to have originated in the Mediterranean and has been used in a culinary capacity since ancient times.

Medicinal: It was soon discovered, however, that it held quite valuable medicinal properties and it has been used throughout recorded history for quite a variety of purposes: for easing flatulence and constipation; as a digestive; in infant colic cures and gripe waters; as a breath freshener; a hang-over cure; even as a slimming aid, the seeds being chewed to ward off hunger pangs. The plant is a mild stimulant and a wash of fennel leaves was used at one time as an eye wash. Hindu and Chinese medical texts recommend fennel as an antidote to snakebite and Indian women have used fennel for centuries to stimulate milkflow during nursing.

Not surprisingly, it was cultivated by the Egyptians, Greeks and Romans for both its stems and seeds, as it is also totally edible, leaf, stem, seed and root. Pliny recommended it as a virtual cure-all and Apicius, the author of the only cookbook to have survived from the Classical Age, mentions its use as a seasoning, a herb and as a vegetable in stews.

Sweet fennel (*dulce*) contains more anethole than its bitter relative, giving it more of an aniseed flavour. It was mentioned in an edict issued by Charlemagne in the 9th century and has been a popular flavouring in fish dishes in Italy and France, including in the Provençal dish, where fish are grilled *au fenouil*, over burning fennel, which imparts a characteristic smokiness. Several Anglo-Saxon recipes also used fennel, especially in those using salted fish, traditionally eaten during Lent. This fulfilled the dual role of both checking flatulence and constipation and also of making the fish more palatable. The third member of the family is Florence fennel or finocchio, the stumpy, thick stalked variety which is used as a vegetable and is very popular in Italy.

Culpeper, the botanist who combined herbalism with astrology, assigned fennel to the planet Mercury.

Anglo Saxon superstition utilised fennel as a ward against evil and disease and it is listed as one of the nine sacred Saxon herbs. It was hung from windows and doors to keep away all harm and evil spirits, small amounts were placed in keyholes to prevent ghosts entering a house, and cows' udders were smeared with a paste made from fennel to prevent their milk from being bewitched.

The herb figures strongly in Greek mythology, too. The Titan, Prometheus was said to have brought the gift of fire to Mankind, hidden in the hollow stem of the fennel plant. As a punishment for this, Zeus ordered that he be chained to a mountainside where his liver was eaten by an eagle. Each night the liver grew back, and each day the eagle feasted again, a torture from which he was eventually rescued by the great hero, Hercules. The links with certain elements in this story of one of the earliest benefactors of Man led to its use in rituals for purification, protection and healing.

Medicinal: thought to somehow defuse harmful carcinogens in alcohol and tobacco that cause cancer of the oesophagus; and niacin - which recent studies have shown may help to prevent certain cancers and lower overall blood cholesterol levels.

The minerals in fennel are sodium, which helps to maintain body fluid balance; potassium, which is good for blood pressure and normal heart rhythm; iron, necessary in the production of red blood cells; magnesium, needed to help the body utilise vitamin C and calcium in the diet and may help in relieving the symptoms of pre-menstrual syndrome; zinc, important in cell growth and repair and the proper functioning of the male reproductive system; a fairly high amount of calcium, which is not only important for bone and tooth growth and maintenance, but is necessary in the proper function of every other bodycell.

Nutritionally, 1 teaspoon of ground fennel weighs around 2g and equals 7 kcalories. It contains some vitamin A, vitamin B1 - good for the nervous system and eyes; vitamin B2 – calcium has also been the subject of various health studies in recent years which have claimed to show a beneficial effect of calcium in helping colonic cancer, heart cholesterol levels, high blood pressure, osteoporosis, pre-menstrual syndrome, and stroke. Maybe Pliny was right!

Fenugreek *(Trigonella foenum-graecum - Bird's Foot, Methi)*.

This leguminous native of southern Europe and Asia is known to be one of the oldest-known plants to be cultivated, rather than gathered from the wild; ancient Egyptian papyri record its routine use medicinally and in the manufacture of the incense, *Kuphi*, used for fumigation and in the embalming process.

Its modern western name, fenugreek is actually an abbreviation of the Latin specific botanical name, which is literally translated as 'Greek hay'. This is generally thought to have been a reference to the practice of using it as a fodder plant and as a booster for inferior quality hay. Both the ancient Romans, in around the 2nd century BC, and Charlemagne, in AD 812, are recorded as doing this, and it is a practice still carried out in the Middle East, although for horses, not milk cattle, as the scent of the fenugreek is carried through to the milk. Its folk-name, *Bird's Foot*, is a descriptive, for the shape of its tri-foliate leaves.

Medicinal: Medicinally, its value has been known since the times of the ancient Greeks, and it was introduced into European apothecaries some time before the 9th century by Benedictine monks.

Over the centuries, it has been found that the high mucilage content of the seeds make them a soothing expectorant for bronchitis and chest complaints; that the mashed seeds make an excellent poultice for skin problems and boils; fenugreek wash will ease mouth ulcers and blistered lips.

The plant has been used in the oldest medical regimes to stimulate lactation in both humans and animals. Unani Tibb, the system of botanical medicine and dietetics developed by the Persian physician Avicenna, lists fenugreek as being an effective curative for coughs, tuberculosis, bronchitis, fevers, sore throat, neuralgia, sciatica, swollen glands, skin eruptions, wounds tumours, sores, asthma and emphysema. In fact, in Eastern medicine, it is prized so highly that The Prophet Mohammed issued the dictum: *"If you knew the value of fenugreek, you would pay its weight in gold."*

During the Middle Ages, fenugreek acquired something of a reputation as an aphrodisiac and was used by 'witches' and folk healers in love potions and as a cure for impotence. Modern chemical analysis has actually detected the presence of a substance, diosgenin, that acts in a similar way to the body's own sex hormones, so, whilst I don't have any actual personal experience as to its efficacy, perhaps they were actually onto something!

This reputation probably led to its subsequent use as a hair tonic; modern Chinese herbalists still recommend its use for impotence and for restoring hair growth. and it is still used in some conditioning powders for horse coats.

Nutritionally, 1 teaspoon of dried fenugreek seed weighs around 3.7g and contains 12 kcalories. It is high in protein and carbohydrate and is cholesterol free. It is a source of vitamins B1, B2, niacin, vitamin C, and the minerals sodium, phosphorous, potassium, calcium, iron, magnesium and zinc. The seed is also higher in folic acid content, by weight, than either dried yeast or liver.

Because it is both a seed and a legume, fenugreek is quite high in protein, elevating it in some countries to food status, not merely a spice. Its nutritional value is also enhanced by sprouting it, like mung or alfalfa seeds, a process which lowers their calorific value and increases their vitamin C content. The differences are quite slight when one considers how much one would have to eat, though, so it is probably best to simply see them as a way to make fresh salad a little more interesting.

Fenugreek is also a vital part of the cooking of the Indian sub-continent, the slightly bitter, 'gold-nugget' seeds giving that characteristic 'curry' taste and aroma. Middle Eastern cookery, too, has its uses for this highly adaptable plant and its products: the seeds being roasted to provide a coffee substitute and also ground with sesame seed to make halva. Another unusual use for fenugreek is as the main flavouring component in synthetic maple syrup.

Today, the largest producers of fenugreek are India, Egypt, the Lebanon and Argentina, although ever-growing demand from a public which is now experimenting with Eastern and Mediterranean cuisine is ensuring a better supply of the locally grown herb.

Personally, we love the stuff. From my favourite Methi restaurant dishes, which employ it in the dried leaf Kasuri Methi form, to its use, simply, as a roasted spice, to enhance that usually bland vegetable, the cauliflower. As regular consumers, we can assure you that our hair is thick and grows very quickly and we very rarely suffer from any type of chest complaint.

The aphrodisiac properties? We couldn't possibly comment - you'll just have to find out for yourself!

Fig *(Ficus carica)*

A member of the mulberry family with pear-shaped, green, brown or purple fruit, it is a native of Asia Minor, a descendant of the wild caprifig, imported into the Mediterranean region and used by the

Egyptians 6,000 years ago. The wild fig is small and dry, and relies on an insect called the '*fig wasp*' for reproduction and so cultivation began early in prehistory in order to provide a better fruit.

Tomb paintings indicate that figs were being cultivated in Egypt by around 1900 BC and by 1500 BC the crop had spread to Crete. By the time of the Roman Empire, new types of fig appeared which did not depend on the *fig wasp* for fertilisation and this was probably when what we know today as the 'common fig' appeared. Pliny (c.AD 77) mentioned 29 varieties of fig known to Rome.

In Ancient Greece and Rome, figs were a staple food, valued for their high sugar and energy content. The Romans especially considered it a symbol of plenty, leading some classical scholars to interpret the use of the fig leaf on statuary as not being so much a preservation of modesty as perhaps a bawdy in-joke. The Greek fig trade gave us the word sycophant, meaning 'one who shows the fig', or someone who has tried to gain favour by informing on fig smugglers, and it is still a very insulting phrase in the Mediterranean countries - 'showing the fig' is even worse, being an obscene gesture with the thumb.

Ironically, for a fruit which has been so consistently associated with the 'baser passions', it was a cleric, Cardinal Pole, who introduced the fig into this country in the early 16th century. A few years later, Cortez introduced the tree to Mexico, from whence it slowly spread northwards, reaching North America by the end of the 18th century.

Dr Andrew Boorde, (1490-1549), a doctor and unfrocked suffragan bishop of Chichester, also associated figs with the earthier side of life, stating in his *A Dyetary of Helth* that they "*doth stere a man to veneryous actes, for they doth urge and increase the sede of generacyon. And also they doth prouoke a man to sweate; wherefore they doth engender lyce.*" Dr Boorde knew a thing or two about such things- he was imprisoned shortly before his death for keeping three prostitutes in his chambers at Winchester. It is not known if he was sweating at the time. Unani Tibb lists the fig as being a laxative; good for curing constipation. Fresh fig is also recommended, split open, as a poultice.

Dried figs, whose nutrients are concentrated around six times those of fresh, are a rich source of potassium and good for calcium, iron and magnesium. The laxative action is provided by the insoluble fibre contained in the fig which helps in moving food through the digestive system. They also contain *pectin*, soluble fibre, which can help to reduce blood cholesterol levels. On the down side, dried figs are prone to mould contamination which contain potentially cancer- promoting toxins, and lots of sugar; high in calories and bad for the teeth.

100g dried figs, without stones give 209 kcalories of energy, 3.3g protein, 1.5g fat, 48.6g carbohydrate in the form of sugar, 6.9g fibre, 230mg calcium, 3.9mg iron, 57mg sodium, 10μg vitamin A, 0.07mg vitamin B1 and 1mg vitamin C.

Galangal *(Alpinia galanga, Alpinia officinarum)*

The spice galangal is the rhizome of an herbaceous plant which is native to China. Similar in appearance and uses to ginger, to which it is related, there are two main types: greater, Laos (*A. galanga*), found in Malaysia and Indonesia, and lesser, Kenchur (*A. offciniarum*), found in Indonesia.

The Latin generic name was given to commemorate Prospero Alpini (1553-1617), an Italian botanist who catalogued as well as described exotic plants. The common name is an adaptation of the Chinese Liang-tiang.

Used in this country from the time of the Crusades, having been brought back from the Middle East, it warrants a mention in Chaucer's *Canterbury Tales*, and is used quite frequently in *The Forme of Cury*, a recipe book written by the cooks of Richard II in 1390.

As with all exotic ingredients, galangal enjoyed a reputation for being powerful in European 'magic'. It was used for protection and health; to encourage lust and desire; to attract money; to enhance and strengthen psychic powers; for breaking evil or malevolent spells.

It has been used medicinally and possesses similar properties to those of ginger: stimulant and digestive.

Garlic *(Allium sativum)*

Its English name is derived from two Anglo-Saxon words - *gar*, a spear, and *leac* (from the same root as leek), a plant - because of its spear-like shape.

Whole books have been dedicated to this pungent bulb and, since time immemorial, it has been used for ritual healing and culinary purposes. Chinese texts from around 3000 BC described it as "the healing plant", showing a long understanding of its benefits to health. The Egyptians are believed to have worshipped garlic and clay model bulbs were found in Tutankhamun's tomb. According to Herodotus, the Egyptians also fed the slave builders of their Great Pyramid at Cheops a daily supply of garlic to ensure strength and stamina and documented its use as a remedy for coughs and colds in the Ebers Papyrus (around 1550 BC). The Romans, too, valued it as a stamina booster and fed it to their soldiers just before battle to give extra strength.

The Ancient Greeks used it to treat gangrene and Hippocrates, the father of medicine used garlic vapours to treat cervical cancers in around 300 BC. They also believed that it would protect the soul as well as the body, and would leave offerings at cross-roads to placate their goddess of the Underworld, Hecate. It was so important in Greek society that a section of the market in Athens was named *ta skoroda* - the garlic.

In the lst century AD Dioscorides wrote about the ability of garlic to de-clog veins and arteries. However, it seems that beyond a use in medicine and as a strengthening addition to the diet of workers and soldiers, the upper classes resisted it. Apicius, the writer of the only cookery book to have survived from classical times, used it very rarely and then only for food for the infirm.

In the Middle Ages, European monks chewed cloves of garlic, or *'the stinking rose'*, as it was then called, to ward off the plague and in World Wars I and II, when antibiotics were not available, garlic poultices were used on open wounds to prevent further infection.

Garlic has had its detractors in droves. In India, Brahmins, the priest caste and the Jain sect are forbidden to eat it, as it promotes 'base passions'. The Prophet Mohammed was said to have waved it away, saying that he was a man who had close contact with others.

In China, in the 1st century AD, Hsuan-Ch'ung issued a rule stating that anyone who wished to eat garlic should do so outside the town. A Turkish legend says that garlic first sprouted where the Devil touched the earth and, in the 14th century, King Alfonso IV of Castille detested the stuff so much that he formed a society of knights who renounced it, on oath. Any knight who had a trace of garlic on his breath was exiled from court for one month.

Mrs Beeton mentioned garlic just once in her *Book of Household Management*, to say that it was "*generally considered offensive and it is the most acrimonious in its taste*" and it seems to be a popular opinion that, until Elizabeth David and her introduction of Mediterranean food to the middle classes in the 1950s, even the mention of garlic and kitchen in the same breath would set the delicate British aswoon.

On the other hand, there are plenty of those who cannot get enough of it. The self-proclaimed Garlic Capital of the World, Gilroy, in California, attracts thousands annually to sample everything, from soups to ice-creams, made from garlic.

A great medical school of the Middle Ages, at Salerno, in Italy, saw both sides of the argument, admitting that it worked against poisons - at a price: "*Since garlic then hath powers to save from death, Bear with it though it makes unsavoury breath*".

Ayurveda, the South Indian study of life forces, calls garlic *Rasona* or 'one taste missing', as described in the ancient Sanskrit texts. It possesses 5 of the 6 tastes: pungent, sweet, salty, bitter and astringent - only sour is missing. It credits it with being able to expel wind, loosen phlegm, as a bacterium, an antiseptic and as an aphrodisiac. Unani Tibb, the Persian medical and dietary regimen established by Avicenna over 1,000 years ago agrees, adding beneficial effects against dysentery, cholera, typhoid, circulation and heart function and urinary stones.

Herbalists use garlic to ease a variety of complaints, including asthma, nasal congestion, warts and verrucas, acne and arthritis. Culpeper, the author of *The English Physician* (1652), noted that garlic had a strong and offensive smell and that it was "*...the poor man's treacle, it being a remedy for all diseases and hurts*".

When the garlic is cut or crushed, allowing the compound, *alliin* to combine with an enzyme, also found in garlic, *allinase*, to form the malodorous *allicin*. A similar process in its cousin *allium*, the onion, produces the tear-provoking reaction when cut. *Allicin* may smell bad, but this is just about the only antisocial thing about it. This compound, in turn, is transformed into diallyl sulphide, which is largely responsible for garlic's medicinal qualities: antibiotic, antifungal, bacteriostatic, bactericidal and a biological insecticide.

Garlic also contains trace minerals; calcium, phosphorous and iron and is rich in vitamins B1 (thiamin) and vitamin C. Add to this the results from ongoing modern scientific research that show that garlic may deactivate carcinogens, suppressing the growth of tumours; that modern research has shown that it lowers blood cholesterol levels, preventing heart attacks, strokes and blood clots; that it promotes good circulation, and one could almost forgive its malodorous tendency.

Over 1,000 studies have been carried out to investigate the beneficial properties of garlic and new results are published on an almost daily basis, adding, it seems, more and more benefits to the list. Scientists at the University of North Carolina recently announced the results of research that indicated that people who eat raw or cooked garlic regularly, face only half the risk of stomach cancer and two-thirds the risk of colon cancer.

It is absorbed so quickly and effectively into the bloodstream, that it is said that if you rub the sole of your foot with a garlic clove, the smell will be detectable on your breath after just two minutes! Perhaps it is this quality that is supposed to ward off vampires, according to folklore. Luckily, there is a counter measure to the smell problem - just chew a sprig of fresh parsley for sweet breath after eating garlic - as long as you're not afraid of vampires, that is!

Ginger *(Zingiber officinale)*

One of the so-called '*Wet Trinity*' of Indian cooking, ginger, takes it Latin generic name, *Zingiber*, from the Sanskrit for 'horn-shaped' -, singabela, emphasising this rhizome's similarity in appearance to deer antlers.

It is thought to have originated in Southeast Asia, but this is difficult to track back accurately, as it is now unknown in its wild state. Cultivated since the 6th century BC by first the Chinese and then the Indians, ginger made its way, courtesy of Arab traders, into southern Europe well before the rise of the Roman Empire. It soon became firmly established in both Europe's kitchen and its medicine chest. Its importance in medicine has been recorded in the very earliest texts; The Koran, The Talmud and The Bible all mention ginger. Confucius wrote about it in his Analects and the Greek physician, Dioscorides, listed ginger as an antidote to poisoning, as a digestive, and as being warming to the stomach in *De Materia Medica*. In Chinese medicine, ginger is *lyang*, hot, and is considered to be good for ailments associated with cold weather, such as colds, chills and poor circulation.

Ginger certainly warmed English hearts very quickly: almost every sauce recipe to survive from the Middle Ages lists it as an ingredient and Tudor England loved it, making it into sweetmeats, cakes and patties. It was said to have been a particular favourite of Henry VIII - perhaps because of its reputation at that time of being a powerful aphrodisiac!

Gingerbread became popular in Elizabethan times and it became a popular practice in Victorian society to nibble crystallised ginger after a meal when it was disclosed that Chinese medicine recommended it for the digestion. British country folklore and 'white witchcraft' used it in a similar way to galangal in 'magic' spells, to enhance and strengthen their power and Culpeper, the astrologer-herbalist, assigned its ruler as the planet Mars.

Medicinal: Ayurveda uses ginger in both dried (*sunthi*) and fresh (*adraka*) forms. It is used for its warming effect and can be used by all three doshas, or life forces. It is said to strengthen the stomach, promote the secretion of saliva, aid digestion and is used as a decongestant and anti-inflammatory. It is also used to treat colds and chills, rheumatism, diarrhoea and constipation. Unani Tibb also uses the rhizome as a digestive and to counter nausea and chest ailments.

Modern science has, of course, analysed it very closely, as it does all foodstuff. One teaspoon of dried, ground ginger weighs approximately 1.8g and has an energy value of 6 kcal. It is high in carbohydrate and has no cholesterol. It does, however, contain vitamins A, Bl, B2, niacin, sodium, phosphorous, potassium, calcium, iron, magnesium, copper and zinc.

Fresh root ginger is high in vitamin C, a powerful antioxidant which helps to boost the immune system and is probably one of the reasons that it is one of several foodstuffs currently being investigated by several U.S. cancer research programmes for its anticarcinogenic properties. Its vitamin C content is almost certainly the reason that it was used by ancient Chinese sailors to prevent scurvy.

Ginger has been used to help eliminate toxins from the body, as it promotes sweating and stimulates the circulation, and its antinausea properties are well-known, having long been used for morning sickness in pregnancy, travel sickness and, more recently, to help combat the nausea associated with chemotherapy.

Externally, too, ginger is a potent weapon and is a major ingredient in anti-spasmodic rubbing oils and is said to relieve aching muscles and cramps and a warm ginger compress will relax menstrual cramps and pains.

Herbs

Early Man found that by using the rather risky process of trial and error, he could expand the range of plants that he could utilise for culinary, medicinal and preservative purposes.

The oldest recorded use for plants is medicinal and references to formal medical practice have been found dating back to 10,000 BC. Ancient Sumerian and Egyptian records, dating from before 2500 BC, indicate a sophisticated and highly skilled knowledge of herbal medicine.

The Ebers Papyrus c.(1800BC), discovered in 1874 by Georg Montz Ebers, details over 800 plants which were commonly prescribed for medicine, ritual and used in the embalming processes. The Babylonians left records showing that they grew bay, thyme and coriander and regularly traded in herbs, spices and aromatic oils with the Egyptians.

Parallel development seemed to occur in China and India. The pharmacopeia compiled on the orders of Emperor Shen Nung, dated at around 2700 BC shows a deep knowledge of medicinal herbalism and the Rig Veda, one of the ancient Hindu scriptures, lists more than a thousand healing plants.

Knowledge spread from Egypt and Mesopotamia to Greece, from where it was gradually absorbed into Roman culture, taken by a flow of Greek physicians who travelled through the classical world. Perhaps the most famous of these early herbalists is Egyptian-born Asclepius who practised in around 1250 BC. The names of his daughters, Panacea and Hygeia, who helped him, are certainly bound to be familiar, having entered modern medical terminology for a universal remedy and sanitary science respectively.

The growth of herbalism, however, was largely dependant upon illiterate itinerant gatherer practitioners to source, evaluate and gather the plants. There was, of course, a good deal of danger attached to this occupation, so it became the practice to use special mystical incantations and rituals to protect themselves against any evil which might befall them, building up a strong framework of 'magic' and belief in the occult.

A more scientific approach, based on diagnosis and treatment, was introduced by Hippocrates (460 - 377 BC). His work was augmented by a Greek army doctor, Dioscorides, who published his work *De Materia Medica*, in the 1st century, in which he describes and lists more than 500 plants. Around the same time, Pliny the Elder (23-79 AD) produced his *Historia Naturalis,* the only one of the 37 books which comprised his encyclopaedia of the arts and sciences to have been preserved, describing plants and their uses.

The Dark Ages brought very little progress and it was not until the 8th century, when Arab physicians started translating early texts, adding their own observances. The most famous of these, the Moslem healer, Hakim Abu Ali al-Husayn Abd Allah Ibn Sina (born AD 980), whose name was, not surprisingly, shortened and changed by westerners to Avicenna, contributed his huge work, *al-Qanun fi al-Tibb* (The Canon of Medicine). Consisting of five volumes, totalling 1,000,000 words, he drew together all the medical knowledge of the period in the work, refining it into a science, and providing the basis for the Unani Tibb school of medicine which is still being practised over 1,000 years later.

The 10th century also saw the first Anglo-Saxon herbal. Written in the common tongue, *The Leech Book of Bald*, placed its emphasis very firmly on magic and ritual. When the printing press was invented in the 15th century, some of the first and most influential volumes were herbals and the Elizabethan age saw a rash of texts appearing all over Europe: *Herbarium viva eicones* (1530), Otto von Brunfels; *Newe Herball* (1551), William Turner; *Historie of Plantes* (including New World plants such as the potato and tomato, 1597), John Gerard.

In 1652, during the Commonwealth period in England, Nicholas Culpeper produced his volume, *The English Physician*, in which he combined both herbal observations and uses with their astrological natures. In 1664 *The Kräuter Buch* (The Plant Book), was published in Basel, by Dr Jakob Theodor Taberaemontanus. Three volumes, providing information on all the possible uses of over 3,000 European plants, both wild and cultivated.

Herbalism still has a strong following today, but practitioners emphasise the importance of using the whole herb, not just the extract, arguing that Nature has provided internal foils for the active principles of the plant which ensure a safe and proper balance in its effects on the human body. For example, ephedrine, an alkaloid found in the Chinese herb, *Ma Huang*, when extracted and used as a drug for the treatment of asthma, was found to produce a dangerous rise in blood pressure levels. However, the whole plant contains another active ingredient which balances this effect by slowing down the heart rate and blood pressure.

Modern herbals often distinguish between culinary and medicinal herbs, but in earlier times, there was no such distinction, as all foods were seen to have an effect, good or bad, upon one's state of health. Most of the common vegetables of today were used in healing potions or poultices at one time or another and, like the Eastern doctrines of Ayurveda and Unani Tibb, the use of herbs and vegetables were largely interchangeable.

Honey

'I eat my peas with honey,
I've done it all my life.
It makes the peas taste funny
- but it keeps them on the knife-' anon.

One of the first things that Man learned to domesticate during his transition from hunter-gatherer to farmer was the honey-bee. It is thought by some scholars that the first use of honey originated in

Central Asia, as a lot of the early names for honey are similar to both the Chinese *Myit* and Sanskrit *Madhu*. Whether true or not, it was most certainly in very deep pre-history, as Stone Age cave paintings near Valencia in Southern Spain depict scenes of a man robbing a wild bees' nest. As with many core foods, honey was regarded as holy - a gift from God and, accordingly, was endowed with mystical attributes.

Honey is produced specifically as a food, as is milk, the first food for all mammals, and so it is natural that much of Man's mythology links the two. The Greek God, Zeus was hidden from his murderous father Kronus, by his mother, Rhea, and fed upon milk and honey. Milk and honey were also the two basic foods which awaited the Israelites in the Promised Land, symbolising God's promise that His children would want for nothing.

Ambrosia, the food of the Olympian Gods, was often assumed to be honey as both were believed to promote longevity. Following this belief, Democritus, the ancient Greek philosopher and physician developed a diet which included honey, to promote eternal life, and, supposedly, lived to 109 years old. The ancients offered honey to their gods, usually in the form of honey cakes, which they placed upon their shrines - although Rameses III of Egypt went a little further, offering the equivalent of 15 tons of honey to the Nile God, Hapi!

The Ancient Egyptians also used honey in cosmetics, and beeswax for, amongst other things, a heat-setting process which set the paint on their sarcophagi. There were even taxes levied, payable in honey. Small wonder then that the first-known records of man-made hives are from Ancient Egypt, in the temple of Ni-weser-Re, dating from around 2500 BC. Ancient Mesopotamian texts relate how Shamash-resh-uzur, the governor of Sukhi and Ma'ar introduced bee-keeping there some 3,000 years ago, probably imported from the Hittites, who were known to be ardent bee-keepers.

Charlemagne, the Frankish King, demanded that bees be kept and that two-thirds of the honey and one-third of the beeswax produced be paid in duty. The French continued taxing hives until as recently as the 1930s.

The link with God and Truth is enduring and seems to have been a world-wide development. The Hebrew word for bee is *dbure*, meaning word, as the bee is said to bring the Divine Word. In places as diverse as Africa, Germany and India, honey was placed upon the lips of infants to endow wisdom and happiness.

The Koran states that honey is a 'medicine for man' and The Prophet Mohammed said that the bee should be treated with deference, as it is the only animal to be addressed by the Lord himself. In Christianity, the Roman Mass is supposed to be celebrated using only beeswax candles, as the bee was blessed by God after the Fall of Man.

In English Country Lore, every event in the family was 'told' to the bees - especially a death - before dawn of the next day, or the bees would die too, and the bees were often taken along to the funerals too.

Medicinal: In medicine, Aristotle and Hippocrates both studied the bee and Hippocrates prescribed cures using honey for skin disorders, ulcers, sores, respiratory complaints, sweats and fever. One medical use dating back as far as 2500 BC, is in the treatment of burns and open wounds. It apparently works by forming a protective barrier, preventing further infection. It is also believed to contain a natural antibiotic, inhibine, and that it draws out water from bacteria, causing them to dehydrate and die. Field surgeons used honey and cod liver oil dressings for open wounds quite effectively in WWI.

Another Old English cure, this time for ear ache, calls for a piece of onion, dipped in honey, to be placed in the ear. Honey has also been used to induce sleep and Ancient Roman physicians used it as a digestive curative and cleanser. There have also been more modern claims that common gut bacteria, such as Salmonella and E.Coli are unable to survive in honey, and an article in one medical journal claimed that a 25% addition of honey to a remedy for diptheria was found to act as an antiseptic and prevented the bacilli from propagating.

Ayurveda classifies honey as an astringent, rather than sweet, taste for its effects. It is energy giving, stimulates the digestion and is cooling. It is used to clean and heal sores and also to help in the healing of fractured bones. It is thought to strengthen sight and voice; act as heart tonic; cure nausea, hiccups, poisoning, asthma, bronchitis, swelling and diarrhoea.

Homeopathic practitioners use local pollen-laden, unrefined honeys to boost resistance to hayfever and it is believed that honeys made from the nectars of health-benefiting plants can help in the same way as the donor plant. i.e. eucalyptus honey may be beneficial in treating respiratory complaints. However, this also works both ways, as pollen from the Rhododendron produces toxic honey which can cause paralysis. But the best known medicinal use for honey is for soothing the throat and even today, some proprietary brands of cough cures still rely on a honey base.

Honey is one of the few foods that has always been used world-wide. The Guayaki Indians of Paraguay do not cultivate the land or trap animals, and only use fishing and hunting in the most primitive forms. Honey is their basic food and their whole culture relies on it. The Maya of Yucatan used several bee ceremonies in their rituals and, like the Egyptian Pharaohs, the Aztec rulers were also offered honey as tributes and a form of taxation. Warriors of the Masai tribe, in East Africa, would traditionally take nothing but honey with them on their long journeys.

Maybe because of its sweet quality, honey has long been associated with youth and love and is yet another one of the long list of foodstuffs which has been attributed with aphrodisiac powers. The 'Honeymoon' was the European tradition, a month during which the newlyweds could enjoy a sweet period in each other's company before the 'real' marriage began. Some Hindu marriages also used a similar analogy: a bowl of honey was placed before the couple, with the groom telling his bride, *"Honey, this is honey; the speech of thy tongue is honey; in my mouth lives the honey of the bee; in my teeth lives peace."*

Honey is produced by bees from plant nectar. It takes the nectar from approximately 1,500,000 flowers to make just one jar of honey.

It is usually made up of around 38% fructose (usually, the clearer the honey, the higher the fructose level), 31% glucose, 2% sucrose, 17% water, and very small amounts of thiamine, ascorbic acid, riboflavin, pantygiothenic acid, rydoxine, niacin, pollen and traces of wax, although modern heat treatments can destroy these, and it is for these nutrient values that it has become more valued than the 'empty' calories provided by refined sugars. It is also thought to be more easily digested by invalids, the sugars having been partially broken down by the bees.

Athletes through the ages, from the first Olympic Games onwards, have used honey as an energy booster, the two main sugars acting in tandem to give two levels of energy: the sucrose being almost instantly absorbed for an instantly, the fructose providing a more sustained supply.

Great beauties throughout history, including Cleopatra, have used honey to prevent wrinkling and to soften the skin, and Queen Anne of England used a 'secret' preparation of olive oil and honey for her famously lustrous hair.

Honey has been used in fermented drinks world-wide and these were said to have been drunk by Dionysius, the Greek god of wine and his Roman alter-ego, before the cultivation of the vine. Historians have found references to mead, the English version, dating back to 334 BC and it remained the staple drink in this country until well into the 19th century. It was also vital to the European economy until the Renaissance and the influx of sugar from exotic parts, until finally sugar replaced honey as the common sweetener and the new practice of using hops and grains for flavouring beers and ales overtook that old favourite, mead. Oh, and by the way, it's great in cooking, too!

Legumes

The second most important plant family used in the human diet, the first being the grasses, and both are thought to have been first domesticated just over 10,000 years ago. Beans, though, are on average, twice as rich in proteins as grains and are especially rich in iron and B group vitamins. This makes them an ideal source of protein for vegetarian communities, such as Southern India, where they form an important part of the diet. Some, like the green pea and haricot, are eaten green and in the pod, when they contain more vitamin A and vitamin C, but much less protein.

In ancient Rome, four of the most prominent families are also the names of legumes: *Fabius* - faba bean; *Lentulus* - lentils; *Piso* - pea; *Cicero* - chick-pea. Beans are a good source of protein, carbohydrates, minerals and vitamins. They are a good source of iron, low in fat and an excellent source of fibre, especially soluble fibre, which may help prevent the erratic blood sugar levels that lead to cravings for sweet foods. Fibre also helps to lower blood cholesterol levels, reducing the risk of heart disease.

All the pulses score well on the Glycaemic Index, the scale invented to help in the treatment of diabetes, which is used to measure the rate at which blood sugar levels rise when a particular carbohydrate bearing food is ingested. Low level GI foods are more complex and hence digested more slowly, ensuring a longer feeling of satiety, longer term energy maintenance and keeping blood sugar levels constant. GI scores below 50 are seen as the best on the scale, whilst those that score above 70 are regarded as best eaten with a lower scoring food - and less frequently.

Broad bean - *Faba vulgaris, Vicia faba*. Also called the faba or fava bean, this was the only bean known in Europe until the discovery of the Americas. Cultivated since Man's earliest times, this humble legume managed to spark a debate which has spanned 26 centuries. In the 6th century BC Pythagoras, the Greek Philosopher and mathematician advised his followers, *"Abstain from beans"*. From anyone else these words might have been taken at face value. But they were spoken, without any further enlightenment as to why, by a philosopher - a positive invitation to further speculation.

One source says that Aristotle believed that they were forbidden because they resemble testicles. Cicero, Plutarch and St. Jerome all held the theory that it was because they possessed aphrodisiac qualities. St Jerome was so convinced that he forbade their consumption by nuns! Roman writer

Diogenes Laertius explained that it was because they contain the souls of the dead, a belief which was also held by the ancient Egyptians, who, even though they cultivated them, regarded them as being unclean.

The Greeks, too, held this same belief and some scholars give as a supportive argument the fact that the Greek word, *anemos*, can be translated as both wind and soul. For whatever reason, this particular conviction was held very widely and almost all the ancient societies used the broad bean as funerary offerings or food in some way. The Celts funeral beanfeasts, for example, gave us the word *beano*.

Another argument which has been put forward for Pythagorus' distrust of the bean is that he may have been a sufferer of favism, a sensitivity to broad beans, suffered by a very small number of people, especially in the Mediterranean, which can lead to anaemia and jaundice.

Writers John Lyly and Thomas Fuller opt for the more prosaic argument that the sage was offering oblique advice to his followers to steer away from politics, as the Greek voting system was based on the use of different coloured beans. Jonathan Swift (1667-1745) certainly had no doubts about the message, clearly stating where he stood on the subject in his advice for conjugal bliss for newlyweds:

> *"Keep them to wholesome foods confin'd,*
> *Nor let them taste what causes wind:*
> *'Tis this the sage of Samos means,*
> *Forbidding his disciples beans."*

The French obviously held no such misgivings about the bean, however: it is said that their common name is derived from the French word for 'good', *bien*.

Medicinal: Nutritionally, the broad bean is good. High in fibre, low in fat, and contains iron, niacin, vitamin E and vitamin C and 100g provides a quarter of the daily requirement of phosphorous, good for healthy bones and teeth. The shelled beans also contain beta-carotene the vegetable form of vitamin A. Broad beans have also hit the news recently as being another food which may help to combat cancer - particularly cancer of the bowel. Scientists have tested the effect of plant proteins, lectins, taken from broad beans on colonic cancer cells and found that they not only improved the ability of those cells to fight the cancer but they also inhibited further growth. The findings, by researchers at both Hammersmith Hospital and the Imperial College of Science, Technology and Medicine, also show that they may help malignant cells become more like normal, healthy cells. G.I. 79

Chick-pea - *Cicer arietinum*. The pulse which gave its name to perhaps the most famous of the four families were sold, mixed with lupin seeds, as a hot street snack in Rome and evidence from archaeological sites in Palestine indicate that it was used around 4000 BC. The specific name refers to the fact that it was thought that the seed resembled the head of a ram, Aries. In the Middle East it forms the basis for many of the dishes, such as hummus (also the Arab name for the chick-pea), rendered into a paste with garlic. In India it is known as *channa* and has been a major food since the 2nd millennium BC. It is used in whole form, as a *dal* (split) and can be milled into a fine flour, *besan*, which is used to make pakoras, battered savouries. Chick-pea flour is also popular in northern Italy, used to make the crisp, light pastry for small pizza. G.I. 36

Common bean - *Phaseolus vulgaris*. Developed by selective breeding into hundreds of varieties, which include the navy, field, pinto, black, haricot, dwarf and red kidney beans, this branch of the family originates in South America. Each variety is seen to fulfil a particular role: white with pork, black with tortillas, and so on. Excavations at Peruvian sites have revealed that Jack beans were being cultivated in around 5000 BC and remains of kidney beans have been found in Mexico which date back to around 3000 BC. Like a lot of the foodstuffs from the continent, they were brought to Europe courtesy of returning Spanish explorers, and rapidly established their place as the most important family of legumes in Europe.

The first beans to reach England, dark and kidney-shaped were duly dubbed 'kidney bean' by the English, whilst the French gamely tried using the Aztec *ayacotl*, which was soon turned into the more Gallic sounding haricot. The most widely used bean in the country, mainly in the form of canned, baked beans, is the navy or pea bean, so-called because it formed part of the rations for the US Navy at one time. Another member of this group which is popular in this country, the red kidney bean, is an excellent source of dietary fibre, potassium and folic acid and a good source of iron. G.I. 31

Lentil - *Lens culinaris*. Probably the first cultivated legume, sometimes linked with wheat and barley, which may have been domesticated at around the same time. Its name is taken from the Latin word *lens*, which is now used to describe a double-convex disc of glass - lentil-shaped. The Bible (Genesis 25:29-34) describes how Esau, the elder twin son of Isaac, sold his birthright to his brother, Jacob, for a bowl of lentil pottage.

It has the second highest protein content in the plant kingdom, next to soy, at 25%, which is why it is such a valued part of any vegetarian diet, especially in Southeast Asia. It is probably also why the lentil plays such a large part in the devout Christian diet during Lent, replacing much of the protein usually gained from meat products at other times of the year - with the added bonus of the opportunity for that English pastime, the play on words - in some areas they are still known as 'Lent tills'.

The lentil is a good source of dietary fibre, rich in folic acid and contains a good amount of potassium. Also, as with the other grains and seeds, it contains phytates, which may ward off cancerous changes in body cells. So, it is good for you - but good enough to pass up the chance to father a nation? G.I. 29

Mung bean - *Vigna radiata*. More familiar in the West for the sprouted form which graces salad bars from California to Bognor, this native of India has been grown since prehistory for human and animal food, and to provide a form of fertiliser. Producing several fast-growing crops a year, the bean is an inexpensive and efficient food source. In India, the beans are also milled, for use as a gram flour and split, as a dal. The split, dried mung beans do not require soaking, as with many other dried pulses, are easily digested and cooked speedily. In China they are used in their sprouted form and as a source of starch to make the almost transparent *fen si* (cellophane noodles). They are a source of manganese, iron, folic acid, magnesium and phosphorous. Sprouted, they are extremely low in calories and high in vitamin C and fibre. G.I. 29

Pea - *Pisum saativum*. Evidence of the use of field-peas and lentils has been found at a site at Jarmo, in Iraq, which dates back to 6500 BC. Remains of peas have also been found at prehistoric lake-site dwellings in Switzerland and Iron Age settlements at Glastonbury. It was grown by both the Greeks and Romans, spreading down to India, where it became very popular. It was introduced into China in the 7th century, where it is known as *hu tou* (foreign legume).

The pea was an important source of protein in the Middle Ages, pease pudding, made from split peas, being almost a staple. When the garden pea made an appearance in the 16th century, it caused quite a stir and, by the end of the 17th century, fashionable ladies on both sides of the Channel were developing what might be regarded as an addiction for eating bowls of small, fresh sweet peas (petit pois). In the Regency period, that famous icon of 'Polite Society', George 'Beau' Brummell (1778-1840), when asked if it was true that he never touched vegetables, apparently replied, "*I once ate a pea*". Proof of the pea's irresistable charm - or its power to repel?

Peas are a fair source of vitamin C, but are rich in vitamin B1 (thiamin), utilised by the body for controlling energy release. They are also a good source of fibre. However, fresh peas start to lose their nutrient value within hours of being picked, making frozen peas, where this loss process is halted, one of the best forms. G.I. 51 (fresh)

Runner Bean - *Paseolus coccineus*. In Central America, where this variety originated, the indigenous population use this variety for its roots, seeds and pods. It was introduced into England in the time of Charles I, by his gardener, Tradescant, for its bright red flowers.

Nutritionally, they are similar to green peas, with a similar amount of fibre, vitamin C and folic acid, 100g providing a quarter of an adult non-smoker's requirement for vitamin C and a fifth of that for folate. However, it is estimated that up to a third of these nutrients are lost to boiling. G.I. 51

Soy Bean - *Glycine maximus*. The soy bean is thought to have first been cultivated in China in the 3rd millennium BC, and it is mentioned in texts which go back as far as 2800 BC. The first seeds were brought to Europe by German botanist, Engelbert Kaenfer in 1692, but it failed to make an impact in Europe at the time as, when treated purely as a bean, the soy is less than impressive, being bitter and tough. In India it enjoys slightly more success and joined their repertoire of pulses under the guise of white gram.

In fact the first use for this highly adaptable foodstuff in the West was for purely industrial purposes, in such things as paints, varnishes and soaps. However, with the advent of the Second World War, things changed. It was soon seen as an invaluable padder for meat products like pies and sausages, an ideal choice, for its amino acid balance is nearly as good as that of meat. Other applications followed; with the invention of hydrogenation, soy margarine appeared and, because of its high protein content, it was soon being used for stock feed.

Soy milk, used by many people who suffer from lactose intolerance, is made from crushed beans which have been boiled and filtered, and has been used in China, where dairy products are not generally consumed, since ancient times. Tofu or bean curd, known as the 'cheese of Asia' is made by grinding cooked soya beans to produce the milk, which is then coagulated using calcium sulphate, making it a good source of calcium, providing roughly a third of the average daily requirement. It is high in protein, low in saturated fats, cholesterol-free and 100g gives an energy value of 73 kcalories and is a fair source of vitamin E and the mineral manganese. The soy bean's fibre is removed during tofu processing, making it easier to digest, but fried tofu can add to the calorie count, as it can absorb up to 15% of the fat used to fry it in.

Soy sauce, the 'salt and pepper of the East', appeared during the Zhou Dynasty (1134-246 BC) and was originally in the form of a thick paste called *mesho*. Eventually this evolved into two products, shoyu, the liquid sauce, and miso, a thick paste. It is made from soya beans which have been fermented over a long period of time, in the case of the 'special' sauces, years, and is extremely high in sodium. Several versions of soy exist throughout the East: the regular light and dark sauces (which also contain wheat and hence unsuitable for those with gluten intolerance); *Kecap*, an Indonesian variety made from black soy beans; *Tamari*, made without wheat from whole beans.

Soya products are rich in isoflavones - hormone-like substances that mimic the effect of oestrogen, phytoestrogens - and these have come under close scrutiny in recent years. It was noticed that Japanese women, who eat rather a lot of soy in one form or another, rarely complain of the adverse menopausal symptoms that seem to affect so many Western women. Separate studies have also shown that women who enjoy a diet which is rich in soya *isoflavones* had a lower rate of breast cancer than women who don't. Japanese men, too, seem to benefit from this *isoflavone*-rich diet, with prostate cancer figures being significantly lower than those for Western men. It is thought that this may be due to the fact that a substance called *genistein*, which blocks the growth of the capillaries which supply tumours with blood, has been found in the urine of people who regularly eat soya-rich food.

However, enthusiasm for these effects is by no means universal. Some scientists believe that although these and other diseases, such as cardiovascular disease and osteoporosis, are lower in such populations, we should beware of a 'jumping on the bandwagon' reaction by flooding the market with phytoestrogen supplements. They say that supplements may not have the same health benefits as the substance as eaten in the foods; although soya food products have been shown to lower blood cholesterol rates there is, as yet, no evidence to show that the extracted phytoestrogen has the same effect in isolation. In fact, some researchers who gave pure phytoestrogens to animals, found that it did not protect them against cancer and in one study, where animals were given genistein, the risk of cancer actually increased. The underlying warning is, as in traditional herbalism, 'Nature probably knows best'; substances in foodstuffs which are beneficial are better when not taken out of the food matrix.

In fact, one research scientist, Dr Richard Sharpe, of the Medical Research Council Reproductive Biology Unit in Edinburgh, has gone on record as stating that he definitely avoids buying anything containing soya products for his children, despite the fact that it has been hailed by so many as an anti-cancer agent. He says that he has seen results of studies which show that, in female animals, soy can produce the equivalent of premature menopause and that the increased intake of oestrogens can lead to lower sperm counts in males, "*Until I have a reassurance that it doesn't have comparable effects on humans, I would rather not give it to my children.*" Professor Tom Sanders, of the Department of Nutrition and Dietetics, King's College, London, says that the effect is not just restricted to children and that a soya-rich diet has been found to have a feminising effect on vegan males and that soya can disrupt the menstrual cycle in women, "*Many vegetarians don't eat meat because they are concerned about the hormone content, but the hormone content of soya is much higher.*" The jury, it appears, is still out. G.I. 15

Lettuce *(Lactuca sativa)*
A large family of plants that include chicory, endive and the thistle, probably grew wild all over temperate Europe and East Asia before being brought under cultivation, probably for the soporific medicinal properties of the latex produced by the wild varieties, and was used in cough medicines until quite recent times. The modern, cultivated varieties also contain the 'lettuce opium', as it is also known, but to a lesser extent.

The Ancient Egyptians used lettuce as an offering to their fertility god, Min, probably because the latex or 'milk' was also believed to be an aphrodisiac, and tomb drawings depicting lettuce have been discovered which date back to around 4500 BC. The Assyrians also believed in its powers of sexual stimulation and it is listed as having been grown in the famed gardens of King Merodach-Baladan of Babylon.

Hippocrates, Aristotle and Theophrastus all mention lettuce and Pliny refers to the plant, saying that the Greeks called it 'poppy lettuce' because of the soporific quality of the milk. The Romans used lettuce, which is where it got its name: *lac* - milk, for the latex becoming *lactuca*, lettuce. It was a popular vegetable, initially used at the end of a meal to help digestion and induce sleep. Towards the end of the classical period, as more varieties with less soporific qualities were developed, the lettuce switched ends and began being used as a starter instead. Apicius, the author of the only surviving recipe book from the period, used lettuce in several recipes, and recommended endive as a winter replacement. Chaucer mentions lettuce, used in a culinary role, in his *Canterbury Tales* in the 14th century, and it was one of the seed crops taken with the early settlers to the New World.

By the time of Andrew Boorde, the traveller, doctor and unfrocked bishop whose 16th century book, *A Dyetary of Helthe*, listed medical and dietary advice, the lettuce had lost its reputation as a love booster. His opinion was that "*Lettyse doth extynct veneryous actes*". Modern herbalists tend to emphasise the calming effects of lettuce, recommending a bowl of darker leaves for stress, restlessness and insomnia.

Medicinal: Nutritionally, the lettuce is a useful source of folates, or folic acid, which is important for women in early pregnancy and those planning a pregnancy, as it helps to prevent birth defects. The darker leafed lettuces, such as cos, are also a good source of beta-carotene, the vegetable form of vitamin A, which is a powerful antioxidant and may help to prevent heart disease and some forms of cancer.

100g of lettuce gives 14 kcalories of energy, carbohydrate, fibre, calcium, iron, sodium, vitamin A, thiamin (vitamin B1) and a very small amount of vitamin C.

Lychee *(Litchi chinensis, Nephelium litchi)*

Originally from China and a member of the family which includes the rambutan (*Nephelium lappaceum*) and longan (*Dimocarpus longan*), the fruit takes its name from the original Chinese name, *li chih* and can be spelt lichee and litchi. The fruit has been cultivated and treasured in the tropical and warmer sub-tropical regions of its home country for about 2,000 years. The fruit was considered a delicacy in the northern regions and there was even a special 'pony express', instituted in the 1st century AD, to bring lychees to the imperial court.

The exiled poet, Su Tung-po was said to have eaten 300 lychees a day, and stated that the fruit would reconcile one to eternal banishment and, during the Sung Dynasty (AD 960-1279), there was special Treatise written, emphasising the importance of the fruit.

The greatest challenge that the lychee posed to early travellers was a description of its exotic appearance and taste to a public that would, in all probability, never see or eat one. In 1684 Vaertijn preferred to not even try, describing it simply as a 'Chinese Chestnut'. In 1824 Bishop Heber proffered the admirable "*a sort of plum, with the flavour of a Frontignac grape*", whilst a gardener from the same period liberally daubs on the purple prose with, "*the lichi, hiding under a shell of ruddy brown its globes of translucent and delicately flavoured flesh.*"

Today, lychees are grown throughout the Eastern tropics, in a band which includes Thailand, Bangladesh and Bihar, Northern India and, in the West, Hawaii and Florida. South Africa is also a major grower. Most of the fruit consumed in this country are canned, but fresh lychees are increasingly available, from November to January.

The longan is slightly smaller and paler than the lychee with the same translucent flesh which surrounds a large, shiny black seed, earning it the metaphoric name, Dragon's Eye.

Their Malaysian cousin, the rambutan takes its name from the Malay word for hair, rambut because of the long, hair-like spines which grow from its skin. All members of the family are good to rich sources of vitamin C.

Mango *(Mangifera indica)*.

The mango has a long and distinguished history. A native of India, it has been cultivated for around 4,000 years and, according to Hindu mythology, it once enclosed the daughter of the sun and Buddha was said to have reposed in a mango grove. Akbar the Great (1556-1605), planted an orchard of 100,000 mangoes near Darbhanga in northern India, assuring and confirming the value of this already important fruit to the country's culture and theology.

Travellers to the subContinent, however, displayed mixed reactions to this unique and exotic fruit. Dr John Fryer, who visited India with the East India Company during the 1670's claimed, "*When ripe, the Apples of the Hesperides are but Fables to them, for taste, the Nectarine, Peach and Apricot fall short.*" But, speaking very plainly for the other side, Fanny Parkes remarks in her Wanderings of a Pilgrim in Search of the Picturesque (1832), "*I was disgusted with them, all those to be had at the time being stringy, with a strong taste of turpentine.*"

The Sanskrit name for the mango was *amra* from which the Chinese derived their *an-mo-lo*. Its English name is from *manga*, used by the Portuguese who occupied Goa, which, in turn was a corruption of the original Tamil, *mankay*.

A member of the evergreen Anarcardiaceae family, which includes the cashew, pistachio, American poison Ivy and the pepper tree, there are currently 41 varieties of mango grown world-wide.

The fruit is oval or kidney-shaped, with a smooth skin, which varies in colour from green through yellow to orange and red, sometimes displaying a pretty crimson blush, although this is no indication as to the ripeness of the fruit. The flesh is yellow or orange and contains a large, flat stone, and the fruit can vary in weight between 255g (½1b) to lkg (21b).

It is notoriously difficult to eat, as the skin is impossible to remove if taken in the wrong direction. The almost universal answer to this problem seems to be to slice the fruit in half lengthways, sliding past the stone, scoring the flesh at diagonals, then turning each half inside out to form a 'hedgehog' of bite-sized cubes. Although true aficionados just soften the mango between their hands, taking care not to split the skin, then make a small hole in the top through which they suck out all the juice.

Another drawback to clean mango consumption is that the fruit is undoubtedly at its best when 'dribbly-juicy', making it the ideal bath-time snack. This is also one of the reasons we can't get the best in this country, as it only ripens to such perfection on the tree. Luckily, March marks the beginning of the season for the best Indian mangoes, and the king of these, the Alphonso, and although you do have to search to find them in the shops here, you can get them - at a price!

India produces an amazing 10 million tonnes of mangoes every year, although, because of the massive domestic demand for the fruit, it only exports about a quarter of these.

Medicinal: Chinese medicine, which regards the diet as a way of balancing health, uses mango to relieve indigestion, ease the symptoms of asthma and to soothe bleeding gums. They advise against eating the fruit after a heavy meal, though, as it tends to swell the stomach and also warn against mixing mango with onion and garlic, as it may cause skin itching.

For fibre and vitamins, the mango is hard to beat. Packed with beta-carotene, the vegetable form of vitamin A - over 1½ times the RDA, a full day's supply of vitamin C for a non-smoking adult, a good amount of potassium and an average-sized fruit supplies 7g of dietary fibre. Beta-carotene is a powerful antioxidant, which may protect against certain types of cancer and atherosclerosis, which can lead to heart attack and stroke, as does vitamin C, which also helps the body to stave off infection.

The dietary fibre is known to maintain bowel regularity, protecting against colon and rectal cancers. However, there is always a viper in paradise: an average mango contains 14% sugar, which, when consumed regularly, is not only bad news for the diet, but for that shiny white smile, too. Amchur, the vitamin C-rich powdered form, is sun-dried mango, ground for use in cooking to add sourness. Ayurveda recommends this easily-digested food-stuff for the elderly, the weak and infirm and for excess of Vata (wind). It is described as soothing colitis and improving the complexion. Another recommended remedy is to grind the roasted stone to make a cure for diarrhoea. Also, ladies beware!

In India, it is said that you can tell that a woman is expecting a baby when she starts craving raw mango!

Marination *(Not just a matter of good taste)*
Marination is a good idea for many reasons - but only under the right conditions. Many advocate it as vital to real taste and others disagree or cannot really be bothered, but few really understand the science behind their reasoning. It acts as a form of pre-digestion: protein-digesting enzymes from plants, such as papaya, fig and pineapple break down muscle and connective tissue in meat and acids, such as vitamin C (lemon juice/orange juice) and vinegars emulate the natural action of lactic acid naturally produced by a living body to break down the proteins for use.

Marination can also be attractive by introducing colour and flavour to the areas in which it comes into contact and in those layers near the surface of the tissue. It is also a useful combatant of harmful bacteria and moulds, its usually acid nature inhibiting their growth, and when an antibacterial spice, such as turmeric, is used in the marinade, this is reinforced.

With a piece of chicken accumulating anything up to 10,000 bacteria per square centimetre by the time it reaches the supermarkets - even under strictly controlled conditions - this is very comforting.

Studies carried out at the Lawrence Livermore National Laboratory in California, indicate that chicken marinated before grilling contains fewer carcinogens, the substances that may produce cancer in living tissues. Dr Mark Knize and his team marinated chicken breast in olive oil, brown sugar, cider vinegar, lemon juice, garlic, salt and mustard. After cooking it for 20 minutes, they found that it had one-tenth the usual level of heterocyclic amines or less.

Quite a powerful weapon in the cook's armoury, one might say. However, as with all weapons, it is a two edged sword. Marination is a chemical reaction and needs the physical contact of marinade and meat tissue. This takes place at the surface. The centre of the meat is still subject to the natural forms of decomposition. Lactic acid builds up and breaks down the protein, naturally tenderising the meat.

The fat tissue within the meat is no longer supplied with white blood cells and antioxidants, so becomes infected and quickly rancid and those meats which are high in unsaturated fats - fish, poultry, pork, lamb and veal are those which spoil the quickest. This is why marination should be under refrigeration, and for a matter of hours rather than days, to allow flavours to permeate - over-marination just leads to mushy tissue surrounding microbe rich centres. Scientists have found that the optimum temperature for tenderisers to work well is between 60°C - 79°C and are deactivated at boiling point - (100°C). So the main tenderising action probably acts upon the muscle tissue in the early stages of the actual cooking.

Whatever the pitfalls of modern marination, it is a vast improvement on the methods used up until the end of the last century. Beef joints were hung in storage until the outsides were literally rotten. The French called this process mortification - but, at the stage of putrefaction they preferred, whose death they were referring to is now lost in the mists of time.

Meat

The actual word 'meat' didn't actually come to be used to describe the flesh of animals until around 1300, until which time it was generally accepted to mean any type of solid food, as opposed to drink.

The whole subject of meat-eating has become quite an emotive one in recent years, with a varied range of arguments being produced by those against. The more scientific points out that evidence exists that proto-human, like the apes, ate a basic fruit diet; that we only started to exhibit ominiverous feeding patterns after the emergence of Homo Erectus. The religious moralists add the argument that, according to the Bible, before Adam and Eve's fall from Grace, they were given herbs, fruits and seeds as foods, and that it was not until after the Great Flood that Man was given *'everything that liveth'* as meat, in recognition of his base nature.

For the opposite lobby, some nutritionists point out that animal proteins supply us with similar and higher quality essential amino acids, needed to provide the proteins required by the body. It also provides us with iron, Vitamin A and some of the Vitamin B group. Strong evidence does exist that early Man was a hunter-gatherer and primitive hunting tools have been found which date back some 15 million years, although the weapons capable of dealing with the larger game didn't appear until around 1 million years ago, and it is generally accepted that our ancestors were largely opportunistic meat-eaters.

The change came in the Neolithic period when agriculture was born. Strains of the grain families and some legumes began to be cultivated, attracting animals like sheep and goats. Such ruminants are timid and easily controlled, can digest the cellulose from discarded stalks, posing little competition for the food needs of the early settlements, with the added bonus of providing milk and wool and hides in payment. The earliest evidence of domestic sheep have been found at sites in Iraq, dated at around 9000 BC, and evidence of goat-keeping has been found at Jericho and dated at 7000 BC.

Dogs and pigs, attracted by the inevitable waste matter from such communities, would have followed, and would have had to be brought under control to prevent danger to the settlement. Canine remains have been found in Iran which date back to 9500 BC, and it is thought that they were probably bred as much for a convenient source of food as a hunting aid. Dog was still a meat animal during the Classical period, enjoyed by both the Greeks and Romans and Hippocrates, the 'Father of Modern Medicine' remarked that he found the meat light and nourishing - as do some Far-Eastern societies, even today.

The Romans also 'battery' bred dormice, which they enjoyed enormously, to ensure a constant supply and Apicius, the only cookbook to survive from the period, includes a recipe for the rodent, cooked with pork meat, pepper, pine kernels, asafoetida and liquamen. South America seemed to have a limited supply of animal protein; the llama having been used almost exclusively for transport and the alpacca for wool, their principal food animal would seem to have been the guinea pig.

Ancient texts mention a great many exotic roast meats, usually at grand banquets, and always to underline the great wealth or importance of the dignitaries being described. Such delicacies would have been the preserve of the privileged few, the masses existing on a basic diet of grain breads, porridges and gruels.

Most historians agree that the human diet from 1400 to 1800 was essentially a vegetarian one throughout most of the world for purely economic reasons: crops can feed up to 20 times the number of population than can be suppported by the animals grazing on the same acreage. The main exception to this rule was in Europe, where a great deal of meat was eaten during the Middle Ages. It is thought that the relatively low population density, together with the availability of a vast amount of high-quality pasturage, may have gone a long way to accounting for this.

However, the population growth from around the 17th century onwards put meat consumption back with the upper classes and during the 17th and 18th centuries, the average European was down to an average of around 10% of their calorie intake coming from meats, much of this salted, as they became more expensive.

North Americans, coming largely from this European stock, shared this meat passion and the abundance of natural game stocks in the New World did nothing to impede the growth in its consumption. And grow it did. The per capita average annual meat consumption of Americans during the decade 1830 to 1840 was 178lb (80.6kg), with salt pork becoming the staple for the masses instead of grain products. The phrase 'scraping the bottom of the barrel' was coined during this time, referring to the barrels in which the pork was stored.

The late 20th century saw a dramatic fall in the consumption of red meat, whilst poultry use has boomed, bolstered by high yielding factory methods which has brought down the cost of raising chickens in large numbers. Economically, however, it still remains a luxury foodstuff. Even today, it takes 900g (2lb) of grain to produce 450g (1lb) of chicken meat, with ratios of 4 to 1 for pork and 8 to 1 for beef. Small wonder, then, that those in the business of mass meat production have, at times, resorted to sometimes scandalous methods of improving the balance sheets. Although medical evidence points strongly in the direction that some meat product consumption is necessary for a healthy, balanced diet, recent research suggests that the average westerner still eats around twice the amount of protein they need for healthy maintenance, most of this coming from red meats, dairy products and eggs.

Meat does benefit from 'ageing'. Historically, meat, especially from game animals, has been seen to improve in flavour and tenderness after a period of 'hanging' or storage after slaughter. It is thought that this is due to a process within the meat tissue whereby the lactic acid, which accumulates in the tissue after death, begins to break down the walls of the cells within the meat which store protein-attacking enzymes.

Flavour changes caused by this process are thought to be caused by the resultant degradation of the meat's proteins into their basic amino acids, which usually have a strong flavour. By means of a similar process, the muscle filaments also start to disintegrate, causing the meat to become more tender. The process is, of course, also known as decomposition, and earlier fashions, especially in early French cuisine, would sometimes see things taken as far as actual putrefaction before the meat was used.

Approximate Dates for Animal Domestication		
Animal	**B.C**	**Region**
Sheep	around 9000	Middle East
Dog	8400	Eurasia, North America
Goat	7500	Middle East
Pig	7000	Middle East
Cattle	6500	Middle East
Guinea Pig	6000	South America
Horse	3000	Northeastern Europe
Chicken	2000	India

Meat has even been used in country medicine: chicken fat was rubbed onto burns and scalds and freshly killed warm chicken flesh was used as a styptic to staunch heavy bleeding. And, of course, who hasn't heard of using a fresh beefsteak to ease a black eye - although I would far rather see it grilled lightly with olive oil and roast garlic, served with a crisp, mixed salad!

Melon *(Cucumis melo)*
Melons are a branch of the squash family and are thought to have originated in southern Africa. The greater family group includes cucumber, musk melon, casaba, winter melon, marrows, pumpkins and

gourds. Taken into India in prehistoric times, the melon became a valuable and popular fruit, finding its way into Egypt by about 4000 BC.

Proper cultivation was instituted by the Arabs in the 12th century. Melons were introduced into the Court of Charles VIII of France from Italy and didn't reach England until the 16th century, when they were grown under glass quite successfully. The French writer, Alexander Dumas, author of the Three Musketeers, was so fond of the melons from Cavaillon that he swapped a complete set of his works for a lifetime's supply of them.

There are five main groups:

Water melon - *Citrullus vulgaris*. Native of Africa and from a different species to other melons. Water melons contain lycopenes, also found in tomatoes, red grapefruit and apricots, powerful antioxidants which protect against cell damage.

Melon - *Cucumis melo*. A variety of shapes and colours with sweet flesh, which include such varieties as Honeydew, Ogen (named for the kibbutz in Israel where it was first grown), Charentais and Cavaillon.

Cantaloupe - *Cucuma melo var. cantalupensis*. Raised in the Papal villa of Cantaluppi near Rome in the fifteenth century, with a warty skin and fragrant orange flesh.

Musk or Netted Melon - *Cucuma melo var. reticulatus*. Round hothouse melons with a raised network pattern on the skin and aromatic flesh.

Cooking Melons - Used in the same way as vegetable gourds in Asian and Oriental cooking these include the Indian Kakri, and Chekiang melon, used throughout Southeast Asia.

Medicinal: The most useful melon, nutritionally, is generally agreed to be the cantaloupe. Its deep orange flesh is packed with beta-carotene, the vegetable pre-cursor of vitamin A, with just half a melon providing more than the recommended daily intake for the average adult. It is a potent anti-oxidant that protects against cancer and the formation of the free radicals that cause cataracts. It is also believed that it helps to protect against infection, that it fights 'bad', or LDL cholesterol, and, that by preventing cell damage, it may be a useful weapon in the battle against the ageing process. It is also high in vitamin C, the same half-melon providing more than double the recommended daily intake for an adult non-smoker. It is also a good source of potassium, which helps to regulate body water balance and normalise heart function, guarding against high blood pressure and irregular heart action. It is also a good source of fibre which helps to regulate bowel action and may help to guard against colon and rectal cancers.

The lighter green and pale yellow flesh melons contain little beta-carotene and less vitamin C, but they are low in calories and their high water content may help the kidneys to work more effectively, flushing the system.

Mint *(Mentha piperita (peppermint), Mentha spicata (spearmint))*

Minthe, who gave her name to this genus of plants, was a nymph who was pursued by Pluto, Greek god of the Underworld. In a fit of rage his wife, Persephone, turned Minthe into a plant, to be trodden underfoot. As a tribute to the nymph, Greek virgins would wear sprigs of mint in their hair on feast days.

Peppermint was used by the ancient Egyptians and the Romans used it for its aesthetic and culinary properties. Pliny wrote about mint in his Natural History (AD 77), *"As touching garden mint, as the very smell of it alone recovereth and refresheth the spirits; so the taste stirreth up the appetite to meat, which is the cause, that it is so ordinarie in our sharpe (vinegared) sauces wherein we use to dip our meats."* In fact, he found the smell of mint so exhilarating that he recommended a wreath of mint for students, to sharpen the mind. He also extolled its virtues in drying up *"the humours that mollifie the grisly windpipe."* and recommended the use of mint juice before any strenuous use of the voice.

In folk legend and country magic, mint was associated with Venus and Mars and was used to invoke protection during travel and exorcism and to attract money, love and healing. One country superstition was to place a few leaves of mint with the family savings in order to make it grow. Peppermint was also used to aid sleep, in purification and to strengthen psychic powers - placing mint on an altar would draw good influences upon rituals and a sprig, placed beneath a pillow, would enable you to see the future in your dreams.

Ayurveda lists peppermint as a pungent taste, strengthening *Vata* (nervous system) and *Pitta* (biochemical body processes), reducing *Kapha* (body fluid balance). A digestive, cleansing and stimulating. Although not used formally in medicine until around the mid-18th century, peppermint, usually in the form of a tea, has been one of the favourite homecures for indigestion since Biblical times, and its anti-spasmodic quality has led to its use to combat menstrual cramps and stomach upsets. Herbalists recommend using it internally for digestion, colds, flu and stomach cramps and externally, as a stimulating rub for aching muscles, in footbaths for tired feet and as an inhaler for catarrh and nasal congestion. Although, always with the rider that pregnant women should avoid using the essential oil.

It has also been used as a form of local anaesthetic: the action of the essential oil, menthol, raises the threshold temperature at which the cold receptors in the skin begin to discharge. However, because of the same reaction, like mustard, it can also be a skin irritant.

Spearmint, its specific name referring to the spear-like shape of its leaves, became a firm favourite in kitchen gardens after its introduction by the Romans. A milder flavour than peppermint and similar, if slightly weaker, medicinal properties.

100g fresh mint provides 39.60 kcalories, 4.70g carbohydrate, 11mg sodium, 3.40g protein, 2425iu of vitamin A, 124.40mg vitamin C and 3.5mg iron.

Mustard *(Brassica nigra, (black); Brassica alba, (white); Brassica juncea, (brown))*

All the varieties are members of the *brassica* family, which includes the radish, horseradish and the cabbage family and it is believed that this branch may have originated in the Mediterranean area where it can be found growing as a weed on untended ground.

The generic name, used by the Romans, is very similar to *Bresic*, the Celtic word for horse and some etymologists believe that this, and the fact that a lot of the brassicas were used as stock forage, may have been the root. The common name is said by some to be derived from the Latin, *mustum ardens*, which means 'fiery must', after the French practice of mixing ground mustard seeds with must (fermenting grape juice). Others, that it is simply a contraction of the Old French *moult ardre*, 'much burning'. But, however it arrived at its name, mustard and Man have been together for a long time - evidence has been found that prehistoric man chewed the seeds along with his meat and Hippocrates, the father of medicine recommended it for cleansing the system.

The ancient Romans believed in mustard as a cure-all: Pliny documented its use in smelling salts; as a curative for toothache; and it was regularly used in poultices for inflamed joints. The Roman army planted it wherever they went, including Britain. In America, the Mohicans treated headaches and toothaches with black mustard seeds and it has long been universally used as a chest rub to help persistent coughs.

A hot mustard bath is an age old domestic remedy for colds, poor circulation and tired feet. Scientists explain that, by irritating the skin, mustard oils draw large amounts of blood to the surface capillaries, relieving inflammation in the surrounding tissue. It is the same effect in the mouth which makes the mustard act as an appetite stimulant Hence, mustard used in this way should come with the warning that those with sensitive skins may experience blistering. Mustard has always been an important spice in Europe, as it was easily grown locally and hence cheaper than its more exotic rivals.

Since 1634, Dijon, in France has been the eponyrnous global capital of mustard making, with over half of all ready-made mustard being manufactured there, usually from a mix of brown and black seeds. England's modern centre, Norwich, only joined the club in the 19th century, when Jeremiah Colman switched from grinding flour to mustard seeds. In 1903 he acquired the London mustard-makers, Keen, the company which supplied the city's chop and ale houses, and whose name inspired the phrase '*As keen as mustard*'.

Before that, Tewkesbury had always been at the heart of British mustard making and the town had become quite famous for their strong mustard and horseradish compound. It was in Tewkesbury, in 1720, that a Mrs. Clement first mastered the art of drying and grinding the seeds to produce a powder, as opposed to a paste. This new process meant that the powder could be kept longer without losing potency and that the mustard made from it would be unsurpassed in strength.

Ayurveda and Unani Tibb both use black mustard seeds (*Brassica nigra*) as a remedy for abcesses and itchy skin. Hot mustard plasters are also used to treat chest pains, coughs, bronchial catarrh and shortness of breath. The warming effect this produces is also used for rheumatic pain and lumbago. Taken internally, it is used to balance Vata and Kapha disorders and expels worms. Tibb also recommends mustard for the treatment of dyspepsia, constipation, delirium tremens, dropsy, hiccups and narcotic poisoning.

Hindus regard the plant as a symbol of fertility, as it grows easily, and its flowering is often seen as the first sign of spring. However, the small black, most pungent seeds are being replaced gradually with the slightly larger brown, which are more easily harvested by mechanical methods. These brown seeds are those from which Pak choi, Chinese mustard greens, are grown. The sweeter, milder, white mustard seeds of the native European plant are actually pale yellow or very light brown and are the variety which produces the ubiquitous mustard-and-cress shoots used in English cafeteria salads.

Medicinal: The mustard greens, such as Chinese cabbage, from the *Brassica juncea* branch of the family, are all rich in beta-carotene, high in vitamin C, a very rich source of potassium and one average portion contains roughly the same amount of calcium as half a cup of milk. The dark green leaves contain substances; phytochemicals called indoles which help to cleanse the body and protect against oestrogen build-up. They are powerful antioxidants which have been shown to slow cancer growth in animal tests and enhance immune functions.

Nutmeg & Mace *(Myristica fragrans, - Jaiphal, Javriti)*

The generic name for the plant that bears the two spices is derived from the Greek for fragrant, *myristicós*, from the same root as the word for Myrrh, with whose scent it has often been compared. The common name, nutmeg probably refers to the fact that it is found within a fruit and is similar in size and appearance to a nut.

Mace, its partner, is actually the aril which surrounds the nutmeg; a clinging, lacy, dark red overcoat, which fades to a lighter orange when dried. The pale yellow fruit which bears both, used to be discarded on harvest but now has started to be used in jams, jellies and syrups, especially in Grenada, where they produce around a third of the world's crop of nutmeg.

These twin spices enjoyed a certain mysticism for several centuries, their origin being unknown even to the Arab traders who brought them to the West. As with most plant products, medicinal uses were discovered quite quickly, the first being recorded from around the 6th century. By the 12th century, nutmegs had found their way onto the spice trains into Europe and were used in the mixture of spices and herbs which were strewn in the streets at the coronation of Emperor Henry VI of Germany in 1191. As spices, and especially nutmeg, were extremely expensive, this would have served the joint purposes of impressing upon the masses an ostentatious show of wealth whilst protecting the royal personage against diseases. In 17th century Venice, plague doctors wore sinister beak-shaped masks stuffed with similar combinations to protect them as they moved around the city.

By the beginning of the 14th century, the Arabs had tracked down the source; the Indonesia Moluccan Islands. However, this did not serve to bring down the cost appreciably as English documents from the period rate 1lb nutmegs as being equivalent to 3 sheep, and the spice was not widely available until the Portuguese opened the first direct sea route at the start of the 16th century. So began the monopoly of nutmegs, along with cloves, by first the Portuguese, then the Dutch. The Dutch were much more serious about their stranglehold. Intent on keeping the only source to themselves, all spices leaving the islands were sterilised to ensure that they could not be propagated elsewhere. This was not enough, however, and to ensure that prices were kept up to a satisfactory level, all the inhabitants of one island were massacred and three quarters of all clove and nutmeg trees were destroyed in order to limit production. Finally, because mace was a more highly prized spice than nutmeg and available in a much smaller quantity, the misguided Dutch inadvertently added yet another factor in keeping its price high by ordering a massive reduction in the number of nutmeg trees, destroying them in order to make way for a plantation of mace trees!

When the British wrested the Spice Islands from the Dutch in 1796, all such silliness stopped and cultivation spread to Penang, Singapore and, finally the West Indies, bringing down prices and increasing availability, enabling nutmeg to be used in almost every sweet dish of the period, whilst mace became a firm favourite in potted meats, fish dishes and farces (stuffings).

All expensive spices found their way into 'magic' potions and nutmeg is no exception. It was used in incense preparations to enliven, sharpen the mind and to increase psychic abilities.

Medicinal: Medicine, too, has valued the spice since the 6th century, and it is mentioned in the vedic texts as a cure for headaches, fever, intestinal upsets and halitosis (bad breath). Until the 19th century nutmeg was thought to be effective against every known ailment and was linked with menstrual flow control and bringing about spontaneous abortions. It is known to be a good soporific and has been used in night-caps, however, its main active ingredient, the phenol myristcin, is also an hallucinogen, also found in minute quantities in black pepper, carrot, parsley and celery seeds, which can cause degeneration of the liver, so it is most definitely not to be overdone! The amount found in quantities of nutmeg, however, is significant enough to have led to its use at one time as a recreational drug among the poor and prison inmates. Malcom X was reputed to have used it whilst in Boston Jail and Charlie Parker, the jazz saxophonist is said to have eaten it.

In fact, most people in this country benefit from the powers of nutmeg oil every winter as, apparently, it is one of the main ingredients in Vick Vaporub. Mace, too has its use, albeit a more cosmetic one, and is used in the production of aftershaves, perfumes and shampoo.

In terms of culinary importance, nutmeg and mace are probably high on the list, being used in possibly the widest spread of preparations: egg and cheese dishes; spinach and green vegetables, having a magical ability to dispel that 'rotting veg' smell; cakes and puddings; sausages and even haggis. Mace, bearing the stronger flavour of the two is also exceptionally good in fish dishes, potatoes and appears in many chutney recipes.

Nutritionally, 1 teaspoon of nutmeg, ground equals roughly 2g, giving an energy output of 12 calories. It contains carbohydrates, protein and slight amounts of vitamins A, B1, B2, niacin, sodium, phosphorous, potassium, calcium, iron, magnesium, selenium, zinc and no cholesterol. The same amount of Mace, ground weighs 1.7g, 8 calories and contains carbohydrate, protein, is rich in vitamin A, B1, B2, niacin, sodium, phosphorous, potassium, calcium, iron, magnesium, selenium, zinc and, again has no cholesterol.

Okra *(Hibiscus esculentus - Bhindi, Gumbo, Ladies' fingers)*

A tropical annual plant which is a member of the mallow family and whose fruits, or pods, are eaten as a vegetable. The fruit pods are slender and tapering and have earned them the common name *'ladies' fingers'*. It is thought that the plant originated in Africa, probably Ethiopia, and managed to spread to Arabia, the eastern Mediterranean countries and India, but as it failed to gain popularity in Europe in the Greco-Roman period, its progress beyond these regions was relatively slow. It was taken to America by the Portuguese and Dutch slave traders, where its Angolan name, *ki ngombo*, already changed by the Portuguese to *quingombo*, was shortened to gombo or gumbo. Its journey eastwards took even longer, arriving in China as late as the 19th century.

The Cajun style of cooking relies on okra for the mucilaginous quality of the pods, its gooey sap being used to thicken the famous gumbo stew. In Eastern cooking, too, this quality is often called for in recipes as a thickener. One Indian method of preparation, however, which involves slicing the pods very finely, deep frying and spicing with amchur, bypasses this effect entirely, and transforms what can be an over-gooey vegetable for some, into a crisp and tasty alternative.

Medicinal: Nutritionally, okra is high in fibre, one of the best vegetable sources, which may help to reduce high cholesterol levels and counter the risk of colon and rectal cancer. It is also a reasonable source of vitamin C and beta-carotene, both antioxidants which help prevent the furring of the arteries which lead to heart attacks and strokes. As far as minerals are concerned, okra is a good source of potassium which works with sodium to regulate body water balance and normalises heart rhythm. Low potassium intake has been associated with high blood pressure and heart arrhythmia. 100g fresh okra = 39 kcalories.

Olive *(Olea europeae)*

The olive tree is one of the oldest cultivated by Man, and archaeological evidence would seem to indicate that it could have begun in Egypt and Ethiopia around 5,000 years ago (or even earlier according to the Isis legend), spreading quite quickly to North Africa, Syria, Lebanon, Israel, Greece, Cyprus and Arabia. Crete, whose modern-day population consumes more olive oil per capita than anywhere else in the world, shows evidence of cultivation as far back as 2500 BC. However, wild olives from oleasters were gathered by the Neolithic population some 10,000 years ago.

However difficult it may be to date the first cultivation, it most certainly would have been after the establishment of the first permanent settlements as, although the olive is a successful crop for otherwise difficult terrain, it does require time and patience to grow and, more importantly, process, the olive and its oil for use and consumption.

The olive became a mainstay in the life of the ancients. Its oil was used to fuel their lamps, to protect their skin, and both the oil and fruit were a central part of their diet. Little wonder then, that it makes an appearance in every ancient sacred text from the region in symbolism always heavily weighted towards that which is fruitful, promising and positive.

In Greek mythology, the olive was a present from the goddess Athena. The legend goes that Athena, goddess of wisdom, and Poseidon, God of the sea, argued over the patronage of a settlement called Kekrops on a rocky outcrop in south-eastern Greece. Zeus, tiring of the dispute between the two gods, decreed that allegiance should be granted to whichever of them could bestow a gift that would benefit the inhabitants there the most. Poseidon struck a rock with his trident, producing a salt water spring to demonstrate his power. Athena caused the olive tree to grow from the barren ground. The gods decided in favour of the goddess, the city was renamed Athens and the olive became a symbol of wisdom, peace and fruitfulness in her honour.

The olive was a central influence in Greek society: several of the major gods in the Greek pantheon were depicted holding olive branches or leaves; young brides carried or wore olive leaves to ensure a fruitful marriage; lekythoi, vases of perfumed olive oil were either broken over graves or placed in tombs at funeral rites, a custom which is still followed at some Greek funerals today. Herodicus (5th century BC), who taught Hippocrates, advocated the use of olive oil as a muscular massage for the athletes who competed in the original Olympic Games. Olive leaves were also used to make wreaths for the victors. The trees used for this were grown at the western end of the Temple of Zeus and were ceremonially cut by a beautiful youth wielding a golden sickle.

The Romans loved the olive, it was mentioned by Homer and Pompeii, buried in detail-preserving volcanic ash by the eruption of Vesuvius in AD79, has revealed that the oil was in use in every aspect of Roman life, used in sacred lamps and for medical cosmetic and culinary purposes. It would be used as a cleanser and skin conditioner and every citizen, when visiting the public baths, would be accompanied by a slave carrying his scented oil. This would be rubbed into the skin after bathing and scraped off with a *strigil*, a curved blade of wood.

The Ancient Egyptians, too, prized both the olive and the oil. Records from the time of Ptolemy II mention 27 varieties by his time and wall engravings in the Temple of Karnak record how the Pharaoh's men were anointed with olive oil on feast days.

Many superstitions have grown up around the olive. In Italy, it was believed that hanging an olive branch above the door of a house would keep away evil spirits and the Venetians believed that an olive branch attached to a chimney would stave off lightning strikes. By the Middle Ages the olive was so vital to the Italians that cutting down a community's or family's olive trees was seen as a more severe punishment than death.

Spanish tradition holds the olive at the centre of happy family life. One belief was that hanging an olive branch in the home would ensure a woman's authority in her house and that eating olives would ensure a husband's fidelity. This was furthered shored up in some areas with the belief that a poor olive crop would result if a man was unfaithful to his wife.

The olive tree is very long lived; it is said that a tree can live up to 1,000-1,500 years still bearing fruit. This has led to the tree being associated with healing and longevity and in Algeria there is one particularly ancient tree which supplicants visit in order to cure whatever ails them.

Olive oil virtually flows throughout the pages of The Bible: '*pure beaten oil of the olive*' was used to light the lamp in the Tabernacle; olive was traded by Solomon; perfumed, it anointed prophets and kings. It was the oil used on the leather shields of the Biblical period and '*oiling one's shield*' became a euphemism for declaring war. In spite of the latter, the olive branch was used to symbolise peace and Noah's dove returned with an olive leaf to the Ark - a sign that the waters were receding - safety.

The New Testament records that Jesus retired to the Mount of Olives before his Crucifixion. The area gained its name for the many olive trees that thrived there; perhaps the choice of the Garden of Gethsemane for his contemplation was linked to the olive's ancient links with wisdom and peace. Interestingly, the name Gethsemane is derived from the Hebrew *Gatshamanim*, which mean oil press.

Because of its long history of symbolism, olive oil has been a favoured oil for ritual and sacred anointing since the very earliest times. The modern Anglican church, for instance, still employ three oils, all using olive as a base: the oil of catechumens, used for baptism, which is basic olive oil; the oil of confirmation and ordination, the Sacred Chrism, a mixture of oil and floral essence; and the oil to anoint the sick, again the same kind of basic olive oil which is used in the kitchen. The oils are blessed on Maundy Thursday by the bishops and distributed amongst the clergy for use during the year.

Olives are still gathered in much the same way as they were in ancient times; vase paintings from around 520 BC show men knocking the ripe fruit onto sheets laid onto the ground. The olives, too, are probably pretty much the same fruit as back in antiquity. Olive trees are clones, one of Man's earliest attempts at genetic engineering. The trees are propagated by cutting off and rooting the small knobs which develop on their trunks, producing genetically identical offspring for replanting, so olives from the very oldest trees are very likely to be almost identical in size and taste as those eaten by the ancients.

As with most other foods, olive oil established its place firmly in Man's medicine chest. Even today many people still swear by a spoonful to relieve constipation and, until its resurgence in popularity in more recent years, the only available source for the oil in many provincial towns was the high street chemist. Warmed olive oil was traditionally used to ease earache and soften hardened earwax and was also used as a massage oil to ease arthritis and rheumatism. Just some of the other ailments which have been treated with olive oil throughout the ages are diabetes, gout, skin infections gall stones, burns, scalds, baldness, smallpox, pleurisy, coughs, yellow fever and even the plague.

Cosmetically, olive oil has been used to protect and smooth the skin, especially during and after exposure to the sun and, apparently, Marilyn Monroe, despite having access to some of the most expensive preparations Hollywood fame could provide used it in preference to anything else on offer.

The oil was also used in agriculture. It was smothered onto fruit trees to deter pests, to protect from the drying effects of the sun and to insulate against winter frosts. In the preparation of textiles, olive oil was used to lubricate both the fingers of the weavers and the fibre being prepared for weaving. In modern times, olive oil is one of the 'wonder foods' which has enjoyed a wide-eyed rediscovery. Scientists, puzzled at the longevity and good health records enjoyed by the Mediterranean peoples, in spite of their heavy smoking habits and high cholesterol intake, investigated the diet of the area further. They found that, whilst the overall fats intake is no less than anywhere in the developed world, in the Mediterranean countries most of that fat is in the form of monounsaturated fats and, in particular,

olive oil. Studies that followed this realisation found that olive oil has a positive effect on blood cholesterol levels, increasing the level of HDL or 'good' cholesterol which has been associated with lower rates of heart disease. This, though, is just one piece of the overall picture as far as the *'Mediterranean Diet'* is concerned. It is thought that the main benefits are enjoyed when taken together with the other good factors in the diet, such as fibre, fish oils and complex carbohydrates.

The tomato, adopted so enthusiastically by the people of the region is another important piece too. It contains the powerful antioxidant lycopene, the benefits of which researchers at Ben Gurion University in Israel have found to be enhanced when taken, and especially cooked, in combination with olive oil.

Olives contain between 4-6 kcalories each and are a good source of vitamin E, although rarely eaten in a large enough amount to significantly affect a dietary intake of the vitamin.

Onion *(Allium cepa)*

A Turkish legend says that when the Devil was cast out from Paradise and first set foot upon the Earth, on the spot where he placed his right foot grew the onion and, on that touched by his left, garlic.

In fact the onion has become so basic a commodity world-wide that nowadays it is not known to have a wild form, making the task of tracing its lineage and origin back to a starting point virtually impossible, although the presence of a wild and distant relative in Central Asia lead some to believe that this may have been the starting point for *Allium cepa* too. There are over 500 members of the allium family, including: *Allium ascalonicum*, the shallot, which has become a virtual cornerstone of 'Modern British' and French 'Haute Cuisine'.

The ancient Greeks were familiar with the shallot, or *askolonion* as they knew it, which, according to Pliny (1st century AD), was so named because it came from Ashkelon in what is now southern Israel. It is from this original Greek word that most of the other names for modern onions are derived, such as 'scallion' which has survived, particularly in the United States, as an alternate name for the spring onion. It is different from A. cepa, being an aggregate onion, growing in a cluster formation which spreads the shallot by a process of division. Other onions that do this are the 'Japanese' onion and the potato onion.

Allium porrum, the leek, whose common name is derived from the Saxon *leac* which they assigned to all the members of the family, such as gar-leac and brade-leac. It is one of the national emblems of Wales, and, although the real reason for this may have been lost in the mists of time, a romantic explanation for this is that it was worn as an identifying bonnet badge by victorious Welsh warriors in a memorable battle against the Saxons in the 7th century. Whether or not this is true, the Celt and Gallic races have developed a true affinity with the leek, producing many classic dishes featuring them, such as Welsh mutton cawl, Cock-a-leekie, Potage Parmentier and 'Poor Man's Asparagus', where immature leeks are served cold and dressed with vinaigrette, parsley and chopped, hard-boiled egg. The leek was popular with the ancients. Leeks are featured in Egyptian tomb paintings and, according to Herodotus, were fed, along with garlic and radishes to the slave force employed to build the Great Pyramid.

Greek and Roman texts, such as the cookery book written by Apicius, featured it as a vegetable in its own right. The Roman emperor, Nero was said to have been very fond of leeks, maintaining that they improved the quality of his singing voice, of which he was already inordinately proud. He is said to have eaten so many that his people gave him the nickname Porrophagus, leek-eater.

Allium fistulosium, the Oriental onion or Welsh onion is another cluster onion which resembles a large ridged spring onion. Despite its English common name, it does not actually come from Wales but from China. 'Welsh' was a prefix which meant 'foreign in Old English and is also the origin of the 'Wal' in walnut, or 'foreign' nut.

According to Pliny both the onion and garlic were deified in Ancient Egypt, a point repeated by Mrs Beeton in her famous *Book of Household Management* and Juvenal said that Egypt was a country where onions were adored and leeks were gods. There does seem to be evidence that the Egyptians swore oaths by both and archaeologists have found funerary offerings in Egyptian tombs. The onion was an important part of the staple diet of Mesopotamia, eaten with bread by the masses. Accounts from the 3rd Dynasty of Ur (early 2nd millennium BC) list bread and onions as a daily ration and in a chronicle from 2100 BC, Ur-Nammu of Ur recorded that he saved his garden of leeks and onions by building a temple to Nannar. Onions were also listed as being grown in the Gardens of King Badalan II of Babylon (8th century BC).

In Ancient Greece and Rome the onion was not as highly regarded as its cousin the leek as they were regarded as 'poor man's' food, although Theophrastus (372-287 BC) mentions several varieties of onion and garlic, indicating enough demand for them to be in daily use in the Greece of his time. He also mentions that when pounded the allia makes a foamy dressing - the forerunner to aioli, perhaps? Apicius used garlic and onion very sparingly in his recipes, hardly surprising, as he tended to concentrate mainly on the less 'humble' ingredients. Horace, too, reinforced the image of the onion as being strictly for the lower classes, when he included it in his 'economical diet'.

Ayurveda, the ancient Indian art of dietetics and medicine doesn't use the onion much in treatment, although it does note that the onion is stimulating, diuretic and an expectorant. Certain sects in India, such as Jains and Hindu Brahmins, are forbidden to eat it, one of the reasons being that it is believed to 'inflame the baser passions'.

Dr Andrew Boorde (1490?-1549), traveller, writer and disgraced cleric concurred with this and noted in his book, *A Dyetary of Helth*, that '*Onyons doth promote a man to veneryous actes, and to sompnolence*'. The good doctor's advice in this region is not to be dismissed lightly, as this unfrocked suffragan bishop Chichester was jailed for keeping three whores in his rooms at Winchester.

Medicinal: The onion has been cultivated for over 6,000 years and as well as its culinary uses, this bulb has been used by healers world-wide to cure almost every ailment. It has been used against infections, as an effective diuretic, heart tonic, contraceptive, aphrodisiac, expectorant, as a treatment for diabetes and as a decongestant (one of my grandmother's favourite cold-cures was a boiled onion, tied around the neck in an old sock!). Far from laughing these claims off, modern science is looking at the onion very seriously. In 1989, a Chinese study found that people who ate the highest amounts of allium vegetables in their diet, i.e. onions, shallots, leeks, chives, garlic, etc., had the lowest rate of stomach cancer. An independent study carried out in the United States at around the same time would seem to reinforce this theory.

The onion is rich in flavenoids, one of which, quercetin, is currently being studied for its apparent ability to deactivate carcinogens and tumour promoters. Those onions that are highest in these flavenoids are red and yellow onions and shallot. A separate investigation by Eric Block PH.D. of the State University of New York, uncovered a sulphur compound in onion that can actually prevent the biochemical chain of events that lead to inflammatory reactions and asthma. Well done, Gran!

The ancient physicians used onion to treat diabetes and, once again, modern studies have only served to proved them right, as recently it has been discovered that onion does indeed play a part in reducing blood sugar levels. Cooked onions are good for the cardiovascular system, taking just about 1 tablespoon to reverse the tendency for the blood to clot after a fatty meal. It is now known to reduce high blood sugar levels and to promote an increase in 'good' cholesterol levels in the blood. In fact, just half a raw onion a day will boost it by 30%.

Pasteur in the mid nineteenth century, declared it anti-bacterial and its essences have been proved to kill harmful bacteria, including E-coli and salmonella. One experiment also found that chewing raw onion for 3-8 minutes made the lining of the mouth sterile.

100g of raw onion equals 150kcalories, is 89% water, and contains 1.2g protein, 0.2g fat, 7.9g carbohydrates, 1.4g fibre, 25mg calcium, 0.3mg iron, 3mg sodium, 2mg vitamin A, 0.13mg Thiamin and 5mg vitamin C.

Oregano *(Origanum vulgare - Wild marjoram)*

Often confused with sweet marjoram, but herbalists believe that oregano is better medicinally. The generic name is said by some to be an amalgam of the two Greek words, *óros* and *gános*, meaning 'mountain brightness' or 'shining mountain'.

An eastern Mediterranean native, the plant has a long history of use in medicine and it was used by the ancient Greeks in poultices for sores, aching muscles and rheumatic pains in limb joints. The herb was taken to the New World by the early colonists largely for the same medicinal uses. They also used it, infused, as a tea to treat bronchitis and asthma and its digestive properties were employed in treating gastro-intestinal disorders.

Oregano contains the antiseptic thymol and also has anti-flammatory, expectorant and digestive properties, and modern herbalists still recommend it for all the above properties, as well as for easing coughs, colds, flu and as an antiseptic mouthwash for mouth and throat infections. The dried herb is very popular in Italian cooking 100g fresh oregano contains 33 kcalories, 5.37g carbohydrate, 3.74g fibre, 1.20mg sodium, 0.92g protein, 575 μg Vitamin A and 3.67mg iron.

Palm *(Elaeis guineensis)*

A native of West Africa, the history of the use of this particularly rich source of edible vegetable oil can be traced back over 5,000 years to the days of the Egyptian Pharaohs.

It is a very productive plant and every part can be used in a wide variety of products, earning it the title, '*Gift from God*' in almost every country where it is grown. The palm fronds and fibres are used in the manufacture of medium density fibreboards, chipboard, paper, matting and mattress fibre, and of course the wood from the trunks can be made into furniture. There is the obvious culinary use of the oil, as well as for the manufacture of polymers, cosmetics, pharmaceuticals, soaps and detergents, and crude palm oil can even be used as a fuel to run cars fitted with modified (Elsbett) engines.

The oil palm is a very productive crop. The plant produces fruit between 2½-3 years after planting, bearing 10-12 fruit bunches annually, each weighing between 20-30kg and carrying anywhere between 1,000-3,000 fruits. Each hectare of plantation can yield up to 5 tonnes of oil each year - 5 to 10 times more than any other commercially grown oil crop. In addition, each palm has a commercially viable life of up to 30 years.

Medicinal: The fruit is processed to produce two kinds of oil: palm oil from the mesocarp, or flesh, and palm kernel oil from the seed or kernel. Freshly extracted palm oil is the richest known natural source of beta carotene, or pro-vitamin A, and also has a high content of both tocopherol and tocotrienol varieties of Vitamin E. Palm vitamin E has been reported as acting as a potent biological antioxidant which helps prevent the formation of cancers, cellular ageing and atherosclerosis. The tocotrienols in particular have been shown to have blood cholesterol regulating properties and are also currently being investigated for their action in inhibiting the growth of oestrogen responsive human breast cancer cells.

Additional studies are also under way at the Center for Membrane Sciences, University of Kentucky which have shown that vitamin E prevents the death of brain cells which have been exposed to a toxic protein found in the brains of Alzheimer's sufferers.

It is a naturally stable oil, with a balanced composition of both unsaturated and saturated fatty acids to complement the high vitamin E level. The unsaturates consist mainly of the much-favoured monounsaturated oleic acid whilst thesaturates comprise 44% palmitic acid and 5% stearic acid. This composition gives the palm oil a semi-solid consistency, which means that, for solid-fat products such as margarine and vegetable ghee, (vanaspati), the oil does not have to go through the expensive hydrogenation process which has come under fire recently after studies have shown that the unnatural trans fatty acids formed during the process are detrimental to health. Like other vegetable oils, such as coconut, palm oil is cholesterol-free and readily digested and utilised as a source of energy.

Crude palm oil is the richest source of the carotenoids with concentrations of around 15 times more than that present in carrots and this is being capitalised upon by the industry in the production of a red palm oil which retains its carotenoids, and which has already been adopted as a natural dietary therapy in the fight against vitamin A induced blindness.

Papaya *(Carica papaya)*

The papaya originated in the Americas, probably Brazil and was cultivated well before the arrival of the Europeans. Papaya fruit is botanically a large berry from a tropical, palm-like, herbaceous plant. It can be oblong or round, smooth or ridged, and has pinky-orange flesh which surrounds a mass of shiny black seeds. The Spanish and Portuguese took it to the West Indies and by 1538 it had arrived in the East Indies via the Philippines. By 1800 it was being grown in nearly all the tropical regions of the world, its original Carib Indian name ababai converted to papaya along the way.

The fruit is often confused with *Asimina triloba*, the pawpaw, which is the fruit of another North American tree, also referred to as Custard apple.

Medicinal: The sweet, juicy, fruit tastes a little like aromatic melon and is extremely nutritious. Like all orange coloured fruits and vegetables, papaya is a good source of beta-carotene, providing one day's recommended intake, and 5 times that provided by an orange. Beta-carotene, the vegetable form of vitamin A is an antioxidant which helps to prevent damage by free radicals that can lead to the formation of certain cancers. One papaya also contains almost three times the RDA for vitamin C for an adult non-smoker, and the fruit is an excellent source of fibre and potassium, which help to regulate bowel function and normal heart function respectively.

The juice of the papaya is a well established cure for indigestion, it has been found to contain an enzyme called *papain*, similar to the pepsin which is produced by the human body to break down protein. The fig-shaped leaves also contain this substance and traditional uses for them include wrapping them around meats as a tenderiser and chewing them to aid digestion and to prevent intestinal worms. Papain is also commonly used in industrial food preparation as a meat tenderiser.

Medicinally, papain has been found to have pain killing qualities and is used in spinal injections to ease the pain accompanying a slipped disc, and an ointment containing papain is used to prevent rough skin forming around wounds.

100g of raw papaya provides 42 kcalories of energy, and contains carbohydrate, sodium, protein, vitamin A, vitamin C, potassium and iron.

Parsley *(Petroselinum crispum)*
An umbelliferous plant, native to the eastern Mediterranean region, related to coriander and celery. The Ancient Greeks called both parsley and celery sélinon, differentiating between the two when the need arose by adding the prefix petro 'rock celery', from which both its modern name and that of celery are derived. Unfortunately for food historians, this makes identification of which member of the family is being referred to in ancient references to the herb very difficult. They regarded parsley as the plant of death, and associated it with Persephone, Queen of the Underworld, death and evil; it was strewn over corpses and included in their burial wreaths and garlands. Interestingly, they also used it in the wreaths used to crown the winners at both the Isthmian and Nemean Games.

The Romans loved parsley for its deodourising qualities and they routinely used it as a breath freshener and as a means of delaying drunkeness. They also believed that parsley was a strong antidote to poison and a custom grew up of diners wearing a small wreath of the herb on the wrist at their banquets. Parsley was one of the plants grown in Circe's pleasant lawn in The Odyssey.

In Medieval times, parsley was used in folk magic to protect, purify and to provoke lust, and several superstitions grew up around the plant.

Parsley is a notoriously difficult herb to grow because of the long germination period needed by its seeds, and the Medieval explanation for this was that the seeds had to pay several visits to the devil before they would grow. It was also maintained, probably for the same reason, that parsley would only grow for the head of the household, and that those in love should never cut parsley, lest they cut their love.

Unfortunately for parsley, the green parts of the plant contain an etheral oil which is composed of pinene, myristicin and apiol, which is a toxin, and so it use in any great quantity has been avoided since antiquity. In addition, some Medieval bright spark unwittingly set its fate, suggesting that sprigs of the herb should be used to decorate dishes, assigning it firmly to the side of the plate for many centuries after. There are those, however, who feel that parsley should have been moved even further from the diner. Ogden Nash, for example, in his *Further Reflections of Parsley*, sums it up quite eloquently for the antipathetic with a simple, "*Parsley - Is gharsley.*" Which is a pity, because, although many find it an unpleasant and unecessary addition to the larder, parsley is, in moderation, a very nutritious and useful medicinal plant.

Medicinal: Since early times, parsley has been a valuable corrective for irregularities in the menstrual cycle: soothing pre-menstrual tension and nerves; acting as a natural diuretic for bloating; stimulating the uterus; relieving headaches and cramps; stimulating and regulating delayed, clotted or irregular blood flow. Herbalists recommend a daily dose of parsley tea to combat the unpleasant affects of menopause.

It has also been used as a treatment for kidney, bladder and urinary tract infections, and the root in particular has been used to make a decoction to combat kidney stones, water retention and jaundice. Parsley tea was used regularly in World War I, to help fight kidney problems following bouts of dysentery. The tea, flavoured with honey and lemon, is also used as a cold remedy. Parsley also has antiseptic properties, and poultices made from its leaves have been used to clear spots and other skin eruptions.

Parsley is also a deodoriser and can be chewed to clean the breath to great effect after eating garlic or onions. Herbalists always warn, however, that parsley root should never be taken in pregnancy and that the seeds should never be used at all.

Nutritionally, parsley is a rich source of vitamin C, containing more by volume than an orange, which, when combined with the other cancer and cholesterol busting substances such as flavonoids, coumarins and monoterpenes, explains why the herb is one of the foodstuffs under investigation by the US National Cancer Institute. It is also a good source of iron, calcium and vitamins A and B12. 100g of fresh parsley contains 39 kcalories, 6.91g carbohydrate, 1.20g fibre, 39mg sodium, 2.20g protein, 5200iμ vitamin A, 90mg vitamin C, and 6.20mg iron.

Pasta/Noodles

One of the most simple and most debated foods, the origins of pasta and noodles are difficult to trace precisely. It is a simple preparation of flour and water whose appearance in Europe has popularly been credited to the writer and traveller, Marco Polo, upon his return from China in the 13th century. However, there would seem to be compelling evidence to show that this basic, boiled unleavened bread was actually known to Europeans well before Signor Polo's travels.

One legend describes the arrival of pasta in Italy, brought by Germanic tribes in the 5th century, the secret of its production passed on to an amorous Roman soldier by the kitchen maid of one of the Chieftans. Even today, in Germany, there exists *Spatzle*, homemade wheat flour, soft noodles.

More concrete proof can be found, however, such as the early Etruscan relief at Caere, dating to around the fourth century BC, which depicts a scene where pasta-making equipment appears to be in use. In Jerusalem, Talmudic debates during the 5th century AD raised the question of whether boiled dough would qualify as unleavened bread under Jewish dietary law and the Persians, who influenced cooking style wherever they went, had a boiled tagliatelle-like dish which they called *lakhshah* (slippery).

From another Arabic source, texts dating from the 10th century mention dried pasta strips, which they called *itriyah*, being on sale from food traders. Interestingly, and probably because of their strong historical links with the Arab world, Sicilians were reported by a 12th century Arab writer and geographer, al-Idrisi, as having a food made from long strings of dough, which they called *trii*. Finally, Genoan archives for the year 1279 list dried macaroni in the details of an estate of a deceased citizen, one Ponzio Bastone. As Marco Polo did not arrive back in Venice until 1298, it is probably safe to say that pasta, in some form or another, was already in use in European kitchens.

No matter how pasta, or to give it its full name, *pasta alimentaria*, evolved, the Italians had decided pretty early on how best it should be prepared. Platina's *De Honesta Voluptate*, written in 1475, gives directions for one pasta dish, stating that it should be cooked only for as long as it takes to repeat 3 Paternosters, indicating that, even then, Italians preferred their pasta *al dente*, with a little 'bite'.

Pasta production was mechanised in Naples in 1878, causing riots of near Luddite proportions, and in 1882, British-made kneaders, extruders and cutters followed. By 1933, at the height of Mussolini's power, the manufacturing company, Braibanti, set up the first fully mechanized, continuous production line.

Nutritionally, pasta is one of the 'good guys'. All forms of pasta score well on the Glycaemic Index. For this reason pasta is a favourite with athletes when preparing for endurance events where stamina is essential. Another surprising fact about pasta is that it is quite a low-fat food, taken with the right sauces. 100g of white, boiled spaghetti contains, on average, 73.8g water, 3.6g protein, 0.7g fat, 22.2g carbohydrate, 0.5g sugar, 1.2g fibre, 7mg calcium, 0.5mg iron and has a calorific count of just 104 kcalories.

Peach (*Prunus persica*)

The peach is thought to have originated in China, where it was probably cultivated from as early as the third millennium BC. It was seen as having very strong divine connections and associated with immortality and longevity; a soul in the Otherworld who ate a peach from the World Tree was said to live for 3000 years.

The fabled peaches of the gardens of Samarkand were never allowed to leave the Imperial orchards at Changan. Eventually, however, the caravans that travelled through Kashmir took the peach to India, Persia and then to Greece and Rome, where they knew it as 'the Persian fruit' - hence the specific name.

Confucius, who wrote down his thoughts about practically everything, wrote about the peach in the 5th century BC and the Classical cookbook by Apicius lists a patina, or paste, made with peaches and served with cumin sauce.

The peach was growing in the London gardens of the wealthy by the late 16th century and the fruit was one of the favourites at the Elizabethan court, although the smoother nectarine was thought to be superior. The Governor of Massachusetts Bay Colony introduced the peach tree to the Colonies in 1629 where it thrived and took so well to the climate in the Americas that some naturalists thought that it must be a native fruit.

Peaches are low in calories, easy to digest and high in fibre, giving a gentle laxative and regulatory effect. If eaten unpeeled they provide over three-quarters of the recommended daily intake of vitamin C for an adult non-smoker and around 10% of the daily requirement of beta-carotene. Dried peaches provide roughly six times the calories of the fresh fruit, weight for weight and just 50g of dried peaches will provide two-fifths of the RDA for iron and one-sixth of potassium. Canned peaches, however, lose over 80% of their vitamin C content.

One fresh peach, with skin, weighs around 100g and gives 35 kcalories energy, 2g dietary fibre, 11.10g carbohydrate, 6.6mg vitamin C, 4701 iµ beta-carotene, 0.11mg iron and a trace of potassium.

Peanut *(Arachis hypogaea – Groundnut)*

Peanuts have been found in ancient Peruvian mummy graves in Ancón and Paracao and there is evidence to show that they were grown in pre-Inca times in Peru.

One of the most important plants to leave the Americas in the so-called 'Columbian Exchange', the groundnut, which is actually a legume, swiftly became a staple in several far-flung corners of the world. In Indonesia and Malaysia they form the basis of most of the salads and sauces and in West Africa, they fill out many of the traditional meat stews.

The oil, when refined, is light and tasteless, making it ideal for the lighter cooking styles, such as Chinese and Thai and its above average resistance to heat, hence burning, makes it doubly attractive to these cuisines, where cooking takes place at extremely high temperatures. And, although high in polyunsaturates, it does not go rancid quickly - important in warmer climates. Peanuts are a concentrated form of energy, an excellent source of protein and fibre, a good source of the B-Vitamin group and vitamin E. However, they are very high in fat.

Unfortunately, nuts, and peanuts in particular, are one of the most common allergen groups, with as many as one in 200 people being affected. In the most extreme cases, the smallest trace of nut can trigger a reaction which leads to a state known as anaphylactic shock, often fatal without a countering adrenaline injection to restore the heartbeat of the victim. Recently, however, research scientists at the John Hopkins University School of Medicine in the United States, have announced that they are currently working on a potential genetic vaccine to be offered to those at high risk. Although this has only been tested on rodents so far, they are confident that this could become a viable option for human patients within a matter of just a few years. Peanuts do score well, however on the Glycaemic Index, at just 14. 100g of roasted, salted peanuts contain 602 kcalories, 24.5g protein, 53g fat, 7.1g carbohydrate, 3.8g sugars, 6g fibre, 37mg calcium 1.3mg iron, 400mg sodium and 0.18mg Thaimin.

Pear *(Pyrus communis)*

The pear is European and Asiatic in origin, centering most probably on the region of the Caucasus, and has been cultivated since well before recorded history. It is thought that it was spread by the migration of the Aryans through Europe and India and the remains of wild pears have been found at Mesolithic sites.

The pear was considered to be a superior fruit by the Ancients, who much preferred it to the apple. The Romans raised its cultivation to an art form. In 300 BC, Theophrastes describes pear growing in detail and Pliny the Elder, the Roman Encyclopaedist lists more pears than apples in his works. The Chinese, too, held the pear above the apple. At the time of the Sung Dynasty, (1279 AD), there was just one variety of apple known to the Chinese, but many pears, and it is the Chinese who claim to have introduced the fruit into India. Cultivation of different strains was so successful that by the height of the Medici 200 varieties were available and records from the Royal Horticultural Society at Kew had identified more than 700 by 1842.

The pear was included in the Westward part of the Columbian Exchange, with seeds being shipped out to the new colony at Massachusetts in 1629. Because they were grown from seeds, they took on new characteristic in their new environment, creating quite distinctive American strains. Pear breeding was at its height in Western Europe by the 18th century and by 1849 the first Doyenne de Comice made its appearance on the banks of the Loire in France.

Medicinal: Nutritionally, the pear is useful for potassium intake and this helps to regulate blood pressure levels. It is also a good source of insoluble fibre, which helps regulate bowel action and may protect against certain forms of cancer. Pear is also a source of soluble fibre, pectin, and one fruit yields around 10% of the recommended daily intake for vitamin C. At 40 kcalories per 100g or 70 for the average pear, it is an ideal snack for weightwatchers - sweet with fructose for easily utilized energy intake - but still only 38 on the Glycaemic Index. Dried pears also contain iron and even higher concentrations of potassium. Pears are also amongst the least allergenic of foodstuffs, and so are popular for use in weaning, exclusion and invalid diets.

Pineapple *(Ananas comosus)*

Pineapple is a compound fruit, native to South and Central tropical America, possibly cultivated initially in Peru from around 1000 AD. The generic name, *ananas*, commonly used to identify it in many European countries is derived from the Brazilian Tupi Indian word *anana*, 'excellent fruit'. Pineapple was given to it by the early Spanish explorers for its fancied pine-cone shape.

It was first seen by Colombus in Guadaloupe in 1493, although difficulties in timing for its transportation meant that its arrival in Europe wasn't until the early 16th century, when it caused quite a stir. It caught the public imagination and soon appeared everywhere. Coats of arms; architectural ornaments; pottery imitations; containers: the ubiquitous exotic shape became almost commonplace in 17th century Europe. Walter Raleigh called it the *"Princess of Fruits"* and it was so admired that European gardeners worked hard on cultivating it, managing the first plants by the early 1520's. The pineapple remained such a curiosity in English society that the presentation of the first pineapple to be raised in England, made by the Royal Gardener, Mr John Rose, for Charles II in 1661, was the subject of a painting by Danckerts. By the mid-16th century the pineapple was being grown in India, from whence it moved quickly onwards to China and, in 1777, Captain Cook took it almost full-circle to the Pacific Islands. Nowadays, the main producers of pineapple on a commercial scale are Hawaii and Malaysia.

Traditional folk medicine credits the pineapple with many healing powers and fresh pineapple juice has been used as a gargle for throat infections, to relieve catarrh, arthritis, bronchitis and indigestion. The fresh fruit contains the enzyme bromelain which breaks down protein and which is so strong that people who regularly work with pineapples in quantity have to wear protective gloves and clothing to protect their skin. The enzyme is sometimes prescribed in tablet form as an aid to those who find it difficult to digest proteins.

Medicinal: Investigations carried out over the past 50 years have produced over 400 extensive papers on the effects of bromelain. Some suggest that it may be of use in the treatment of heart disease by helping to disperse blood clots. Other studies have presented evidence that it may help to combat sinus congestion, urinary tract infections and that it may augment the effects of antibiotics. Bromelain is also an anti-inflammatory and has been used in the treatment of both osteo- and rhematoid arthritis. It also appears to accelerate tissue repair and is used in several applications marketed for the treatment of sports injuries. However, the canning process destroys the bromelain but not the vitamin C content. Fresh pineapple provides almost a quarter of the recommended daily intake for vitamin C for a non-smoking adult, but not much in the form of other vitamins or minerals.

100g canned in juice provides 47 kcalories energy, no fat, 12.2g carbohydrate in the form of sugars, 0.5g non-soluble fibre, 8mg calcium, 0.5mg iron, 1mg sodium, 2μg vitamin A, 0.09mg Thiamin and 11mg vitamin C. Pineapple has a score of 66 on the Glycaemic Index.

Pistachio *(Pistacia vera)*

The pistachio is one of only two nuts to be mentioned by name in the Bible, the other being the almond, and it was probably brought under cultivation initially for its oil. The nut is the fruit of a small tree, native to Western Asia and the earliest evidence of it being consumed has been found at sites in Turkey and the Middle East, dating back to 7000 BC. It came to Europe via Rome from Syria and so became known as the '*Syrian nut*'.

Pistachios, when ripe, are open at one end and the people of Iran, where most pistachios are grown nowadays, called this state *khandan* which means laughing.

Uniquely in the nut world, the healthy kernel of a pistachio is green, due to the high presence of chlorophyll, a colour to be avoided in other members of the family, as an indicator of poison. Ancient writers mention it as a luxury food, as it still is, used mainly in rich, festive dishes such as fancy desserts and as a garnish.

Unani Tibb is the only medicinal regime which mentions a use for the pistachio and then just for the skin of the nut, which is listed as a combative to diarrhoea.

Plantain *(Musa sapientum)*

The plantain is also known as the cooking banana and is a staple food in Eastern and Central Africa, and is also used widely in other tropical regions. The fruit is thicker and larger than the dessert varieties and their skins can be pink, green, red, orange or black-brown.

Unani Tibb, the dietetic and medicinal doctrine founded by the Arab physician, Avicenna, lists its properties as being astringent, demulcent (containing a viscous substance which soothes inflamed tissues), and expectorant. The hakims, or healers, are advised to use the roots and leaves in their preparations for blood disorders and as a coolant and diuretic.

The plantain is also used to combat coughs, irritated throats, gastritis, respiratory problems and to eliminate mucus and catarrh. Externally, the leaves are crushed to produce a paste which soothes cuts, wounds, sores, insect bites and haemorrhoids.

Plants

Plants form the largest and most easily obtainable type of food, providing nutrients from all groups; carbohydrates, fats and proteins. They are also fairly easy to catch, most need no special preparation before being ready to eat and, with the exception of the poisonous few, do not fight back. Early settlers also found that quite a few could be grown to order. This discovery probably happened quite by accident, when discarded seeds from gathered edible plants began to thrive in the fertile middens and refuse heaps. All but a few of the common vegetables have been eaten since pre-history by Man, although it was not until the 16th century and the growth of wider trade links and communication that a greater variety of produce became available to any one culture.

The first plants to have been brought under cultivation, some 10,000 years ago, are thought to have been the grains and legumes; the richest sources of proteins and carbohydrates in the plant world. It is believed that fruits and vegetables would have followed quite a bit later as, although they contribute vitamins and minerals, they offer less in the way of the more filling and energy-giving carbohydrates, and so would always has been considered supplements rather than staple foodstuffs.

Primitive Europeans still had quite a range to choose from. They were able to grow wheat, beans, peas, carrots, turnips, radishes and onions, and by around 3000 BC, most of the native Mediterranean food plants were already in use by the Egyptians and Sumerians.

In Central America, maize, beans, avocados and tomatoes were all being grown by around 3500 BC, with the Peruvians already reliant on the potato as their staple. Asia's earliest crops were millet, rice, wheat, banana and the coconut palm, which provided so much more than simply food. Early societies also developed a taste for flavoured foods, with the Europeans and Asians using mustard seeds and ginger, whilst the indigenous Americans started using chillies. By 2500 BC the embryonic spice trade had been established by the naturally nomadic Arab traders and in 1200 BC it was recorded that Rameses III had given offerings of huge amounts of cinnamon, a native of Ceylon, an indication of just how widespread the trade had grown.

In the Classical world, the Greeks were very fond of lettuce and ate fruit at the end of their meals. Black pepper from India was in use in Europe by 500 BC and very quickly became the most popular and highly prized spice in the ancient world. It flavoured staple gruels and had the added benefit of both hiding and retarding food spoilage. The Romans also loved all other spices, especially cumin, the use of which they spread further west, together with their fruits, vines and cabbages.

Lines of supply were, naturally, weakened after the fall of the Empire with interest being rekindled after the visit of Haroun al-Raschid, the Caliph of Islam immortalized in 1001 Nights, to the Emperor Charlemagne in around 800 AD.

In ancient Rome, vegetables were regarded as hors d'oeuvres with fruit as a dessert, and like the Greeks, who provided most of their cooks, they too served lettuce both at the beginning and end of the meal, as they believed that the leaves would enable them to drink more wine without ill-effect.

By the beginning of the Christian era, the earliest form of genetic engineering – grafting – had been well-developed by both the Greeks and the Romans. The Romans, through a combination of discovery and cultivation, developed 25 varieties of apple and 38 of pears. They also refined the grafting method for the propagation of olive trees, still in use today, leading to most of the trees being clones and virtually identical to those grown by the ancients.

The Renaissance brought the so-called 'Colombian Exchange', bringing a veritable cornucopia of exotic, new plant foods: maize, common bean, squash, tomato, hot and sweet peppers, potato, groundnut, avocado and the pineapple. The mis-named 'French' bean was an immediate success, but outside Italy, where they have an eye for a good thing, the tomato was grown purely for ornament and corn and the potato soon became cheap staple crops for the poor masses.

The Exchange was two-way and by the end of the 16th century sugar cane and East Indian spices were being successfully cultivated in the new plantations in the West Indies. The 17th and 18th centuries then saw a further development, caused by the setting up of these colonial estates. Watermelon, okra and black-eyed peas spread to both the Americas and Europe, carried by the slave trade from Africa to the colonies.

By the 18th century a novelty appeared; the salad became fashionable. French food hygienists recommended eating fruit at the start of a meal and salad at the end, reasoning that the salad would moisten and refresh the stomach, encourage sleep, enlarge the appetite, temper the '*ardors of Venus*' and appease the thirst. And to think, the Romans and Greeks did exactly the same thing for the less romantic reason of being able to drink more.

The word fruit is derived from the Latin word *frui*, meaning to enjoy or delight in and originally meant any food plant, although it gradually came to mean just the edible layer of flesh which surrounds seeds. Fruit phrases entered the language, almost always being associated with pleasure or beauty, with the rare exceptions, of course, such as the raspberry and the lemon. Perhaps one of the reasons for this positive view of fruit is that they tend to be sweeter and generally have a higher sugar content: 15% on average, for temperate zone fruits, up to 60% in the tropics, with the lemon coming in at just 1%.

In the 18th century, botanists specified that a fruit is the organ derived from the ovary and surrounding the seeds. Around the same time, vegetable, from the Latin *vegere* meaning to enliven, came to be used for plant foods eaten as an accompaniment to a meal, as opposed to its original meaning of simply a plant.

In contrast to the more romantic phraseology linked with fruits, however, the poor old vegetables became linked in speech with boring, stupid or dull associations, with perhaps just the carrot coming out best, being used to illustrate a reward. The issue of what constitutes vegetable or plant, however, still raged on. Lots of plant foods labelled as vegetables are technically fruit: green beans, aubergines, cucumbers, marrows and sweetcorn have been so defined by common usage.

On the tomato debate, no less a body than the U.S. Supreme Court officially designated the fruit to be a vegetable when, in a case at the end of the 19th century, a New York produce importer lost his battle with the Customs authorities. He argued that, as a fruit, the tomato was not subject to import duty. However, the Court ruled against him on the grounds of linguistic custom, citing that tomatoes "....*are usually served at dinner in, with or after the soup, fish or meat, which constitute the principle part of the repast, and not, like fruit, generally as dessert."*

Plum *(Prunus domestica)*

Evidence of plum-eating has been found in Switzerland at prehistoric lake-sites and it is thought to be native to a wide band from Anatolia, the Caucasus and northern Persia. Mesopotamian records mention that they were grown in the orchards there and an Assyrian herbal recommends that they are eaten with honey and butter.

The Romans were fond of plums and experimented a great deal, as they did with all the fruit plants they liked, with grafting and cultivation techniques, to produce a great number of varieties. As Pliny the Elder, the 1st century encyclopaedist put it *"a great throng"*. Their genetic tinkering probably ensured that the plum reached the status of having more varieties than any other stone fruit today, with a staggering total of something over 2000.

The Latin generic name is used elsewhere, in varying forms, such as the French prune, as the common name for the fruit but in England, this term has been used exclusively for the dried form since Medieval times. In the Middle Ages, the contrary English also used the word plum to mean almost any kind of dried fruit too, leading to quite a bit of confusion as to the original recipes for those British classics such as plum pudding and cake - Little Jack Horner could have pulled out a large raisin or cherry.

Culpeper, the herbalist who mixed astrology in with his botany, assigned the plum to Venus, reasoning that the fruits were very much like women - "some better and some worse."

Nutritionally, plums are a good source of Vitamin E, an antioxidant which helps to protect body cells from the damage caused by 'free radicals', and may help to combat the effects of ageing.

Medicinal: Umeboshi, brine-pickled plums are used in traditional far-Eastern medicine to treat digestive problems. When dried, - prune - plums become a concentrated source of fruit sugars, an ideal energy food and they also provide potassium, iron and Vitamin B6.

They are also a useful source of dietary fibre which helps to avoid constipation and may help to combat certain cancers, like those of the colon and bowel. In addition, studies carried out in the United States are thought to indicate that the soluble fibre found in prunes may help to lower 'bad' or LDL cholesterol levels. Prunes also lower the levels of certain acids in the body, which may also help to protect against colon cancer.

Prunes are also a good source of beta-carotene, iron, which is necessary in red blood cell manufacture, copper, which prevents blood clots, thus avoiding thrombosis and stroke, and boron, important in helping post-menopausal women retain the oestrogen that is needed for calcium absorption, so guarding against osteoporosis.

A 100g serving of fresh plums, with skin = 36 kcalories, 8.8g carbodhydrate in the form of sugars, 1.6g fibre, 13mg calcium, 0.4mg iron, 2mg sodium, 49 µg Vitamin A, 0.05mg thiamin, 4mg vitamin C. 100g prunes =141 kcalories, 34g carbohydrate as sugar, 5.4g fibre, 34mg calcium, 2.6mg iron, 11mg sodium, 23 µg Vitamin A, 0.09mg thiamin, and no vitamin C.

Pomegranate *(Punica granatum)*

The pomegranate probably originated in Asia Minor and it has been a favourite fruit in the mythology of the region since earliest times. Assyrian art and monuments feature the pomegranate; remains of pomegranate have been found in Bronze Age tombs at Jericho, and carbonised fruits have been found amongst the funerary offerings and gardens of Ramesses II, dating them to 13th century BC.

Its common name is derived from the Latin *poma granita*, seeded apple, but the ancient Romans also called it *pomum punicum* as the fruit was introduced to them via Punica, or Carthage, in North Africa.

This link also gave rise to its botanical generic name with the *granatum*, many seeds, added as its specific name. This multi-seed structure has ensured a close link to mysticism since earliest times, particularly in the fields of life-force and fertility and it is one of the fruits which has been identified as the possible 'forbidden fruit' of the Garden of Eden.

The Ebers Papyrus, dated at around 2000 BC mentions the pomegranate, it appears in the Old Testament and ancient Sanskrit texts also indicate early cultivation in India.

In Greek mythology, the fruit plays quite an important part in the story of Persephone's abduction and the creation of winter. Demeter, her mother, was so upset that she suspended all growth on earth, preventing trees and plants from bearing fruit. Whilst in Hades, Persephone had vowed not eat, but was eventually tempted by a pomegranate and swallowed just six seeds. When Pluto finally relented and gave Persephone back to Demeter, he insisted that she should return to Hades each year, spending a month for each of the seeds she had eaten, triggering Demeter's grief and thus creating winter.

Ironically for the fruit which was associated with the onset of winter for the Greeks, the Hittites used it as the prime symbol of their god of agriculture, Ibritz, and its strong fertility symbolism earned it a place on both the Royal badge of Katherine of Aragon, one of the wives of Henry VIII, and the blazon of the Royal College of Physicians.

The Spanish city of Granada is named after it, as it was thought that its rather scattered layout would look like a half-opened pomegranate. Less pleasant things have also acquired their name from inspiration taken from this delicious fruit. When ripe, the pomegranate bursts and scatters its seeds in all directions around it and so, in the 1590s, when a bomb was invented which scattered metal fragments in much the same way, one name seemed appropriate - grenade.

The pomegranate has been used in healing for centuries with Pliny, the Roman Encyclopaedist, recommended using pomegranate root bark to expel tapeworm. The Indian holistic doctrine Ayurveda uses pomegranate rind to treat dysentery and its astringent properties are also useful in the treatment of diarrhoea. Under their classification system, pomegranate is listed as sour and is attributed with the ability to increase saliva flow, thus aiding digestion. The juice is also said to be cooling and nutritious and good in the treatment of bleeding gums. Pomegranate leaves are also used for their antibacterial properties and were traditionally applied to open wounds and sores.

Unani Tibb, the eastern dietetic and medicine philosophy founded by the physician Avicenna, also uses pomegranate as an astringent, using its leaves and flowers as a styptic and a tonic. Tibb also recommends the use of pomegranate for curing worms, although with care, as large doses can cause vomiting and giddiness. The rind is used to combat diarrhoea, haemorrhage, cancers and ulcers of the uterus and rectum and is also used to treat fevers. A tea is also made from the bark to eliminate tapeworm. Refreshingly, the Tibb doctrine has only one use for the fruit flesh itself - food.

As a food, the pomegranate is a very important ingredient in Middle Eastern cookery, used to flavour meat stews and the dried seeds being used as a garnish. Indian cuisine uses it too, sometimes using the seeds in stuffings for savoury breads and pastries and are used as a refreshing change of taste and texture in salads and drinks. The juice is also used to make drinks, desserts and is, of course, the base for the liquor, grenadine.

Nutritionally, pomegranate is a good source of vitamin C and useful for fibre intake when the seeds are eaten. 100g pomegranate flesh gives and energy value of 72 kcalories, 1.0g protein, 16.6g carbohydrate, 1mg sodium, 379mg potassium, 13mg calcium, 12mg magnesium, 0.7mg iron, 0.17mg copper, 0.3mg niacin and 7mg vitamin C

Poppy *(Papaver somniferum)*

Recorded use of the poppy dates back well over 5,000 years, to the time of the ancient Sumerians and it was used by all the great civilizations; used by the Egyptians, Greeks and Romans and cultivated in China, India and Iran by the 8th century AD.

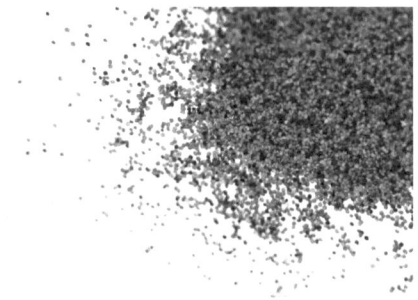

The drug opium is obtained from this species of poppy, a thick, milky latex which is extracted from the unripe seed heads, which contains some 25 different alkaloids, notably morphine and codeine, both powerful painkillers. This, of course, has led to its use as a medical painkiller since the earliest times. It has also been used for its sedative, antispasmodic and expectorant properties. Eighth century Arab physicians formulated a cough syrup, based on opium, which was in common use up until the 17th century. During the Middle Ages, sponges impregnated with poppy juice, mandrake, hemlock and ivy were used as an early form of anaesthesia during medical operations.

The Victorian era saw opium abuse, with tinctures of opium and laudanum, used routinely for pain control and opium smoking became a fashion among the creative and arty set. Opium mis-use continues today, with heroin, a morphine derivative high on the list of so-called 'recreational' drugs. However, the ripe seeds contain none of these narcotic alkaloids and neither does the oil extracted from them, and the tiny, nutty seeds impart a wonderful flavour to foods such as cakes, biscuits and breads. Poppy seeds are very popular in Indian cookery, where they are used not just to flavour, but as a very effective thickening agent too.

Potato *(Solanum tuberosum esculentum)*

The potato is a native of highland South America, with evidence of use in Peru dating back to at least 3000 BC. Since maize, the staple for most of the Americas, does not grow well at altitude, the potato, a hardy plant which takes a lot of punishment, became the staple of the American mountain dwellers. It can grow at altitudes as high as 4,000m (13,000ft) and can even grow on the snowline. Firm evidence of cultivation in Peru has been found dating back to 750 BC and archeologists have also found remains of a dehydrated potato product, *chuño* which seemed to form an important part of winter food stores and a potato flour, produced by a similar process, called *tunta*. Pottery items in the shape of potatoes have also been found at some sites, suggesting that it may also have been worshipped.

There are several claims for its discovery and transport to the 'Old World', but first off the mark may have been the Spanish explorer, Gonzalez Jiménez de Quesada, who first came across it in 1536, mistaking it originally for a new variety of truffle.

The idea that Sir Walter Raleigh is responsible for bringing it from the 'New World' seems to now be generally regarded as a modern myth and Lindsey Bareham in her '*In Praise of the Potato*', 1995, quotes a theory as to why the connection was established, put forward by the American foodwriter, Waverley Root:

"*In 1586, Sir Walter Raleigh's cousin, Sir Richard Grenville, sailed to do battle with the Spaniards in the Caribbean, and the story goes that he was asked to drop off some provisions in Virginia for premature colonists. One of Raleigh's men, Thomas Hariot, went along for the ride as far as Virginia and on arrival they discovered that the colonists wanted out. Around that time Sir Francis Drake was about to set sail for England after a successful series of battles against the Spaniards in the Caribbean.*

"*Drake stocked up with provisions for the return journey at Cartagena, Colombia, and included some potatoes. Next stop was Virginia to pick up the colonists. They returned via Ireland and Raleigh is supposed to have planted some of the tubers in his property at Youghal, near Cork. But, by the time the ship arrived in England, the potato and the Virginian settlers became inextricably entwined and potatoes became Virginian potatoes.*"

Reaction to its introduction was mixed, to say the least. As a member of the solanaceae, its 12 European cousins include such varieties as mandrake, henbane, woody nightshade, deadly nightshade and thorn apple, leading many to regard it has having similar, poisonous properties. However, the Americas have over 1,000 members of the genus, including the tomato and chilli.

Even its common name became subject to confusion. Another tuber, the Sweet Potato, brought back by Columbus from Haiti, and called *batata* by the natives there was often confused with the ordinary potato and so the original Peruvian papas was soon forgotten. The Spanish changed it to *patata*, the English to potato and most of the rest of Europe seem to have opted for variations on an 'earth-apple' theme - *pomme de terre* in France.

The potato was taken to India in the early 17th century where it did little to challenge rice and pulses as a staple, but did gain acceptance as a vegetable. John Gerard listed the plant in his herbal in 1597, by 1650 it had become the staple food in Ireland and by 1840 it had been attributed with causing over-population in Ireland. In 1845 and 1846 the potato famine affected the population badly enough to trigger mass emigration to America and Britain.

However, not all the Celts took to it. In Northern Ireland and Scotland, Protestants refused to use it as it was not mentioned in the Bible, but the canny Roman Catholic Irish overcame this particular theological problem by 'baptizing' seed potatoes with Holy Water and planting them on Good Friday.

The resourceful Irish also found another use for their new staple. They mashed them up then boiled and distilled them to produce the sometimes lethal *Poteen* (pronounce pocheen). Frank Muir, humourist and author, writing in 1976 on the subject, pointed out that in many cases this moonshine *eau de vie* turned out to be *eau de mort*.

European leaders seized upon the easily grown, filling crop as a means of feeding the masses; Frederick the Great of Prussia ordered mass cultivation and several European governments issued edicts promoting the tuber. The English also saw the great potential of the potato, although they regarded it initially as a medicine and, typically for the times, an aphrodisiac, as highlighted by its inclusion as such in Shakespeare's 'Merry Wives of Windsor'.

The French, on the other hand, reviled it, and it was only used on a very small scale until pharmacist, Antoine-Auguste Parmentier, recommended the use of the potato as a solution to the country's recurring famine in the early 1770s. However, the French were less than enamoured of this ugly, unprepossessing tuber and resisted strongly. Feelings against the potato were so high that a rumour even existed that it would cause leprosy. So Parmentier indulged in a little reverse psychology; gaining permission from Louis XVI to plant a small field of potatoes just outside Paris, he posted a very conspicuous guard. This was enough to pique the interest of the contrary French temperament with Parisians, who had initially turned up their noses at the tuber, plundering the crop and giving the potato a new-found 'chic'. To reinforce this new growing popularity, M. Parmentier demonstrated a genius for marketing that many modern companies would envy in organizing a royal banquet, at which every course contained potatoes in some form and the Royal couple wore potato flowers, his name gaining synonymity with the potato for posterity in France.

In folk medicine, potato and milk poultices are used for cuts and wounds, skin infections and swellings; raw potato juice is used for gastritis and stomach swellings and it is believed that its alkaline properties make it good for combating uric acid retention, rheumatism and arthritis.

Today, the potato is the third most important crop in the world and, according to figures from the Potato Marketing Board, we eat an average of 100kg (242lb) per person, per annum.

Nutritionally, the potato has had some unfair press over the years, being falsely labelled 'stodgy' and 'fattening'. In fact, it is not the potato itself which piles on the calorie count, but whatever cooking method or accompaniment one chooses. An example of this is the fried potato crisp or chip. Labelled as junk food or 'empty calories', they are actually an excellent source of potassium and a good source of vitamin C. An average bag of crisps (35g) provides just under a quarter of the recommended daily allowance for vitamin C in an adult non-smoker.

The BIG drawback is that they have a huge fat content. Because of the large surface area afforded by their shape, they absorb 1/3 of their weight in fat. Another high-fat British favourite, the chip, (ironically dubbed French-fries by the Americans and Pommes Anglaise by the French), is also high in fat. But this can be reduced by various methods. Using fresh potatoes, rather than frozen will help - frozen chips absorb fat more readily. Oven chips, however, are lower in fat by comparison to deep fry. In addition to this, the cut of the chip will also affect final fat content. Weight-for-weight, the thinner a chip is cut, the greater the surface area created and hence in contact with the fat, and fat absorption increases. Needless to say, crinkle-cut increases the surface area even more! Oven chips contain around 5%, medium-cut 10% and thin cut, or string, 20%. A 225g (8oz) potato, boiled, steamed or baked contains just 160 calories and is composed of 81% water, 16% starch, 1% minerals and trace elements, 0.79% vitamins, 0.6% fibre, 0.35% protein, 0.27% sugars and 0.08% fats.

One medium potato supplies, on average, 30mg vitamin C, nearly as much as in a glass of tomato juice and 1.5mg iron, which is around the same amount as in an egg. However, long storage times, soaking, boiling and salt in the cooking water can drain out some of the precious nutrients, which are mainly found just under the surface of the skin. For this reason, some people advocate using potato cooking water for soup stocks, gravies and cooking other vegetables and always cooking them in their skins. Potato juice has also been used for some time in Germany as an effective antacid.

The potato also contains thiamin, riboflavin, nicotinic acid and a significant amount of potassium at 844µg per 100g. When potatoes turn green, however, throw them away. When exposed to light in bad storage, poisonous solanine levels rise rapidly, causing them to be unfit for consumption when levels rise above as much as 0.1%. Even in small amounts, solanine can cause drowsiness and migraines in those sensitive to its effects.

Pumpkin *(Cucurbita pepo)*

Fragments of pumpkin have been found in Mexico which date back 4,000 years, giving a fair indication of just how long this has been a food crop. Etymologists believe that the common name is derived from the classical Greek *pepon*, meaning melon, via the Old French, *pompon*.

Pumpkin seeds, taken with castor oil, have been used as a traditional method to expel intestinal worms and they have also been used to combat urinary tract infections and their hormone-like action is capitalised upon to ease prostate problems. Easily digested, pumpkin rarely triggers allergic reactions and scores quite a high 75 on the Glycaemic Index.

Medicinal: As with all orange fruit and vegetables, red pumpkin is an excellent source of beta-carotene, the plant pre-cursor which is converted to vitamin A by the body, a powerful antioxidant, as is vitamin E, also found in pumpkin. Both are quite powerful anti-oxidants which may prevent the damage caused to body cells by free radicals which, in turn, can cause ageing and certain types of cancer.

Pumpkin seeds, too, are quite nutritious. Used sometimes in Middle Eastern and Indian cookery, they are an excellent source of iron and phosphorous and a good source of potassium, magnesium and zinc. 100g pumpkin flesh give 15 kcalories, 0.5g fibre, 0.6g protein, 3.4g carbohydrate, 1mg sodium, 310mg potassium, 39mg calcium, 8mg magnesium, 0.4mg iron, 0.08mg copper, 5mg vitamin C, and 1500µg carotene.

Radish *(Raphanus sativus - Daikon, Mooli, Spring radish)*

Commonly taken to mean the swollen parts of the roots of a family of cruciferous plants which are related to cabbage, turnip, horseradish, Brussels sprouts, cauliflower, etc. The plant is thought to be an 'Old World' native from a region which stretches as far as Japan, but it is difficult to pinpoint where it first occurred accurately as it has been used from the Mediterranean to the Orient as far back as it is possible to trace. Herodotus, writing in the 5th century BC, includes the radish in the list of vegetables which were supposed to have been used by the Egyptians to feed the slaves who built the Great Pyramid.

The botanical name is from the Greek, *raphanos*, and the Latin *raphanus*, both versions of the same word which these ancient societies used to describe any of the radish family known to them at the time.

The common word, radish, however, is a direct descendent of the Latin *radix*, meaning root. It reached Britain in the mid-16th century and by 1633 Gerard was able to record four varieties of radish; to be made into a sauce to accompany meats and to stimulate the appetite, eaten raw with bread. This latter practice survived quite a while in the case of the small red spring radish, packed as it is with similar glucosides to mustard, giving it a sharp peppery tang, which would also be covered in butter and salt before eating with the bread.

The larger radishes, known as Mooli in much of Asia, Chinese Icicle Radish in America, where they were taken by Iberian explorers in the 17th century, or daikon in Japan, are long and white, shaped like large carrots. They are valued for their ability to withstand long cooking without losing shape or too much texture, and for their ability to absorb flavours whilst retaining their individual character. Always used peeled, they are used in much the same way as potatoes, carrots or turnips.

Medicinal: Radish is a useful source of vitamin C, necessary for the production of collagen which is used in skin, bone, cartilage, teeth and gum development and in the healing process. They are also low in fat and calories and have been used in herbalism as a diuretic, so, although an ideal light snack for slimmers, they are not to be overdone.

In Ayurveda, the ancient Indian holistic method of balancing one's life and health, the radish and its relations are listed in the pungent category; seen as cleansing, increasing the flow of saliva, hence aiding digestion, absorbing excess liquids and used sometimes as a gentle expectorant. Interestingly, Romany gypsies, who can trace their ancestry back to the same roots as these practitioners, use horseradish juice, a plant which is another member of this cruciferous group, mixed with honey, as a treatment for bronchial complaints.

Unani Tibb also value the radish for its medicinal properties. Among the uses listed by the hakims are to combat coughs, rheumatism, gallbladder problems, flatulence, diarrhoea, headache and insomnia. Its juice is also used as a mouth cleanser in Tibb to prevent dental caries. It was also grown as a 'proper' vegetable, for its leaves as well as the root, as the daikon still is and the beta-carotene commonly found in such dark, green leaves, is known to be a powerful antioxidant, and is under investigation by several study groups for its ability to either combat or prevent many types of cancers.

100g **red, raw radish** = 15 kcalories, 93.3g water, 1.0g fibre, 2.8g carbohydrate, 1mg protein, 59mg sodium, 240mg potassium, 44mg calcium, 11mg magnesium, 1.9mg iron, 0.13mg copper, 0.1mg zinc, 0.04mg vitamin B1, 0.02mg vitamin B2, 0.4mg niacin, 25mg vitamin C and 24μg folates.

100g **white/mooli**, raw = 24 kcalories, 93g water, 1g protein, 0.1g fat, 4.3g carbohydrate, 27mg sodium, 228mg potassium, 27mg calcium, 15mg magnesium, 0.4mg iron, 0.15mg copper, 0.2mg zinc, 0.02mg vitamin B1, 0.03mg vitamin B2, 0.7mg niacin, 42mg vitamin C.

Rice *(Oryza sativa)*
'Rice is a necessary and appropriate food for a virtuous and graceful life' Confucius
Rice is the staple food of over half the world's population, and there are three basic varieties - long grain, short grain and glutinous - spread across the 19 species of this member of the grass family.

A tropical plant, it requires quite high temperatures and humidity to grow successfully. The plant has a hollow stem which carries oxygen down to its roots, an evolutionary adaptation to growth in flooded areas, although it is thought that the now long-established paddy-field cultivation by man, which nowadays is where 90% of the world's rice is grown, was probably not developed as an agricultural skill until late in the Neolithic period, probably around 3000 BC. The remainder, which does not need to be flooded, growing much like any other cereal crop, is known as upland rice.

Wild rice, the dark grain which has been fashionable, sometimes mixed with American long-grain for some time now, is not a true rice at all, but the seed of an aquatic grass, *Zizania aquatica*. It grows in the swamps and shallow lakes of central North America and was once the staple food of several Native American tribes, who used to harvest it by shaking the ears of grass over their canoes to collect the seeds - a method which is still used today.

Theories differ widely as to exactly where and when rice cultivation first started. Some scholars believe that it first appeared in the Ganges Delta, in India, around 3000 BC, moving eastwards as early trade movements began during the Chinese Bronze Age. Other sources claim evidence exists in excavations in Eastern China dating back to 6000 BC, whilst yet another group point to food remains found in a cave in Northern Thailand, dating back to around 6000 BC, as the earliest evidence of Man's cultivation of this basic foodstuff.

It is mentioned in several very early texts: *Susrutha Samhita* a medical work from around 1000 BC classifies the then existing strains in India, including advice on nutritional value; Greek texts from around the time of Alexander's invasion of India in 320 BC refer to rice as being an Indian grain; Aristobulus, writing in 280 BC mentions that rice was being grown in Babylonia, Bactria and Lower Syria. Rice was slow to emerge any further Westwards from Asia, probably because of its expense and resistance to transplantation in cooler climes. It warrants no mention at all in the Bible. The Ancient Egyptians, keen horticulturists and ever ready to try a new food, did not grow it, despite the ideal conditions along some stretches of the Nile, and the Greeks and Romans regarded it as an expensive novelty to be used a medicine.

Eastwards its progress was more successful. It is thought that rice spread with the movement of South Chinese immigrants to the Philippines before the first millennium BC, reaching Japan by 1st century BC.

A charming Chinese legend explains the origin of rice, attributing it to Kuan Yin, the goddess of compassion, also know as *Sungtzu niang-niang*, the lady who brings children. The story goes that the rice plant had always existed but, at first, its ears were empty. Seeing that Mankind were suffering and hungry, Kuan Yin went into the rice fields and emptied the milk from her breasts into the barren plants. Before she had filled all the plants, however, she had pressed so hard that blood began to flow with the milk. That is why there are two types of rice, white and red.

The earliest appearance of rice in written records in this country is a quantity itemised in the household accounts for the court of Henry III in 1234, and when the cereal finally arrived in any quantity, it was the glutinous, short-grained variety which found favour, for use in milk puddings. Initially, the rice/milk pudding was a costly and indulgent luxury, containing refined sugar and spices as well as the equally expensive grain itself. Rich Elizabethans tended to reserve it for nursing mothers, whilst by the time of Charles I it was regarded as an aphrodisiac.

Pudding rice remained the British favourite until Anglo-Indian dishes, such as *Kedgeree*, found favour in Victorian England. Adapted from the Indian mix of rice and dal, *Kitcheri*, the British (and Scottish regiments in particular) in India added smoked fish and chopped, hard-boiled eggs, dropping the lentils somewhere along the way, and the dish was almost a mandatory part of the British breakfast sideboard for decades.

Thailand is currently one of the world's greatest producers of quality rice, having three to four harvests annually. In fact, rice is so ingrained within Thai culture that a common phrase to express hunger is 'I have an appetite for rice'.

Rice is far more adaptable than many people give it credit for. It is used to brew beers; to make fermented wines; distilled to make spirits. It can be ground to provide a flour for pancakes, dumplings

and breads. By cooking , wrapped tightly, in either in banana leaves or cooking foil, rice can also be 'compacted' into sliceable loaves and makes it an interesting way to serve it as the central carbohydrate in a meal.

The most enduring recipes, however, can be traced back to the Sassinad Persians from around the 10th century AD. Modern dishes such as the Iranian Polo, Indian Pilau, Spanish Paella, Italian risotto and French Pilaf all bear traces of influence of their Arab forebears. Moghul rulers of India loved pilau and, to add to the sensual enjoyment of the dish, would have their rooms filled with the fragrance of saffron before it was served.

Ayurveda values brown, unpolished rice as being effective on all three forces which affect bodily and mental functions, the tridoshas - Pitta: Sun (metabolism); Kapha: Moon (body fluids balance); Vata: Wind (nervous system). It is regarded as being sweet, cooling, diuretic, beneficial to the eyesight and a strengthening tonic for the heart. Unani Tibb believes that rice increases pleasant dreams and '*produces an abundance of semen*'.

Nutritionally, brown rice, which still has the vitamin and nutrient bearing bran worn away by milling, is far superior to the polished white. Modern processing methods, parboil the grain before milling, causing some of the nutrients to migrate from the outer coat to inner parts of the grain. Even so, all the essential nutrients are dramatically reduced, if not wiped out completely.

A nutrition comparison between the basic types shows that the Vitamin B1 is reduced considerably by polishing, as are many other nutrients and valuable dietary fibre. It was the loss of the vitamin B1, however, which led to beri-beri outbreaks in the Far East at the end of the 19th century. *Beri-beri*, which takes its name from the Sri Lankan word for weakness, causes mental confusion, loss of feeling in the feet and legs, paralysis of the eye muscles, muscular degeneration, heart irregularities and emaciation.

Nutritional Chart

Per 100g	Water	Dietary fibre	Energy	Value	Protein	Fat	Carbohydrate
	g	g	k cal	kj	g	g	g
Brown raw	13.9	4.2	357	1518	6.7	2.8	81.3
Long Grain Polished, raw	11.7	2.4	361	1536	6.5	1.0	86.8
Parboiled, raw	12.4	N	364	1523	6.7	1.0	78.7
Red raw	13.2	N	354	1481	7.4	1.6	76.0
	Na	K	Ca	Mg	Fe	Cu	Zn
	mg	mg	mg	mg	mg	mg	mg
Brown raw	3	250	10	112	1.4	0.85	1.8
Long grain polished, raw	6	110	4	13	0.5	0.06	1.3
Parboiled raw	2	150	7	N	1.2	N	N
Red raw	2	195	18	N	1.2	N	N

Vitamins	Thiamin (B1)	Riboflavin (B2)	Niacin (B3)	Folacin (Folic Acid)
	mg	mg	mg	ug
Brown raw	0.59	0.07	5.3	49
Long grain polished, raw	0.08	0.03	3.0	29
Parboiled, raw	0.20	0.08	2.6	N
Red, raw	0.30	0.10	4.2	N

In 1886 the Dutch East India Company began investigations into the cause of the disease, but it was not until 1911, when a Polish chemist named Cosimir Funk found that an extract of rice hulls could be used to prevent the disease. He originally believed it to be a nitrogen-bearing compound, or amine and, as it seemed vital to life he dubbed his new discovery 'vitamine', a contraction of vital amine. It was later discovered that the substance wasn't actually an amine and so the 'e' was dropped. The word vitamin, however, had arrived to stay. Rice bran is also a good source of vitamin K, which helps blood clotting and in the absorption of calcium, and vitamin E, which has been attributed with helping to slow down all the harmful oxidation processes in body cells, such as ageing and the formation of free radicals which can trigger cancers and damage heart tissue.

The Glycaemic Index rates brown rice at 66, Basmati rice at 58 and white rice at 72. The lower the rate, the slower the digestion rate, keeping blood sugar levels more constant.

As with all highly nutritious foods, however, there is always a danger that other organisms get to them before we do. The spores of the organism *bacillus cereus* germinate rapidly and produce toxins in batches of cooked rice which has been left to stand in warm, moist conditions. Unfortunately the toxins cannot be destroyed by normal cooking methods, and symptoms, which include stomach pains, vomiting and diarrhoea, occur as quickly as 1 hour after eating contaminated food.

Rosemary *(Rosemarinus officinalis)*

Both its systematic generic name and the common are said to be derived from *ros marinus*, dew of the sea, after its tendency to grow in coastal regions where it is found wild in the Mediterranean. The ancient Greeks believed that it improved the power of the mind and wore garlands of it around their heads during examinations. Rosemary was also used in Classical Rome but primarily as a medicine, and it was taken with them to their colonies.

Later its associations grew to include remembrance and mourners who would often carry sprigs to toss into the grave, to indicate that the deceased would not be forgotten. Shakespeare reflected this when writing for Ophelia's pre-suicide ramblings, (Hamlet, Act IV, Scene IV), *"There's rosemary, that's for remembrance; pray you, love, remember."*

Rosemary was also worn at weddings to signify fidelity and was traditionally incorporated into the bridal bouquet; Anne of Cleves wore a wreath of rosemary on her marriage to Henry VIII - either proving it totally ineffective in this capacity, or the king's immunity to herbal cures. Had he been more susceptible to rosemary's charms, Henry may also have been able to avail himself of another benefit of the plant; rosemary oil is a traditional remedy for gout, a disease from which he suffered very badly. The oil is also used in herbalism to ease muscular aches and pains and was the active ingredient in 'Hungary Water', a preparation made by a hermit for Elizabeth, Queen of Hungary, in around 1235. A distillation of rosemary, lavender and myrtle, it is said to have restored life to her paralyzed limbs.

Its antiseptic properties have been well-known throughout the ages. During the 15th century, rosemary branches were burnt to protect homes from the Black Death and during World War II rosemary and juniper branches were burnt in French hospitals to prevent the spread of infection. In popular magic, rosemary is said to be ruled by the sun and is used to promote sleep, enduring youth, protection, love, mental awareness and purification. One superstition held that if rosemary sprigs were placed under the pillow, it would banish evil spirits and the nightmares they bring.

Used in incense for purification and insight and may be slightly hallucinogenic, as it was inhaled by practitioners to promote visions and 'the sight'. It was also used as a cheaper alternative to frankincense.

The flowers of the rosemary were said to have once been white, turning blue after the Virgin Mary rested her mantle over them.

Culinary use of the herb is usually restricted to the savoury side, for roasts such as lamb, flavouring vegetables and for stuffings for poultry and fish. Slender rosemary branches can also be used to make skewers which flavour meat from the inside-out to stunning effect. It is said to stimulate the circulatory, nervous and digestive systems, relieving indigestion and flatulence. A herb for all uses, rosemary has also been used in cosmetics throughout the ages. The oil is used to stimulate the head and scalp being a common ingredient in many hair tonics and shampoos. Herbal medical practitioners also use weak rosemary tea to relieve headaches, dizziness, neuralgia and colds and its antiseptic properties makes an infusion of rosemary an ideal gargle.

Modern medical scientists are also exploring the cancer-busting properties of the herb. Apparently, it contains substances known as *quinones*, which have been shown in laboratory tests to inhibit carcinogens and cocarcinogens, chemicals which enhance the action of cancer-causing substances.

Saffron *(Crocus sativus - Kesar - Saffron crocus)*

Perhaps one of Man's earlier spice 'finds', the flower that produces the stigmas that comprise this highly prized - and priced - spice was represented in Cretan art dating back to 1600 BC. In Greek legend, Crocus was a beautiful young man who played a game of quoits with the messenger god, Mercury. One of the god's quoits hit Crocus on the head, killing him instantly. His friends grieved for him and where his blood had spilled on the grass, saffron crocuses sprang up.

The common name for the spice is derived from the Arabic root *assfar*, meaning 'yellow', as it was, originally, mainly for the intense yellow colour obtained from the stigmas that this spice was used.

The plant is perennial and rarely grows in the wild, and has been cultivated in Europe since the 12th century. From the 14th century up until the early 20th century, the Essex town of Saffron Walden was the English growing centre. Saffron is the most expensive of the spices (over £2 per gram, more than £56 per ounce), due to the fact that each flower yields just three stigma, and, due to the variation in the length of each of them - up to 5cm - it can take anything between 200,000 to 300,000 to make 1lb in weight; add to that the fact that each stigma must be picked by hand, and it is little wonder that this is the gold of the spice world in more than one sense.

Hardly surprising, also, are the recorded instances of criminals being burned or buried alive in 15th century Germany as a punishment for ruining or tampering with saffron crocus crops.

Probably because of the cost, giving it strong associations with wealth and power, saffron was attributed with ritual and caste significance, and was used to dye the robes of royalty and holy men and to produce the caste marks worn on the forehead in India, to where it was taken in around the 3rd century AD by the Moghuls.

These associations survived its passage across geographical boundaries, with most cultures linking it to fertility and harvest rites, physical strength, sexual and psychic prowess and with royalty. John Gerard, in his book *The Herbal*, published in 1597, claimed that saffron possessed life-restoring properties and, in 1670, the German scholar, J.F. Hertodt devoted a whole book, *Crocologia*, to the spice, in which he stated that it will cure both toothache and plague!

Saffron was one of the earliest trade spices and was brought into Spain some time during the 10th century, where it was adopted enthusiastically. Nowadays, Spanish saffron, grown in the flat central plains of La Mancha is regarded as being the very finest, and over 70% of the world's saffron now comes from Spain, although it is also grown in Greece, Iran, Morocco, Kashmir and Italy.

The ancient Romans used it to tint and scent their bathwater and used saffron-scented oils for massage, introducing it to England during their stay here.

The ancient Greeks valued it as much for its subtle honey-scent and earthy flavour as for its colour, and in Medieval Europe, it enjoyed popular use as a hair dye and aphrodisiac amongst the wealthy classes.

The saffron stigmas contain three chemical compounds: *Picrocrocin*, which provides the bitter, earthy flavour; a glycoside, *safranal*, which gives the spice its characteristic aroma; *Crocin*, a carotenoid, which releases the intense dye with its ability to colour up to 150,000 times its volume in water. It is this colouring power upon which the quality of a particular variety of saffron is assessed.

Mancha Selecto, regarded as the very best, must score a colour factor of at least 180 times the stigmas' weight, although some brands exceed the minimum requirement with ease, and this is reflected in their price. Inferior saffron is coarser, paler and sometimes includes other parts of the flower to pad it out, thus affecting the colouring power and providing a much more bitter taste.

Saffron was traditionally used in English cooking in sweet dishes, such as apple and pear pies, custards, creams, syllabubs and the famous Cornish saffron buns and cakes - although many of these products actually contain little or none of this expensive commodity nowadays, having been largely replaced with artificial colourings.

Most other cuisines, however, see it in a more savoury light: Italian rissottos, Spanish paellas, French bouillabaisse, and Persian pilaffs all require that little pinch of culinary gold.

Nutritionally, saffron has very little to offer. A massive 1 tsp., ground, an amount that no cook would ever envisage using, weighs 7 grams and has an energy value of just 2 kcalories. It contains very little in the way of vitamins - a little B2, and contains sodium, phosphorous, potassium, calcium and iron.

However, in spite of its lack of food value, herbalists have long been convinced of its powers as a digestive and appetite stimulant and in Persia, pregnant women traditionally wore a ball of saffron tied around the base of the stomach to ensure an easy delivery.

Sage *(Salvia officinalis - Garden Sage)(Salvia officinalis purpurea - Red Sage)(Salvia sclanea - Clary Sage or Clear Eye)*

The botanical generic name for all the sage family is derived from the Latin *salvere*, to save, cure or thrive, a lasting testament to its ancient reputation as a medical cure-all. So strong was the faith in sage that, by around the 10th century AD, it had acquired the reputation of being able to confer immortality.

Folk magic and Culpeper assigned the planet Jupiter as the ruling astrological object for garden sage, and it was used in country magic to generate money, protection, longevity, wisdom and used in the granting of wishes. It was said that you should carry sage if you wish to be wise and that you should eat a little every day - especially during May - for a long life; one old proverb asks, *"how can a man die, who has sage in his garden?"*

It was thought by some to reflect the business fortunes of the man of the house, flourishing or withering with the state of his finances. Confusingly, another belief also held that garden sage only grows well when a woman rules the roost, as it reacts well to the imposition of 'gentler values'. Sage was the herb originally used in Europe for making tea long before the introduction of Indian tea and the Chinese traded their own green tea with the Dutch in return for supplies of the herb. The Chinese healers considered it to be strengthening to the digestive system and calming to the nerves.

Medicinal: Garden sage has antiseptic and antibacterial properties and an infusion has traditionally been used as a mouthwash to cure mouth ulcers and gum infections and as a gargle for sore throats. Herbalists also claim that sage can aid digestion of heavy, rich foods and can help to combat a tendency to sweating. This cooling property also makes it an ideal remedy for fevers and flushes, especially those experienced during the menopause. Even just the leaves, rubbed gently across the teeth, will freshen the mouth and strengthen the gums. However, it is advised not to use too much during pregnancy and in not too large an amount on a regular basis for all.

Sage has had its cosmetic uses too; the ancient Romans used a strong infusion of the herb to darken their hair.

Sage is also very attractive to bees and the honey is highly regarded by aficionados, but even so, it was only relatively recently - the 16th century - that sage has been given kitchen space. Gaining favour as a flavouring for pork and poultry, especially in farcies, or stuffings, it may have initially been used in this way for its reputation as a digestive and an aid to absorbing heavier meats and any toxicity which may be present. It is an essential ingredient in the Italian dish, *Saltimbocca*, ('jump in the mouth), veal layered with ham and sage and the Italians use it rather effectively with calves liver and eels.

Other favourite culinary sages are: Greek Sage, *Salvia fructiosa*, a lighter, more subtle variety; Pineapple sage, *Salvia rutilans*, with a scent reminiscent of the fruit; American Blue sage, *Salvia clevelandii* and the variety which has a slightly lavender scented aroma, *Salvia lavandulifolia*. Red sage has, as can be gathered by its name, dark purple-red foliage, but its seeds will revert to the green variety. It is thought to be more effective in countering sore throats than ordinary garden sage and, like its sibling, is also used for bleeding gums and mouth sores and ulcers.

In the kitchen, it can be used in exactly the same way as garden sage, adding a little more colour. Clary sage is the largest member of this little group, growing larger and with large leaves and its common and specific name is derived from the Latin *clarus*, clear as in its folk name, clear eye. This is due to the fact that traditionally the seeds are soaked in water to produce a mucilaginous liquid which was then used to clear the eyes of grit and foreign bodies.

The leaves, together with elderflowers, were also used to flavour some German wines, especially more potent Muscatels, hence the common German name for the herb is *muskatellersalbei* or simply, *muskateller*. The plant is also used in perfumery and aromatherapists use it for its warming, uplifting and soothing properties to relieve tension, stress, muscular aches and period pains. Interestingly enough, in old folk medicine, strongly mixed with the lore of country magic, the ruling body for the clary sage is the moon, linked to its cycles and, for that reason, used to aid and regulate the menstrual cycle.

Salt *(Sodium Chloride, NaCl)*

Salt, or sodium chloride, is such a basic requirement for life, that all animals are equipped with special taste-buds in the tongue in order that we may detect it. Salt, or more specifically, the sodium component of the compound is needed to maintain proper fluid balance and to control nerve and muscle activity and so all our body fluids contain salt, which is why tears and blood always taste salty. Even saliva, derived from the Latin word for salt, *sal* contains salt.

Migration patterns for early Man, historical events, riots, revolutions and even wars have been motivated by this need for salt. It is thought that only once Man had discovered agriculture and added more vegetables and grain to his diet did he develop this growing need for sodium; totally carnivorous beasts do not have the same supplementary requirement, gaining all the sodium needed from the muscle tissues of other animals. It is said that the closer you are to true vegetarianism, the more salt you will desire.

Salt is extracted from natural sources by several methods. Rock salt is obtained by mining or by using a 'well'. This method entails forcing water down one of the well tubes, which then dissolves the salt, the resulting brine being extracted through other tubes. Once at the surface the salt solution can be purified using a method of evaporation. Different methods of evaporation are available: solar; steam evaporation in vacuum pans; evaporation in pans and kettles using direct heat. Most commercial salt uses either steam or direct-heat evaporation, as solar options, such as the traditional methods used in the Mediterranean, using shallow coastal saltpans, is time consuming and expensive.

Religions worldwide have given salt a prime place in their observances. Judaism prescribes it as a prime offering to God and it symbolizes His Covenant with his chosen; salt is sprinkled on bread at the start of the Sabbath and, in the New Testament, Jesus refers to his followers as 'the salt of the earth' in the Sermon on the Mount.

Country witchcraft, too, placed a great importance on this basic commodity. Witches and the agents of the evil powers could be identified by placing salt on their backsides, thus preventing them from sitting down, and the superstitious, reflex action of throwing a pinch of spilt salt over the left shoulder, stems back to a belief that it would scatter the evil spirits that were supposed to gather there.

It is hard to believe in modern times, when salt is plentiful and cheap, that it played an enormous part in the social, economic, political and even religious development of most cultures. It has been used in the religious rites of the Greeks, Romans, Hebrews and Christians. This is most evident in the legacies of the ancient Roman Empire. The number of words we have inherited from them which have a common root in *sal* indicate just how central a part of their society salt was. Salad from the extended form *salata*, salted; salami; sausages; sauces, via salsa; salary, from salarium, the payment made to Roman soldiers for their salt allowance. Herbs and oils were also added to augment and complement foodstuffs, *sal conditus*.

The face of the planet was also altered in great part due to the movement and trade of salt; the Via Salaria, a highway built by the Romans which stretched right across Italy from the Mediterranean to the Adriatic was in direct response to the need to transport salt to their outposts. Venice, a clever city state, rich in business acumen and eye to the spice trade upon which it built much of its wealth, was only augmenting its already vast wealth created by its saltpans, carved to harvest this treasure from the sea.

Salt was a preservative too, enabling the export and long-term storage of food, especially fish which degenerates rapidly.

In some countries, salt was so important that the state often either took control at some stage or levied special taxes on its sale and distribution. In China salt was the subject of a state monopoly from before the 7th century BC. France had La Gabelle, the despised salt tax, which prompted the nation into revolution and Ghandi led his famous long march in protest at the British salt tax which outlasted domestic abolition (1825) in the colonies. His mass protest march to the sea to gather a free supply in 1930 was much publicized and can be said to have lead, ultimately, to the end of the British Empire. Even today, Italy taxes salt, to the extent that it is sold alongside that other treasury booster, tobacco.

The quest for salt can even have been said to have led to the foundation of the great American oil industry. Subterranean salt deposits sometimes force a dome of salt to ground level, indicating sizeable supplies beneath. In 1901, a party drilling into one of these domes came upon quite a different treasure - black gold.

Medicinal: Ayurveda values salt as it is one of the basic tastes needed to ensure perfect balance of the doshas, or life forces, as it calms all three. However, most texts on the subject recommend sea salt as being the most therapeutic, as it contains other valuable minerals, such as iron and magnesium. It is said to strengthen eyesight, stimulate poor digestion, act as a heart tonic, and even act as an aphrodisiac.

Ayurvedic practitioners also believe that salt changes the consistency of saliva, creating energy to soften food and putting an edge on the appetite; It helps to break down food tissue and promotes salivation, hence digestion and regular bowel movements.

However, too much sodium may cause high blood pressure and those on high salt diets are at greater risk of developing stomach and gastrointestinal cancers. Salt is normally excreted in urine, but some people retain the excess salt. This causes a sodium overload; the body retains water to compensate; blood volume increases; the heart works harder to pump the extra fluid; blood pressure rises: high blood pressure.

A lot of nutritionists believe that diet patterns in the developed world are leading to over-consumption by as much as 200-300% and the World Health Organisation have laid down guidelines that we should limit ourselves to around 2,400mg per day - just under 1 level teaspoon. However, it should be pointed out that this is not the added salt from the condiment pot, but includes all hidden salt intake too. For instance, just one hamburger from a fast food outlet can contain up to 1,200mg - around half the day's allowance, cornflakes can contain up to 360mg per average serving, which, surprisingly, easily outstrips the much-maligned packet of crisps which weighs in at a more humble 270mg average. When viewed in this way, one can see how very quickly the total can rise in a society which relies so heavily on processed convenience foods and snacks.

Because the growing awareness of this problem, several low-salt products are making an appearance on the market. These preparations generally cut the sodium content by half by substituting potassium in its place and should be avoided by people with kidney problems and those who have been diagnosed as suffering from diabetes. These groups often experience difficulty in excreting excess potassium and can build up dangerously high levels unless they watch their intake.

Sesame *(Sesamum indicum Gingill)*

Most people associate the name sesame with the command given by Ali Baba to gain access to the thieves den in the Tales of 1001 Nights. It is thought that the bursting and scattering action of the ripe seed pods inspired this somewhat tenuous link.

Sesame is a native of the region which stretches from East Africa to Indonesia with evidence of its first cultivation found in the Middle East, dating back to around 3000 BC. Sesame oil was used in Mesopotamia and tablets detailing accounts and receipts for the day-to-day running of the palace of Nebuchadnezzar, (600BC), list *'best quality sesame oil'*, backed up by histories written by the ancient Greek scholars record that the plant was cultivated for the oil extracted from the seeds in Babylon in the 1st century, Dioscorides described how the inhabitants of Sicily sprinkled sesame seeds over their breads.

Its name is believed to be derived from the Ancient Egyptian word, *sesemt*, one of the few to have passed to us in modern times, and records indicate that it was cultivated there by around the 4th century BC. It was also grown further south on the continent and gathered from the wild, especially in West Africa, where it was known as *benni*, a name the slaves from the region took with them to the Americas when both were transported there by the slave trade.

A fragrant, nutty seed, prized for its oil throughout the ages, even though it is one of the lowest-yield crops, averaging a mere 150kg per hectare, (135lb per acre). It is, however, one of the highest quality oils, high in polyunsatruated fatty acids, delicately flavoured and slow to spoil.

It arrived in India quite early via Persia, and the seeds became quite popular, ground into a paste as a thickening agent or used, as it is in the Middle East in a variety of *halwa*. This paste also appears in the eastern Mediterranean countries, on its own as *tahini* or blended with chickpeas to make *hummus*. The Persians also took sesame eastwards to China, where it became much prized, gaining the name 'fragrant oil' and used as a condiment in order not to lose the precious scent. As do the Japanese, who are thought to have used it originally as their exclusive cooking oil.

The seeds themselves have been adopted as coatings and coverings wherever they were taken and, in northern Europe, this seems to have been the only use for them for quite a while. Ayurveda lists sesame oil in the sweet category, said to promote growth, to strengthen the memory, acts as an antitoxin, helps aganist burning sensations and promotes lactation in nursing mothers. Unani Tibb uses sesame as a mild laxative, in hair preparations and in liniments and poultices.

100g **sesame oil** gives 881 kcalories energy, 0.1g water, 02g protein, 99.7g fat, 0.1g carbohydrate, 2mg sodium, 20mg potassium, 10mg calcium, 0.1mg iron, 0.01mg vitamin B1, 0.07mg vitamin B2 and 0.01mg niacin

100g **sesame seeds** = 588 kcalories, 4.8g water, 26.4g protein, 54.8g fat, 6.4g carbohydrate, 40mg sodium, 407mg potassium, 131mg calcium, 347mg magnesium, 7.8mg iron, 10.3mg zinc, 40μg carotene 0.72mg vitamin B1, 0.09 vitamin B2, 12.6mg niacin.

Sichuan Peppercorns *(Zanthoxylum simulans)*
The dried berries of a small bush related to the citrus family and to Zanthoxylum piperitum, Japanese Pepper or Sansho. Known throughout the rest of the world as Sichuan pepper as they are characteristic

of the food produced in that province of China, renowned for its hot and spicy cuisine, but called 'flower peppers' within China as they are said to resemble opening flower buds. They are actually not a true pepper, but when dried, the fruits are similar in appearance to small, red-brown peppercorns.

Spinach *(Spinacia oleracea)*

Both the botanical and common name for this plant are derived from the original Persian *aspanakh*. It is thought to have originated there; first evidence of cultivation is centered there, (before 4th century), and exiled communities from that country, such as the Parsee population around Mumbai, in India, use it a great deal in their cooking.

Its journey from Persia took it through Nepal to China by the mid-7th century AD, but its journey westwards was a little slower, reaching Europe only through the Moorish occupation of Spain during the 11th century, and Britain had to wait another 500 years or so before the plant was established here.

Spinach is yet another plant which started out as a medicinal aid, used as a laxative for the purgative action of the oxalic content - also found in rhubarb. In this country, it was also one of the 'spring greens' - young vegetable tops, nettles etc., which were eaten in the Spring to 'clear the blood' after a Winter of stodgy - and sometimes dodgy - food.

A versatile leaf, spinach has been used as a filling for pastries, pasta and tarts, is a perfect foil for eggs in such dishes as Oeufs Florentine, and the juice is a perfect natural colouring wherever a deep green is needed. During Medieval times, spinach was also used to make sweet dishes and some food historians see the habit that some of us have acquired of adding a little nutmeg when cooking spinach as a remnant of this practice.

During the middle of the last century, spinach gained a reputation of being packed with iron, and children were forced to eat it in the belief that it would build them up and make them big and strong. A cartoon character, Popeye the Sailorman, was created to back up this food propaganda. Ironically, later analysis revealed that, somewhere along the line, a food chemist had misplaced a decimal point, leading to the belief that spinach contained 10 times more iron than it actually does.

However, spinach is an excellent source of beta carotene, which is converted by the body into vitamin A and a good source of vitamin B6, folic acid (very important if you are in the early stages of pregnancy or even thinking about it), iron, (although absorption of this is hampered by the presence of oxalic acid, which hampers mineral absorption) and potassium. One way of helping the body to absorb the vitamins and minerals is to eat it with a sprinkling of lemon juice or with capsicums or tomatoes, all of which are rich in vitamin C, which helps the body's uptake of iron especially. It is also a fair source of riboflavin, vitamin C, calcium and magnesium.

During World War I, spinach juice was mixed with red wine and given to French soldiers who had suffered heavy blood loss and, as spinach is rich in folates which help blood formation, this may have been based on more than just old wives' tales.

Spinach is also a rich source of other carotenoids such as lutein, which have an antioxidant effect and recent research at the Harvard Medical School has indicated that a diet rich in carotenes may reduce the risk of age-related macular degeneration, a common cause of blindness in the elderly.

100g frozen spinach, boiled = 21 kcalories, 3.1g protein, 0.5g carbohydrate, 0.3g sugars, 2.1g fibre, 50mg calcium, 1.7mg iron, 16mg sodium, 640µg vitamin A, 0.06 mg thiamin, 6mg vitamin C.

100g fresh, raw spinach = 26 kcalories, 90.7g water, 3.2g protein, 0.3g fat, 3.7 carbohydrate, 71mg sodium, 470mg potassium, 93mg calcium, 88mg magnesium, 3.1g iron, 4860µg carotene (vitamin A), 0.10mg vitamin B1, 0.20mg vitamin B2, 1.1mg niacin, 51mg vitamin C. Total folates 123µg.

100g canned, drained solids = 24 kcalories, 91.4g water, 2.7g protein, 0.6g fat, 2.7g carbohydrate, 236mg sodium, 350mg potassium, 118mg calcium, 63mg magnesium, 2.6g iron, 4800µg carotene, 0.02mg vitamin B1, 0.12mg vitamin B2, 0.3mg niacin, 14mg vitamin C.

Star Anise *(Illicium verum)*

Native to China, the use of star anise by Man has been traced back to around 100 BC. Its generic name is derived from the Latin verb *illicere*, to attract, because of its pleasant smell.

An evergreen, related to the Magnolia family, the tree only produces its small, compound fruits after 15 years and then yielding just three annual harvests. The fruit itself is unique with eight rough, dark brown carpels, around 1cm long, containing a shiny, light brown, almost bronze, seed, radiating from a central stalk to produce a 'star'. Cultivation is difficult and transplantation problems mean that it is almost exclusively grown in South China and northern Southeast Asia.

It is said to have first been brought to Europe by an English sailor sometime in the 16th century, and was soon adopted for use in jams, puddings and syrups. Although totally unrelated, it contains the same essential oils as anise, (anethole and anisole), but with a spicier, warmer flavour, with just a hint of bitterness.

Ayurveda and herbal medicine use star anise as a digestive, relieving flatulence and stomach disorders and Oriental medicine use it in a linked way to cure colic.

In Chinese cooking, it is one of the ingredients in five-spice powder, which consists of equal quantities of star anise, cassia or cinnamon, fennel seeds and Sichuan peppercorns, ground to a fine powder with a half-quantity of cloves.

Sugars

Naturally sweet-toothed, Man has explored many sources of natural sugar and with his innate ingenuity has found many. Germinating seeds produce a disaccharide, maltose, to serve as food for the potential young plant; honey, a combination of dextrose and fructose which are split away from flower nectar by the enzymes which occur naturally in bee saliva; manna, a substance found on some plants and trees; palm sap, used to manufacture the strong, sweet jaggery found in southern India; corn syrup, produced by breaking down the starches found in maize.

But the two main sources, used throughout the modern world, are cane sugar (*saccharin officinarum*), thought to be a descendent of a now extinct grass originating in New Guinea, and beet sugar (*beta vulgaris*).

Sweetest: lactose (milk), maltose (germinated grains), glucose (honey, fruit & vegetables), sucrose (cane and beet), fructose, fruit and honey.

India seems to be the only place where sugar has always been as popular as honey. So, being able to gather supplies from vegetable sources, they were less reliant on bees. Archaeologists also believe that the Dravidians, the early inhabitants of the Indian subcontinent, knew how to make a form of treacle from sugar cane, which they called *guda* and that they may even have learned this process from even earlier ancestors. So sophisticated had their sugar processing become by 1000 BC, that they had developed a machine for extracting cane sugar juice and a sugar and spice mix was used to produce a milk-curd recipe called *payasyâ*.

Alexander the Great (334-324 BC) sent some cane sugar back to his Mediterranean headquarters, telling of yet another wonder of the mysterious Indies; "a solid honey not made by bees". The earliest written reference to sugar is thought to be a love poem in the Atharra-veda, and a Persian tablet, dated at around 510 BC, refers to solid sugar from the Indus Valley. In fact the Persians were the next society to make an improvement in the refining process, in the 7th century AD, by introducing the use of lime to remove proteins and impurities, producing the first 'white' sugar.

Europe was largely dependent upon honey as its main sweetener and what little sugar trickled through was so expensive and rare that it was used almost exclusively as a medicine. After the arrival of the Moors in Spain in the 8th century, sugar cultivation began there, but the product was still regarded as a medicinal resource rather than a culinary one. The Iberian explorers took canes to their outposts, the Spanish establishing crops in the Canaries and the Portuguese, Madeira. In 1493 Columbus took sugar cane to the Caribbean, where it has thrived and become a main cash crop.

In England, the demand for sugar only grew with the introduction of tea and coffee a mere two hundred years or so ago, honey having served well as medicine, sweetener and popular drink base for much of its history. The Venetians, ever ready to exploit new demands for the exotic and valuable commodity, added sugar to its already expansive range and were the main suppliers for most of northern Europe. Slowly, as crops began to thrive in the various colonies, cane sugar became more plentiful, but still quite expensive, having to be transported from such distant places, and so other sources of sweeteners were still explored.

In 1590 a French botanist, Olivier de Serres, managed to extract the first sugary syrup from beet, but it was not seen as a viable process at the time and nothing much happened until 1747, when German chemist, Marggraf extracted the first sugar. Even then, it took a student of his, Karl Franz Achard, to gain the necessary patronage to produce sugar from beets in any great quantity.

In 1800 he persuaded Frederick the Great of Prussia to set up the first beet refinery in Silesia - more than 200 years after the first syrup had been extracted. Another step forward for beet sugar came when in 1812, at the height of the Napoleonic Wars, supplies of cane sugar to France were cut off, triggering a direct order from Napoleon to cultivate and exploit the alternative source from beet. Today much of the sugar eaten in northern Europe is that derived from beet.

Modern medicine may not see sugar as a curative, but early medical texts, such as those of Ayurveda, value sugar as a diuretic and apurient, promoting the excretion of waste products. Ayurveda also sees it as a useful tool for those suffering from kidney disease, being protein free and easily digested. Similarly, in cases of hepatitis, Ayurveda sees sugar as offering some protection to liver cells unable to tolerate fats or proteins during the illness.

Another benefit is that of the sweetness 'telling the brain' that the appetite has been satisfied when eating something sweet at the end of a meal, triggering a feeling of satiety and suppressing hunger.

Sugars exist, in one form or another, in all living things. Together with the other carbohydrate group, starch, they provide energy. They are broken down by the body's digestive processes to form glucose, which is carried in the bloodstream to provide fuel for organs, muscles and body cells. The level of glucose is controlled by the action of two hormones; insulin (reduces glucose), and glycagon, (increases glucose).

It is estimated that around one-fifth of the middle-aged population of Britain is glucose intolerant to some extent. That is, their blood sugar levels are slow to return to normal after a high carbohydrate meal, indicating that they are at risk of developing diabetes and/or heart disease. Glucose is the main fuel for the brain, which cannot store its supply and so relies on a consistent source from the bloodstream. A sudden drop in levels, or hypoglycaemia, can lead to mood swings, irritability and, in very severe cases, coma and death.

Most sugars, especially the simple monosaccharides are digested quickly and provide a quick boost of energy. However, the quicker blood sugar levels rise, the faster they fall afterwards, which can lead to a drained, lethargic feeling - sometimes within 20 minutes. This can be avoided by eating small, regular meals which are higher in complex carbohydrates which take longer to be broken down by the body. This means that the glucose created is released more slowly into the bloodstream, providing a more sustained, consistent flow of energy. The ideal is to eat small, regular meals using plenty of complex carbohydrates to help the body to maintain normal blood sugar levels.

No links have been found to suggest that excess sugar causes heart or kidney disease, or that it leads to diabetes. Studies have even been carried out in which thin people have been found to eat more sugar than those who are fat, leading to doubts even that it causes obesity. Excess sugar which is not secreted or stored in the liver can end up helping to form fatty deposits around the body.

To help in the tricky balancing act required in estimating a healthy intake, nutritionists have developed the Glycaemic Index, which is used to measure the rate at which blood sugar levels rise when a particular carbohydrate bearing food is ingested.

Low level GI foods are more complex and hence digested more slowly, ensuring a longer feeling of satiety, longer term energy maintenance and keeping blood sugar levels constant. This group include unrefined, high fibre, high protein foods such as beans, lentils, grains, dried fruits and pasta. High scoring foods, such as sugar, processed foods, potatoes, fruit juices and white breads should be offset with lower scoring foods.

One recent theory linking diets high in refined sugar with hyperactivity has caused a certain amount of controversy. Chromium, necessary for the metabolism of sugar, is removed during refining and without it insulin is less effective in reducing blood sugar levels. This led the researchers to suggest that this could increase the symptoms of hyperactivity such as aggression and behavioural problems. However, with a lack of firm scientific evidence with which to back this up, the medical establishment have yet to accept this theory.

The most common proven worry with excess sugar, however, is that of tooth decay. All starches contribute to this and gum disease, because bacteria in the mouth break them down into acid that destroys tooth enamel, so sugar itself is not seen to be particularly detrimental to the health - as long as the overall diet is adequately balanced.

Sunflower *(Helianthus annuus)*

Introduced into Europe from South America in the 16th century, its botanical name means 'flower of the sun' - *helios* (sun), *anthos* (flower). This is because the flower heads appear to follow the course of the sun, turning to face it, hence also their Spanish and French names, *girasol* and *tournesol*, respectively.

In ancient Peru, where they are thought to have come from originally, the sunflower was the Inca symbol of their sun god. Sunflower headdresses were worn by their priestesses and golden representations decorated Inca temples.

As a food, the native Americans used dried and roasted seeds to produce a kind of cake and were also able to extract a culinary oil from them, and the young flower buds can also be steamed or boiled and eaten in much the same way as artichoke.

Not surprisingly, the first European country to receive the sunflower was Spain, from their newly discovered lands in the Americas. However, it was initially seen as a decorative plant, not being seen as a food source until its arrival in Russia in the 18th century. At that time the Orthodox Church forbade the consumption of oil-yielding plants on fast days, but the sunflower, being a new introduction was excluded and the seeds became a popular snack, roasted or salted, causing Russia to become the largest producers of sunflowers. Then, in the 1720s oil extraction was perfected in Bavaria, leading to massive production all over Eastern Europe.

In European folklore sunflowers were believed to make wishes come true: pick a flower at sunset, make a wish and, by the time the sun has come round again, your wish should have been granted. It was also believed in some countries that the flower was a means of divination and that placing a sunflower under the bed would reveal the truth of any particular matter to the sleeper.

In country magic the sunflower was said to be ruled by the Sun and was linked to fertility, wisdom and health, and a popular charm for a woman who wished to conceive was to eat sunflower seeds. In holistic medicine, such as Ayurveda, sunflower seeds are used as an expectorant and diuretic, used in the treatment of coughs, colds, bronchitis and kidney troubles.

Nutritionally, the roasted seeds are high in the B vitamins, are a useful source of vitamin E and are high in linoleic acid, needed for the maintenance of cell membranes. The oil is also high in oleic acid, another polyunstaurated fatty acid which makes it a good cooking medium for those interested in avoiding rising bad, or LDL, cholesterol levels.

Sweet Potato *(Ipomoea batatas)*

Remains of sweet potato have been found in Peruvian caves known to have been inhabited by Man since around 8000 BC. The tuber of a convolvulus vine from the same family as the 'Morning Glory', it is thought to have been brought under cultivation by about 200-100 BC, well before the time of the Incas, becoming one of the staple carbohydrates in the tropical Americas.

Its use as a food spread eastwards to the Caribbean islands and it is thought that early trans-Pacific migration took it westwards into the Pacific Islands, reaching as far as New Zealand by the early 13th century. This theory would seem to be supported by the fact that many of the words used to describe the tuber in the region differ only very slightly from the original Peruvian name, *kumara*. Discovered by Colombus' expedition of 1492 in Haiti, where it was called *batatas* by the local population, the sweet varieties soon found favour with the Spanish explorers. They took it with them to the Phillipines from where the Portuguese transported it to the East Indies. It was also via the Phillipines route that the sweet potato was to find its way into China: a famine in the Fujian Province in 1593 prompted an expedition to the islands in search of food plants; the ships returned a year later bearing, amongst others, the sweet potato. It was such a success in the province that when it travelled onwards to Japan in the 18th century the Japanese called it the 'Chinese potato'.

It is believed that the slave trade was responsible for the arrival of the sweet potato in Africa, where it was accepted as another type of yam, which it resembles.

Europe and the more northern countries were a different matter. However, unlike its namesake, the white potato, a solanaceae tuber which grows well in cooler climates, the sweet potato only thrives in warmer regions keeping it firmly in the novelty food bracket until the more efficient and speedier trans-global transportations methods of modern times.

Nutritionally, the sweet potato is a good source of potassium, a useful source of vitamin C and the deeper orange the potato, the more beta-carotene it provides, which may help to prevent certain forms of cancer.

100g raw gives, on average, 91 kcalories energy, 1.2g protein, 0.6g fat, 21.5g carbohydrate, 19mg sodium, 320mg potassium, 22mg calcium, 13mg magnesium, 0.7mg iron, 0.16mg copper, 4000-1200µg carotene, 0.10mg vitamin B1, 0.06mg vitamin B2, 1.2mg niacin, 25mg vitamin C. 100g, boiled in salted water, gives 84 kcalories of energy, 1.1g protein, 0.3g fat, 20.5g carbohydrate, 11.6g sugars, 2.3g fibre, 23mg calcium, 0.7mg iron, 32mg sodium, 660µg vitamin A (beta carotene), 0.07mg Thiamin, 17mg vitamin C.

Tamarind *(Tamarindus Indica, Imli)*

The plant is thought to have originated in tropical Africa and the use of its products in India is first documented at the end of the 13th century AD. It made its first appearance in Britain in the 16th century, then taken further west by the Spanish. Cultivation is now widespread throughout India and Southeast Asia.

The tree is a tall evergreen, which produces long green seed pods that look rather like round broad beans. As these pods ripen, the flesh turns to a dark chocolate-brown. These pods can be found in some specialist food stores, although it is the block form with which we are more familiar in this country. The pods are harvested, peeled, seeded, semi-dried and compressed into rectangular blocks which can be re-hydrated and sieved to produce the tamarind paste used in many Indian recipes. However, even this seems rather a laborious way to use tamarind nowadays, with the advent of so many concentrates and powders available in retail outlets - and not just in the Asian stores.

Most people in this country would probably be under the mistaken impression that they have never encountered tamarind, but they would be very wrong. It is one of the major ingredients in that great British contribution to world cuisine - Worcestershire Sauce - although, even today, only four people in the whole of Lea & Perrins actually know how much of it goes into the recipe.

In India, the whole plant is used: the pulp as a souring agent; the leaves and flowers as vegetables; the seeds in much the same way as a grain or pulse - ground to a flour to make cakes. In China, it is used in crystallised form to obtain their sweet and sour effect. In fact, the main use of tamarind is as a souring agent, lending a characteristic zing to a dish, tempered with just a hint of sweetness. As with all plants, tamarind has not escaped the attentions of the herbalist, especially in the holistic Ayurvedic tradition of medicine. Ayurveda lists tamarind as sour within the six tastes, which means that its properties are heavy, hot and oily. This group includes those plants which contain oxalic and fruit acids, such as blackcurrant, rosehip, the citrus family, mango and pomegranate.

Medicinal: Its uses in Ayurveda are mainly as an aid to stimulating appetite, digestion and as a system cleanser, and is also listed as being an effective antidote for alcoholism. Mixed with sugar and a little salt, it is used for sunstroke, fever, biliousness and acute diarrhoea, and tamarind concentrate is a good, mild laxative. Nutritionally, tamarind yields an energy value of around 70 calories per oz and is a fairly good non-animal source of calcium.

Tea *(Camellia sinensis, Camellia thea)*

The earliest written reference to tea-drinking is to be found in a Chinese dictionary of AD 350, although it is quite likely that the practice began much earlier than that. Some sources say that the tea plant was indigenous to southeast Asia and was brought to China and Japan by travelling Buddhist monks.

However, if a popular legend is to be believed, it began much earlier than that, in around 3000 years BC, when a Chinese emperor, Shen-Nung was sitting under a Camellia tree waiting for his servant to boil him some water. A leaf blew down from the tree and the emperor, on tasting the resulting brew, decided that he liked it, and *Tchai* or *Tay*, as it was called, was a popular drink in China from then on.

India and Japan have startlingly similar legends to explain the introduction of tea where, respectively, Darma and Dharuma, during seven years of sleepless contemplation, grew tired. In the Indian version, Darma chewed some leaves from the Camellia and was instantly alert. In the more grisly Japanese version, Dharuma cut off his own eyelids, threw them to the ground, where they sprang up as tea plants which then revived him.

Early methods of tea production involved making the dried and powdered leaves into a cake first, together with other flavouring ingredients, ready for use after rehydration. It was not until the 15th century, during the Ming dynasty, that the more familiar process to us, of steeping the leaves in hot water, was developed.

The Dutch brought tea to Europe in around 1610 and Britain was introduced to it at a relatively late date, in 1657, by a London coffee house owner, Thomas Garway, who claimed that it made the body active and lusty and that it cured *'gripping of the guts, cold, dropsies and scurvey'*. Interestingly, Mr E.C. Dozey, quondam Examiner at the University of Calcutta during the 1930's, mentions in his 1937 work, *Darjeeling, Past and Present*, that he managed to track down a reference to "tea pott" in the accounts of Bess Hardwicke, Countess of Shrewsbury in 1583 - almost three quarters of a century before the beverage itself made its appearance.

To make up for this slow start, however, the enthusiastic English had adopted the brew as their 'national drink' by around the mid-18th century. By the 19th century, the Duchess of Bedford hit upon an idea to fill in the long gap between luncheon and supper with the new fashion of taking tea, and the marriage was well and truly cemented, and today, around 70% of the British public drink tea at least once a day.

During the 18th century, the English East India Company held sway in the world trade in tea, playing a major role in the introduction of China and India teas into England and colonial America. According to Mr Dozey's research, the company imported 1 million pounds of tea into Britain in 1720, retailing at 30 shillings per pound. Just five years later the figure had risen to five million pounds and kept on rising until, in 1773, the company held over 17 millions pounds (imperial measure) of tea in its warehouses.

However, tea was still a very expensive commodity and the average Englishman spent as much as one third of his weekly wages in order to satisfy his thirst during this period. In 1773, British Parliament made matters even worse for the common man, passing the notorious Tea Act, raising heavy taxes even further, and granting permission to the East India Company to export their huge surpluses to America.

This huge and sudden demand on them, for what they saw as "taxation without representation", precipitated the famous 'Boston Tea Party' when 342 chests of tea were dumped into the harbour, leading ultimately to the American Revolution. Not surprisingly, the taxes were not popular on the domestic front, either and, despite being closer to the excise men, by the simple expedient of smuggling it in, managed to get away not paying duty on as much as two-thirds of the tea being drunk in Britain during that time.

Originally China held the monopoly of the trade in tea with Europe and formed the most valuable part of the East India Company until its charter expired in 1813 and control of the trade passed back to the Crown. The directors of the company decided to source other supplies, shipping in plants from China to the Himalayas, the eastern frontiers and Nilgiri, blissfully unaware, according to Mr Dozey's book, that the plant was already growing quite happily in Assam and other places in India and that the local population had been growing, manufacturing and drinking tea without any help whatsoever from the esteemed company!

In 1904 there came a new development in tea drinking - as always almost unintentionally. One Richard Blechynden was promoting Indian tea at the St Louis World Fair and found that, due to the scorching weather, there seemed to be very little interest in his product. In a moment of inspiration, he started to pour the tea over ice cubes, inventing iced tea.

The Cantonese call tea *ch'a* and the Fukienese call it *t'e*. The Cantonese word was adopted by Japan, India and Russia, whilst the Dutch, who brought tea to Europe, adopted the Fukienese. The English wavered between the two, with early references to chah and chai, strengthened by our very obvious, strong links with the Indian sub-continent. However, this was replaced in polite society with the more refined-sounding *tay*, staying that way until late in the 18th century, when it was converted, finally, to tea.

Tea is divided into three categories: fermented, usually referred to as black; unfermented, or green and semi-fermented, or oolong.

With black tea, the leaves are fermented, or oxidised until they turn a warm, coppery colour. Green tea is steamed in cylinders or boilers and oolong teas, which have some of the characteristics of both black and green, are partially fermented before drying.

Nutritionally, tea has very little to offer, although the stimulants it contains, such as caffeine can increase heart rate, increase alertness and dilate the airways in the lungs, aiding respiration. One average cup of tea contains around 40mg caffeine, almost twice that found in cola, and about two-thirds of the amount found in a cup of instant coffee.

One of the drawbacks with tea is the presence of tannins, which not only interfere with iron absorption, but also stain the teeth, a process which is ironically accentuated if a mouthwash containing chlorhexidine is used immediately before drinking tea. So be careful with that morning cuppa!

Also, those suffering from peptic ulcers should avoid strong black tea as, like coffee, it stimulates gastric acid secretion, causing irritation and some studies have linked tea to migraines in sensitive people, although it is not quite clear whether this is triggered by the tannins or by the caffeine.

On the good side, however, various teas, or more exactly the bioflavonoids, naturally occuring antioxidants in teas, are being investigated for their anti-cancer properties and, although the jury is still out on this one, green and oolong teas in particular have been associated with lower rates of heart disease and cancers.

An infusion of dried black leaves gives, per 100g weight, 99.7g water, minimal traces of protein and carbohydrate, 2mg calcium, and very little else. Chinese green tea, per 100g weight, 99.6g water, minimal traces of protein and carbohydrate, 2mg calcium and 0.1mg iron. Any calorific values gained from teas come from the accompanying sugar and milk used by many people.

Thyme *(Thymus vulgaris, zattar)*

There are many species of this herb, giving quite a wide variety of slightly different options for flavouring purposes. Two explanations have been put forward for the derivation of its name; one being that it is from the Greek word for courage - thyme motifs were often embroidered onto a knight's vestments to inspire courage before a joust; alternatively, that it is derived from a Latin term which meant to fumigate, cleanse in a sacrificial fire. In fact, all through the Middle Ages, sprigs of the herb were burned in houses as a kind of air freshener and to protect the occupants from plague.

Ancient Greeks and Romans used thyme as a temple herb and to bathe in it for vigour and grace. Some parts of the ancient world, however, associated the herb with death; the Egyptians used it in their embalming processes and the Welsh traditionally planted it upon the graves of their dead. In country magic, thyme is ruled by Venus, imparting courage, love, psychic gifts, health and sleep, and it was believed that placing thyme under the pillow would prevent nightmares. It was also thought that planting thyme in the garden would attract fairies and that wearing a sprig would enable you to see them.

Medicinal: Ayurveda, the ancient Indian study of life, lists thyme under its pungent section: strenghening and cleansing. It recommends its use externally as a disinfectant, mirroring the cleansing uses in Europe and, internally prescribes the herb as an expectorant and to expel worms. European herbalists, too, use thyme quite a lot. Thymol, its essential oil, is a strong antibacterial agent, and is active against salmonella and staphylococcus bacteria, hence the reputation as a cleanser and disinfectant; thyme tea is a traditional remedy for gastrointestinal complaints and the oil was taken to expel hookworm.

Thyme is also an antispasmodic, making it effective in combating sore throats, irritable coughs and bronchitis. Thyme is also good for settling the stomach and 2-3 teaspoons taken three times a day will settle diarrhoea. In addition, a thyme mouthwash will help mouth infections and thyme oil was used during World War I as an antiseptic and is still used today in some proprietary preparations for fungal diseases of the skin.

Its culinary uses are quite extensive too. Sausages, meatloaf, terrines and stuffings have all benefitted from the addition of thyme, both for its preservative and taste properties. It is an important herb in Mediterranean cooking, especially southern France and Greece and Cajuns and Creoles in the States use it as one of their key notes, and thyme is an important flavouring in Benedictine liqueur. Persian thyme, or *zattar* to give it its Arabic name, is also known as wild thyme, which not only contains thymol, but also carvacrol, essential oils which give the oregano flavouring favoured in Mediterranean and North American foods.

Tomato *(Lycopersicon esculentum)*

Tomatoes were first introduced to Europe by the Spanish, possibly from Mexico, but more likely from Peru. A work written by the Dutch herbalist Dodonaeus in the mid-1500s gives the common name 'pomi del Peru' to the tomato, indicating that its origin was thought at that time to be Peru.

The tomato still grows wild in the Peruvian Andes, the land of its origin, but the small, wild tomato does not bear a great deal of resemblance to the plump, red, juicy food item that you are likely to pluck from the vegetable bin at your local supermarket. It seems, though, that the ancient Peruvian tribes who would have discovered the plant made scant use of it as a food source. That privilege belonged to the more northerly tribes of Central America. It seems an unidentified wild ancestor of the tomato somehow made its way north.

The Aztecs called it xitomatl while other Central American tribes called it tomati. The Spanish called it manzana or apple, apparently because that is what they thought it was. From Spain it made its way to Italy where this "apple" was named pomi d'oro (golden apple). Obviously a yellow or golden tomato variety, one writer described it as being eaten with "oil, salt and pepper".

Red tomatoes were also known, but not yet in Italy. It is said that they were introduced, not from Spain but from Morocco. When they arrived, to differentiate them from their yellow skinned counterparts, they were given the name of *pomo d'Moro* (apple of the Moors). A French visitor, intrigued by this new food of his Italian hosts, mistranslated that when he reported it upon his return home. For him it became *pomme d'amour* or "love apple." Thus began its reputation as an aphrodisiac, and to this day there are some who cite the tomato's rich, red color; its heart shaped fruit, and its long established reputation as "proof" that eating fresh tomatoes increases sexual desire.

The tomato that first reached Europe in 1523, brought from the 'New World' by the Spanish, bore little, if any, resemblance to the uniformly glossy, scarlet globes used in modern kitchens. Small, yellow, ridged and flattened, almost star-like in shape, this little native of the Andes was regarded, along with its cousin the potato, with a great deal of suspicion, as they are members of the poisonous Solanum family, which includes the Deadly nightshade; and its Latin name, *Lycopersicon esculentum* or 'edible wolf's peach' bears more than a little echo of this doubt, perhaps.

The Italians still call it *Pomodoro* or golden apple, a name logically arrived at, considering that tomatoes were originally yellow in colour, before early genetic engineering methods altered them to the red we expect today.

The name tomato is derived from the Aztec word meaning 'plump fruit, *tomatl*. However, they also used it, prefixed with xi- for the forebear of the tomato with which we are familiar and the prefix mil- to describe the Mexican husk tomato, or tomatillo, small tomato, (Physalis ixocarpa), which is a very important flavouring component in Central American cooking. The Spanish ignored the prefixes, calling both *tomate*, causing a little confusion for a while. There has also been some confusion as to whether the tomato is actually a fruit or vegetable. In the 18th century, botanists specified that a fruit is the organ derived from the ovary and surrounding the seeds.

Unfortunately, at the end of the 19th century, the U.S. Supreme Court officially turned this scientific classification on its head when it designated the fruit to be a vegetable, at the end of a case in which a New York produce importer lost his battle with the Customs authorities. He argued that, as a fruit, the tomato was not subject to import duty. However, the Court ruled against him on the grounds of linguistic custom, citing that tomatoes "*....are usually served at dinner in, with or after the soup, fish or meat, which constitute the principle part of the repast, and not, like fruit, generally as dessert*".

Interestingly, even the Ministry of Agriculture, Farming and Fisheries in the UK, lists the tomato as a vegetable, presumably on this same rule of 'linguistic custom' - Botany? Schmotany, as they might say in Queen's.

Its acceptance at the table was quite slow, and after a fairly short flirtation with the court tables in Elizabethan England it was dismissed almost generally as a nasty, sour little thing that was liable to make one sick. Ironically, the tomato was seen as little more than an ornamental plant in North America too and was not cultivated as a food crop there until well after the Declaration of Independence.

By the mid-nineteenth century, however, attitudes, and the tomato, seemed to have changed markedly, and Mrs Isabella Beeton simply glowed with approval in 1859 when she wrote, *"In this country it is much more cultivated than it formerly was; and the more the community becomes acquainted with the many agreeable forms in which the fruit can be prepared, the more widely will its cultivation be extended. For ketchup, soups, and sauces, it is equally applicable and the unripe fruit makes one of the best pickles."*

The late twentieth century finds it even more in favour as nutritionists and modern science discover more about its chemistry. Studies at Ben Gurion University in Israel and more recently in other universities have found that the carotenoid lycopene, found in tomatoes, may be very effective in helping to protect against cancer, heart disease and degenerative eye disease, and that these antioxidant elements are more readily absorbed into the bloodstream when the tomatoes are cooked with an oil high in monounsaturates, such as olive.

Perhaps this is yet another reason that the so-called 'Mediterranean Diet' is associated with reduced risk of heart disease and some cancers, such as cancers of the cervix, prostate, bladder and pancreas.

Medicinal: In its natural form, lycopene has been found to be the most potent antioxidant discovered to date and that it helps to prevent the formation of oxidised LDL or 'bad' cholesterol which can build up as arterial plaque, leading to heart attack and stroke.

Separate studies on a group of 47,000 adult males by researchers at Harvard University in the USA over a period of six years have found that lycopene seems to activate DNA damage control. The research group there suggest a possible 40-45% decrease in the risk of prostate cancer in men who eat at least 10 servings a week of tomato-based foods.

Even better news is the fact that lycopene seems unaffected by processing and is also present in tomato products such as tomato juice, purées, passata and pastes. Tomato is also high in the natural immune booster, vitamin C; an average 100g serving contains 22mg - more than one third of the RDA for non-smokers and lg fibre, which may help to prevent cancers of the colon and rectum.

Chinese medicine recommends one tomato sweetened with sugar for bleeding gums and, for all those 'morning after the night before' sufferers, one to two tomatoes, first thing in the morning, taken on an empty stomach is recommended for those bloodshot eyes. There is a down side, though, the salicylates which are also found in tomatoes and other nightshades may trigger a painful reaction in arthritis and gout sufferers. 100g raw tomatoes give 17 kcalories energy, 0.7g protein, 0.3g fat, 3.1g carbohydrate, 3.1g sugars, 1.0g fibre, 7mg calcium, 0.5mg iron, 9mg sodium, 105 μg vitamin A, 0.09mg thiamin, 17mg vitamin C

Turkey

Several theories abound as to how this modern symbol of Christmas fare got its name. It originated in Mexico where it was called *uexoloti*, so it was hardly surprising that a new name had to be found for this strange creature.

One theory holds that the turkey,'s head was supposed to resemble those of 'T'urkish soldiers, whose helmets were blue to the shoulders which bore red lapels. Another has it that the name comes from the bird's 'turk, turk' call. The most logical explanation, however, is that the birds were first imported into England in quantity in the 1540s by traders from the Levant, who were known as *'Turkey Merchants'*. The birds became known as Turkey birds, which was soon shortened to turkey.

Elsewhere, too, the bird's origin seems to have caused perplexity when choosing its new name. In Germany it is known as *Calecutische Hahn* - Calicut Hen. The French, receiving the bird in around 1520 from the Spanish Indies, as Spain's colonies in the Americas were known at the time, called it Coq d'Inde, which became shortened to *dindon*. The Dutch also favoured Calicut with their *Kalkoen*.

Ironically, India was nearer the mark with the name *Peru* - but only by being on the right continent! The man attributed with bringing the first turkeys to Britain was William Strickland from Bridlington, North Yorkshire, He was a cabin boy with the explorer, John Cabot, and sailed with him around the coast of South America in 1526. The crew traded with the natives during the trip, and William came home with six turkeys which he sold in Bristol at tuppence (just under lp) each. With each progressive trip he made, his profits grew and he was eventually able to charter his own ship. Fortune and a knighthood followed, and, as a tribute to the bird that made him, his coat of arms proudly bore a turkey.

The bird was a natural for feasts and royalty took to it immediately. Henry VIII loved it and Archbishop Cranmer tried to curb the gluttony that it seemed to inspire, by trying to limit the number of turkeys served to just one per feast. In the mid-eighteenth century, George II had developed such a taste for turkey that a section of Richmond Park was sectioned off exclusively to rear them. The bird's popularity grew and, during the 18th and 19th centuries vast flocks set out in August, driven on foot, to the London markets from Cambridgeshire, Suffolk and Norfolk.

By the end of the Victorian era, turkey had gained its place at the centre of the Christmas feast and Charles Dickens, author of '*A Christmas Carol*' didn't just feature it in his work. According to his wife Kate, in her book, '*What Shall We Have For Dinner?*', written in 1852, he ate it at his own Christmas celebrations, too.

In the modern era, cold roast turkey can lay claim to being the first meal ever eaten on the moon! Nowadays, the turkey is no longer kept just for the rich on high days and holidays, and quite rightly so! It's is arguably the best meat we can have in our diet. It is very low in fat, containing just 1g per ounce of skinless flesh - most of that being polyunsaturated. Not surprisingly, with this level of fat content, it is also extremely light on calories at just 140 per 100g (3½oz). The same serving provides almost 50% of the recommended daily allowance of folic acid, vital in protecting against birth defects, and also useful in combating certain cancers and heart disease. Turkey is also an excellent source of Vitamin B1, and all the other B vitamins, especially niacin, providing around 93% of the recommended intake.

On the minerals side, turkey is a good source of potassium, essential for maintaining normal heart function and blood pressure, and phosphorus, necessary in bone and teeth production and in the efficient conversion of energy from our food, Turkey contains over one-third more zinc than chicken, a 100g serving providing just under half the daily recommended amount. Zinc plays a major part in cell growth and repair, is critical for the proper functioning of the male reproductive system, is instrumental in maintaining a normal sense of taste and smell, and recent studies have found that it could be a booster to our immune system.

Turmeric *(Curcuma longa, Huldi)*

The Latin genus name is derived from an Arabic word, *Kurkum*, which means saffron, a yellow dye. As with its cousin, ginger, it is the rhizome which is used to produce this intensely yellow, bitter, spice. The brown-skinned tuber is boiled to activate the carotenoid Curcumin, then peeled, dried and ground to a yellow powder. The plant is grown in China, India, Java, Taiwan, Indonesia, Vietnam, The Philippines and Central America. India produces approximately 12,000 tons of the spice annually, of which 10,000 tons are for export.

Its use as a dye has been very important throughout history; for cloth, leather and even the skin, cosmetically. In South East Asia, turmeric plays an important part in rituals and religious customs:

traditional weddings see its use as a dye for the arms of the bride and groom; Indonesians use turmeric water as a cologne; Malays believe that it offers protection from evil spirits and rub it on the stomachs of women who have given birth and on the umbilical cord of their infants. However, these practices are not just a question of superstition. Turmeric helps to calm inflammation and has an antibacterial action and, originally, its use in fish dishes was probably more for this latter property, preventing spoilage, than for any attractive colouring effect. Turmeric amulets are also worn to bring good luck in many regions. Some Indian communities see turmeric as a charm for newborn babies; a piece of turmeric is hung around the baby's' neck, or turmeric water dabbed onto its head, until it has learned to walk. Whilst in Bengal, a burning piece of turmeric would be waved under the nose of a person believed to be possessed by a tree spirit, as it was believed that ghosts and evil spirits were said to be unable to bear the smell.

In cooking, it can be used as a saffron substitute; it was known in this country as Indian Saffron during the Middles Ages and even now the French still call it *safran d'Inde*. However, the taste is very different, with a hint of bitterness. It has been used for many years in European kitchens to dye butter, margarine, cheeses, fish, batters and breadcrumbs.

Medicinal: In 2009 Professor Murali Doraiswamy, of Duke University in North Carolina, said *"there is evidence that people who eat a curry meal containing turmeric two or three times a week have a lower risk of dementia and Alzheimer's. The key ingredient is curcumin, a component of the spice turmeric. Curcumin appears to prevent the spread of amyloid protein plaques - thought to cause dementia - in the brain"*. This created numerous media stories of how eating curry will stave off dementia as well as suggestions of other ways turmeric can be ingested such as with scrambled eggs!

Homeopathy uses turmeric for jaundice, liver complaints, ulcers and digestive problems. It is said to improve circulation and the powder will staunch bleeding. It is even used by some herbalists as a cold cure, mixed with hot milk and sugar.

Externally, Indian medicine has used turmeric in poultices and ointments for skin sores for thousands of years and, until quite recently, the yellow lint pads on sticking plasters contained it. It is also believed, in India, that turmeric will discourage the growth of facial hair.

Nutritionally, 1 teaspoon of dried turmeric weighs around 2.2gms and gives 8 kcalories, containing carbohydrate, protein, fibre, fats, and no cholesterol. Turmeric also contains vitamins B, B2, niacin, vitamin C, sodium, phosphorous, potassium, calcium, iron, magnesium and zinc.

Vanilla *(Vanilla planifolia)*

The dried fruit pods of a climbing orchid, native to Central American tropical forests and, in particular, those of Mexico. It is indigenous to the region, with attempts at transplantation to other countries meeting with little success until a way was found to simulate the pollination which occurs naturally in the wild, and which enables the formation of fruit.

In the 19th century a Belgian botanist, Charles Morren, discovered that, in its natural habitat, only one species of bee and one species of hummingbird were the means by which the plants were pollinated. But it was a slave in Réunion, Albius, who discovered a method of hand pollination which meant that the plant could be grown successfully in other tropical areas such as Mauritius, Réunion and Madagascar. Of course, this labour-intensive method of pollination does make the spice very expensive, and so finding a synthetic form of the flavour has occupied food scientists for many years. In 1874 the first synthetic *vanillin*, the essential oil which gives vanilla its flavour, was extracted from a certain variety of conifer by German chemists. By 1925, a successful synthetic chemical was produced, using oil of cloves and subsequent methods have utilised coal tar extracts and even wood waste. But, no matter how successful the scientists have been in matching the chemical signature of *vallinin*, purists still insist that they lack the subtle spiciness of 'the real thing.'

Despite the expense, vanilla has been a popular flavouring worldwide for confectionary and thrifty cooks would make the pods last longer by storing them in jars of sugar and using the flavoured sugar produced in their dishes instead of lavishing the actual pods on just one recipe.

In country magic, a small amount of vanilla sugar was added to love potions in order to make them more effective.

IF FOOD BE THE FUEL OF LUST....

Since time immemorial, food and love have travelled arm-in-arm: a good dinner is an almost universal prelude to a good night's passion, sharing food for some being a prerequisite to sharing love. The less serious, though, should be warned, as in some cultures, the union that follows is intended for life, not just one night. Little wonder, then that through the ages man, and his sometime accomplice in such matters, woman, should have wanted to make sure that the food matched the occasion.

Aphrodite, from whose name the word '*aphrodisiac*' is derived, has cast her mantle over many foods through the ages and the following is just a small list of candidates.

Naturally, spices, expensive and aromatic, have long been regarded as love boosters. Cardamom, second only to black pepper in importance on the Malabar Coast, has been used since the 5th century BC and Nicholas Culpeper, who combined herbalism with astrology assigned it to Venus, even though it is strictly a member of the ginger family, which is ruled by Mars, for this reason (*The English Physician*, 1652).

Black Pepper, another expensive spice in classical times, was also seen as a powerful aphrodisiac. Greek and Roman courtesans used a mixture of black pepper and myrrh, mixed with equal quantities of two scents named Cyprus and Egyptian as a love potion.

Coriander, with the slightly narcotic properties that earned its early European name of '*dizzycorn*', was used, along with cumin by the early Egyptians, as an important ingredient in magic love potions and made into eau-de-toilette in 17th century Paris. Cumin is also valued in witchcraft as an ingredient for ensuring fidelity.

Fenugreek, the spice that gives curry its characteristic smell, contains diosgenin, a substance that acts in a similar way to the body's own sex hormones and is recommended by Chinese herbalists to cure impotence and the Prophet Mohammed decreed that its seeds should be valued "*as much as the gold they resemble*".

Saffron, the most expensive spice, probably gained its status in this category of foods because of its high value and its use as a dye for royal and holy garments, making it a symbol of power and status since the earliest times - and power and wealth has always been the strongest aphrodisiac.

Cinnamon, a beautiful, sweet spice, is not traditionally regarded as an aphrodisiac, but it has been shown to help insulin work more efficiently in converting glucose into energy - and plenty of that is needed in seduction.

Ginger, hot and lusty, was regarded as 'nookie nosh' in the Tudor period and was Henry VIII's favourite spice for this very reason! It is actually a very good digestive and probably helped him recover more from those extravagant banquets he loved more than anything else.

Nuts and lentils - so important in South Indian cuisine, are high in manganese, a mineral that assists in the production of a substance that transmits sensual experiences to the brain's pleasure centres.

Vegetables too play their part. Those high in vitamin C, such as okra (bindi), sweet peppers, tomatoes (strictly a fruit), etc. may prevent DNA damage in sperm, helping to prevent infertility.

Foods high in vitamin A, such as dark green vegetables and yellow or orange fruit, and vegetables, such as carrots, pumpkin, yam and yellow squash are worth looking out for too, as vitamin A is essential in the production of sex hormones. In women, it counteracts excess oestrogen, which, in quantity, can reduce sex drive. Another useful vitamin is B6, found in brown rice, fish and peanuts. Figs were a staple food in ancient Greece and were fed to athletes to improve stamina whilst oysters, being high in zinc, are certainly good for male potency.

The most unlikely of all aphrodisiacs must be garlic and onions, whose properties are said to *'inflame the baser passions'*. This is one of the reasons that Hindu Brahmin and Jain sects ban them from their diet. This theory was also put forward by Andrew Boorde in the 16th century. In his *'A Dyetary of Helth'* he said that *'Onions doth promote a man to veneryous acts'*. Obviously the man had no sense of smell! Even this can be countered by a sprig of parsley, giving you a shot of vitamins C and A, both good for the sex drive!

VEGETABLES, FRUITS, AND SPICES USED IN WESTERN EUROPE

Mediterranean Area Natives, Used BC
mushroom - onion - apple - basil - dill - beet - cabbage - pear - marjoram - parsley - radish - lettuce - cherry - oregano - fennel - turnip - artichoke - grape - mint - bay - carrot - cucumber - fig - rosemary - caper - parsnip - broad bean - dates - sage - fenugreek - asparagus - pea - strawberry - savory - garlic - leek - olive - thyme - mustard - anise - poppy - caraway - sesame - coriander - saffron - cumin

Asian Natives, Imported BC
citron - cardamom - apricot - ginger - peach - cinnamon - turmeric - black pepper

Later Additions
spinach - celery - rhubarb - cauliflower - broccoli - Brussels sprouts

Imported Later
yam - lemon - clove - water chestnut - lime - mace/nutmeg - bamboo - orange - tarragon - eggplant (aubergine) - melon

New World Natives, Imported 15th-16th Centuries
potato - kidney bean - pineapple - allspice - sweet potato - lima bean - red pepper - pumpkin - sweet pepper - vanilla - squashes - avocado - tomato

Food History Time Line

4.6 million - 2000 BC

Precambrian period	
4,650,000,000 700,000,000 B.C	Paleozoic
570,000,000 BC	Shellfish - Trilolites
500,000,000 BC	Fish - Chordates
430,000,000 BC	Vascular Land Plants
395,000,000 BC	Amphibian - Insects
345,000,000 BC	Fern Forests
320,000,000 BC	Reptiles
Mesozoic	
225,000,000 BC	Triassic - Dinosaurs - Mammals
200,000,000 BC	Pangaea - one landmass attached to Antartica
195,000,000 BC	Jurassic - Birds
180,000,000 BC	Pangaea splits into Laurasia and Gondwanaland
136,000,000 BC	Cretaceous - Primate - Flowering Plants
100,000,000 BC	Supercontinents split to make Atlantic
Cenozoic	
65,000,000 BC	Dinosaurs disappeared
65,000,000 to 12,000,000 BC	Tertiary - Grazing and Carniverous Mammals
2,500,000 BC	Pleistocene - Human beings - Late in Pleistocene humans crossed over to the New World via the Bering land bridge.
2 million BC	Earliest tool making in East Africa.
500,000 BC	Cave dwellers use fire (Homo Erectus), but only from natural sources. Making of recognisable tools.
300,000 BC	Ice Age reaches Europe. Southern Europe turned into chilly tundra.
250,000 BC	Indian sub-continent first populated.
200,000 BC	Neanderthal Man evolves in Asia and colonises Europe.
150,000 BC	Homo Sapiens evolve in Africa and start to move outwards to Nile Valley, India, Malaysia and to Australia and through Russia to China and to Europe.
125,000 BC	Ice Age forces Neanderthals into Near East. Homo Sapiens migrate to Near East.
50,000 BC	Plants and animals used as more than mere food in, and near China.
40,000 BC	Homo Sapiens sweep into Europe in large numbers
38,000 BC	Crudely fashioned fish hooks in evidence.
33,000 BC	Homo Sapiens arrive in the Americas from Asia.
30,000 BC	Neanderthal Man extinct. - Bow and arrow invented
14,000 BC	Dogs tamed in S.E. Europe
12,500 BC	Ice retreats.

12,000 to 9,000 BC	Early manipulation of plants and animals.
10,050 BC to 10,000 BC	End of Ice Age. End of Paleolithic era - Mesolithic era begins. Possible time of Osiris supported by many astrological theories.
9,000 BC	Sheep and goat farming in Eurasia, plus wheat and barley. Open settlements in Iraq, Jericho and Jordan. First pottery appears in Japan.
8,900 BC	Evidence of farming at Sharidar in Kurdistan.
8,000 BC	Neolithic Man learns to make fire by friction. Large animals start to disappear as climate heats up. Start of cultivation in Mesoamerica, Middle and Far East. Intensified exploration of resources and technological innovation. Jericho exists as a city of 10 acres. Fishing traps in use.
8,000 BC	Cattle in Eurasia.
7,900 BC	Oldest known surviving piece of pottery found in China dated to this period.
7,800 BC	Nautufian Jericho the oldest recorded town
7,000 BC	Chillies are gathered in South America - lima beans in Peru.
6,500 BC	Cattle farming known - also pigs, chickpeas and lentils.
6,000 BC	Millet popular in north China. Olive Oil known. Wine making is started, probably in Caucasia or Mesopotamia. Pottery appears in East Mediterranean basin to Zagros (Iran). Peasant farming in Greece. Catal Huyuk in Turkey is a town of 32 acres. Britain becomes an island.
5,000 BC	Rice farming in Yangtze Delta - short and long grain. Peasant farming in South Balkans. Sumerians rule in Mesopotamia. Earliest use of the wheel. Kept sheep, cattle, donkeys and cultivated dates and cereals. Primitive farming in Tehuuacan, Mexico. Chillies are cultivated in South America
5,000 – 4,500 BC	Metallurgy spreads from Balkans.
4,300 BC	Nile Valley settled by two tribes under the Pharoah.
4,241 BC	Egyptians create the calendar.
4,000 BC	Cattle farming expands. Raised bread starts. Large farming villages exist in China (Yellow River). First city state founded in Mesopotamia. Neolithic cultures from East introduce agriculture to Aegean. Farming in Lower Thames Valley in Britain
3,600 BC	Troy founded by Neolithic settlers from Kum Tepe by the Dardenelles.
3,500 BC	Winter squash, tomatoes, avocadoes, beans, corn, used as staples in Central America. Potatoes in Peru, plus millet, rice, wheat, coconuts, bananas in Asia. Two wheel carts exist in Sumeria.
3,200 BC	Silk weaving discovered in China.
3,100 BC	Egypt unified. Archaic Period (Dynasty 1 - II) to 2686 BC
3,000 BC	Lebanon settled by Canaanites, later known as Phoenicians. Ur in Mesopotamia are eating cereals and vegetables flavoured with watercress and mustard seeds and leaves and invent beer. Cuniform writing started by the Sumerians. Shen Nung assembles the first documentation on herbs. Turmeric, cardamom and pepper are grown in India and mustard in China. Shortly after this, ginger and cinnamon arrive from the tropical forests of Southeast Asia and Ceylon (Sri Lanka). Vines cultivated in Egypt and Phoenicia for wine-making. Horses in Russia. Mesopotamia well versed in beer brewing. Llama and alpaca domesticated in Andes.
2,852 BC	China ruled by The Three Sovereigns.
2,800 BC	Cretans already an influence in Aegean, having originally come from the Levant. Cultivation of rice evident in China
2,700 BC	Silbury Hill created.
2,700 BC	Rhubarb used for medicinal purposes in China
2,686 – 2,181 BC	Old Kingdom in Egypt (Dynasty III - VI)
2,680 - 2,565 BC	Pyramids built in Egypt.

2,500 BC	Olive oil popular in Crete. Thriving community in Indus Valley. Rice in Central India to Taiwan. Ancient Egyptians regularly using spices, especially cumin, anise and cinnamon in their embalming processes. Others starting to be mixed into cosmetics, purifying incenses and foods. Egyptian sailors trading for cassia and cinnamon in the Land of Punt (Somalia). First sea spice routes established, passing up the west coast of India, along the Arabian coast and through the Red Sea to Egypt. The Bible refers to spices as part of everyday life during the period: In Ezekiel, cassia and calamus is placed in Phoenicia; Moses is said to have used myrrh, cinnamon and calamus in the oil prepared to anoint the Ark of the Covenant; Joseph, of the many-coloured coat fame, was sold by his brothers to a camel train carrying spicery, gold and myrrh. Cumin, anise and cinnamon used for embalming in Egypt.
2,300 BC	Cheese used in Egypt.
2,200 BC	Semite Amonites settle around Babylon.
2,070 BC	Hitites attack Mesopotamia, introducing horses for war.
2,000 BC	Greek speaking peoples emerge ruled by a heroic warrior class. Winemaking now widespread throughout Greece. Chickens recorded in India.

Food History Time Line

2000 BC to Year 0

2,000 - 1,500 BC	Abraham (Abram son of Terah, descendent of Shem also Ibrahim, ancestor of Arabs through Ishmael) lived in Ur on the Tigris. Crete was the centre of the Minoan civilisation - 8,000 live in the capital, Cnossos. Myceans come to Greece from the north. Aryans from Russia and Turkistan invade India over the Hindu Kush. Stonehenge in England built. Ice cream in China (2,000 BC) - a soft milk and rice concoction. Period of Hsia Dynasty (2000-1520 BC)
1991 - 1786 BC	Kingdom in Egypt (XII Dynasty)
1786 - 1552 BC	Second Intermediate Period in Egypt (XIII - XVII Dynasty)
1552 - 1069 BC	New Kingdom Period in Egypt (XVIII - XX Dynasty)
1520 - 1030 BC	Shang Dynasty in China encourages food preparation and service is ritualised.
1500 BC	Aryans invade India
1262 BC	The Exodus of the Children of Israel from Egypt.
1200 BC	Trojan Wars. Break-up of Empire of Crete. First swords made from iron in Egypt.
1180 BC	Troy falls to the Acheans. Phoenicians are the world's great traders.
1069 - 525 BC	Third Kingdom in Egypt (XXI - XXVI Dynasty)
1000 BC	Phoenicians invent phonetic alphabet. Winemaking comes to Italy, Sicily, N. Africa.
950 BC	The Queen of Sheba visits King Solomon in order to promote the spice trade.
814 BC	Phoenicians colonize Carthage.
800 BC	Rome founded.
800 - 400 BC	The Upanishads form basis of Indian religion
776 BC	First Olympiad held.
753 BC	Romulus founds Rome according to legend
750 BC	Homer produces his epic Iliad and Odyssey.
700 BC	Wheaten bread a luxury in Athens - the poor live on cake, breads and mashes.
609 - 593 BC	Phoenicians circumnavigate Africa in the reign of Pharoah Necho.
600 BC	Darius of Persia invades the Punjab. First Emperor of Japan Jimmu Tenno
563 BC	Siddhartha Gautama (Buddha) born in Northern India
551 BC	Birth of K'ung-Fu-tzu (Confucius)
546 BC	Cyrus of Persia conquers Ionian Greece then Athens beats him at Marathon.
540 BC	Mahavira born who founded Jainism in India
539 BC	Cyrus of Persia takes Babylon.
525 - 332 BC	Later Period in Egypt (XXVII - XXXI Dynasty)
510 BC	Romans expel last Etruscan King.
500 - 600 BC	Traditional time of Prophet Zoroaster but probably nearer 1500 BC
500 BC	Fine food common in Greece and the first cookery book is produced by Hesiod of the Epicurians. Winemaking spreads to France - Marseilles the oldest region, followed by Languedoc in 200 BC.
489 BC	Death of Buddha
479 BC	Death of Confucius
480 BC	Xerxes tries again and fails. Carthage invaded by Greeks at the same time and is beaten, as were the Etruscans. The Greeks developed an after-dinner wine game called Kottabos.

469 - 399 BC	Sokrates.
450 BC	Herodotus writes his 'History' in which he tells how the Arabians cover themselves in animal hides in order to gather cassia from shallow lake-lands, infested by giant bat-like creatures and that cinnamon is obtained by tricking large birds which make their nests on mountain precipes.
448 BC	Athens defeated in the Nile Delta.
447 BC	Parthenon built under Pheidias.
429 - 347 BC	Plato.
415 BC	Athens tries to invade Sicily and Greater Greece (Southern Italy).
405 BC	Sparta crushes Athens with the help of Persian finance.
400 BC	Hippocrates, the Father of Modern Medicine. Leavened bread introduced.
384 - 322 BC	Aristotle.
359 BC	Philip becomes King of Macedonia.
356 BC - 323 BC	Alexander the Great founds Alexandria in Egypt, which becomes the main spice trading centre of the known world.
350 BC	Greeks and Romans are now regular spice users, growing caraway, cardamom, anise, mustard and fennel and importing pepper, cassia, cinnamon and ginger along the Old Silk Road between India and the Mediterranean
341 - 270 BC	Epicurius, founder of Epicureanism for qualified hedonism and peace, and was a great influence later on Christians.
336 - 328 BC	Alexander brings rice to Europe.
332 - 30 BC	Ptolemaic Period in Egypt
331 BC	Alexander the Great builds Alexandria. Ruled by Cleopatra 47-30 BC and destroyed by an earthquake in 335 AD.
300 BC	End of the Kushans from China in India. Rice cultivation in Japan. Meze invented in Greece.
287-213 BC	Archimedes of Syracuse.
286 BC	Rice introduced to Greece from India.
269-232 BC	Ashoka the first Buddhist King comes to power in India - the son of the first great power there, Chandragupta.
264 BC	Rome starts her conquests.
228 - 210 BC	Great Wall of China built
217 BC	Hannibal is served raw, cured ham in Parma on his way to fight the Romans.
206 BC	Stir-frying appears during the Han Dynasty.
202 BC	Hannibal of Carthage defeated. Greeks taken as slaves into Italian kitchens.
200 BC	Pyramids in Mexico built at Teotihuacan.
150 BC	Euthydemus writes 'On Vegetables'.
146 BC	Romans sack Corinth and control Greece until 395 AD. Greek cooks come to Rome - most breads originate from Greeks.
110 BC	Oysters are cultivated near Naples. Fine food in Italy. Favourite sauce is garum, made with fish, salt, dill, rue and mint.
100 BC	Pepper reaches Rome.
55 BC	Julius Caesar invades Britain
44 BC	Julius Caesar murdered.
6 BC	Communication by mule-track meant that Chinese silk and Greek bronze found together in tomb in Stuttgart.
5 BC	Greek cookery schools and dining clubs appear as Greek cooks become more in demand.
4 BC	Archestratus writes 'Life of Luxury'.
0 AD	Jesus born leading to start of Christianity

Food History
Time Line

A.D. 1 - 1499 A.D.

0 - 35 AD	In Israel, the pharisees pay their tithes in cumin seeds.
40 AD	Apicius writes 'De Re Coquinaria' in the reign of Tiberius. A Greek, Hippalos, discovers how to use the monsoon winds in the Indian Ocean to speed up sea voyages. The Romans follow suit, thus weakening the Arab monopoly and ensuring a more reliable supply of pepper from India and cinnamon from Ceylon.
43 AD	Roman conquest of Britain begins under Claudius I
50 AD	London founded
79 AD	Pompeii buried.
92 AD	The trade grows enough for Rome to build special pepper warehouses.
330 AD	The Emperor Constantine founds Constantinople, which becomes the centre of the spice trade. Cloves and nutmeg start to arrive in the West from the Moluccas.
335 - 375 AD	Samudra Gupta becomes India's Napoleon.
350 AD	The Champagne wine district is founded.
408 AD	Rome pays Alaric the Visigoth 3,000lb (1,360kg) in pepper, together with silver, gold, silks and furs to raise their blockade on Rome.
410 AD	Alaric the Visigoth sacks Rome.
451 AD	Attila and Huns invade.
577 AD	Matches are first made by ladies of the Court in China.
570 AD	Mohammed is born
500 AD	Coffee drinking becomes popular in Arabia.
622 AD	Mohammed 's famous Hejira to Medina
630 AD	Islam is born.
712 AD	Muslims capture Sind.
745 AD	Boat loads of Parsees fleeing Islam arrive at Gujarat in India.
800 AD	Alsace wine region is founded.
982 AD	Extra Christmas and Easter taxes, payable in pepper, are levied by King Aethelread II on German ships which come up the River Thames to trade at London Bridge. The Vikings take cardamom from Constantinople to their homes in Scandinavia. Ginger has become popular in Germany since its introduction there sometime in the 9th century and reaches Britain by the 10th century. Saffron growing starts in England (Saffron Walden) and caraway is found growing naturally in Europe.
997 AD	First use of pizza as a name at Gaeta between Naples and Rome.
1066 AD	Normans invade England and popularise the use of pepper.
1096-1097 AD	First Crusade.
1116 AD	Ottomans overrun Syria, Egypt and Arabia.
12th - 1300s AD	Series of Crusades begins
1200 AD	Spices become a status symbol in England.
1204 AD	Venetian ships plunder Constantinople and bring back enough wealth to establish Venice as the new centre of the spice trade.
1206 AD	Kutbuddin is Sultan of Dehli. Chenghiz Khan rules China - dies 1227 to be followed by Kublai 1259.
1275 AD	Marco Polo in China.

1279 AD	Pasta first mentioned in Genoa
1297 AD	Marco Polo entrances Italy with tales of spices and exotic goods in the Far East and the race for spice trade superiority in Europe starts in earnest. The Venetians pass a law stating that all spices from the East are to pass through Venice.
1398 AD	Tamerlane plunders Delhi.
1400 AD	Orange introduced to the West.
1400 - 1800 AD	Most of the world eats a mainly vegetarian diet, except Europe.
1471 AD	The Portuguese cross the Equator.
1486 AD	Bartholomew Diaz sails around the Cape of Good Hope.
1492 AD	Columbus sets out from Spain, reaches San Salvador in the Bahamas and discovers red chilli peppers in Santa Domingo (Cuba).
1493 AD	On his second voyage to the New World, Columbus finds paprika being used to flavour local dishes in Hispaniola (Haiti).
1497 AD	Vasco da Gama sails around the Cape of Good Hope to Malabariu, India, returning with cinnamon, cloves, ginger, pepper and precious stones.
1498 AD	Vasco da Gama discovers sea route to India.

Food History Time Line

1500 A.D. - 2000 A.D.

1500 AD	Red Pepper (Capsicum Annum) introduced to Europe from 'New World'.
1509 AD	Allspice, so called because its berries are thought to taste like a combination of cinnamon, cloves, nutmeg and pepper, is discovered by the Spanish in Jamaica.
1510 AD	Portuguese gain control of Goa.
1511 - 14 AD	The Portuguese take control of the Malabar coast, Java and Sumatra and successfully capture the Moluccan nutmeg trade.
1519 AD	Mexico conquered by Hernan Cortes. Spanish take pigs, chickens, cattle, cereals, vegetables, olive oil, sugar cane, citrus fruits and wine to Mexico. Ferdinand Magellan sets out from Spain and finds nutmeg growing on the Indonesian island of Tidore. Magellan killed in the Phillipines, but the solitary ship that does make it back safely from the expedition is laden with a cargo of nutmegs, mace, cinnamon and sandalwood.
1520 AD	Tomato brought to Spain from Peru or Mexico.
1526 AD	Babur's Mughal Empire is started. He dies in 1530 and is replaced by his son, Akbar.
1535 AD	Pineapple comes from South America to Europe.
1536 AD	The Portuguese occupy Ceylon. The potato is discovered by Jiminez de Quesada in Peru.
1559 AD	Tea first mentioned in Europe.
1579 AD	Sir Francis Drakes presents Elizabeth I with a gift of cloves.
1586 AD	Potato comes to Britain from Mexico, via Virginia. Ginger plantations established by the end of 16th century by the Spanish in the West Indies.
1599 AD	East India Company started by the English to break Portuguese/Dutch monopoly.
1600 AD	Coffee introduced to Europe.
1602 AD	The Dutch East India Company is founded in order to found a Dutch empire in Asia.
1605 - 1621 AD	The Dutch succeed in driving the Portuguese out of the Spice Islands.
1608 AD	First British ship arrives at Surat for East India Company
1612 AD	English establish first trading post in India.
1636 AD	The Dutch capture Ceylon (Sri Lanka).
1651 AD	The Dutch now control the clove, nutmeg and cinnamon trade and forbid the uncontrolled planting of spices under pain of death.
1657 AD	First tea reaches London.
1700 AD	Vegetables become true dishes rather than just garnishes. Salads become popular.
1757 AD	Last Nawab of Bengal dies at Battle of Plessey
1765 AD	The word 'restaurant' in its modern context introduced by Boulanger.
1770 AD	Pierre Poivre, the French Governor of Mauritius, smuggles cloves, nutmeg and cinnamon cuttings out of the Spice Islands and establishes a plantation in Réunion, the Seychelles and other French colonies.
1773 AD	Curry appears on a menu for the first time in Britain at a Coffee House in Norris Street, London.
1776 AD	The first French cloves are harvested and plants reach the English colonies.
1780 AD	First commercial curry powder on sale

1795 AD	The first non-Indian pepper cargo sets out from Salem. Boston, Portsmouth, Bath and New London become major spice ports.
1820 AD	Calcutta created as British capital in India.
1824 AD	The Dutch and the British sign a treaty which divides up all the spice growing regions between them.
1826 AD	Modern matches created.
1835 AD	Vanilla, originally from South America, is grown in India.
1840 AD	Confectionary eating chocolate invented.
1843 AD	Nutmegs planted on Grenada.
1857 AD	The Indian Mutiny and British troops, women and children were massacred in Delhi, Cawnpore and Lucknow. Order restored in mid-1858.
1859-61 AD	Mrs Beeton's Book of Household Management is published.
1900 AD	Charles Candler brings Coca Cola to Britain.
1907 AD	Lyons' Coventry Street Corner House opens in London, eventually to cater for 4,000 covers.
1912 AD	Lyons' Strand Corner House opens in London.
1914 - 18 AD	First World War
1931 AD	First commercial yoghurt created (Danone).
1933 AD	Maison Lyons opens near Marble Arch, London, seating 2,000.
1939 - 45 AD	Second World War
1940 AD	Sugar, butter and bacon rationed in Britain.
1946 AD	Bread rationed in Britain until 1948.
1947 AD	Indpendence for India and Pakistan (August 15th)
1948 AD	First tandoor in a restaurant used in Moti Mahal in New Delhi
1949 AD	Sweet rationing in Britain ends temporarily.
1954 AD	War-time rationing of goods in Britain comes to an end.
1967 AD	Asians expelled from Kenya
1971 AD	Independence for Bangladesh (26th March)
1972 AD	Asians expelled from Uganda
1974 AD	Turkish invasion of Cyprus.
1997 AD	Hong Kong handed back to China.

FOOD ORIGINS

Apricot	China	**Maize**	Mexico
Banana	Asia	**Melon**	Near East
Broad Bean	South America	**Nigella**	Damascus
Broccoli	Italy	**Nutmeg**	Moluccas
Cactus	Mexico/South America	**Okra**	Africa/Asia
Capers	Mediterranean	**Olive**	Mediterranean
Capsicum (Bell Pepper)	South America	**Onion**	Israel to India
Cardamom	Southern Asia	**Oregano**	Eastern Mediterranean
Carob	Babylon	**Parsley**	Eastern Mediterranean
Carrot	Afghanistan	**Parsnip**	Eurasia
Cauliflower	Cyprus	**Pea**	Western Asia
Celery	Mediterranean	**Peach**	China/Persia
Cherry	Europe/Western Asia	**Peanut**	South America
Chicory	India	**Pear (wild)**	Middle East
Chili	Mexico/South America	**Pepper (Piper Nigrum)**	India
Chives	Mediterranean	**Pineapple**	South America (Brazil)
Cinnamon	Sri Lanka	**Pistacchio**	India
Citrus fruits (Lemon/Orange/Lime)	Southeast Asia	**Plum**	Caucasus
Cloves	Eastern India	**Potato**	Peru
Cocoa	Mexico	**Pumpkin**	Mexico/South America
Coffee	Abyssinia	**Radish**	E. Mediterranean
Coriander	North Africa	**Rhubarb**	China (medicinal) Banks of Volga (edible)
Courgette	Mexico/South America	**Rice**	India
Cucumber	India/Africa	**Saffron**	Orient
Cumin	Mediterranean	**Sesame**	South America
Dill	Eastern Mediterranean	**Shallots**	Mediterranean
Eggplant (Aubergine)	India	**Spinach**	Southwest Asia/Persia
Endive	India	**Star Anise**	China
Fennel	Mediterranean	**Tarragon**	Russia
Fenugreek	South Europe/South Asia	**Tea**	Tibet/Assam
Garlic	Mediterranean	**Tomato**	Mexico/Peru
Ginger	Southern Asia	**Tortillas**	Mexico
Mace	Moluccas	**Turmeric**	Southern Asia
		Vanilla	Mexico

The Authors

Husband and wife team Peter and Colleen Grove have written numerous books in their journalistic careers ranging from children's books (Bornington Chronicles) to science fiction (The Levellers) and The Ergo-Economics of Sports and Leisure Facilities and Sports Form Guide to The National Hotel Directory (Guide to UK Hotels with Leisure Facilities).

Initially trained in economics, Peter moved into sports journalism as the result of being an international swimmer and county water polo player and was later joined by Colleen at All Sports International, supplying international sports news and information on 82 sports to national newspapers and other media working closely with both the Daily Express and Daily Mail.

In 1989 they produced The National Restaurant Directory sponsored by Carlsberg, which later broke down into The Real Curry Restaurant Guide covering over 9000 Indian restaurants in the UK. They then published The Oriental Restaurant Guide followed by The Italian and lastly The Mood Food Restaurant Guide covering Mexican, Greek, Spanish, Caribbean, etc. food.

In 1994 at the request of a group of top Indian restaurants they set up The National Dome Grading Scheme which has been providing an inspection service to the industry ever since and operated an annual '*Best In Britain*' Awards to highlight excellence in the industry for 15 years.

As a result of their experience they have written much of the market research that has appeared in recent years published by a variety of marketing groups and newspapers and have appeared on radio and television talking about ethnic food in general and Indian in particular.

They also edited Spice N Easy and Masala magazines for a short while and have edited Mood Food Magazine for over fourteen years, in addition to www.fedrest.com, an internet restaurant guide for The Federation of Specialist Restaurants, originally started in April 2000, enjoying 1 million visitors a month.

Although they both remain registered sportswriters, the demands of the ethnic food and drink sector leave them little time for active participation so you are more likely to see them at a restaurant or chatting to chefs, rather than attending a World Cup or Olympic Games.

In 2007 they started The Restaurant Hall of Fame at www.resthof.co.uk and continue to organise National Curry Week first started in 1998 to raise funds for charity. In 2008 they founded The Curry Tree Charitable Fund.

Their forte has always been research. They were credited by the Daily Telegraph with discovering details of Dean Mahomed – First Man of Curry- in 2005 leading to a City of Westminster plaque being placed on the wall where his 1809 restaurant once stood.

Tim Joiner, Mayor of Westminster City Council said, on unveiling a plaque marking the site of Britain's first Indian restaurant;

> **"We have historians Peter & Colleen Grove, our foremost experts on Indian restaurants to thank for discovering the information on Sake Dean Mahomed - first man of curry."**

This work took 6 years to complete and has been written with the aim of providing a standard volume for the industry that will remain a classic work of reference for many years.

Prior to this work they wrote and published the very popular, "Curry Spice and All Things Nice" and "Curry Culture – a very British love affair" (IBSN 0-9548303-0-X).

BIBLIOGRAPHY

Our grateful thanks to the contributors named in this work and the authors and publishers of these and many other books and avenues of research that went into producing this volume -
Peter & Colleen Grove

Title	Author	Publisher
Royal Recipes	Michele Brown	Pavilion
Legacy of the Indus	Samina Quraeshi	Weatherhill
Archaeology of the World	Courtlandt Canby	Chancellor
A Dash of Spice	Hawkins & Duff	Readers Digest
A History of Roman Britain	Peter Salway	Oxford University
Bengali Cooking	Chitrita Banerji	Serif
Bridge on British Beef	Tom Bridge	Piatkus
The Chinese Cookery Encyclopedia	Kenneth Lo	Collins
The Complete Meze Table	Rosamund Man	Garnet
Indian Cookery	Mrs Balbir Singh	Mills & Boon
Traditional Greek Cooking	George Moudiotis	Garnet
The Food of Italy	Claudia Roden	Arrow
Traditional Spanish Cooking	Janet Mendel	Garnet
50 Great Curries of India	Camellia Panjabi	Kyle Cathie
The Complete Mexican Cookbook	Loudes Nichols	Piatkus
The Food Medicine Bible	Earl Mindell	Souvenir Press
The Book of Fruit & Fruit Cookery	Paul Dinnage	Sidgwick & Jackson
The World Atlas of Food		Spring Books
In Search of the Trojan War	Michael Wood	BBC
Mythology	Richard Cavendish	W.H.Smith
World Prehistory	Grahame Clark	Cambridge University
Fabulous Feasts	Madelaine Pelner Cosman	George Braziller
The Food of Japan	Wendy Hutton	Periplus
Curries & Bugles	Jennifer Brennan	Viking
Savouring The Past (The French Kitchen Table 1300-1789)	Barbara Ketcham Wheaton	Chatto & Windus
The Oxford Companion to Food	Alan Davidson	Oxford University
On Food & Cooking	Harold McGee	Harper Collins

Title	Author	Publisher
A History of India	Romila Thapar	Penguin
The Dawn of Civilization	Stuart Piggott	Thames & Hudson
The Might that was Assyria	H.W.F.Saggs	Sidgwick & Jackson
History of Hospitality	David Goymour	
The Great Household in Medieval England	C.M. Woolgar	Yale University
Hobson-Jobson	Henry Yule & A.C.Burnell	Wordsworth Ref.
Harvest of the Cold Months	Elizabeth David	Michael Joseph
The Genesis Secret	Tom Knox	Harper Collins
Beeton's Book of Household Management		Chancellor Press
Food (An Oxford Anthology)	Brigid Allen	Oxford University
The Raj at Table	David Burton	Faber & Faber
The Roots & Tales of Bangladeshi Settlers	Yousuf Choudhury	
The Peopling of London	Nick Merriman	Museum of London
The Carlsberg National Restaurant Directory	Peter & Colleen Grove	Belgrove Publishing
London & Its People	John Richardson	Barrie & Jenkins
London a Social History	Roy Porter	Hamish Hamilton
Food in Antiquity	D. & P. Brothwell	Thames & Hudson
Savouring The East	David Burton	faber & faber
Food - The Gift of Osiris	Darby, Ghalioungui & Grivetti	
In Praise of the Potato	Lindsey Bareham	Penguin
Food	Clarissa Dickson Wright	Ebury Press
A Concise History of the Darjeeling District since 1835	E.C. Dozey	Under the patronage of Rt Hon Baron Carmichael of Skirling G.C.I.E. K.C.M.G. first Governor of Bengal
History of the World	W.N. Weech	Odhams
The Frank Muir Book	Frank Muir	Wm Heinemann Ltd
Myths & Legends - China & Japan	Donald A. Mackenzie	Gresham Publishing Co.
The Travels of Dean Mahomet	Dean Mahomet	University of California Press

Last but certainly not least –

Many of the photos in this book have been taken from http://www.sxc.hu – all of the photographers were contacted individually, as per their request, to thank them.

Also, many thanks to the wonderful photos – pages 67, 111, 117 - from Tanvi Hathiwala of "The Hathi Cooks" - http://thehathicooksblogspot.com

www.ingramcontent.com/pod-product-compliance
Lightning Source LLC
Chambersburg PA
CBHW040901020526
44114CB00037B/27